THE WAR IN AMERICAN CULTURE

The *War* in *American Culture*

SOCIETY AND CONSCIOUSNESS DURING WORLD WAR II

EDITED BY

Lewis A. Erenberg and Susan E. Hirsch

The University of Chicago Press

CHICAGO AND LONDON

The University of Chicago Press, Chicago 60637
The University of Chicago Press, Ltd., London
© 1996 by The University of Chicago
All rights reserved. Published 1996
Printed in the United States of America
14 13 12 11   6 7 8
ISBN: 0-226-21511-3 (cloth)
      0-226-21512-1 (paper)

Library of Congress Cataloging-in-Publication Data

The war in American culture : society and consciousness during World War II /
   edited by Lewis A. Erenberg and Susan E. Hirsch.
      p.   cm.
   Includes index.
   1. United States—Civilization—1918–1945.   2. World War, 1939–
1945—Social aspects—United States.   I. Erenberg, Lewis A., 1944–
II. Hirsch, Susan E.
E169.1.W273   1996
973.7—dc20
                                             95-35334
                                                 CIP

The University of Chicago Press gratefully acknowledges a subvention from
Loyola University of Chicago in partial support of photographic reproduction
and permissions costs of this volume.

♾ The paper used in this publication meets the minimum requirements of the
American National Standard for Information Sciences—Permanence of Paper
for Printed Library Materials, ANSI Z39.48-1992.

To

Jesse and Joanna

CONTENTS

Contents

ACKNOWLEDGMENTS

Many people helped make this collection possible. First we wish to thank the contributors to *The War in American Culture* for all they did to make the original conference a success. Ever since we gathered at Loyola University in March 1992 for a series of wonderful and provocative panels, lectures, and discussions—as well as a typical Chicago blizzard—they have been unstinting and timely in meeting our many editorial demands.

We also want to thank Scott La France, co-curator of the Chicago Historical Society exhibit "Chicago Goes to War," for his enlightening discussion of the exhibit. In addition, several of our colleagues in the History Department of Loyola University helped create the intellectual and scholarly atmosphere of the conference: Walter Gray, Ann Harrington, Cheryl Johnson-Odim, Theodore Karamanski, Janet Nolan, and Harold Platt. Most important, the late Robert McCluggage suggested the idea of a conference to commemorate World War II. The chair of the department, Joseph Gagliano, went out of his way to encourage and support both the initial conference and this volume. Russell Lewis eagerly agreed to have the Chicago Historical Society cosponsor the conference along with the Illinois Humanities Council and Loyola University's Endowment for the Liberal Arts. Dean Kathleen McCourt helped us come up with additional money.

Our editor at the University of Chicago Press, Douglas Mitchell, has been enthusiastic and encouraging in our efforts to turn these papers into a book. We received able help from his associate, Matt Howard, and from Alice Bennett, senior manuscript editor. Our research assistants, Julia Foulkes, Katie Dishman, and Scott Newman, were indispensable to its completion.

Finally, we dedicate this book to our children, Jesse and Joanna, as an expression of our profound hope that they "won't have to study war no more."

Lewis A. Erenberg and Susan E. Hirsch

INTRODUCTION

Released in the heat of the most destructive war in history, the film *Lifeboat* (1944), directed by Alfred Hitchcock and scripted by John Steinbeck, reveals the crisis that World War II posed for American culture. Adrift in a lifeboat, survivors of a luxury liner torpedoed by a German submarine must face the central issue raised by the conflict: Can a divided democracy heal its internal differences of class, race, and ethnicity so as to defeat an external enemy, a monstrous Nazi superman bent on its destruction? A microcosm of America, the lifeboat is sharply split between the wealthy passengers of the liner, led by a businessman and a socialite photographer, and its crew, a radical Czech American merchant seaman, a black steward, and a German American sailor. Taking advantage of democracy's failings, the ruthless Nazi submarine captain deftly divides and conquers to lead this ship of fools—a metaphor for the ship of state—toward ruin. In the end the passengers avoid catastrophe by submerging their differences, symbolized by the love affair between the socialite and the radical seaman.

In its depiction of a new American national ideal, *Lifeboat* parallels the "ethnic platoon" of World War II films in which upper-class Protestants, working-class ethnics, and African Americans cooperate in the nation's defense. As Richard Slotkin points out, this vision of America was "markedly more liberal, tolerant, and integrated than the one in which most of the movie audience lived." *Lifeboat* elevates utopian melting pot values to "the symbolic equivalent of a war aim." All could work together for a common political ideal, unhampered by ethnic, racial, or class differences. By showing the courage and humanity of the black steward, the film raised the question whether black Americans and other non-

Figure 1. "We're all in the same boat" in this scene from *Lifeboat:* from left to right, the Nazi U-boat captain, the working-class merchant seaman, the celebrity photographer-reporter, the big businessman, the German American swing fan, the dazed mother of a drowned baby, the young English girl, the African American steward, and the English merchant seaman. Courtesy of the Academy of Motion Picture Arts and Sciences.

whites could be part of the melting pot in the face of a white supremacist foe. The demands of war thus required a profound reworking of American national identity.[1]

The contributors to *The War in American Culture* explore the way World War II represented a major turning point in American culture. It should be apparent that they all challenge the paradigm of World War II as the last "good war." Instead, their essays focus on the tremendous but paradoxical effects the war had on American identity, racial and ethnic subgroups, and women's roles long after the conclusion of hostilities. With only one exception, the pieces included here were first presented at a public symposium held at Loyola University of Chicago on 20–21 March 1992 commemorating the fiftieth anniversary of United States entry into World War II. The two-day conference, "The War in

American Culture," sponsored by the History Department of Loyola University, the Chicago Historical Society, and the Illinois Humanities Council, created a forum for scholars, students, and the general public to examine how World War II affected the nation's political, social, and cultural fabric. Given this purpose, these essays focus less on international and military aspects of the conflict, important as they are, than on the much less examined territory of the home front and the meaning of the war in the lives of ordinary Americans. It is for these reasons that so much emphasis is placed on the everyday aspects of people's lives and the popular culture that reveals so much about the consciousness of average people.

In raising questions about "the good war" as the organizing construct for understanding World War II, of course, the editors and authors are aware of the many reasons, at the level of popular understanding, why Americans believe the war was good. At its conclusion, the world had been liberated from fascism, the United States was the richest and most powerful nation on earth, and unlike its allies or its enemies, the country had not been physically and economically devastated. Having waged a necessary war of self-defense that ended in the defeat of international bullies, moreover, ordinary citizens could feel proud of their sacrifices. That the war ended the depression, ushered in an era of unprecedented prosperity, and brought the nation's citizens together in a united effort only underscores the memory of this as "the last good war" and the last time Americans felt truly united as a nation.

More recently, however, "the good war" has lost some of its luster. No one goes back to Charles Beard to argue that the war need not have been fought.[2] Beginning in the 1960s, however, revisionist historians argued that American diplomatic and military decisions, especially the decision to build and drop the atomic bomb, contributed to the onset of the cold war.[3] In the 1970s, moreover, scholars began to explore the effects of the war on American society. John Morton Blum in V Was for Victory and Richard Polenberg in War and Society surveyed on a general level how the war reoriented political energies toward the expediencies of victory and away from the reform agenda of the New Deal. Business regained lost power and prestige, and labor radicalism declined. The federal government went only as far as victory required and no further in ethnic and racial policy and in ideas about women and industrial relations. Blum, especially, sees no radical break between the 1930s and the 1940s; war measures were shaped by extant attitudes toward women and racial and ethnic minorities. The war heightened the dissatisfaction of minorities but did not seem to grip and transform their thinking. A well-known popular work, Studs Terkel's *"The Good War,"* emphasized the negative side of the war, highlighting the irony of any war's being perceived as good, a strategy pursued at length by Paul Fussell in *War-time.* As part of this general onslaught, numerous more specialized works have examined class, gender, and racial and ethnic conflict in the defense industries. Popular memory rightly recalls the unifying aspects of the war and the willing sacrifices, but the massive changes it brought also raised many points of conflict. Although previous authors challenged the popular conception of the war years as a time of unity and amity, this remains the image of the era and the "standard" used since then to judge the home front in wartime.[4]

The War in American Culture suggests a different interpretation of the war as a turning point. The essays reveal a much deeper transition from a New Deal paradigm of society, culture, and politics to one associated with the war. At one level the war made it official, as Richard Slotkin pointed out, that the national identity of the United States was no longer exclusively white or Protestant. The terrible demands of total war required that former outsiders be included in a new pluralistic national self-definition. Without the New Deal, radical labor efforts, and the challenge to class domination by older elites during the 1930s, the redefinition of American national identity would not have been possible. But though wartime propaganda made great efforts to fulfill the New Deal's original impetus, there was a crucial distinction. To be included now required patriotic dedication to unity and suppression of one's class dissatisfactions. The transition occurred in part because of the state's manipulating and controlling society and consciousness through censorship and propaganda. In many ways Americans were encouraged to support the war effort because the nation would provide them with an abundance and acceptance long denied.

Yet Americans were not merely passively shaped by a powerful and order-conscious state. It is here, we believe, that *The War in American Culture* offers a unique contribution to our understanding of wartime culture. By focusing on the popular culture of the era and on the cultural and social practices of diverse Americans, the contributors show that the war redirected American culture because of the interaction between the ideology created by government and media and the consciousness and self-assertion of various racial and cultural groupings in American life. Ordinary Americans actively shaped official conceptions of the war but also resisted them, and they helped create a whole set of unanticipated consequences that had a profound effect on American culture and racial relations. The new nationalism, for instance, not only had to include African Americans because of that group's growing political power, but also encouraged blacks and other minorities to demand their birthright as Americans and to resist attempts to suppress their awakened American identity. Just as the war increased the idea of new opportunities for all Americans, so wartime racial hysteria, racially changing workplaces and neighborhoods, and government's attempts to manage racial demands all led to wartime explosions. If the official ideology expected racial minorities to be content with symbolic recognition, their demands for true inclusion and equality transformed the meaning of American pluralism.

In many ways these essays establish that the war had a much larger impact on people's lives than historians have previously realized. Here too the effects were paradoxical. Mobilizing at home and abroad made extraordinary demands on people and their values. Despite official messages of an orderly domestic world, in fact, the war was a liminal period for people's personal lives. Geographically, for example, the war uprooted servicemen, families, and job seekers from traditional areas of settlement and scattered them across the country. Living and working with new people challenged old stereotypes, and problems that had been predominantly regional—such as race—became the focus of intense national attention. The entrance of women and African Americans into previously white male workplaces, moreover, posed new challenges to older folkways. Women's new jobs were but one aspect of the challenge to traditional gender roles; their new sexual freedom was perhaps even more unsettling. Yet mobilization required unity, and the drive for unity championed continuity and conformity in behavior and beliefs. It is the concern of the following chapters to explore both the attempts to create a unified American culture and the conflicts this effort engendered.

No matter how varied the experiences, the war deeply affected everyday life and consciousness. Perry Duis's "No Time for Privacy: World War II and Chicago's Families" reveals how wartime demands intruded into home and family life, producing a loss of privacy and lessening control over personal time. Duis's detailed study of daily life counters the premise of Blum and others that the war had only minimal influence on Americans far removed from the battlefield. Duis implicitly questions the major role assigned to propaganda in transforming popular consciousness by showing how rationing, work schedules, civil defense procedures, and government production schedules forced drastic changes in personal behavior and family life. These created, he finds, the conditions that made the postwar "return to the home" a popular movement, one abetted by producers of consumer goods and advertisers but not created by them. With lives disrupted by the war, many Americans wanted to recapture the sense of privacy, "normal" domesticity, and personal freedom that advertisers promised.[5]

Although historians have emphasized the overt and explicit attempts to mold public opinion, several of these essays explore new aspects of how government and the media attempted to shape American consciousness. George Roeder's "Censoring Disorder: American Visual Imagery of World War II" reveals the subtlety of the federal government's propaganda effort when compared with the heavy-handed endeavors of the Creel Committee during World War I. Using the National Archives' collection of censored material, dubbed the "Chamber of Horrors," Roeder analyzes the visual images government censors believed would harm a unified war effort and hence withheld from the public. Censors tried to maintain the idea of a war of absolute good versus unmitigated evil and to promote confidence in American institutions and ensure their stability. Americans were flooded with visual images, but they had no way of suspecting what they did not see, and thus how much the government attempted to manage their thinking.

It was not just that the federal government tried to impose a unified national consciousness on Americans. Many artists and intellectuals saw the need to strengthen the bonds of American culture for the duration. The movie industry, popular music, radio, and advertising played critical roles, to an extent not seen in any previous war including World War I, when the media of electronic communications were still relatively undeveloped. World War II was very much, as Paul Fussell puts it, "a public relations war." Belief in the cause often led intellectuals and entertainers to engage in propaganda efforts. This explains John Steinbeck's role as screenwriter for *Lifeboat* and also suggests why the film's celebrity photographer is excoriated as an aesthete until she deigns to participate in the dirty business of war. In using art as a weapon, artists and intellectuals continued the depression era's preoccupation with art as a social tool. During the war, however, the goal was not criticism of American economic, social, and political arrangements, but defense of America as a democracy under attack.

Filmmakers, many of them political radicals, played a large role in constructing portraits of a unified American identity in order to contain disruptive forces. The demands of war, Lary May tells us in "Making the American Consensus: The Narrative of Conversion and Subversion in World War II Films," led to a depiction of American identity as one of nonconflictual class unity and a healthy ethnic pluralism worthy of defense against fascism. To achieve this sense of unity, however, popular filmmakers were forced to abandon former New Deal narratives of class conflict. Characters in war movies who criticized their superiors or the unequal distribution of wealth and power were labeled subversive. May thus sees moviemakers as promoting a more conservative politics of consensus and sowing the seeds of the Red scare that was soon to come. Yet at the heart of the propaganda, as *Lifeboat* shows, lay the utopian belief that European immigrants could be full Americans.

This vision of national pluralism and unity could be seized by certain groups to mark and legitimize their full participation in American life. In "The Working Class Goes to War," Gary Gerstle shows why working-class Americans of French Canadian and, more generally, European immigrant backgrounds, more so than management, actively supported the war with bond drives, care packages, and patriotic benefits and pageants. The New Deal had nurtured a sense of a working-class Americanism even in isolated industrial communities. As the official goals of the Four Freedoms meshed with New Deal pluralism, these workers turned enthusiastically to the war effort to claim their full status as Americans. Whereas other scholars have focused on the shop floor struggles between labor and capital during the war, Gerstle reveals that workers as well as intellectuals and advertisers had a part in shifting the political focus from economic redistribution to pluralism as the cornerstone of Americanism. Their patriotic support of the war and its new national ideal undercut their class politics.

Nowhere was the official version of unity more conservative than in its support for traditional gender roles, and nowhere was it more in tune with popular beliefs. In "Rosie the Riveter Gets Married," Elaine Tyler May explores the ways traditional gender ideology prevented women from developing long-term commitments to women's rights and employment. In a parallel to Gerstle's view of workers as having a dual identity composed of ethnic and class allegiances, May stresses that women were not just workers. They also thought of themselves as mothers and wives, lovers and girlfriends, separated from their male loved ones. Wartime prosperity encouraged women to dream of marriage and families, something made difficult first by the depression, second by the war's separation of the sexes, and third by the disruption of domestic existence Duis describes. Yet the war also opened up for many women the possibility of autonomous sexual lives outside the purview of parents, husbands, or neighbors. The injunction to support "the boys" encouraged many young women to attend USO events and date servicemen; some went further and violated taboos against casual premarital and extramarital sexual affairs. May reveals that the war's effect on women was less in broadening their employment options than in expanding their sexual autonomy, a situation that created a whole new set of fears after the war.

The drive for unity drew on the American entertainment industry in an unprecedented manner to make the war part of public life and personal consciousness. In "Swing Goes to War: Glenn Miller and the Popular Music of World War II," Lewis Erenberg demonstrates how popular swing bands joined the war effort. Air Force Major Glenn Miller sought to transform military bands with a swing music that glorified and defended an idealized and commodified home front—the embodiment of the American dream. For young men and women separated by war, Miller's lush ballads incarnated the longing to recreate domestic happiness and achieve romantic love as a goal for the postwar world. Erenberg, like Elaine May, shows us the clash between the image of women as the embodiment of home front values and the potential for newfound sexual experience that the war unleashed. If Miller helped make jazz-inflected swing an expression of true American values and the freedom of American culture, his version of American music was a white one that included the children of immigrants but excluded the originators of jazz—black musicians. Erenberg stresses that Miller's music, like the other official versions of Americanism, could not contain the issue of race.

One of the great ironies of the war is that as ethnic, and to a lesser extent racial, pluralism became a new national ideal at home, racial tensions increased and intensified. Many of the essays wrestle with this paradox. John Dower explores the large gulf between the official goals of the war and the realities of race. Nowhere was this more apparent than in depictions of the enemy. As Dower shows us in "Race, Language, and War in Two Cultures: World War II in Asia," Americans viewed the Pacific war as a racial conflict in which an inferior race of "yellow monkey men" deserved annihilation by white men. In popular cartoons and magazine graphics, film depictions, and the pronouncements of civilian and military leaders, the Germans were a human enemy misled by Nazi leaders, but the Japanese were a subhuman race. Comparing American and Japanese popular images of each other, Dower discovers that the Pacific war was filled with racial animosity and brutality on both sides. For Americans the racial nature of the Pacific war undermined official ideology—yet as Dower reveals, racial stereotypes could shift quickly. The same racism that led to a policy of extermination of the enemy could aid the relatively benign postwar occupation.

Reed Ueda's "The Changing Path to Citizenship: Ethnicity and Naturalization during World War II" suggests the malleability of racial thinking in another way. The war had a paradoxical long-term effect on the role of Asians in American life. Fear and hatred of the Chinese had led white Americans to bar Asian immigration and to resist Asians' attempts to become citizens. When the war broke out, white Americans could not conceive of second-generation Japanese Americans as the citizens they were and unceremoniously herded them off to concentration camps with their unnaturalized parents. Ueda shows, however, that the needs of wartime diplomacy forced the United States to liberalize its laws toward its ally China and to create new images of the Chinese as democracy-loving brothers-in-arms. The long-term effect was a liberalization of immigration and citizenship laws toward all Asians and, beginning with the Chinese, a reconceptualization of their racial character and acceptability.

During the war, however, this first step was overshadowed by the pervasiveness of racism against people of color. Carol Miller's sensitive reading of works by Leslie Marmon Silko and N. Scott Momaday in "Native Sons and the Good War: Retelling the Myth of American Indian Assimilation" demonstrates the mixed legacy of new ideals and traditional behavior. Native Americans fought proudly in World War II, expecting that their bravery and sacrifice would lead to acceptance, yet the results were disillusioning. Underneath the novels of despair, there lies a sense of great expectations that were not fulfilled. For the first time Native Americans expected both cultural autonomy and justice within

American, not just tribal, society. Instead, many veterans did not find acceptance in the larger world and also were cut off from the old rituals and cultures of their people.

The most explosive confrontation between the ideal of pluralism, official war aims against white supremacy, and popular racial attitudes occurred over the role of African Americans in American society. The historic migration from the rural South to the defense industries of the North and West placed black-white racial issues on the national agenda for the first time since Reconstruction. New opportunities for jobs arose from the threat of a "March on Washington" organized by A. Phillip Randolph and the Brotherhood of Sleeping Car Porters. Susan Hirsch's "No Victory at the Workplace: Women and Minorities at Pullman during World War II" shows the roots of Randolph's movement in the struggles of Pullman Company employees and assesses the gains achieved by black men and women and white women under government protection. She shows how management's attempt to maintain traditional gender and racial patterns of job holding led to a redrawing of boundaries that left white women in the fastest-growing area for employment—clerical work. When government action against discrimination ceased after the war, black men and women made no further gains. Although no victory at the workplace occurred, those black workers who gained a foothold in industry during the war became the bedrock of a postwar black working class and the foundation for a mass Civil Rights movement in the future.

As Shirley Ann Moore attests in "Traditions from Home: African Americans in Wartime Richmond, California," political consciousness and resistance were rooted not only in the workplace but also in community cultures. When African Americans migrated from the Southwest to the shipyards of Richmond, they brought their musical culture with them. Their familiar ways and institutions differed from those of Californians, white and black, and the migrants experienced hostility from both groups. The newcomers stood up to both, enjoying rhythm and blues clubs that seemed "low class" to Californians, and using them to begin a local chapter of the National Association for the Advancement of Colored People to fight discrimination in housing and employment.

In "Zoot-Suiters and Cops: Chicano Youth and the Los Angeles Police Department during World War II," Edward Escobar shows that Mexican Americans, another group that faced harsh repression in the contest over opportunities and acceptance, created cultural forms of popular resistance during the war. Young men and women assumed new modes of dress, behavior, and even language—all symbolized by the zoot suit—to set themselves apart from both Anglo culture and their parents. The *pachuco* style mocked and confronted Anglo society, and escalating racial conflicts between police and young "zoot-suiters" culminated in a full-scale race riot between white servicemen and young Mexican Americans. This cultural movement had a political impact in the postwar years, as the tense relations led to the growth of a nascent Mexican American consciousness and the first attempts of Mexican Americans to run for political office. Escobar shows, however, that the war was a turning point not only in Mexican American consciousness, but also in police ideology. The hostile relations between Mexican Americans and police created a belief among the police that race and crime were inextricably linked. In the postwar years they extended this ideology to other racial minorities and became an army of occupation in the ghettos of Los Angeles.

By war's end, a new political consciousness and level of mobilization existed among African Americans and other racial minorities. Popular movements in local communities, as well as the ideology and propaganda of American unity, put pluralism and especially race in the forefront of politics. In the closing chapter, "World War II and American Liberalism," Alan Brinkley explores how political leaders responded to these imperatives and conflicts and transformed the New Deal political heritage into postwar liberalism. Ending their focus on class conflict, liberals upheld the values of stability, prosperity, ethnic pluralism, and racial justice within a modified capitalism and an economically productive corporate order. As Brinkley shows, race and ethnicity rather than class or gender would become the overarching "radical" issues of the postwar world. In this way, he disputes views that America became more conservative; rather, the nature of liberalism changed. The war played a formative role in this new agenda and in the ways class, race, and gender were perceived in American life.

Different conceptions of politics, national identity, racial and ethnic rights, and gender roles would become the subject of fierce political and cultural debate in the postwar era. The war experience created the conditions for that debate by encouraging both a new vision of Americanness and the assertiveness of racial and ethnic minorities. At the same time, the war years established a new set of options for women and a heightened yearning for domesticity as the American dream. At the level of popular culture, wartime demands for mass consumption and abundance created the basis for a new-style liberalism. Similarly, the war's restrictions on the individual set in motion a radical cultural emphasis, embodied by hipsters and then beats, on personal freedom and existential identity. In various ways the war awakened many of the forces that shape our political and cultural lives today. It created both new possibilities and new conflicts.

Notes

1. Richard Slotkin, *Gunfighter Nation: The Myth of the Frontier in Twentieth-Century America* (New York, 1992), 318–26.

2. For Charles Beard's antiwar stance and what it represented, see David Noble, *The End of American History: Democracy, Capitalism, and the Metaphor of Two Worlds in Anglo-American Historical Writing, 1800–1980* (Minneapolis, 1985), 41–64, and Noble's essay "The Reconstruction of Progress: Charles Beard, Richard Hofstadter, and Postwar Historical Thought," in *Recasting America: Culture and Politics in the Age of the Cold War,* ed. Lary May (Chicago, 1989), 61–75.

3. Gar Alperovitz, *Atomic Diplomacy: Hiroshima and Potsdam* (New York, 1965), and Martin Sherwin, *A World Destroyed: The Atomic Bomb and the Grand Alliance* (New York, 1975), are two examples. Members of the revisionist cold war school are too numerous to list.

4. John Morton Blum, *V Was for Victory: Politics and American Culture during World War II* (New York, 1976); Richard Polenberg, *War and Society: The United States, 1941–1945* (Philadelphia, 1972); Nelson Lichtenstein, *Labor's War at Home: The CIO in World War II* (Cambridge, 1982); Karen Anderson, *Wartime Women: Sex Roles, Family Relations, and the Status of Women during World War II* (Westport, Conn., 1981); D'Ann Campbell, *Women at War with America: Private Lives in a Patriotic Era* (Cambridge, Mass., 1984); Maureen Honey, *Creating Rosie the Riveter: Class, Gender, and Propaganda during World War II* (Amherst, Mass., 1984); Alan Bérubé, *Coming out under Fire: The History of Gay Men and Women in World War Two* (New York, 1990); Robert Westbrook, "I Want a Girl, Just Like the Girl Who Married Harry James," *American Quarterly* 42 (1990): 587–614; Studs Terkel, *"The Good War": An Oral History of World War II* (New York, 1984); Paul Fussell, *Wartime: Understanding and Behavior in the Sec-*

ond World War (New York, 1989). There are also important state studies. Among these see Allan Clive, *State of War: Michigan in World War II* (Ann Arbor, Mich., 1979), and John F. Zwicky, "A State at War: The Home Front in Illinois during the Second World War" (Ph.D. diss., Loyola University of Chicago, 1989).

5. Dana Polan, *Power and Paranoia: History, Narrative, and the American Cinema, 1940–1950* (New York, 1986); Frank Fox, *Madison Avenue Goes to War: The Strange Military Career of American Advertising, 1941–1945* (Provo, Utah, 1975).

The Quest
for National Unity

Perry R. Duis

ONE

No Time for Privacy: World War II and Chicago's Families

During World War II, Mrs. Frances Jankowski rose at 4:45 A.M. six mornings each week. After feeding her family and riding a streetcar to the Swift and Company stockyards plant, she spent the next eight hours trimming pork scraps for sausage. After the ride back to her South Rockwell Street home, she did the family shopping, cleaned their six-room apartment, cooked dinner, and still found time to cultivate a victory garden of two thousand square feet, collect scrap, and participate in neighborhood civil defense exercises. On Sundays she did the washing and ironing. Her husband John had spent the day as an elevator operator, the only job he could hold because of a decade-long illness. Together the Jankowskis invested 15 percent of their family income in war bonds to hasten the safe return of three sons and a daughter who were in military service.[1]

The *Chicago Tribune* lauded the Jankowski family as an ideal home front household, but their hectic domestic schedule was far from unique. During World War II families all over Chicago and America balanced extended working hours plus scrap drives, civil defense exercises, victory gardens, neighborhood ceremonies honoring those entering the service, and countless other demands made on the time of good citizens. All of these endeavors were encouraged by official propaganda claiming that military success abroad depended on home front support, requiring citizens to sacrifice domestic comforts and conveniences in exchange for the protection of the American family.[2] What the federal government implied but did not openly say was that victory overseas required an unprecedented invasion of home front duties into the private lives of its citizens.

The routes and methods of this domestic invasion grew out of the urbanization that produced a complex system of interdependencies. Those who lived in cities relied on someone else for almost everything needed to operate their households, and this gave the federal government its most effective means of enlisting civilian support for the war effort among city dwellers, whose concentration made them most vulnerable to enemy attack.[3] Home front programs had far less impact on rural America, where families were much more self-sufficient for everyday necessities. At the same time, much farm labor was exempt from the military draft, and there was no real need for extensive civil defense programs except where the farmsteads were close to cities.[4]

The penetration of urban domestic life also depended on manipulating people's sense of time. The war seemed to accelerate the pace of life. Even by today's standards, the speed with which things were organized and built during World War II remains impressive.[5] This hurried-up world of patriotic production outside the home altered the lives of those within it. Whereas farm life continued to be controlled largely by the seasons and people's internal clocks, cities had always been governed by signals and schedules that were more public and social. The factory whistle, the school bell, the public clock, the commuter train timetable, and the signals that opened the doors of downtown stores and offices controlled the schedules of adults and children. Each rush hour was a public accounting of the transitions between different phases of the workdays of hundreds of thousands of Chicagoans.[6] The disruption of these rhythms of everyday life greatly altered the private world.

Prewar Patterns of Time and Privacy

During the half century before 1941, the uses of domestic space and time in Chicago and elsewhere already had undergone changes that would shape the patterns of home front participation. The prewar years had witnessed a growing fascination with the efficiency movement launched by Frederick Taylor to reduce the waste of time. Timesaving schemes marked the new quest for "scientific management" in the operation of factories, stores, and offices, while early expressways like Chicago's Lake Shore Drive and faster speeds for public transit were supposed to reduce the time spent traveling between work and home.[7]

Meanwhile, at the other end of the commuter's journey, the traditional view held that families functioned most effectively when they could build social barriers around themselves. Supposedly, privacy allowed the family to be a sheltering institution. A backyard kept young ones off the street; a piano in the parlor and books to read obviated the need for commercial amusements. Privacy also permitted personal modesty: a family needed its own bathing and toilet facilities, and children of different genders needed separate bedrooms.[8]

Traditionally, income had been the primary determinant of how much privacy and space a family could attain. The poorest Chicagoans had always lived on the street or in other public places, in full public view. A trickle of income put a family into a crowded tenement, where at least they were behind walls part of the time. Additional income might bring a modest cottage on a small lot, and greater wealth bought more space that was also functionally specialized.[9]

This traditional goal of insularity for the household, and its relation to wealth, had begun to erode well before World War II. New household appliances were supposed to free housewives' daytime hours for other pursuits, many of them outside the home.[10] Department store shopping and commercial amusements, for instance, drew middle- and upper-class people out of their private worlds. On the other hand, the automobile gave even working-class families a measure of privacy from crowded mass transit and independence from its schedules in their pursuit of leisure or on the commute to work. Further, as consumer goods came within their reach, working-class families still made the ultimate decisions about what radio programs and Victrola records they would hear, if any, what newspapers and magazines entered their homes, and what prepared foods were found on their tables.[11]

No development, however, disrupted the traditional idea of proper privacy as much as the Great Depression, with its devastating impact on families. Accounts of the suffering of the 1930s often include descriptions of the way middle-class people tried to hide their plight. The trip to the welfare agency, being seen on a WPA work crew, the public humiliation of eviction—all these sad events represented not only a loss of status and pride, but also a loss of privacy. Adult children and parents, as well as other extended family members, moved in together. Although the arms buildup of the late 1930s began a return to prosperity, Pearl Harbor occurred before many of these effects of the depression could be healed. The decade of suffering, in essence, had helped soften the walls of privacy and, to a substantial extent, made it that much easier for the home front programs to penetrate the privacy of the family.[12]

Fear and Enthusiasm, 1941–43

Although America had been moving toward involvement in world war for at least two years, the attack on Pearl Harbor constituted a sudden invasion of the American consciousness that enabled other intrusions into domestic life. During the first months of the war, most home front projects in Chicago were met with nervous enthusiasm prompted by a general belief that the city might be bombed. The entire civil defense program, with its responsibilities shared by as many people as possible, required at least a minimum of fear to guarantee participation. For most families, involvement also became an adventure, a way every citizen could feel he or she was making an important contribution to the war effort. Families learned not only how to use twenty-four hour "military time," but also how to calculate local time in distant parts of the world where loved ones might be serving.[13]

This atmosphere of involvement, in turn, helped generate a willingness to compromise family privacy for the patriotic good. Collecting salvage to be recycled into war goods required an especially complete intrusion into the home. Advertising, posters, radio, and neighbors exhorted housewives to collect kitchen grease for conversion into nitroglycerine, search cupboards and attics for unused aluminum cooking utensils and other metal junk, and bundle newspapers and magazines to be reprocessed into shipping containers for war goods. Their husbands pulled old tires and discarded iron and steel items from basements and garages, while youngsters scoured alleys, vacant lots, and other play places for anything salvageable. The private satisfaction of helping often was subordinated to organized scrap drives that became a form of team sport, with neighborhoods and assorted organizations vying to collect the most.[14]

Civil defense exercises were an invasion of privacy that was welcomed by Chicagoans who feared enemy attack. Not only were families asked to give up some of their spare time to attend meetings and study the official literature, but the local civil defense program fingerprinted as many as 100,000 Chicago volunteers and investigated their backgrounds.[15] Some training exercises, especially blackouts, directly altered life at home. To block all light that might be seen from outside, home-

Figure 1.1. Children bringing in scrap to a civil defense office in Chicago, 1942. Courtesy of the Library of Congress.

Figure 1.2.   Chicago area family hears war news, 1942. Courtesy of the Library of Congress.

makers had to take time either to find cloth and make blackout curtains or to buy them. These curtains were to be put in place for every test, and even then residents were asked to turn off their radios because the tubes glowed and to avoid smoking lest the light be visible around the edges.[16]

Meanwhile, one of the duties of the civil defense block captain was to gather information about everyone in the jurisdiction. In an attack it would be vital to know something about the layout of each dwelling, when a family might be home, where its members worked, and other details. Knowing about the neighbors also enhanced the block captain's security function of reporting draft dodgers and suspicious characters who might be spies. Training sessions early in 1942 schooled block captains in the techniques of keeping card files on neighbors and getting the necessary information without seeming nosy or pushy.[17]

Finally, compliance with the ideals of home front unity sometimes required public forms of patriotic behavior to demonstrate one's private loyalty. Defying the city ordinance against ragweed might mean a householder did not care about the efficiency of defense workers who had hay fever. Colorful window stickers and posters told neighbors that a family bought bonds, contributed to scrap drives, planted victory gardens, and had someone serving in the armed forces. Failing to advertise one's loyalty might arouse suspicion of being a "mattress stuffer"—hoarding money instead of buying bonds—or worse.[18]

War and the Private Family, 1941–43

The war affected every aspect of domestic life in Chicago, including family formation. After Pearl Harbor, couples flooded the Cook County marriage license bureau at more than twice the usual rate. Many chose mass-produced weddings that were sold as a package by downtown department stores and hurried through by churches or local judges. There was no time for even the longest-standing family traditions, such as using an heirloom ring or exchanging gifts, and the honeymoon sometimes consisted of a few nights in a Loop hotel before reporting to duty.[19]

For thousands of war brides, this rush of events was followed by months, even years, of delay before they could establish a household. Not only were these times marked by worry and long lapses of communication, but there was also a substantial loss of privacy. Letter writers were pressured to use V-mail, a compact format that was reduced to microfilm to save precious space in overseas shipments, then printed photographically for the recipient. V-mail also helped military censors obliterate any information that might tell where military personnel were or were going. Packages from home were inspected so thoroughly that by late 1942 platoon commanders were, in effect, dictating what families could and could not send as holiday gifts.[20]

At home new brides often lost spatial privacy. Lacking money and unable to make firm domestic plans, many newly formed "households" consisted of what could fit in a few suitcases or trunks. War brides often moved back home with their parents or lived in a succession of rooming houses. Many military wives also joined one of the dozens of support groups that started during the holiday season of 1941 and found themselves revealing their most intimate fears to people who had been strangers only a few weeks earlier. One war bride confided to a University of

Chicago graduate student, "Before our separation, we talked quite frankly (albeit sadly) of the possibility of extra-marital relations. We both felt unsure about this; we really could not decide whether it would be condoned in our consciousnesses. But the important point here is that we did not blind ourselves to its likelihood."[21]

Many women also were advised to lose their worries outside the home by plunging into volunteer programs like Bundles for Blue Jackets, Red Cross, and dozens of other war-related charities. Even such traditional tasks as knitting or baking cakes and pies took on new significance if the products made their way to soldiers and sailors. Besides the private satisfaction of helping, there was informal pressure to contribute more baked goods than other neighborhoods to the Chicago Service Men's Centers and similar organizations.[22]

By March 1942 a grim realization had set in that the war would change the way everyone lived, regardless of social class. Early Allied defeats foretold a long conflict that could be shortened only by the total commitment of every individual.[23] This grim need-to-win attitude coincided with disappearing supplies of consumer goods and the depletion of private stocks of rationed items. The intrusion of wartime was accelerated by the complex interdependencies of urban life. Unlike rural people, city dwellers grew very little of their own food. Home refrigerators were inefficient, with tiny freezers, and because preservatives and individual packaging were little used, many foods had a short shelf life. The most effective way to slow down the buy-and-consume cycle was through canned goods, but lack of space limited how much apartment dwellers could store. Many urban families were immediately vulnerable to rationing, which began with sugar in the spring of 1942. An elaborate system of coupons and tokens, designed to ensure an equitable distribution of scarce commodities, imposed universal guidelines on diets and caused families to lose control of many private shopping decisions. Cooks had to alter treasured recipes and drop some favorite dishes altogether. The new Chicago Nutrition Association and similar groups joined with the press, utility companies, and department stores to reeducate homemakers.[24]

The invasion of the dining table also included the element of time, as families lost control not only of what they ate, but also of when. Ration coupons carried expiration dates, so the use of sugar, canned goods, coffee, and other regulated items had to be paced to cover a week or month. Sometimes a family had to force themselves to finish a supply

The Chicago Daily News Ration Calendar for AUGUST

SUN.	MON.	TUES.	WED.	THURS.	FRI.	SAT.
STAMPS GOOD TODAY BLUE R, S, T Through Sept. 20 RED U Through Aug. 31	2	3	4	5	6	LAST DAY FOR BLUE STAMPS N, P, Q
RED V STAMP GOOD THROUGH AUG. 31	9	10	11	12	13	14
LAST DAY SUGAR STAMP 13 RED W GOOD Through Aug. 31	SUGAR STAMP 14 GOOD	17	18	19	20	21
22	23	24	25	26	27	28
29	30	LAST DAY FOR RED STAMPS T, U, V, W.	SUGAR: Stamps Nos. 15 and 16 in Book One good for five pounds each for home canning through Oct. 31. FUEL OIL: Coupons No. 1, New Book Good for 10 Gals. each in Region 6 of OPA from July 1 through Jan. 4, 1944. Coupons No. 5, Old Book Good for 11 Gals. each in Region 6 through Sept. 30. SHOES: Stamp No. 18, Book One Good for one pair through Oct. 31. Stamp exchangeable among members of family. GASOLINE: Coupons No. 7, New Book Good for 4 Gals. each through Sept. 21. TIRE INSPECTIONS: For A Books, must be completed by Sept. 30; for B Books, Oct. 31, and for C Books, by Aug. 31.		

Figure 1.3. Monthly ration calendar (*Chicago Daily News,* 2 August 1943, 4)

of some item because time was running out on the next coupon period. The press counseled self-control, chiding imprudent families that used their coupons or tokens too quickly and found themselves either hungry or left with only less desirable unrationed items. The Office of Price Administration added to the confusion by frequent adjustments in the point value of rationed commodities. Many Chicago families found their shopping lists determined by full-page tables that they clipped from the newspaper and posted on the kitchen wall.[25]

Rationing produced some unexpected results. Short supplies of meat forced many pet owners to abandon their dogs and cats, causing a severe animal control problem with the rapidly growing number of strays.[26] Rationing also contributed to the long-term movement of some family functions outside the home. Unable to obtain either new washing machines or repair parts for old ones, many families turned to commercial laundries. Long lines and spot shortages of food items meant wasted time going from store to store. Often it was easier to purchase bread and pastries from a bakery than to assemble the needed ingredients. The inconvenience of rationing also lured families to restaurants, whose advertising stressed not only the time saved, but also the savings in points and coupons. Although some restaurant supplies were limited—one lump of sugar and no coffee refills, for instance—and servers were often inexperienced and slow, dining out increased dramatically in Chicago during the war years.[27]

Food shortages also encouraged widespread planting of victory gardens as a way to regain some independence from rationing, but even this project tended to take families away from home. Although those who owned or rented single-family houses could plow up part of the backyard, the official victory garden program sponsored by the Office of Civilian Defense and the Chicago Park District used free seeds, water, and advice to promote communal plots designed to increase neighborliness and participation in other civil defense programs. In either case, rationing transformed the leisure time of 300,000 Chicagoans who spent evenings and weekends laboring in the fields. And when the harvest was in each fall, families who had never canned fruits and vegetables found themselves sterilizing jars in a steaming copper boiler.[28]

The need to replenish nondurable household items also took time and entailed the invasion of privacy. Fuel was used up and clothing wore out. Here the government used rationing not only to distribute goods more equitably but also to slow down consumption of items using raw materials needed for military production, and it manipulated the relationship between manufactured products in a way that the public often did not understand. For instance, it was natural rubber shortages caused by the war in the Pacific, even more than the need to reduce petroleum consumption, that forced the nation into gasoline rationing. Cars that could not be driven would not wear out tires.[29]

Every American driver had to submit an application to the local rationing board and reveal details of automobile use to justify the mileage driven. Many families who had just bought their first cars since the depression found the restriction on leisure driving difficult to bear. Automobile vacations and Sunday drives had become the custom, and guidebooks produced by the WPA Illinois Writers Project during the depression had given official sanction to tourism as a way of improving the economies of states, cities, and towns. But tire and gasoline rationing allowed no frivolous travel. Even those who had managed to save coupons found that the windshield sticker revealed their ration classification to anyone interested enough to look. Illinois vacationers sometimes found themselves fined for illegal trips into Wisconsin.[30]

Selective cutbacks in transportation affected everyone. City dwellers could no longer depend on those who picked up garbage and delivered coal, milk, newspapers, and department store merchandise—services that were severely restricted by conservation of motor fuel and tires. On occasion, Chicago families complained about contradictions within federal rationing policies. Consumers with the space and money had traditionally avoided autumn price increases and delivery delays by filling their coal bins in summer—a practice lauded as prudent in peacetime but condemned as "hoarding" after Pearl Harbor. As the war progressed, however, shortages of heating fuel and cutbacks in autumn delivery services prompted federal officials to encourage families to begin buying some—but not too much—coal during the warm months. No one was sure what that meant, since they continued to condemn those who could fill their basements with enough fuel to make it through the winter. The policy shifts confused most people, who also encountered other cutbacks because urban housing depended on utility grids that supplied gas, water, electricity, telephones, and sewage disposal. At one time or another during the war all these services but sewage disposal were reduced in Chicago because priority was given to defense plants.[31]

Replacing items that broke or wore out also made new demands on people's time. Early in 1942 the federal government issued a series of edicts that prohibited the manufacture of nearly six hundred consumer goods, both durable and nondurable, to conserve raw materials for the war effort. This quickly led to an endless string of shortages. Rumors of large caches of rubber pants for babies led desperate Chicago parents to downstate stores, while small-town residents headed to the city. On occasion, crowds in search of a particularly scarce item damaged store interiors, leading one department store chain to pass up an opportunity to sell a shipment of nylon stockings. All the government seemed willing to do was suggest that consumers visit the used-merchandise "exchange shops" that appeared in unprecedented numbers or buy some items, when available, with a neighbor. In at least two instances, however, public reaction forced changes in federal policy. During early 1942 the government, citing military priority, prohibited the sale of radio tubes to the general public. But when family radios began to malfunction, the need to maintain morale through public amusement and to funnel information and propaganda into the home brought back civilian sales. Similarly, because of a decision not to "waste" metal on bread-slicing equipment, bakeries were ordered to sell only uncut loaves. Public indignation forced a reversal.[32]

The war immediately altered clothing choices—both fabrics and styles. Metal zippers and low hemlines on women's dresses disappeared, as did men's two-trouser suits, patch pockets, vests, and pants pleats and cuffs. National regulations on clothing manufacture evoked mixed reactions. Some people were hesitant to venture out with incorrect styles lest they appear either unpatriotic or out of fashion. Others welcomed the opportunity to be innovative, and in the early months of the war there were several Chicago-area contests to design not only factory apparel for women but also street clothing that was properly patriotic in its use of raw materials.[33]

These intrusions into the private realm also disrupted the rhythm of the year. The college term was accelerated to cut down the time of training needed for the war. Rationing and unavailability interfered with seasonal purchases of clothing and other consumer goods. And though city life had already moved away from the natural planting and harvest cycles of the farm, cold weather brought a constant reminder of dependence on coal delivery or gas pipes. Warm weather brought efforts to channel some of children's outdoor play into patriotic activities. Youngsters were especially crucial in the scrap drives because they knew their neighborhoods so well. Many children between eight and eighteen who did not belong to the Boy Scouts or Girl Scouts were gently urged to join the new American Youth Reserves. This group, founded in Chicago, stressed organized athletics and community service through local civil defense structures. The truly patriotic adults in the family, meanwhile, spent their summer days laboring in victory gardens. The war also brought severe restrictions on vacation travel, which became subject to official scrutiny. It was very difficult for civilians to obtain space on railroads for anything but defense-related travel, since carriers had to account for every seat.[34]

The Industrial Miracle, 1943–45

By the end of 1942 Chicago's war production was about to enter a new phase. For two years Mayor Edward J. Kelly and other civic leaders had complained that although the city had received a number of defense orders in such established industrial areas as steel, railway car construction, and food processing, it had yet to obtain its fair share of the major contracts. That began to change by mid-1942, and by the end of the war 24 billion federal dollars had been spent among more than 1,400 contractors in the Chicago region. The industrial boom included the construction of 320 new factories, including four major aircraft plants.[35]

Although much of the workforce needed to operate the new factories was drawn from those already living in Chicago, thousands more poured in from rural Illinois and other parts of the nation. Among them were over 20,000 Japanese Americans who were moved from desert relocation camps and over 65,000 African Americans who migrated from the South.[36] The demand for living space they generated quickly evaporated the surplus of housing that had characterized the city during the 1930s. Rent control, established nationwide during spring 1942, limited inflationary pressure for those who had apartments, but it did not increase the total space available. During the summer of 1943, federal housing officials pressed the Chicago City Council to temporarily suspend the building code in two critical areas. It lowered standards on new construction to conserve materials, thus paving the way for hundreds of previously forbidden townhouses, single-family structures built below code requirements, and residential units carved out of basements and commercial structures. And many property owners were allowed to subdivide existing apartments, reducing the amount of private space for each tenant.[37]

The number of newly constructed units and conversions never caught up with the demand created by the influx of workers. Several months before the new aircraft plants were completed, the lack of space was already so severe that neighborhood civil defense workers were going door-to-door pleading with families to take boarders in their unused bedrooms. These efforts fueled rumors that the federal government was about to enact a domestic billeting plan forcing those fortunate enough to own homes to share their living space and privacy.[38] African American families faced a problem within a problem, a preexisting housing shortage compounded by newcomers seeking work in wartime industry. At the same time, the housing shortage in the surrounding white neighborhoods tightened the long-standing wall of segregation that encircled the so-called Black Belt, overcrowding dilapidated structures still further, with an attendant decline in privacy.[39]

Regardless of where they lived, Chicagoans not only shared in a level of economic prosperity that few had seen in years, but also found their everyday lives—especially the sense of time within the family—altered by new conditions generated by the workplace. The war deeply affected the city's temporal rhythm in several ways, each contributing in turn to a further penetration of family life. First, on 20 January 1942 President Roosevelt signed a law establishing nationwide daylight saving time for the duration of the war. By shifting an extra hour of light from the morning, when most people were asleep, to the active hours of the evening, the administration hoped to save electricity. Though most Chicagoans appreciated the time for working in their victory gardens, many had to commute to work in darkness.[40] Second, the return of prosperity greatly increased traffic during the normal rush hours, just when fuel and tire rationing forced riders from private autos to public transit. To alleviate the burden on an aging and bankrupt transit system that could not handle the extra riders, the city began urging employers to show their patriotism by staggering shift changes, so that employees could arrive and depart when there were empty seats.[41]

Many workers also found commuting times much longer because the new defense plants were on the urban periphery. The lack of adequate public transportation to many of these sites, and the rationing of gasoline and tires on their own cars, forced them to join car pools that put them at the mercy of the group's schedule. Those who had been accustomed to driving to work alone viewed the new commuting experience as imposing on their privacy. Not only did many have to share space with strangers, but those who drove alone found themselves shunted to the least convenient parts of plant parking lots.[42]

The industrial buildup made Chicago more of a twenty-four-hour city than it had been in years. Although a lively nightlife had long been present in the Loop, Near North, and Uptown areas, and though some prewar factories had worked every hour of the week, the new production urgency forced Chicagoans to reset their personal clocks. Nighttime job training, for instance, brought people to Chicago public high schools and other technical education centers, which ran mechanical shop classes in three shifts, around the clock.[43]

The war also placed great pressure on factories and workers to meet the rigorous schedule typified by the new Douglas Aircraft factory. Land clearance began in June 1942, but the new plant surpassed its "Fly by July" promise when it completed its first C-54 transport plane only eleven months later. Every department of every defense supplier was expected to become equally efficient, and all contracts had time limits written into their performance clauses. For 233 Chicago companies, the reward for cooperating with the speedup was the coveted army-navy "E-Award," which recognized superior corporate effort and included on-time delivery as one of its criteria. And when Congress enacted tax withholding, or the "pay-as-you-go" system, in 1943, workers learned that Uncle Sam also wanted immediate payment of income taxes.[44]

The new work schedules of the defense plant ultimately invaded the home. Many factories required three full shifts, often seven days a week, to meet production deadlines, forcing family timetables to conform to work orders. First, many workers faced expanded schedules of forty-eight or even sixty hours a week, especially during the labor-scarce final year of the war. But many companies also spread the burden of the night work among employees, many of whom had had no experience with the 11 p.m. to 7 a.m. shift. This "swing shift" meant that the work hours for hundreds of thousands of Chicago's industrial employees changed every few weeks.[45] Swing shifts disrupted not only the temporal pattern of domestic life, but also the play of neighborhood children. In January 1943 Mayor Kelly announced the formation of the Greater Chicago Noise Reduction Council, asking children and adults living near war workers to maintain quiet so that night shift workers could sleep during the day.[46]

Wartime disruption of personal time was even more complete when both parents worked. At the beginning of the war, social workers and other experts advised married women, especially mothers, against taking jobs. And in Chicago, at least, initially there was little interest in hiring mothers with small children. But as the labor shortage grew into a crisis by late 1943, women found themselves regarded as unpatriotic in some quarters unless they left their labors at home. Recruiting teams from Johnson and Johnson, Douglas Aircraft, and other war contractors went door-to-door selling women on a temporary industrial career. The prospect of employment created a dilemma for many. The additional income was tempting to those who still faced debts from the depression, and military pay sent home by servicemen did not go far in a boom civilian economy. But thousands of Chicago women also were mothers of young children, mostly depression-delayed first births as they were nearing the end of their childbearing years.[47]

Women's choosing to work outside the home removed the person whose traditional domestic role was the most predictable. Homemakers got the family up and going in the morning, prepared the meals, and tucked the children in at night. Women who decided to join the labor force often faced the problem of child care. When parents' work schedules meshed, the fathers usually took over child care for at least part of the day. But because of swing shifts and absent mates, even preschool youngsters might spend a third or more of each day outside their own homes. Often, friends and neighbors established informal networks of child watching, but by 1945 young Chicagoans were enrolled in 117 day care centers, operated initially by the WPA and later by the Board of Education and the Park District.[48] The least fortunate were left home alone, the so-called latchkey kids or eight-hour orphans. Occasional fires and other accidents that befell them evoked angry editorials and demands that neighbors report such abandonments, adding to the irony that wartime employment made home a dangerous place for a child during much of the day.[49]

The intrusion of the war spared few children, even when their parents were at home. Each holiday season brought more toys with war themes, everything from dolls to tattoos to model planes, and with them came a continuing debate over how much parents should shield their offspring from news of the conflict. Youngsters who had escaped disruptions at home or day care encountered the war at school. Some had classmates whose fathers or uncles had died in the conflict, and whole classes were asked to write letters to servicemen. The child also became a pipeline into the family for propaganda and information about civil defense and other home front activities. In Chicago the curriculum on all levels reflected the times, with an increased emphasis on patriotism, world affairs, and interracial and interethnic harmony as well as vocational skills useful in defense work. Many extracurricular projects, including scrap drives and the construction of model aircraft used in flight training, focused on neighborhood schools.[50]

Growing Impatience, 1943–45

The war had made Chicagoans—and Americans in general—willing to accept what might be called a "substitute culture" of temporary replacements for artifacts, institutions, and social relationships. In the consumer goods that were still available, plastic and wood often replaced the iron, steel, brass, and aluminum needed to make the weapons of war. Workers who once made jukeboxes now turned out weapons guidance systems. Great Lakes fish, Spam, molasses, and other unfamiliar foods filled plates that had once held steaks and sugar confections. A tour of local museums would have to do instead of the customary fishing vacation to northern Wisconsin. Women took the jobs previously held by men. Day care and eight-hour-orphan arrangements served as stand-ins for what society regarded as normal families. Everywhere average Chicagoans turned, they encountered something familiar—yet different.[51]

During 1943 Americans began to lose their tolerance for home front substitutions at about the same rate that their optimism for an early victory, especially in the Pacific, disappeared.[52] The press documented a slowly rising tide of impatience and waning enthusiasm for home front programs—even anger and resistance. Some commentators complained that as women joined the workforce and gained independent incomes, they were more prone to waste time and money shopping for frivolous clothes.[53] There were also signs during 1943 of a growing intolerance of the rationing system. A chorus of complaints greeted the decision by the local Office of Price Administration to force Chicago's 560 undertakers to collect the ration books of the deceased.[54] Chicago-area informants for the federal Office of War Information noted rising anxiety and anger over the complexity of the new point system and a growing belief that the upper class used influence to get away with hoarding. The first newspaper accounts detailing a widespread "black market" also began to appear during 1943. Although a hidden trade in illegal tires and gasoline had existed since the first twenty-four months of the war, reporters now described networks of dealers in counterfeit and stolen coupons, street peddling of liquor and cigarettes, and price gouging. The underlying theme of the revelations was a concern that such easy secret sales were undermining consumers' wartime discipline. Those trading on the black market often agreed with the principle of rationing but regarded their own transactions as a private matter that should be of no interest to those administering the law.[55]

Boredom and an inability to sustain the frenzied pitch of enthusiasm took their toll. The last citywide civil defense drill took place on 23 May 1943, soon to be followed by an admission that most of the 200,000 Chicagoans who had initially signed up for neighborhood defense programs had stopped attending meetings. Officials claimed that workers were too tired from their extended workweeks. Civil defense leaders also admitted that few of their followers still believed Chicago was vulnerable to bombers. It became increasingly difficult to meet scrap drive goals, and bond drives began door-to-door solicitation for the first time to fill their quotas. In February 1944 Mayor Edward J. Kelly, the local Office of Civilian Defense director, appointed civic leaders to a new Committee for Patriotic Action, charged with reviving enthusiasm, but to no avail. The only program to expand late in the war was gardening, which, following a slump in 1943, rebounded after the most serious food shortages of the war spoiled many 1944 Christmas feasts.[56]

The focus of fear about the consequences of war also seemed to shift in Chicago. During the early months the possibility of bombing had threatened the safety of society as a whole, with the individual playing a subordinate role. By mid-1943, however, anxiety was more personalized and private. This change was rooted not only in the growing belief that Chicago would always be safe from enemy bombers, but also in the soaring number of families that had seen a loved one go off to war. The draft now reached more deeply to take fathers and eighteen-year-olds. By November 1943, tearful families were photographed at the first of hundreds of dedication ceremonies for new plastic signs designating intersections nearest the homes of those killed in action as "memorial squares." Meanwhile, the honor rolls of neighborhood residents away in service had grown noticeably longer. At the time of the D Day invasion, 6 June 1944, each Chicago block had on average seven men or women in uniform.[57]

The second half of the war also was marked by a growing fear that the conflict was creating a generation of juvenile delinquents. Some blamed the war for prematurely terminating childhood as a special time of life. School dropout rates rose sharply as teenagers tried to get established in jobs before veterans returned. Underage girls from across the Chicago region, flocking to downtown Grant Park to be picked up by military men, justified sexual liaisons as a patriotic duty to those who might soon die in combat. Who was to blame? Most sociologists commented that the long hours at work had removed parents from the home, with its primary-group influences and controls, leaving children vulnerable to this "life is short, have a fling" mentality that throve in public places and among the anonymous crowd.[58]

The concern about rising juvenile delinquency also was part of a grow-

Figure 1.4.   Ceremony dedicating neighborhood honor roll, 1942. Courtesy of the Library of Congress.

ing preoccupation with the nature of the postwar world. During the last two years of the war, prognosticators sorted themselves into two groups. Pessimists viewed the future as part of a repeating cycle and expected a recurrence of the problems that had appeared after World War I. Thus delinquency portended a recurrence of the wild youth of the 1920s, which they considered a reaction to the discipline of wartime. Predictions that postwar divorce rates would soar were based not only on the number of hasty marriages, but also on what had happened when the doughboys returned. Similarly, because there had been a sharp economic downturn in 1919–20, many commentators forecast a return of the Great Depression after the artificial stimulus of defense spending was withdrawn.[59]

Others looked to the future with optimism. They were willing to draw parallels with the past, but they saw the war as part of a linear development, with the future building on the most positive aspects of the past. They were especially hopeful about the way science and technology would change the everyday lives of Americans. This attitude was stimulated in part by the government decision during 1944 to allow manufacturers to divert some of their resources to plans for resuming domestic production. But the way the war was promoted on the home front also may have contributed to it. Displays of "hardware" had been an integral part of the defense bond campaigns throughout the war, but during the final eighteen months of the conflict the American public learned the details of such feats as the B-29 bomber, radar, the automatic pilot, and the mass production of sulfa drugs and penicillin. The atomic bomb would be the final proof that science and engineering, as well as bravery on the battlefield, were responsible for victory. The situation advanced an old theme: the expositions of the 1930s had amplified the promise that science and technology would end the depression and create a better everyday life. The long deferment of that dream during the war made it that much more fascinating and exciting.[60]

In part the growing interest in the future also sprang from the public's bifurcated experience of time. The speed of change and the control of the temporal rhythm of everyday life had been an essential element in instilling a desire to participate in home front endeavors. Yet just when the world seemed to be changing so rapidly, many aspects of Chicagoans' personal lives had been, in effect, frozen in place for four years. Decisions that had been rehearsed over and over in daydreams would now be made in reality. Returning military personnel had careers to begin; reunited couples had families to start and homes and consumer goods to buy. Thoughts of what would happen when servicemen and servicewomen came home became a national daydream.[61]

Conclusion: Speed up, Slow down "for the Duration"

Government policies often affect more than their creators expect. There is no evidence of a central plan by the federal government to manipulate time to force the war into the domestic lives of Americans. Only daylight saving time and tax withholding even resemble such a scenario. But federal officials faced two tasks that involved the temporal rhythm of society. One was generating enormous amounts of weapons and other war-related goods as quickly as possible. The nation had to upgrade industrial capacity that had been allowed to deteriorate during the depression, retrain its workers, and marshal raw materials. The last requirement, in turn, made it necessary to slow down, if not eliminate, the diversion of resources for what were deemed nonessential uses. Official policy held that direct interference with the free market mechanism not only would make scarce raw materials last longer, but would also help maintain civilian morale through an equitable distribution of goods. Domestic life was caught between the speedup and the slowdown.

Controlling the pace of events was one way home front programs affected the life rhythm of average Chicago families. Coordinating or synchronizing people and their activities was a second. The sirens that announced civil defense drills were a loud manifestation of what went on in many subtle ways. The government issued specific and publicly stated deadlines and amounts for bond campaigns, defense contracts, salvage drives, civil defense rosters, and almost everything else. Large thermometer-style signs, pie charts, and similar gauges let the average citizen not only estimate progress and the size of the task remaining but also respond in harmony. These visual devices functioned in wartime society much as factory clocks and whistles had synchronized the lives of nearby workers during earlier decades.

The manipulation of time ultimately aided the goal of enlisting every American in the urban home front effort. The interdependency that characterized urban life drew everyone into the rhythms of consumption and preparedness established by the federal government. Workplaces,

★ ★ ★

The **Sixth War Loan**

calls

EVERY ILLINOIS WOMAN

to buy

"E" BONDS

See What ONE
$100 Bond Will Buy:

2 Seawater Desalting Kits	· · · · ·	$30.00
3 Oars, Metal Sectional	· · · ·	30.00
Signalling Mirror	· · · · · ·	8.00
Fishing Kit · · · · · · · ·		4.50
First Aid Kit · · · · · · ·		2.50
		$ 75.00

<u>Your</u> Boy May Need This
Sometime

★ ★ ★ ★ ★

MC CORMICK & HENDERSON — 100M — 11-23-44 — CHICAGO, ILL.

Figure 1.5.   War bond flyer, 1944

school systems, organizations, local governments—all joined in making sure the program worked by penetrating the walls of family privacy. The broader the participation, the less the individual burden and sacrifice. The war impinged on the privacy even of the very wealthy, who may not have entered the factory workforce but nonetheless participated in civil defense, salvage, Red Cross, and other volunteer efforts. The home front crusade in Chicago proceeded with urgency and enthusiasm for about two years before a combination of complacency, boredom, and frustration seriously eroded the diversion of interest away from the family and other private concerns.

After the war, as Americans focused on creating a domestic world that restored their lost privacy, the intrusions of war shaped their efforts. Wartime predictions for the postwar world had included new automobiles that would glide down superhighways, free from car pools and transit schedules. The popular press also foretold a return to the detached house, with new building materials transforming the basement into a "family room" where parents and children could stay home and watch television. War-spawned appliance technology would return cooking and laundry to the home, yet free housewives from drudgery and give them more time for themselves and for taking care of their youngsters rather than remaining in the workforce. Moreover, with construction techniques developed during the war, whole towns of prefabricated houses could be erected on site in hours. The nature of wartime sacrifice helped shape the postwar American dream around the central pillars of consumer goods and a suburban home.[62]

Notes

1. *Chicago Tribune*, 16 July 1944.

2. Robert B. Westbrook, "Fighting for the American Family: Private Interest and Political Obligation in World War II," in *The Power of Culture: Critical Essays in American History*, ed. Richard Wightman Fox and T. J. Jackson Lears (Chicago, 1993), 194–221.

3. Stuart A. Queen and Lewis F. Thomas, *The City: The Study of Urbanism in the United States* (New York, 1939). The classic statement, Louis Wirth, "Urbanism as a Way of Life," *American Journal of Sociology* 45 (1938): 1–24, had appeared only three years before Pearl Harbor. Wirth occasionally contributed to efforts by the Office of War Informa-

tion to gauge the mood of America. Louis Wirth papers, box 28, folder 10, Special Collections, University of Chicago Library.

4. Faith M. Williams, "The Standard of Living in Wartime," *Annals of the American Academy of Political and Social Science* 229 (1943): 125–26; on efforts to create civil defense programs in semirural parts of the Chicago area, see Perry R. Duis and Scott LaFrance, *We've Got a Job to Do: Chicagoans and World War II* (Chicago, 1992), 51.

5. Ibid., 77, 98.

6. The growing literature on time and society includes Wilbert E. Moore, *Man, Time and Society* (New York, 1963); Eviatar Zerubavel, *Hidden Rhythms: Schedules and Calendars in Social Life* (Chicago, 1981); Michael Young and Tom Schuller, *The Rhythms of Social Life* (London, 1988); Michael Young, *The Metronomic Society: Natural Rhythms and Human Timetables* (Cambridge, Mass., 1988); see also Amos Hawley, *Human Ecology: A Theory of Community Structure* (New York, 1950), 288–316; and Kevin Lynch, *What Time Is This Place?* (Cambridge, Mass., 1972), passim.

7. On Taylorism, see Michael O'Malley, *Keeping Watch: A History of American Time* (New York, 1990), 164–71, 227–36, and Thomas P. Hughes, *American Genesis: A Century of Invention and Technological Enthusiasm* (New York, 1989), 187–201.

8. Gwendolyn Wright, *Building the Dream: A Social History of Housing in America* (New York, 1981), 125–28.

9. This framework of class and space shapes Perry R. Duis, *The Saloon: Public Drinking in Chicago and Boston, 1880–1920* (Urbana, Ill., 1983).

10. Susan Strasser, *Never Done: A History of American Housework* (New York, 1982), 213–19.

11. S. P. Breckinridge, "The Activities of Women outside the Home," in *Recent Social Trends in the United States,* ed. President's Research Committee on Social Trends (New York, 1933), 709–50, and William F. Ogburn, "The Family and Its Functions," in ibid., 661–79. Lizabeth Cohen, *Making a New Deal: Industrial Workers in Chicago, 1919–1939* (New York, 1990), 104–47.

12. Ernest R. Groves, "The Family," in *Social Changes in 1931,* ed. William F. Ogburn (Chicago, 1932), 942–45; [Louis] Studs Terkel, *Hard Times: An Oral History of the Great Depression* (New York, 1970), 453–500; Ruth Cavan and Katherine Ranck, *The Family and the Great*

Depression (Chicago, 1938), 176–49; Cohen, *Making a New Deal,* 214–18.

13. *Chicago Daily News,* 21 May 1943; *Chicago Tribune,* 20 February 1932, 25 February 1945; "24-Hour Clock Used by the Navy and Army," *Science Digest* 12 (November 1942): 12; "War News for Your Radio," *Popular Science* 140 (May 1942): 204.

14. Duis and LaFrance, *We've Got a Job to Do,* 34, 43, 47–50.

15. *Civilian Defense Alert* 1 (28 April 1942): 1; 1 (19 May 1942): 1; 2 (12 May 1943): 7.

16. Duis and LaFrance, *We've Got a Job to Do,* 36, 39, 40; "Manual for Practice Blackout, August 12, 1942," typescript, Blackout Collection, Chicago Historical Society Library; *Civilian Defense Alert* 2 (12 December 1942): 1.

17. *Civilian Defense Alert* 1 (11 March 1942): 1; 1 (31 March 1942): 2; 1 (21 July 1942): 1; *Chicago Tribune,* 31 May 1942.

18. *Civilian Defense Alert* 1 (21 July 1942): 2; *Chicago Tribune,* 14 February and 7 July 1942; *Chicago Daily News,* 3, 12, 17 June 1943.

19. Doris Weatherford, *American Women and World War II* (New York, 1990), 243–64; *Chicago Daily News,* 27 March 1943, 6 June 1944.

20. Duis and LaFrance, *We've Got a Job to Do,* 6–7; Judy Litoff and David Smith, " 'Will He Get My Letter?' Popular Portrayals of Mail and Morale during World War II," *Journal of Popular Culture* 23 (1990): 21–45.

21. Quotation from Augusta Kanthak, "Term Paper: Mobility Effect on Life of a Family," typescript, Ernest Burgess papers, box 170, folder 4, Special Collections, University of Chicago Library; *Chicago Tribune,* 12 January and 1 February 1942, 12 June and 26 July 1944.

22. The "Women in War Work" column in the *Chicago Tribune,* daily from 8 January 1941 through 18 November 1944, has hundreds of listings; on pies, 8 January, 13 and 21 March 1942.

23. *Chicago Daily News,* 8 June 1942.

24. Duis and LaFrance, *We've Got a Job to Do,* 18–22; Chicago Nutrition Association, *Annual Reports,* 1942–45; *Chicago Herald-American,* 8 October 1942; John F. Zwicky, "A State at War: The Home Front in Illinois during the Second World War" (Ph.D. diss., Loyola University, Chicago, 1989), 203–309.

25. *Chicago Tribune,* 3 May 1942; *Chicago Daily News,* 24 March, 29 April, 16 May, 4 June 1943.

26. *Chicago Daily News,* 16 April 1943.

27. On laundries, *Chicago Daily News,* 26 June 1942, 16 June and 14 July 1943; on restaurants, ibid., 4 January and 12 May 1943; *Chicago Tribune,* 27 February and 1 May 1942, 18 and 28 July 1944.

28. "Report of the Victory Garden Department, Office of Civilian Defense, Chicago Metropolitan Area from Its Inception in 1941 to December 31, 1943," typescript, Chicago Historical Society Library; Duis and LaFrance, *We've Got a Job to Do,* 45–46.

29. Zwicky, "State at War," 310–13.

30. Ibid., 305, 314–15; Duis and LaFrance, *We've Got a Job to Do,* 25–26.

31. *Economist* 107 (20 June 1942): 16; *Chicago Daily News,* 2 November 1943.

32. *Civilian Defense Alert* 1 (9 June 1942): 5; *Chicago Daily News,* 6 August 1943; Duis and LaFrance, *We've Got a Job to Do,* 14–15.

33. Men's clothing, *Chicago Tribune,* 4 and 28 March 1942; *Chicago Daily News,* 17 May 1943. Women's clothing, *Chicago Daily News,* 7 June 1943; *Chicago Tribune,* 19 and 20 March 1942, 2, 9, and 10 May 1942, 5 June 1942, 25 May 1943.

34. "First Youth Reserves Organized in Chicago," *Civilian Defense* 1 (May 1942): 44; on vacations, *Chicago Daily News,* 8 May 1942, 2 July and 11 August 1943; *Chicago Tribune,* 1 August 1944, 18 February 1945; Mary Watters, *Illinois in the Second World War* (Springfield, Ill., 1952), 1:411.

35. Duis and LaFrance, *We've Got a Job to Do,* chap. 3; Zwicky, "State at War," 82–123; Mary Watters, *Illinois in the Second World War,* vol. 2, *The Production Front* (Springfield, Ill., 1952), passim.

36. Masako M. Osako, "Japanese Americans: Melting into the All-American Pot," in *Ethnic Chicago,* 2d ed., ed. Melvin Holli and Peter d'A. Jones (Grand Rapids, Mich., 1984), 526–28; St. Clair Drake and Horace Cayton, *Black Metropolis: A Study of Negro Life in a Northern City* (New York, 1945), 174–213.

37. Zwicky, "State at War," 317–19; Duis and LaFrance, *We've Got a Job to Do,* 27–30.

38. *Civilian Defense Alert* 1 (26 May 1942): 1; *Chicago Tribune,* 31 May 1942.

39. Paul T. Gilbert and J. M. Klein, *Some Light of Truth on the Negro Housing Nightmare* (Chicago, 1945); Robert C. Weaver, "Race

Restrictive Housing Covenants," *Journal of Land and Public Utility Economics* 20 (August 1944): 183–93; *Chicago Daily News*, 22 May 1943; *Chicago Defender*, 31 May 1943.

40. *New York Times*, 4 and 21 January 1942; *Chicago Tribune*, 21 and 22 January 1942; on the daylight saving time issue during World War I, see O'Malley, *Keeping Watch*, 259–95.

41. *Economist* 108 (5 December 1942): 13; *Chicago Tribune*, 12 and 17 January 1942; *American City* 60 (December 1945): 7.

42. *For Action Now: A Program to Promote Car Sharing in the Chicago Metropolitan Area* (Chicago: Office of Civilian Defense, Chicago Metropolitan Region, July 1942); *Microphone* (Western Electric Corporation) 18 (November 1942): 2; *Civilian Defense Alert* 1 (14 July 1942): 5, 2 (6 January 1943): 1, 4.

43. "Training Workers for Defense," *Commerce* 38 (February 1941): 13–15, 39–40; Duis and LaFrance, *We've Got a Job to Do*, 82–85. Some neighborhood civil defense watches and blackouts were also staged after midnight; see *Civilian Defense Alert* 1 (29 September 1942): 1.

44. *Chicago Tribune*, 10 June 1942; [Douglas] *Chicago Airview News* 1 (8 June 1943): 6, 1 (29 June 1943): 4–5, 1 (14 September 1943): 3; Watters, *Illinois in the Second World War*, 2:290–91; James P. Baxter, *Scientists against Time* (Boston, 1946).

45. *Civilian Defense Alert* 2 (20 January 1943): 3; *Chicago Tribune*, 13 October 1943.

46. "Sleep Tips for Swing Shifters," *Popular Science* 142 (May 1943): 98–99; *Chicago Daily News*, 13 October 1943; Watters, *Illinois in the Second World War*, 2:286, 287, 292; *Civilian Defense Alert* 2 (20 January 1943): 3.

47. *Chicago Tribune*, 8 May 1942; Zwicky, "State of War," 154–56.

48. Watters, *Illinois in the Second World War*, 2:350–54; *Chicago Tribune*, 26 June and 2 July 1944, 19 February, 27 and 28 March 1945; *Chicago Daily News*, 18 March 1943.

49. *Chicago Daily News*, 1 July 1942, 17 March 1943. There are many requests for hour reductions in the files of the War Manpower Commission, Record Group 211, box 3567, National Archives, Great Lakes Regional Depository, Chicago.

50. *Chicago Daily News*, 22 April 1943; Thomas J. Crawford, "The Participation of the Chicago Public High Schools in the War Effort" (M.A. thesis, DePaul University, 1946), 90–95; Duis and LaFrance,

We've Got a Job to Do, 4–31, illustrates many wartime toys; "War Toys Not Harmful to Minds of Children," *Science News Letter* 41 (16 May 1942): 309.

51. *Chicago Daily News*, 17 December 1941, 6 July 1942.

52. Paul D. Casdorph, *Let the Good Times Roll: Life at Home in America during World War II* (New York, 1989), 78–79, 136. George Gallup, *The Gallup Poll, Public Opinion, 1935–1971*, 3 vols. (New York, 1972), 1:329, 399, 427, 452.

53. *Chicago Daily News*, 31 January, 25 August, 22 September, and 17 December 1943.

54. "Report of January 18–23, 1943, Rationing," 1–2, in Chicago Files, Office of War Information, Record Group 44, boxes 1939–40, National Archives, Washington, D.C.; *Chicago Daily News*, 17 November 1943.

55. Watters, *Illinois in the Second World War*, 1:330–32, 339, 341; *Chicago Daily News*, 10, 24, and 26 May, 16 July 1943; Weatherford, *American Women and World War II*, 213; Zwicky, "State at War," 309–10, 313–17.

56. Watters, *Illinois in the Second World War*, 1:79; Zwicky, "State at War," 331–32; *Chicago Daily News*, 27 January and 9 February 1944.

57. Victor Kleber, *Selective Service in Illinois, 1940–1947* (Springfield, Ill., 1948), 170, 173, 229–34; Watters, *Illinois in the Second World War*, 1:223; issues of the *Civilian Defense Alert* during 1943 chronicle the shift in neighborhood concern to memorials.

58. *Chicago Daily News*, 11, 14, and 18 January 1943, 22, 24, and 25 February 1943, 25 March 1943, 25 September 1943, 15 November 1943, 19 January 1944, 11 May 1944; *Chicago Tribune*, 28 February 1945; Watters, *Illinois in the Second World War*, 1:372, 374–75, 383, 386-87. The contemporary sociological literature on delinquency is voluminous, but excellent summary articles may be found in topical issues of *Annals of the American Academy of Political and Social Science:* "The American Family in World War II," 229 (September 1943), and "Adolescents in Wartime," 236 (November 1944).

59. The divorce literature in also voluminous, but see *Chicago Daily News*, 3 and 24 June 1943; *Chicago Tribune*, 11 November 1944, 26 January 1945. On other aspects, see Duis and LaFrance, *We've Got a Job to Do*, 115–21.

60. Duis and LaFrance, *We've Got a Job to Do*, 97–102; Donald G.

Cooley and the editors of *Mechanix Illustrated, Your World Tomorrow* (New York, 1944), passim, and numerous articles in *Popular Mechanics* and *Popular Science* during the years following 1943 provide an unusual look at technological optimism.

61. See especially the series of columns by Tom Collins, *Chicago Daily News*, September and October 1943, and *Chicago Tribune Magazine*, 25 March 1945, for predictions about Chicago's air future.

62. *Chicago Daily News*, 8–10 December 1943; *Chicago Tribune*, 24 September 1944, 21 and 28 January 1945. It is useful to note, however, that William H. Whyte Jr., *The Organization Man* (New York, 1956), which studied the new Chicago suburb of Park Forest during 1952–53 and 1956, found a society marked by intrusive neighboring and communal sharing of consumer goods.

George H. Roeder Jr.

TWO

Censoring Disorder: American Visual Imagery of World War II

The photographic essay that provoked the angriest responses from *Life* magazine's readers during World War II had no apparent connection with the war.[1] It depicted a 1942 Cambridge, Massachusetts, production of *Othello* that featured the black actor, singer, athlete, and activist Paul Robeson. Some of the photographs showed Robeson onstage as Othello with his wife Desdemona, played by white actress Uta Hagen. The resulting letters of protest included one from a Houston reader who found it "more than I can stomach" and another from a South Carolinian who warned that "such pictures have a tendency to create in some Negroes a longing for something that cannot be theirs." A Kentucky reader expressed horror that there were "white men with so little respect for themselves that they would cause to be printed the picture of a Negro man with his arm around a white woman." By that reader's definition the *Life* editors must have regained their self-respect, because they did not run another picture showing a black man in physical contact with a white woman during the remaining three years of the war.[2]

Because of such incidents, military and civilian officials in the United States usually assumed that they were more likely to get in trouble by releasing potentially controversial visual images than by withholding them. During the entire period of American involvement in World War I, authorities did not allow publication of a single photograph of a dead American soldier. Although President Franklin D. Roosevelt's government eventually released some photographs of the American war dead during World War II, censorship remained a major component of the effort to shape public opinion. It worked. Things unseen had as least as great an influence on American understanding of World War II as things seen.

What was seen did matter. Despite the difficulty of evaluating how visual imagery affects individual and collective attitudes, abundant public opinion polls, wartime studies by agencies such as the Office of War Information (OWI), and other evidence suggest that the themes emphasized in wartime posters, movies, and news photographs did influence Americans. The imagery that had the greatest impact drew sustenance from, and helped reinforce, assumptions deeply rooted in the culture. Negative images of Japanese were not a post–Pearl Harbor invention, although such images became more numerous and vicious after 7 December. Wartime imagery perpetuated traditional hierarchies of white over black and male over female even as it advertised some new economic opportunities for African Americans and women.[3]

Many scholars have documented the power of active propaganda in the United States during World War II. John Dower argues convincingly that images of one another by Americans and Japanese before, during, and after the war affected perceptions and thus behavior. Karal Ann Marling and John Wetenhall tell wonderfully the story of the origins and exploitation of the war's most famous American image, Joe Rosenthal's photograph of the second flag raising at Iwo Jima. Essays in *Behind the Lines: Gender and the Two World Wars* include a few of the many recent studies that explore the nature and influence of the imagery of gender, class, ethnicity, and race in different places and times. Clayton R. Koppes and Gregory D. Black make extensive use of official records to measure the considerable energy the United States government expended during World War II to ensure that Hollywood movies served the propaganda needs of the war effort. But Koppes and Black show that OWI suggestions for excisions from movie scripts were at least as urgent as their requests for additions. Important as officials perceived active propaganda to be in achieving intense, unified support for the war effort, they believed its effect would be undercut if it was not combined with vigorous censorship of contradictory messages. This belief was especially strong because memories of World War I excesses had created skepticism toward active propaganda among both leaders and the public. Thus censorship proved a more reliable device for shaping public opinion than pro-war visual messages, even though public and private organizations churned them out in unprecedented abundance.[4]

So what was missing? I will answer this question mainly through an examination of censored photographs now declassified and accessible to researchers at the National Archives. The largest number of these photographs are in a file in the Still Picture Branch marked "RG 319-CE." The World War II photographs in this file, taken by Army Signal Corps photographers, were kept out of view for the duration of the war and for decades afterward. The National Archives' holdings reveal that the photographs most likely to be censored, excluding those of strategic value such as pictures of new weaponry and aerial photographs of terrain, were those that blurred the distinction between friend and foe, suggested the war might bring about disruptive social changes, or undermined confidence in the ability of Americans to maintain control over their institutions and their individual lives. My shorthand terms for these overlapping categories are confusion, disruption, and disorder. As I note at several points in this chapter, consideration of photographs not subject to military censorship, and of posters, editorial cartoons, newsreels, and movies, would provide a sometimes different but in most ways similar answer to the question, What is missing? Before examining the categories of censored photographs, it is important to note briefly the origins of United States censorship policy and changes that occurred.

Early in 1941 the Joint Army and Navy Public Relations Committee had proposed, at an initial cost of $50 million, a system for "complete censorship of publications, radio, and motion pictures within the U.S.A." Finding the proposal "fishy," President Roosevelt emphatically rejected this "wild scheme," noting that the joint committee "obviously . . . knows nothing about what the American public—let alone the American press, would say to a thing like this." Roosevelt, serving an unprecedented third term, did know something about the public and the press, and how they would resist domestic censorship policies that announced themselves too flagrantly. When he set up an Office of Censorship shortly after Pearl Harbor, he gave it authority much less sweeping than that envisioned in the joint committee's plans. The office had power of mandatory censorship over all international communications not covered by military censorship and over domestic information originating from military installations and certain industrial plants with military contracts. Its monitoring of most other domestic information, however, relied on voluntary compliance with its guidelines by the press and public. Consequently some images generated and published within the United States during World War II, as well as some from noncombat areas outside the country, did indeed provide visual evidence of confusion, disruption, or disorder. But such images were the exceptions.[5]

There was nothing voluntary about censorship in American combat zones, where the military allowed only its own photographers or accredited nonmilitary photographers pledged to abide by its rules. These rules varied over time and among services, but typically photographers submitted exposed film to field censors, who classified photographs in accordance with policies set by military and civilian leaders, then sent them back to the United States for further review and for distribution. Because they were far more likely to get in trouble for letting through a photograph they should have blocked than for restricting one they might have released, in doubtful cases censors were more likely to stop an image than to let it pass. In the case of Army Signal Corps photographs, most had to be approved by field censors, then by the War Department's Bureau of Public Relations (BPR) in Washington before being released for publication. Censored photographs ended up in a separate file, housed by midwar in the newly constructed Pentagon.[6]

Elmer Davis hoped to liberate some images from this file, although he probably did not know that BPR personnel referred to it in their internal correspondence as the "chamber of horrors." Davis, appointed director of OWI, formed in June 1942 to coordinate the flow of war-related words and images from government to public, was a respected radio commentator and Rhodes scholar with no previous government experience. He recognized that his primary responsibility was to maintain a high level of public support for the American war effort. Thus, although OWI had no formal powers of censorship—as its relations with Hollywood attested—the agency sought to keep out of view material that might weaken this support. But Davis also took seriously his promises "to tell nothing but the truth" and "to see that the American people get just as much of it as genuine considerations of military security will permit." Even as Davis acknowledged that "security" required something short of full disclosure of all war news, the adjective *genuine* announced his intention to use sparingly this excuse for keeping information from the public.[7]

Others were less reluctant. Shortly after Davis took office he received a prescient letter from George Creel, former head of the Committee on Public Information, which during World War I had combined functions now divided between Davis's office and the Office of Censorship. Creel noted that rather than having the freedom to build his own organization "from the ground up," Davis would have to piece together OWI out of existing agencies that had been "running wild due to divided authority." Because Roosevelt hated to fire anyone loyal to him, OWI inherited much "deadwood." Nelson Rockefeller's maneuvering would allow him as coordinator of inter-American affairs to compete with OWI for control of information flowing to and from Latin America. Most serious of all, "your control over Army, Navy and State is not real in any sense of the word." Supposedly those departments were to establish information policy in consultation with OWI, but "'coordination by conference' never worked and never will work." When a conflict arose, the habitually restrictive military would use its pivotal role in the transmission of information to control access to it. "He was about right on all points," Davis later noted on the bottom of Creel's letter. Despite Davis's conviction that Americans wanted their war news to be brutally frank, for nearly two years the photographs that best fit this definition accumulated in the "chamber of horrors," whose very existence remained secret.[8]

Davis achieved partial success in August 1943, when President Roosevelt and Secretary of War Henry L. Stimson instructed the military to make available to OWI for public release some photographs of American dead. Davis's threat to resign if this was not done perhaps contributed to the policy change, although he had made this threat before. More important, the events of 1943 replaced earlier administration fears of widespread demoralization with new concerns that public overconfidence would make workers less reluctant to strike, miss work, or leave essential jobs and would reduce the effectiveness of war bond and conservation campaigns. The Allies had gained control of all North Africa in May. By about the same time they had countered the U-boat threat effectively enough to ensure Allied dominance in the Atlantic. Negotiations were under way that led to Italian surrender in September, and American forces were on the verge of dramatic advances in the Pacific. An OWI survey of public opinion completed one week before Davis threatened to resign suggested that although dissatisfaction with official information was not as great as it had been the previous winter, it was on the increase again. On the day Davis gave his ultimatum, OWI's regional observers reported rising optimism about the war that might lead to complacency and thus "lagging production," but they also noted

growing resentment that "the war news is incomplete and sugar coated."
The proportion of Americans who believed that government news releases made the situation look better than it was went from 28 percent
in July 1942 to 39 percent in June 1943. Officials hoped that greater
candor about the realities of war might reduce public skepticism. The
first, carefully selected photographs of dead Americans appeared in September 1943. To keep pace with the lulling effect of further Allied
advances, the government released the bloodiest images of American
death in the war's final year. Despite these significant variations in policy,
officials consistently censored, and kept out of view for the duration,
most photographs that suggested confusion, disruption, or disorder.[9]

Confusion

To maintain clear distinctions between friend and foe, propagandists
produced images that contrasted the admirable qualities of American
soldiers and their allies with the brutality, even bestiality, of their enemies, especially the Japanese. Censors kept out of view photographs that
cast doubt on these neat categorizations. Released photographs created
the impression that American bombs, bullets, and artillery shells killed
only enemy soldiers. Pictures of young, elderly, and female victims always ended up in the files of censored images. So did photographs of
the residents in allied and occupied countries who had been unintention-
ally run over by American soldiers or killed in traffic accidents involving
military vehicles. Wartime necessity often required weary soldiers to
rush these vehicles through unfamiliar terrain. Investigators visually recorded the numerous casualties that resulted. Authorities censored all
the documents they produced, such as a poignant photograph showing
a little Italian girl just killed by an army truck when American troops
occupied the southern part of her country.

The enemy committed all the visible atrocities. Officials released photographs showing American soldiers whom Germans troops had killed
after their surrender near Malmedy during the Battle of the Bulge in
December 1944, but they suppressed photographs of GIs taking enemy
body parts as trophies, an especially common occurrence in the Pacific
war. On rare occasions visual evidence of this practice slipped through
holes in the censorship net, as when *Life* published in its 22 May 1944
issue a photograph of a prim woman from Arizona looking at a Japanese

skull that her navy boyfriend had managed to get smuggled home to her. He and thirteen friends had signed it and added an inscription, "This is a good jap—a dead one picked up on the New Guinea beach" (see p. 179 below). *Life* noted that "the armed forces disapprove strongly of this sort of thing." Because of this disapproval officials censored, for instance, a photograph of a Japanese soldier's decapitated head hung on a tree branch, probably by American soldiers, as a warning to others. Censored photographs lend support to the observation of John Dower and other scholars that Americans were far more likely to commit such atrocities against the Japanese than against European foes. In reviewing thousands of censored photographs and tens of thousands of uncensored ones, including some taken by soldiers for their own use, I never have encountered one documenting that American soldiers took as trophies body parts of European soldiers.[10]

Censors also withheld photographs likely to invite sympathy for the enemy, such as figure 2.1, which the army captioned, "This patrol captured two Nips alive." The suggestion of possible mistreatment of the prisoner, his obvious vulnerability, likely to elicit an empathic response from some viewers, and the possibly unsportsmanlike expressions of onlookers all would have encouraged the censors' decision. Also censored because they might elicit sympathy were pictures of wounded enemy soldiers receiving treatment from American medics, and others showing enemy soldiers convicted of war crimes being given last rites by a minister, priest, or monk, although censors did allow publication of some images that depicted the presence of clerics at executions.[11]

The sharpest challenge to the clear distinctions between allies and enemies required by polarized wartime ways of seeing came from the presence in the United States of a few hundred thousand Asian Americans. Henry R. Luce, born of missionary parents in China, was especially concerned lest Americans confuse residents of Japanese and Chinese ancestry. Shortly after Pearl Harbor the magazines he published, *Time* and *Life*, ran detailed, illustrated articles, based on highly dubious assumptions about connections between ethnicity and behavior as well as appearance, titled "How to Tell Your Friends from the Japs." Filmmakers found easier ways of identifying the ethnic affiliations of characters so that the audience could sort out good and bad. Among the onlookers at a military parade depicted in *Shores of Tripoli* was a spectator who waved an American flag and wore a sign that said "Me Chinese." News-

Figure 2.1

reels featured stories such as "Chinatown Hails Captured Jap Sub" to emphasize the difference.[12]

Not even the Constitution restrained the imperative to maintain clear distinctions between enemy and ally. Arguably the government violated at least half of the ten amendments composing the Bill of Rights with its decision to remove Americans of Japanese ancestry, most of them United States citizens, from the communities where they lived and worked and to place them in guarded camps in sparsely inhabited areas of the West. This move was dictated primarily by political expediency (the action won widespread approval) and by fears of espionage, later discredited. Other reasons included concern over violent attacks on Japanese Americans by hostile neighbors and the greed of some of these same neighbors, who were able to buy much of the detainees' property at a small fraction of its value. But the relocation removed 110,000 confusing reminders that the bestial Japanese faces glowering from wartime posters and cartoons did not tell the whole truth.[13]

The government acknowledged visual motivations for its actions. An OWI bulletin sent to the motion picture industry emphasized that Japanese Americans were sent to relocation centers partly because they *"look like* our Japanese enemies." Relocation actually complicated the visual distinctions Luce had tried to maintain. Because it placed actors of Japanese ancestry behind barbed wire, it ensured that Chinese American actors would be cast in roles such as the interrogating Japanese general in *Purple Heart,* played by the omnipresent Richard Loo. It also meant that when Twentieth Century–Fox filmed *Little Tokyo, U.S.A.,* it used neon signs in Los Angeles' Chinatown as a substitute for those in that city's Japanese business and entertainment district, darkened by the internment. This mattered little. Because relocation was more about perceived threats and differences than substantive ones, it helped maintain the wartime illusion of clear distinctions.[14]

The "censorship" of living human beings accomplished by relocation was reinforced by actions that kept out of view photographs revealing ironies of the process. One, a 1942 Dorothea Lange photograph taken during her brief stint with the War Relocation Authority (WRA), showed a Japanese American, apparently a retired veteran, reporting to the Santa Anita Park assembly center, a first stage in the relocation process, dressed in his military uniform. The uniform markings and ribbons showed that he had served in the United States Navy for at least twenty years, stretching back to World War I. WRA's internal shelflist of negatives says this photograph was one of several "impounded by Major Beasley," and as far as I know it was not released during the war years. As the camps were being set up, the Office of Censorship and the BPR coordinated their efforts to review all photographs taken inside them. They released those that served the dual purpose of proving the inmates were confined securely enough to make certain they posed no threat to the country's safety yet showing they were not being mistreated.[15]

Censorship of potentially confusing images of Japanese Americans helped keep intact unambiguous categories of friend and enemy. For similar reasons officials suppressed evidence of disunity within the Allied camp, such as postwar photographs of the bloody interior of the apartment of an English officer whom two Americans had beaten. These photographs had been shot as part of a court martial investigation. The RG 319-CE file contains other photographs taken for this reason, including many, often gory, of victims of GI rapes and murders. GI criminals as well as GI crimes remained largely out of sight, although *Life* and others published photographs that recorded crimes committed in areas not subject to military censorship. The Office of War Information made elaborate behind-the-scenes arrangements to ensure that Americans saw pictures of civilians in state prisons going through self-imposed marching drills as a sign that even this most marginalized part of the population stood solidly behind the war effort. At the same time, BPR withheld photographs showing drills carried out by GIs sentenced to army stockades abroad for crimes committed while in the military.[16]

Soldiers themselves, by contrast, often encountered stern visual warnings that the wrong sort of behavior would send *them* to the stockade. Here as in other areas, officials produced for soldiers imagery that might raise troubling questions if presented to the civilian population. To emphasize the differences between clean-fighting Americans and the tricky enemy, the government did not release to the general public training posters such as figure 2.2, which taught soldiers the value of sneak attacks, although *Life* and others did publish some verbal and visual reports of these practices.[17]

Disruption

Authorities could not deny that war was disruptive. But they did minimize attention to potential disruptions within American society that were

Figure 2.2

related to the war effort. Race was the touchiest issue. Wartime imagery urged blacks and whites to work harmoniously in the common cause, but it reassured the white majority that this did not require violating widely accepted social norms. Propaganda took care of the first task, censorship the second. During 1943 publication in several places of photographs of African American GIs in England dancing with white women caused controversies similar to that provoked by the *Life* article on Robeson's *Othello*. In response the BPR hastily ordered military censors to stop all photographs showing blacks mixing socially with white women. In the war's final year black troops' "vigorous protest" of this practice led General Dwight David Eisenhower to call for a slight modification of the restrictive policy. He agreed that publishing such photographs would "unduly inflame racial prejudice in the United States" but suggested that the BPR allow blacks to mail home their own photographs

Figure 2.3

after censors stamped them "For personal use only—not for publication." Figure 2.3, an official army photograph of the winners of a dance contest at the Red Cross Colored Club in Italy, is an example of a photograph censored by the BPR for racial reasons. For part of the war the army also refused to release pictures showing wounded members of the black Ninety-second Division or burials of soldiers from that unit because of the "tendency on part of negro press to unduly emphasize" its achievements. Without knowledge of this order it would be difficult for researchers to understand why the files of censored material include, next to images showing horribly wounded whites, apparently innocuous photographs of slightly wounded blacks.[18]

Not all censors worked for the government. Local newspapers refused a Maryland post commander's request to run a photograph showing an African American GI (Dempsey Travis, now a successful Chicago realtor) who had won a prize for the best-managed post exchange. Such images threatened a racial status quo based on the assumption of black subordination. The activities of Milton Stark show how intertwined government and private efforts could become. Stark, a white who owned several movie theaters with a largely black clientele as well as a photographic supply store in Baltimore, also worked as a "racial liaison" for the Office of Emergency Management. During the 1943 Detroit riots he reported to OWI that he was concerned because All-American News, a company that made newsreels for theaters serving mostly blacks, had sent cameramen to Detroit. He hoped the company would not use footage shot there in its newsreels, because that "would serve only to spread further disunity and racial prejudice throughout the entire country." Stark claimed he should have no trouble persuading the company to withhold scenes of the riot. He had talked to the company head, Edward Gluckman, who assured him "that all material in the reels will be *favorable* rather than inflammatory." Stark added, "I feel I can control this to a large degree, since contracts for the newsreel service to theaters which I control personally will represent a large percentage of the total income possibilities of the project." He exaggerated his own economic power, but Stark's position was consistent with that of others in government and business whose support All-American depended on. The company never ran a story on the Detroit riots. On rare occasions other outlets such as *Life* did run dramatic pictures of wartime riots in Detroit and elsewhere, but the government was able to censor photographs even of racial conflicts taking place on domestic military bases.[19]

Increased interracial socializing was not the only opportunity for disrupting conventional gender relations that wartime circumstances created. For many, military life meant spending extended periods exclusively with their same sex. Censors, especially those distant from combat zones, took care to conceal visual suggestions that this had any effect on sexual identity or behavior. Despite its clearance by a field censor, the BPR withheld from publication a photograph showing enlisted men wearing Women's Army Corps (WAC) uniforms. Perhaps what seemed natural or entertaining to those in military encampments where men outnumbered women by over fifty to one seemed not only undignified but even subversive to those living in the very different conditions of wartime Washington. Some authority, probably the BPR, also censored a photograph, cleared in the field, showing two WACs, bivouacked in temporary quarters in a cold climate, embracing each other to keep warm.[20]

Disorder

The category of disruption spills over into the final category of disorder. Indeed, by a broad definition "disorder" becomes the most comprehensive category, accounting for virtually all the censored photographs. Reduced to its essence, the message of wartime propaganda was that Americans lived in a well-ordered society that was threatened by Axis aggression. Images that hoped to win official approval might point to correctable imperfections in American society but must not question this basic premise. They could document meaningful sacrifices that Americans made for the larger cause, eventually including even death, but could not demonstrate how thoroughly war could disorder—rip asunder—their individual lives and bodies.

Throughout the war officials censored photographs of the American dead that showed decapitation, dismemberment (with a few exceptions), and limbs twisted or frozen into unnatural positions. The latter feature no doubt contributed to censorship of figure 2.4, an army photograph of one of the Americans that German soldiers killed at Malmedy. Censors also would have suppressed this image because of its overall grisly nature and because of the number placed on the soldier, which could have been perceived as dehumanizing, although its purpose was to aid a war crimes investigation into the massacre.

The government censored disturbing images of war's mayhem as it affected Americans for many reasons: out of respect for the feelings of citizens worried about family members in combat zones, because of a widely shared sense of propriety (most publications would not have used them even had they been released), and for the practical reason that horrific pictures of the American dead seemed unlikely to help the government's ongoing effort to keep the ranks filled with new recruits. But censoring such images was also a way of shielding apprehensive citizens from full knowledge of war's transformative power, a power so great that no particular person, family, community, or social institution could be certain of escaping its often unpredictable effects. This led the army to censor not only photographs of a field littered with bits of human flesh

Figure 2.4

after the explosion of an ammunition truck, but also images, such as one of a soldier who fell to his death from a window and numerous others documenting GI suicides, that would not fit seamlessly into a master narrative emphasizing that "we have everything under control."[21]

For the most part news and entertainment media shared this goal. Numerous publications did run stories describing government misman-agement, but photographs and film footage from combat areas almost always were presented so as to reassure readers that the American war effort was rational not only in its overall goals but in all its details, including the mission assigned to every soldier. *Life* accompanied its first photograph of Americans killed in the war—George Strock's powerful, elegantly composed picture of three American soldiers lying dead on Buna Beach in New Guinea—with a full-page editorial. The editors drew on familiar sports imagery to guide viewers' responses: "We are still aware of the relaxed self-confidence with which the leading boy ran into the sudden burst of fire—almost like a halfback carrying the ball down a football field." Such presentations, reinforced by censorship of photographs showing American corpses piled on top of each other or being tossed onto trucks, placed each American death in a context consistent with a well-ordered life and world.[22]

Maintaining this impression of order required the suppression of images that revealed incompetence, irrationality, or loss of control. Photographs censored at least in part because they fit into this broad category ranged from those that showed Americans and others killed or wounded by Allied "friendly fire" or other military blunders to one showing turkeys intended for soldiers' Thanksgiving dinner carelessly strewn over the floor of an army warehouse. In addition to suppressing evidence of organizational disorder, the army censored photographs that might raise doubts about how well individual American soldiers controlled their own behavior. Without such control, how could they consistently resist sliding into undisciplined acts attributed only to the enemy?[23]

This concern led the army to censor photographs that recorded sexual energies unleashed by the American war effort. In addition to their discomfort with documentation of wartime disruptions of conventional patterns of sexual identity, officials recognized that any sexually charged photograph could subvert the illusion of control. The government also was unwilling to alarm spouses, lovers, and parents waiting at home. One censored photograph showed two young military policemen, apparently quite satisfied with their assignment, accompanying Neapolitan prostitutes to an army medical center for "treatment and confinement." Another depicted WACs somewhere in Asia. According to the caption they were "watching elephants bathe." This alone would not have kept the picture out of even the *Saturday Evening Post,* but half of the women were looking with more interest than the censors could accept at the elephants' handler, a young Asian man naked except for a narrow loincloth. Other censored photographs in the RG 319-CE file included, to give a few examples, those of clinics set up to help soldiers avoid venereal disease after sexual encounters and one showing a hospitalized American soldier receiving an alcohol rub that some viewers might have interpreted as sexually arousing. Despite this thorough government censorship, some photographic documentation of GI sexuality appeared in nonofficial sources, especially near war's end.[24]

If sexually charged photographs suggested that personal loss of control was possible, others—of soldiers in the midst of mental breakdowns—dramatically revealed this loss. No army had ever made a greater effort to recruit only the mentally healthy. Through preinduction examinations the United States military rejected 970,000 men, approximately one of every eighteen tested, because of "neuropsychiatric disorders and emotional problems." Even with this extensive screening, such are the stresses of modern war that over a million American soldiers, more than three times the number who died in combat, "suffered psychiatric symptoms serious enough to debilitate them for some period." A secret study carried out by the Office of the Surgeon General concluded that "psychiatric casualties are as inevitable as gunshot and shrapnel wounds." Contrary to assumptions about the "battle-hardened veteran," the longer a soldier fought, the greater was the probability of emotional breakdown. The study found that on average an infantryman could "last" about two hundred days before breaking down.[25]

Censors kept emotionally wounded Americans out of sight throughout the war and after, despite their large numbers. BPR policy concerning pictures or other publicity on "psychoneurotic" casualties remained one of "complete silence" until May 1944, then loosened only slightly. This policy is hardly surprising in view of the emphasis the government placed on presenting the American war effort, however grim a task, as carried out in orderly fashion. None of the censored pictures I have encountered in my research illustrate more vividly the human inability to keep complete control over war's chaos than those of "shell shocked" soldiers screaming and flailing out at their fellows and at the horror of their situation.[26]

Conclusion

Some official censorship policies, such as those that slighted the contributions of African American soldiers, were clearly wrong. But other decisions responded to wartime necessity or displayed an appropriate respect for the privacy of soldiers and their families. Even some fifty years after the event, I have chosen to exclude one category of photographs from my book on these issues, *The Censored War: American Visual Experience during World War Two*. My own self-censorship is in part a consequence of these policies. The photographs I chose not to use plainly showed the faces of young soldiers in the midst of severe mental breakdowns. In 1993 the subjects of these pictures would be men in their late sixties, whose earlier images might be quite recognizable to friends and family. Because the United States government kept evidence of psychiatric casualties invisible during the war years, many Americans presumably believe such casualties were rare and therefore might interpret these photographs of breakdowns as evidence of individual weaknesses rather than general conditions.

Thus I chose to use in my book figure 2.5, an image that documents government censorship of pictures of psychiatric casualties but does not expose the face of the afflicted soldier. The photograph also bears witness to the incompleteness of the army's explanation—made in defense of its decision to suppress for over three decades John Huston's film *Let There Be Light*—that it censored visual records of World War II–era psychiatric casualties solely to protect the rights of the soldiers depicted. If that were the only reason, this photograph would not have ended up in the RG 319-CE file. But to put government policies regarding release of visual imagery in context, we must recognize that they were not much different from standard practices of the news and entertainment media in the 1940s. On at least one occasion, to prove this point the army challenged the media with material they were not prepared to publish. When the BPR released a few especially shocking pictures of the American wounded in September 1943, almost all newspapers and magazines declined to run them. The photo editor of the *New York Daily News* explained that he decided not to use a close-up of the leg of a soldier whose foot had been shot away because "I personally try to select pictures that will go down well with my coffee in the morning."[27]

Whatever the wisdom of the censorship policies, they had costs. From Bill Mauldin in the 1940s through Paul Fussell in the 1990s, many have testified that the war plunged participants into a chaos beyond the imagining of distant observers. Censorship of images that revealed war's chaos enlarged this inevitable gap in understanding. Withholding evidence of atrocities committed by American soldiers encouraged excessive confidence in the rectitude of American goals and tactics in cold war conflicts, including early phases of the war in Vietnam. During World War II the United States government suppressed all pictures of American and western European war dead stacked in piles or being handled like inanimate objects, although they let pass some such pictures of Asians and

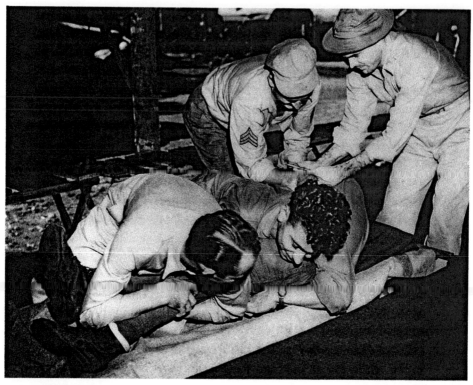

Figure 2.5

eastern Europeans. This dissociation of Americans from mass death
made it easier for many to distance themselves emotionally from pictures
of the Holocaust that appeared at war's end. Refusal to publish pictures
of African American soldiers in leadership positions sustained postwar
assumptions of white supremacy. Most generally, the images Americans
encountered during World War II sustained a less complex understanding of the nature and meaning of that war than they would have attained
had they also seen the censored images.

Some of the things that can be learned from exposure to war's com-
plexities are revealed by a letter that Marine Corporal J. B. Sacks wrote
to his family in July 1944, describing his landing at Saipan. Sacks reported that he had been shaken by seeing dead American marines for
the first time, but had been helped through the crisis by the "welcome"
sight "of *many good japs* (dead ones) strewn all over the place." He
continued, "When we were heading for Carapan, we all talked about
how we were going to kill any jap we saw. Young and old, male or

female. But, we really changed our minds when tattered, terror, and hunger stricken kids, the age of Harvey, Linda, and even carrying babes as young as Bobbie, came out of holes and caves waving a torn white rag. Well this was really a sight that put a lump in your throat. The killing was confined to those japs who preferred dying for their emperor rather than surrender."[28]

Sacks's letter lets us compare his response to visual encounters with wartime realities with the reaction of those who experienced combat areas only through censored images. The casual attitude toward killing soldiers expressed in his final sentence was often displayed in wartime imagery, but photographs, newsreels, films, advertisements, and posters never suggested that Americans might consider indiscriminately killing civilians. Indeed, these images almost never reminded viewers that there were Japanese children, women, old people, and gentle men. When Americans at home did get a glimpse of Japanese children, as in Frank Capra's *Why We Fight* film series, they usually saw their elders training them for military duty or otherwise regimenting them. The scant evidence available suggests that Americans on the home front did not respond to wartime images in a passive and uncritical manner. As they viewed these images in the light of their own experience, no doubt many recognized limitations in the way the government and media depicted the war. However, the imagery would have made it difficult for them to undergo the type of transformation Sacks experienced or to make any emotional connection between the Harveys, Lindas, and Bobbies in their lives and those feeling the consequences of American military effort. Sacks's own response demonstrates that it was not impossible to reconcile awareness of these consequences with full commitment to the necessity of winning the war. Release of some of the censored photographs might have allowed more Americans to achieve such a mature understanding. A population so informed might have devised less costly ways of responding to the imperatives of the postwar world.

Notes

1. I excerpted some parts of this chapter from my book *The Censored War: American Visual Experience during World War Two* (New Haven, 1993).

2. "Life Goes to a Performance of Othello," *Life,* 31 August 1942, 82–95; letters in *Life,* 21 September 1942, 11.

3. Studies attempting to measure the impact of propaganda and other forms of verbal and visual persuasion on audiences number in the tens of thousands. Some of those most pertinent to the study of the American experience in World War II are discussed in Frank W. Fox, *Madison Avenue Goes to War: The Strange Military Career of American Advertising, 1941–45* (Provo, Utah, 1975), 3–9, and in David Culbert, ed., *Film and Propaganda in America: A Documentary History*, vol. 2, *World War II: Part 1* (New York, 1990), xxii–xxiv.

4. John Dower, *War without Mercy: Race and Power in the Pacific War* (New York, 1986); Karal Ann Marling and John Wetenhall, *Iwo Jima: Monuments, Memories, and the American Hero* (Cambridge, Mass., 1991); Margaret Randolph Higonnet et al., eds., *Behind the Lines: Gender and the Two World Wars* (New Haven, 1987); Clayton R. Koppes and Gregory D. Black, *Hollywood Goes to War: How Politics, Profits and Propaganda Shaped World War II Movies* (New York, 1987). For more detailed discussion of issues covered in this essay, including more information on relevant bibliography, see my book *The Censored War*.

5. Roosevelt memo, 20 February 1941, Army Adjutant General (hereafter AG) 000.7, Record Group (RG) 407, 22 January 1941, entry 360, box 3, National Archives (hereafter NA).

6. Roeder, *Censored War*, 9. In my research I have not found a single example of a censor's being reprimanded for *not* letting material through, although sometimes censors would receive directives telling them to start releasing certain categories of previously withheld material. For an example of censors' being "disciplined" for letting too much through see Secretary of War Stimson to Secretary of Navy Knox, 29 September 1942, AG 000.73, RG 407, entry 360, box 3, NA.

7. Elmer Davis and Byron Price, *War Information and Censorship* (Washington, D.C., 1943), 46. The phrase *chamber of horrors* is mentioned on page 7 of an internal study of the Pictorial Branch of the News Division, War Department Bureau of Public Relations (hereafter BPR), undated but with a cover letter of 3 November 1942, 020.4–5, General Records of the Army Staff, PR Division, RG 165, entry 499, box 10, NA.

8. Creel to Davis, 4 August 1942, Elmer Davis papers, Library of Congress (hereafter LC). Davis's handwritten note is on the copy of the letter in his records at LC. On internal changes and struggles at OWI see Allan Winkler, *The Politics of Propaganda: The Office of War Information, 1942–1945* (New Haven, 1978), esp. p. 37.

9. "Minutes of Meeting of War Information Board," 30 August 1943, RG 208, entry 16, box 105, NA; memos from Corr Panel Sections to Clyde W. Hart, 23 August 1943, and Clarence Glick, 30 August 1943 ("Lack of Realism about the Fighting Front—Its Effects"), ibid., box 1710; "Current Surveys," OWI, issue 16 (11 August 1943), ibid., box 1715.

10. Malmedy photographs in *Life*, 5 February 1945, 27; photograph, "A head of a dead Jap hanging in a tree on the Burma Road . . . is a symbol of the Japanese defeat in Northern Burma," 6 February 1945, 319-CE-10-SC271823, Still Picture Branch (hereafter SPB), NA; Dower, *War without Mercy*, 66.

11. "This patrol captured two Nips alive," Southwest Pacific, 8 June 1945, 319-CE-130-SC262353, SPB, NA. For an example of a classified photograph showing American soldiers helping a wounded Japanese soldier, see photograph, 16 October 1942, 80-G-12463 in SPB, NA.

12. *Time*, 22 December 1941, 33; newsreel from ca. 8 November 1942 described in file, "United News," RG 208, entry 285, box 1520, NA.

13. On widespread public support for the relocation, see Hadley Cantril, ed., *Public Opinion, 1935–1946*, prepared by Mildred Strunk (Princeton, 1951), 380.

14. Special Bulletin, 24 October 1942, OWI Bureau of Motion Pictures, in Film Study Center, Museum of Modern Art, New York (emphasis in original). On Little Tokyo and other ironies of wartime film imagery of Chinese and Japanese, see Koppes, *Hollywood Goes to War*, 72–74.

15. The War Relocation Authority's (hereafter WRA) internal shelflist of negatives is available in the WRA file, SPB, NA. On the censorship policy, see N. R. Howard, Press Division, to Gen. A. D. Surles, Director, BPR, 25 April 1942, in RG 165, entry 499, box 10, NA.

16. "Bloody door of English captain assaulted by American soldiers," Rome, Italy, 3 March 1946, 319-CE-66-SC241464, SPB, NA. On OWI public relations use of prisoners see Edward Lauber to Richard Russell, 16 August 1944, RG 208, entry 2, box 12, NA; undated memo in file marked "Prison Industries," ibid., entry 285, box 1519. For censored photograph of GI prisoners drilling, see 319-CE-2-SC236841-w, SPB, NA. For published photographs of GI criminal activity see *Life*, 12 March 1945, 17–18.

17. "Surprise . . . A Powerful Weapon," a poster prepared for the

Army Orientation Course by the Army Service Forces, Newsmap Series, 29 November 1943, available in Department of Special Collections, University Research Library, UCLA. *Life*, 22 March 1943, 4–6, showed such an attack as part of an article on Gjon Mili, who took the photographs for the poster. *Life*, 26 July 1943, 47 showed a still from an army training film depicting an American soldier gouging out the eye of a German soldier.

18. Memo BPR to CG, USFOR, ETO, London, 2 August 1943, 062.1–589, Public Information Division, RG 165, entry 499, box 25, NA; Supreme Headquarters Allied Expeditionary Forces to BPR, 6 March 1945, and related memos in 062.1–104, ibid., box 67. On black protest, ibid.; on the Ninety-second Division, Allied Force Headquarters, Caserta, Italy, to WD, 26 January 1945, in ibid., 062.1–6. On the policy of also restricting written descriptions of black troops "intermingling" with whites in England, see staff memo of 23 February 1945, 000.73–13, Public Information Division, RG 165, entry 499, box 61, NA. For figure 2.3 see photograph, "These are the winners and partners who participated in the dance contest of the Red Cross Colored Club," Italy, 24 April 1943, 319-CE-65-SC237349, SPB, NA. For an example of a published photograph of integrated social activity, see the Toni Frissell photograph accompanying the article "Red Cross Looks after Service Man's Welfare in England," *New York Herald Tribune*, 21 February 1943, sect. 5, 1. Thanks to Nicholas Natanson at NA for this reference.

19. Studs Terkel, *"The Good War": An Oral History of World War II* (New York, 1984), 157; author interview with Dempsey Travis, 18 August 1988; undated memos, Herb Miller to Lowell Mellet and Milton Stark to Barry Bingham, in file marked "Newsreel Material—Miscellaneous," RG 208, entry 185, box 1519, NA; Report on "Special Directive on Treatment of Negro and Other Minority Problems," 9 October 1944, RG 208, entry 359, box 116, NA; H. F. Gosnell to Dr. Herring, 13 February 1943, in La Mar Seal MacKay papers, Hoover. Professor Thomas Cripps of Morgan State University provided me with additional biographical information on Stark, who also used the name Milton Stone. Neil A. Wynn, *The Afro-American and the Second World War* (London, 1976), 86, noted that Fox Movietone decided never to show its item on the Harlem riot of 1943. For an example of vivid photographs that were published, see *Life*, 5 July 1943, 93–102.

20. Director, BPR, to Col. R. Ernest Dupuy, PR Officer, Supreme

Headquarters, Allied Expeditionary Force, 23 February 1944, PR Division, RG 165, entry 499, box 33, NA. For the women embracing, see photograph, SC197886 in the SPB, NA. Markings on this photograph indicate that it was cleared in the field 14 December 1944, then marked "confidential," apparently by BPR, on 8 January 1945. For a discussion of related issues, see Allan Bérubé, *Coming out under Fire: The History of Gay Men and Women in World War II* (New York, 1991), especially chap. 3, "GI Drag: A Gay Refuge."

21. Photograph, American soldier killed at Malmedy "on or about 17 December 1944," 319-CE-6-SC236624, SPB, NA; photograph, body of soldier who accidentally fell to his death, New South Wales, Australia, 18 March 1944, 319-CE-3-SC268444, SPB, NA. For more on which Malmedy photographs were published and which censored, see visual essay 1, "Playing the Death Card," in Roeder, *Censored War*.

22. Photograph, "Three dead Americans on the beach at Buna," *Life*, 20 September 1943, 35; sports comparison, ibid., 34.

23. For the turkeys see photograph, 319-CE-3-SC171051-W, SPB, NA. For a victim of American "friendly fire" see photograph, 319-CE-65-SC236949-W, SPB, NA.

24. Photograph, "American military police take prostitutes to a hospital for treatment and confinement," Naples, Italy, 5 April 1944, 319-CE-65-SC236296, SPB, NA.; photograph, "WACs watch elephants bathe while the elephant driver stands by," 8 June 1945, 319-CE-130-SC235985, SPB, NA; photograph, "Individual booths at a U.S. Army prophylaxis station," Naples, Italy, 17 April 1944, 319-CE-66-SC246942, SPB, NA; photograph, "Filipino nurses' aide gives alcohol rub to American soldier in facilities set up by 36th Evacuation Hospital in a church," Palo, Leyte, Philippine Islands, 24 December 1944, 319-CE-124-SC237674, SPB, NA. For an example of published photographs of sexuality, see *Life*, 26 March 1945, 102.

25. Richard A. Gabriel, *No More Heroes: Madness and Psychiatry in War* (New York, 1987), 4, 72–74, discusses the screening efforts; surgeon general's report described in Martin Gilbert, *The Second World War: A Complete History* (New York, 1989), 599.

26. Director, BPR, to Commanding Generals in all Theaters of Operation, 30 April 1944, 000.7–77, Public Information Division, RG 165, entry 499, box 6, NA.

27. Photograph, "Lt. Allen Enzor . . . administers sedative to psycho-

neurotic patient in admission tent," Dobodura, New Guinea, 18 June 1943, 319-CE-121-SC236850, SPB, NA; *Daily News* editor quoted in *Newsweek*, 20 September 1943, 98.

28. Sacks letter, 14 July 1944, in Preston Sturges papers, box 38, folder 19, UCLA. Sacks's sister, Israel Sacks, sent a typed copy of the letter to Sturges along with a letter of her own, dated 11 August 1944, praising Sturges's film *Hail the Conquering Hero.*

THREE

Making the American Consensus: The Narrative of Conversion and Subversion in World War II Films

The principal battleground of this war is not the South Pacific. It is not the Middle East. It is not England, or Norway, or the Russian Steppes. It is American opinion.

Archibald MacLeish[1]

Shortly before the end of World War II, the future head of the Motion Picture Producers' Association, Eric Johnston, wrote the best-selling book *America Unlimited*. A business reformer who led the United States Chamber of Commerce during the late thirties, Johnston gained fame arguing that business should put aside laissez-faire capitalism and cooperate with labor and government to realize the miracle of economic growth and "democratic capitalism." As President Roosevelt's business adviser during World War II, he believed that the defense mobilization brought to fruition his dreams of a new order. Claiming that in the past New Dealers had preached an "un-American" class conflict, Johnston saw that in the war people discarded mass organizations as tools of reform, embracing instead the politics of economic growth and productivity. In his opinion, Americans could envision a future where their desire for personal happiness centered on dreams of the consumer-oriented home presided over by an attractive new woman. Yet since the nation now faced another foreign threat from the Soviet Union and worldwide communism, he believed that the wartime consensus must continue into the postwar years. To ensure that unity, one of Johnston's first acts as head of the Motion Picture Producers' Association was to tell members of the Screen Writers Guild, "We'll have no more *Grapes of Wrath*, we'll have no more *Tobacco Roads*, we'll have no more films that deal with seamy side of American life. We'll have no more films that treat the banker as a villain."[2]

Fifty years after these events, Johnston's view that moviemaking in the war years revolved around a contest over Americanism seems almost incomprehensible. Liberal historians have taught us that the New Deal and then World War II expressed the continuous triumph of reform, saving the United States from totalitarianism of the Left and Right. New Left historians have countered that the New Deal expressed a conservative defense of liberal capitalism that failed to address the inequities of race and class.[3] Yet despite their vast disagreements, all concur that with the exception of the occasional film or artifact critical of the status quo, a constant commitment to liberal capitalism and consumerism informed the popular arts from the 1930s through the 1950s. Following the lead of Warren Susman's pioneering work on the culture of the depression era, Alan Trachtenberg argues, "The stereotype of the 1930s as a decade fired up by ideological passion and conflict proves, on close examination, not really to have existed . . . this was an era more of consensus than dissent. . . . In the 1930's the cry was not so much for change as 'recovery,' a return to basic values, to fundamental Americanism."[4]

The problem with this view is not that it is wrong but that it is one-sided. By way of contrast this chapter shows that a large body of World War II films were engaged in reshaping American culture and political ideology. In these works the cooperation necessary to win the war meant that the heroes and heroines had to identify with large organizations and patriotic causes that stressed class unity. In the process, they labeled as subversive a counternarrative of American identity in which citizens grounded in regional or ethnic communities were critical of monopoly capital. On the screen this transformation gave rise to a "conversion narrative" in which the protagonists put aside the class and ethnic consciousness that had informed politics and popular art in the thirties. As a result, the "American way" that historians saw as indicative of the cold war era was significantly different—in its uniformity—from earlier visions of cultural authority and gender relations. Further, the loss of that earlier democratic ethos generated the search for an alternative realm of freedom that now came to center on women and the consumer-oriented home.

In showing that the American way arose during World War II, this essay also demonstrates how the idea of the "classic American cinema" and the monolithic "Hollywood discourse" that media scholars have seen as pervading moviemaking during this era is fundamentally mistaken.[5] On the contrary, Hollywood moviemaking from 1930 to 1945 was part of a competitive civic sphere in which national myths and symbols were constantly reworked and contested. By the civic sphere I mean that space between state power and private life where, in democratic states, artists and citizens can engage in a debate concerning the nature of political and social values.[6] To show how the changing nature of film form and content was part of a reformulation of national values and traditions over the period, I do not just examine films I label representative—the usual pattern among scholars of the media. Rather, my conclusions derive from a systematic exploration of plots presented to film distributors in the film industry's major trade journal from 1930 to 1950.[7] By submitting over 240 film plots to a set of narrative conventions, this database provides a way to calculate changing film formulas over time and demonstrate that a contest over culture and political values was at the heart of filmmaking from the depression through the war.[8]

This evidence reveals that moviemakers and their fans were haunted by the memories of political conflict in the Great Depression, but that during World War II government leaders called on the film industry to promote an unprecedented class and cultural consensus as the very essence of the American way. This was no small task, since the collapse of capitalism in the depression called into question established institutions and beliefs. Industrial and political leaders such as Henry Ford and Herbert Hoover were vilified in the thirties as symbols of a political and economic order that could no longer deliver on its promise of prosperity. In response much of the nation's electorate turned to radical social movements, ranging from populism to labor unions, and for the first time injected voting by class into the two-party system. As these voters generated the political realignment that laid the basis for the social reforms of the thirties, laborers created a new "working-class Americanism" that promoted democratic ideologies critical of monopoly capital, racial exclusion, and imperialism.[9]

Yet when the nation was attacked in 1941, the president replaced "Dr. New Deal" with "Dr. Win the War," and businessmen became central to the management of the state. Now government demanded that labor and management cooperate, since this consensus promised to bring victory and realize the hope of abundance that had been so central to the popular dreams and social upheavals of the depression era.[10] In the film industry this created a twofold approach. Government created wage and price controls to promote cooperation and displace labor radicalism in Hollywood, and government leaders looked to the film industry to dramatize this new spirit of cooperation on the screen.[11] To further that task, the government created the Office of War Information (OWI). Guided by interventionist New Dealers, the OWI wanted Hollywood to use its great skills to promote the spirit of war to a population removed from the fighting. As Elmer Davis, director of the OWI, explained, the "easiest way to inject propaganda ideas into most people's minds, is to let it go in through the medium of an entertainment picture when they do not realize that they are being propagandized."[12]

Though disagreements would occur between the OWI and moviemakers over how to dramatize the merger of art and propaganda, it was clear that many Hollywood artists were willing allies. To start with, the war was popular, making it possible for film profits to increase by a third above their very best year during the depression. Even before the Japanese attack on Pearl Harbor, Warner Brothers studio made *Confessions of a Nazi Spy* (1939) because their emissary in Berlin, Joe Kaufman, had been killed by Nazis because of his Jewish ancestry.[13] On the home front, personalities identified with the political and labor battles that consumed the film capital in the thirties—James Cagney, Pat O'Brien, Edward G. Robinson, Myrna Loy, Carole Lombard, and John Garfield—avidly volunteered to promote "victory parade" tours in every major city across the country. Writers moved between Hollywood and Washington, D.C., to make films that merged "characterization and the world struggle against fascism."[14] Further, movie houses sold over 20 percent of all war bonds. The government built battleships named after Will Rogers and Carole Lombard, the famed comedienne and wife of Clark Gable who died in an airplane crash while entertaining the troops.[15]

This wartime enthusiasm created an unprecedented merger between the state and the movie industry. Before the war Hollywood had operated in a commercial marketplace relatively free of state control. In this autonomous civic sphere, producers had deflected government efforts to control their art by creating internal boards of censorship.[16] But now that the OWI, the producers, and the people saw the aims of the war as good, many directors could agree that our "primary responsibility was not to the box office, nor to our paychecks. It was a special responsibility . . . to the men who wore the uniform" of the armed forces.[17] Director John Huston observed that movies now functioned as the "conscience of our people," spurring audiences in a "blinding flash of truth" to shed "race prejudice" and divisions. Robert Andrews, the writer of *Bataan* (1943), maintained that his writing movie scripts during the war was no different from his covering gang killings as a journalist in Chicago. The purpose then was to "wake the good citizens to what they were up against. That's all I'm trying to do today. . . . And I am determined to write a picture so shocking that people would say to themselves, if this is what our men have to stand up to, we've got a job to do." The effect made the audience "depressed." But soon "you find yourself getting angry—angry that such things are being done to us."[18]

Transferred to the screen, these concerns generated a distinct change in film form and content. "No longer . . . is it necessary," observed a trade reporter, "to cloak the more serious thoughts and aspects behind a melodramatic yarn or sugarcoat the message with the public. . . . Such terms as 'Fascists' and 'appeasers' can be used without offense."[19] Many writers saw their task as dramatizing the tie between "characterizations . . . and the world struggle against fascism." On the screen, this official view was encouraged by authoritative overhead narrators, written epilogues and maps that told the audience how to think correctly about the action.[20] As this linked everyday life and belief to state aims, directors reshaped a style of cuborealism that had been popular in the thirties. Here the camera moved inside the frame and the action to display like a microscope the real truth occurring beneath surface events, while drama as well as dialogue unfolded simultaneously in the foreground, background, and middle ground. During the thirties this style had emphasized that all groups were tied together in a reciprocal social environment. But now that the aim was to infuse the environment with symbols of unity and authority, the same environment was permeated with religious and patriotic rituals. Repeatedly the screen was filled with Christmas and Easter scenes or the marches of John Philip Sousa and George M. Cohan. As this clear line of authority permeated the screen, it created what one director called a "unified morality" in a world "divided by explosively antithetical moralities."[21]

The ensuing division of the world into antithetical moralities also produced a change in story content. A government pamphlet titled "Manual for the Motion Picture Industry" outlined the broad contours of that shift. Whereas World War I was clearly identified with a nationality grounded in Anglo-Saxon exclusion and Victorian values of scarcity, the manual insisted that World War II would be fought in the name of American pluralism and abundance.[22] As the authors expressed it, this was not just a war. It was a revitalization movement that would eliminate from the world as well as the home the fears of "fascism, or the brutality, cruelty, treachery and cynicism of the enemy." According to the manual, Hitler and Mussolini embodied the spirit of "Caesar and Pharaoh" that many immigrants had left behind in the "Old World." Whereas in the past southern and eastern European immigrants and racial minorities had been outside the boundaries of official Americanism, now they were included in the fight. The authors thus saw that the "people" were very much against "any form of racial discrimination or religious intolerance, for special privileges for any of our citizens are manifestations of fascism and should be exposed as such." The United States was thus a great "melting pot" of "many races and creeds, who have demonstrated that they can live together in freedom and progress." In fighting against the enemy's doctrines of racism we were "not involved in a national, class or race war." Rather, unity would realize "the dreams of a world free of fear and want" for the "common man."[23]

No matter what the genre, themes of revitalization appeared endlessly. Musicals like *This Is the Army* (1943), *Star Spangled Rhythm* (1942), and *Yankee Doodle Dandy* (1942) featured the rise into American life of ethnic showmen and black boxers like the world champion Joe Louis. *The Fighting Sullivans* (1944) dramatized how an Irish Catholic working-class family gave five sons to defeat the Japanese. Laborers and factory owners in films like *Pittsburgh* (1942) and *American Romance* (1944) created the unity necessary to build munitions without strikes or labor disruption. Abroad, heroes in *Airforce* (1943), *Life Boat* (1944), *Bataan* and *Back to Bataan* (1945), *The Fighting 69th* (1940), and *Sahara* (1943) created ethnically and racially balanced military units and platoons composed of Texans, Jews, Italians, and African Americans (see fig. 3.1).[24] Further, *Casablanca* (1942) and *Lifeboat* shed the black stereotypes that had been so much a part of American popular culture. African American writers pointed out that for black soldiers films like *Lifeboat,* where the black actor participates in disarming a Nazi agent, just "did wonders for

Figure 3.1. *Bataan* (1943). The new pluralistic American national identity symbolized by the ethnic platoon. Note the presence of racial minorities: an African American, fifth from left, and a Mexican American, sixth from left. Courtesy of the Academy of Motion Picture Arts and Sciences.

the morale of the Negro GIs who talked about it for days. To them it was the symbol of changing times, of acceptance, of full integration into the pattern of American life."[25]

Yet the ethos of ethnic and racial pluralism was also a modernized form of an older code of assimilation. Members of formerly ostracized racial and ethnic groups participated in public life as valued citizens and soldiers. But the patriotic demands for unity also meant that memories that collided with national purpose were labeled subversive. Even before films were produced, OWI directives noted that since we must "believe in the rightness of our cause," we could no longer focus "attention on the chinks in our allies' armor," for this "is just what our enemies might wish. Perhaps it is realistic, but it is going to be confusing to American audiences."[26] Within this atmosphere, the famed director Orson Welles and screenwriter Philip Dunne found the Federal Bureau of Investigation probing into their past. The reason? Welles had been engaged in radical New Deal causes and had made *Citizen Kane* (1941), which the FBI believed defamed the publisher William Randolph Hearst. Dunne had written the pro-labor film *How Green Was My Valley* (1941) and promoted social movements in Hollywood. When the FBI made it impossible for him to receive security clearance to make documentaries with John Ford, Dunne noted: "The hurt and the humiliation were not so easily exorcised. Apparently the only way citizens can be sure of remaining 'clean' in the eyes of their own government is to abstain entirely from any political activity: in other words, abdicate their responsibilities as citizens in a democracy, and that is one of the worst crimes committed in the name of 'security.'"[27]

Such crimes did not stop with preproduction censorship. During the thirties Frank Capra rereleased *Lost Horizon* (1937), one of his most noted films. Whereas in the thirties this film was part of Capra's populist criticism of imperialism in the Far East, OWI officials now cut a speech where the hero asks a British official, "Did you say we saved ninety white people. Good. Hooray for us. Did you say we left ten thousand natives down there to be annihilated. No. No, you wouldn't say that. They don't count." Capra himself dismissed writers from his government-sponsored *Why We Fight* series (1942–45) because the House Committee on Un-American Activities investigated them and because they depicted the actions of the Japanese as a response to unresolved class conflicts.[28] Director John Huston found his documentaries *The Battle of San Pietro* (1944) and *Let There Be Light* (1945) unacceptable to the War Department. The first showed that the fighting in Italy led to needless slaughter and the second underlined how the shock of war drove men temporarily insane. Even commercial films were not immune. OWI officials were not happy that a Bette Davis film, *Mr. Skeffington* (1944), dealt with anti-Semitism and finance capital. They observed that it was "gravely detrimental to the War Information Program . . . the Jewish question is presented in such a way to give credence to the Nazi contention that the discrimination for which Americans condemn the fascists, is an integral part of American democracy."[29]

Most important, the call to redefine America's core versus alien values provided the axis around which wartime moviemakers dramatically reoriented the conversion narrative that had provided the staple of depression era moviemaking. A generation of scholars has told us that moviemaking

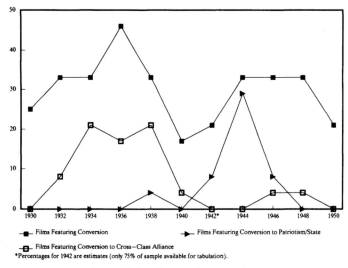

Figure 3.2.   Conversion narratives

tended to deflect audiences' attention from the class and political conflicts of the day. Yet a look at data we have gathered from a systematic analysis of plots appearing in the industry's major trade journals leads us to revise this view. Although many films promoted escapism and reinforced the myths and symbols of liberal individualism and conformity, there were also many movies that promoted what one contemporary screenwriter called the "spirit of the New Deal broadly defined." To overcome social and economic corruption, heroes commonly shed their loyalty to the rich and moved toward cross-class alliances with the lower orders. This conversion from goals centered on individualism to goals centered on collective solutions to problems increased from none in 1930 to over 20 percent by 1938 (fig. 3.2).

As the ensuing cross-class alliance by the new urban hero emerged, characters engaged in a new style of progressive reform, in which they no longer sought to moralize the population with small-town values hostile to the diverse peoples of the city. Rather, they now aligned with racial or ethnic groups in a common effort to realize a modern culture rooted in abundance and a revolution in morals. This category fluctuated, but it was higher in the 1930s than in the 1940s (fig. 3.3). Indicative of that transformation in values, plots where actions of the wealthy villains endangered the heroes increased from less than 10 percent from 1920 to 1930 to over 50 percent by 1936 (fig. 3.4). Films that featured heroes

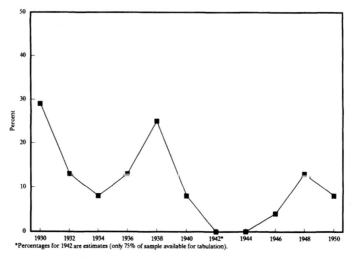

Figure 3.3. Films featuring progressive reform of society, 1920–50

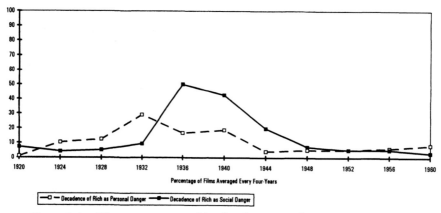

Figure 3.4. Films portraying wealthy decadence as a danger to individuals or society

from the new trades of the city—newscasters, aviators, singers, radio announcers, dancers, composers—rose to prominence, replacing the old middle-class ideal of the professional or big businessman (fig. 3.5). Reflecting on this change in film content, one fan noted that his favorite Hollywood productions of the thirties—the Marx Brothers or Frank Capra films—taught him not only to be suspicious of all "mass politics" but also to see all wars and patriotism as the siren call of the devil.[30]

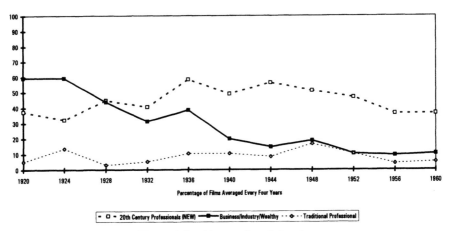

Figure 3.5.   New trades of the city

The advent of the war sparked a very different conversion narrative. Now the basis of authority was realigned from the grass roots to the official institutions and patriotic causes dedicated to saving the nation from foreign rather than internal enemies. Nowhere was that new conversion narrative more evident than in one of the first wartime films of two artists who had become famous in the thirties for making films at odds with official values and traditions. John Ford and Greg Toland created *December 7* (1942), written and directed for the navy, to promote the new ethos of class and cultural consensus.[31] The film opens in the Hawaiian Islands, where Uncle Sam, played by Walter Huston, embodies American values before the advent of the war. Coming to the islands before the attack on Pearl Harbor, he tolerates labor strife and supports an autonomous series of public arenas where men and women of different races mingle. He also approves of the traditions of the Japanese Americans on the islands. But then his conscience explains that these ideas are dangerous. The Japanese Americans are "hyphenated" people who have separate schools and languages and practice a Shinto religion that deifies the Japanese emperor. In this divided world, the Japanese civilians are subversive. Mingling with the Americans in bars and nightclubs, they obtain military secrets that they pass on to the imperial navy that soon attacks Pearl Harbor on 7 December 1941. In the wake of this reality, Uncle Sam undergoes the wartime conversion experience. The descendants of the Japanese must shed their distinct ethnic traditions as class conflict and an autonomous public life are elimi-

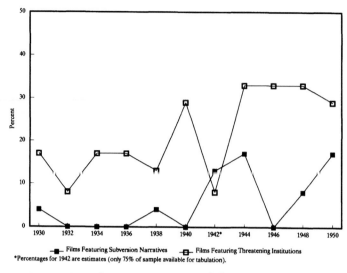

*Percentages for 1942 are estimates (only 75% of sample available for tabulation).

Figure 3.6.   Subversion narratives and threatening institutions

nated. Once this process is completed, the film shows all groups cooperating to win the war and produce abundance for the "common man."

Since no Japanese Americans were found guilty of subversion, though the fear of it led to their internment on the West Coast, the ideological message that emanates from this film has to be seen as part of a much larger transformation in American culture. Though the story is clearly about Pearl Harbor, the authors want to explore why the war came to the country. The actions of the enemy are a factor, but most attention is on the home front. Here it is not the earlier expansion of the United States into the Pacific that has led to conflict with Japan. It is false values, symbolized by Uncle Sam, that have created the problem. In the thirties Sam allowed ethnic groups to maintain traditions in partial opposition to the mainstream. Labor conflict made Uncle Sam weak. And equally important, consumerism and the open mingling of men and women in mass amusements provided the means for enemy agents to prey on the people's softness and gain national secrets. In response to these dangers, the means to a stronger society is to identify with patriotic causes that not only destroy the enemy at home and abroad, but displace one's older political values. In other words, the wartime conversion experience makes consensus the nation's core value, whereas distinct ethnic as well as class interests are now seen as alien to public life.

Most important of all, the themes unfolding in *December 7* were not

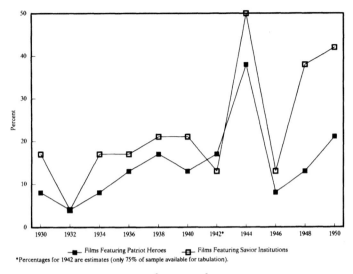

Figure 3.7. Patriot heroes and savior institutions

idiosyncratic. Rather, the perception of danger coming from American institutions controlled by the enemy, in the form of either subversion or threatening institutions increased from less than 20 percent in 1930 to almost 40 percent in 1944 (fig. 3.6). Themes of subversion in films increased from none to almost 20 percent in the same period. Together these dangers have to be seen as two sides of the same coin. Indeed, one or the other theme informed over 50 percent of all wartime films. Each provided the means for delegitimizing dissent within the civic sphere and identifying the skills of the modern middle-class hero with large state or economic institutions (figs. 3.2 and 3.7). Although the world is still a dangerous place, now the threat comes not from big businessmen or corrupt politicians, but from a foreign enemy and subversion at home. The main characters still identified reform with making a better world, but this goal was now to be accomplished through "patriotic causes" and official "savior institutions," state-sponsored groups such as the military and the FBI that promote class consensus. Not surprisingly, films featuring heroes aligned with patriotic categories went from 10 percent in the thirties to almost 40 percent by 1944 (fig. 3.7), while characters threatened by the wealthy decreased from 50 percent to 20 percent from 1936 to 1944 (fig. 3.4). This did not mean that movies celebrated big business, since often the subversives were aligned with greedy corporate leaders. But that the disruption was linked to enemy actions rather than the faults of industrial leaders at home suggests that disorder was not seen as emanating from the patriotic capitalists promoting the war effort.

The dialectic of subversion and conversion informing the World War II films identified disorder at home with treason and the shedding of values associated with the thirties' discontent with patriotism and unity. Consider *Americans All* (1941). The film begins with an overhead narrator explaining that this is a nation composed of diverse ethnic and racial groups. But the Japanese, Italian, and German Americans' loyalty to their ancestral past leads them to use their foreign language press and radio stations to advance the cause of the enemy, while blacks participate in communist-led parades that spur class conflict and disloyalty. As the war comes, more loyal minorities help the FBI master the enemy.[32] In the world outside the United States, *Across the Wide Pacific* (1942) showed the discontent of Japanese plantation laborers in Panama leading them to revolt. But this is not due to economic grievances, as it might have been in films of the thirties. Rather, they are aligned with the Japanese navy's effort to create an airfield to bomb installations at the Panama Canal. Similarly, *Keeper of the Flame* (1942) portrayed a famous reporter, played by Spencer Tracy, who admires a wealthy businessman who uses populist rhetoric to gain a following for his attacks on the nation's involvement in the war. The reporter sheds these values, however, when he discovers that the businessman, who is half Huey Long and half Charles Lindbergh, is really a Nazi agent who has duped the people. Additionally, the hero in *Mission to Moscow* (1943) finds that those who wish to keep the population isolated from Europe serve the enemy. "And I say, gentlemen," says an isolationist congressman, "not only can we do business with Hitler but we can make a nice profit doing so. . . . It's going to be Hitler's Europe and I say, what of it." And in *The House on 92nd Street* (1945), the Nazis are profiteering transvestite spies who promote sexual deviance and national weakness.[33]

On the other hand, the expurgation of subversive tendencies served positive purposes. It identified the state rather than autonomous social movements as the source of security and prosperity for the people. A classic example is *Sergeant York*, winner of the Academy Award for best picture in 1942. The story depicts the life of Alvin C. York, a poor Tennessee farmer who became the single most decorated soldier in World War I. As one critic put it, the film charts the epic of a "mountaineer" who put "aside his religious scruples against killing for what he felt was the better good of his country and the lasting benefit of mankind." Before the conflict the hero is a young pacifist who enjoyed "hell raising" in local saloons. He is also angry that the rich own all the good farmland. He is a dispossessed yeoman farmer unable to achieve individual autonomy. His mother says at prayer, "Dear Lord we thank thee for this food and that we are beholden to nobody." Given these traditional American values, it is not surprising that when World War I breaks out Alvin is a potential subversive. He refuses the draft, and when forcibly inducted, he refuses to fight. But when a wise officer gives him an American history book to read, he is reborn. Seeing his old values as mistaken, he becomes a soldier who captures 132 Germans. When he comes home a hero, the prosperous and unified state rewards him with a lavish farm, showing that wartime cooperation has made it possible for capitalism to reward formerly poor boys. In case audiences might miss the message that this applied to World War II as well, the star, Gary Cooper, and Alvin York himself were invited to the White House, since the film encouraged enlistment in the military.[34]

Alvin was not alone in his conversion. In the Academy Award–winning film of 1944, *Mrs. Minever,* a middle-class youth dislikes the snobbish British aristocracy. The war teaches him, however, to give up his class animosity and cooperate with the upper orders to defeat the foreign enemy. Similarly, in the *Fighting 69th* James Cagney plays a rebellious Irishman whose hatred of established leaders leads to subversive acts. To redeem himself he saves his unit from disaster. A young girl and her father in *The White Cliffs of Dover* (1944) initially see that the American ethos of individualism and freedom is at odds with the English aristocracy of the "Old World." But as World Wars I and II come, the girl marries an aristocrat and gives her son to defend a new Atlantic civilization rooted in class unity. Along similar lines, *Airforce* showed a bomber flying to the Hawaiian Islands late in 1941 with a crew made up of the nation's diverse people: a Yankee pilot, a working-class mechanic, and a Brooklyn Jew. John Garfield portrays John Winocki, a Polish American tail gunner who hates authority because he believes his commander has stymied his efforts to become a pilot. Carrying the anger of many working-class ethnics, Winocki hates the Anglo-Saxon captain and the "system." When the Japanese attack Pearl Harbor, however, he abandons these subversive tendencies and joins the "team." The screenwriter,

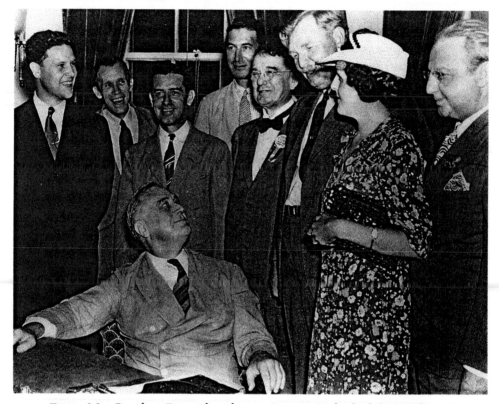

Figure 3.8. President Roosevelt welcomes Sergeant York, third from right, after a White House showing of the movie. Courtesy of the Academy of Motion Picture Arts and Sciences.

Dudley Nichols, noted that "now Winocki has found something real to direct his embittered feeling against and his eyes grow hard."[35]

Just as characters like Winocki replaced their class hatreds with new enemies, consensus also demanded a reorientation of the depiction of the nation's place in the world. This was no small matter, for criticism of war and imperialism was a part of working-class politics in the thirties and appeared on the screen in popular films such as *All Quiet on the Western Front* (1930), *The Informer* (1935), and *Mutiny on the Bounty* (1935). But if the heroes in *Airforce* were now united in war to save democracy, what were those European colonies and American bases doing in the Philippines and Pacific Islands? In a typical cinematic answer to this question, *Back to Bataan* charts the adventures of an American officer, played by John Wayne, who mobilizes the Filipino resistance

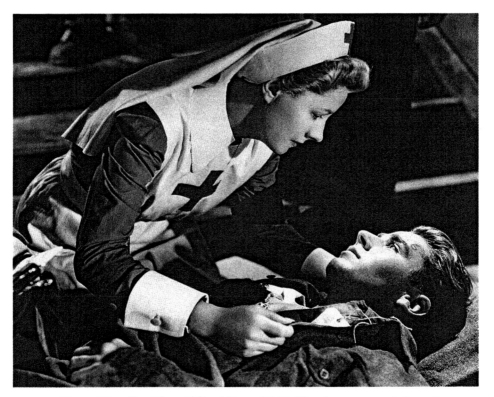

Figure 3.9. *The White Cliffs of Dover* (1944). The dying son symbolizes the unity of Britain and the United States. Courtesy of the Academy of Motion Picture Arts and Sciences.

to the Japanese. Early in the film the audience hears the enemy, via a radio station, ask the Filipinos why they are not joining their fellow Asians, the Japanese invaders, to throw out Western imperialists. This question haunts the resistance leader, played by Anthony Quinn, the grandson of a Philippine patriot who fought against the American invaders in the 1890s. Not only is he restless under white domination, but his lover has become the radio announcer who supports the Japanese invasion. Yet once he sees that the Japanese are evil, he and his lover shed their subversive ideas and expel the Japanese.[36]

The struggle against subversion did not simply focus on enemy agents or the hero's false ideas. It also came to center on another potential source of disruption: women's desire for independence and more egalitarian family and social relations. In film after film the heroines were empowered women like those who came to prominence in movies of the

Figure 3.10.   *Mrs. Miniver* (1944). In the congregation, two formerly warring classes convert to wartime unity. Courtesy of the Academy of Motion Picture Arts and Sciences.

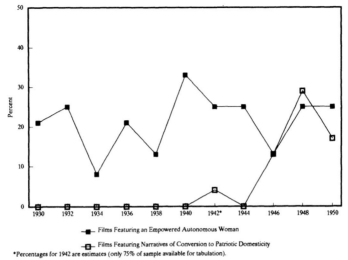

Figure 3.11. Empowered women and conversion to patriotic domesticity

twenties and thirties. Appearing in between 10 percent and 30 percent of films in the thirties, this heroine, personified by stars like Bette Davis, Vivien Leigh, Joan Crawford, and Myrna Loy, also worked in the new trades of the city as secretaries, singers, and reporters (fig. 3.11). Not only were they erotically attractive, but in the most popular films of the era such as *Meet John Doe* (1941), *The Thin Man* (1934), and *His Girl Friday* (1940), they helped the heroes solve social problems.

Although the category of empowered women rose slightly in the films of the 1940s—reflecting the move of women into the workforce as men went to war—the young heroine's independence in public life nevertheless was seen as potentially subversive. Heroines in *Foreign Correspondent* (1940), *Back to Bataan, Notorious* (1946), *The White Cliffs of Dover*, and *Across the Wide Pacific* vacillated between betraying and supporting their men's commitment to the war. To prove their loyalty, either they were revealed to have been innocent all along or they too underwent a conversion. Indeed, since the cause of patriotism demanded eliminating conflict from the public realm, the heroine's identity became split. She saw her work as a means to support her man fighting abroad, yet she focused her identity on providing in the home the freedom and personal fulfillment that were being lost in the larger public realm.[37]

Why women would make this choice received its fullest answer in *Since You Went Away*, which won the Academy Award for best picture in

1944. The epilogue explains that this is the story of that "unconquerable American fortress, the American Home." The wife is played by Claudette Colbert, a star identified in the public mind with her well-known role as the rebellious woman of Frank Capra's hit film *It Happened One Night* (1934). Carrying into the war years some of the élan that marked her performance in the 1930s, she and her two daughters work as nurses and in a factory. However, the heroine has undergone a transformation in values. With their husbands and lovers committed to military organizations, women are expected to channel their potentially dangerous desires for freedom and sexual expression away from public life into the home. There they will remove the irrational power of uncontrolled sex and female independence, and they will provide a vision of freedom that men are losing in the public domain. In other words, women will now embody the "American" ideal of democracy and personal fulfillment that is being eroded by the loss of autonomy in a public life pervaded by state ends.

In dramatizing this change, Claudette Colbert suppresses her desire for romance and the old world of nightclubs and dance. She rejects a naval officer who wants to take her out and condemns as subversive a female friend who sees prosperity as the chance to have a good time. As Colbert's character explains, "I have a husband who went off to fight for this home and for me. I have children who have shown courage and intelligence while their mother lived in a dream world. Well believe me I've come out of it. . . . I want to do something more." Responding to men's being at war while women remain in safety, she goes to work in a munitions factory. But though her employment symbolizes women's participation in the war effort, her purpose is not her own pleasure. Instead, work is an extension of her new identity as mother and wife. Symbolic of the way the self has become absorbed in the larger patriotic cause, a refugee from the Nazis explains that Colbert embodies "America." With highlights of the Statue of Liberty in the background, the clear message is not only that ideal women will make the guns to win the war, but also that their true identity is found in creating a vision of love and beauty that men can expect to find when they return from the front. Indicative of that ideal, the final scene shows her receiving a letter on Christmas saying that her husband is coming home. As the camera pulls back to show the home of his dreams, an epilogue says,

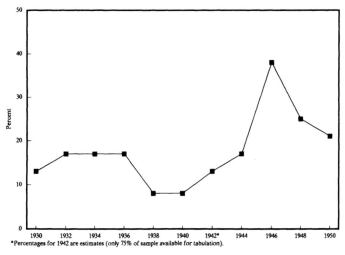

*Percentages for 1942 are estimates (only 75% of sample available for tabulation).

Figure 3.12.   Films featuring antiheroes, 1930–50

"BE OF GOOD COURAGE AND HE SHALL STRENGTHEN YOUR HEART ALL YE THAT TRUST IN THE LORD."[38]

With the themes of consensus displacing a counternarrative of American identity, two relatively new categories also rose to prominence. The first was "patriotic domesticity" on the part of women, a theme that received its best dramatization in *Since You Went Away.* In this formula the "empowered woman" continued to move into the economy. But by 1945 almost 20 percent of all films showed these women focusing their energies on making the home the ideal that the men would return to when the war was over (fig. 3.11). At the same time, a rising number of films suggested that the men and women who gave up their independence to fight in the war, and looked to home and women for a vision of freedom, were in fact rebellious antiheroes or "vamps" (fig. 3.12). Often these stories portrayed men and women who rebelled against the institutions of the war but eventually saw the light. But amid the change, these characters give voice to discontent and a growing alienation from the proscribed male and female roles unfolding in the wartime state.

Typically film historians have seen the rise of these alienated characters as foreshadowing the "film noir" that gained great popularity after World War II. Focusing on deranged characters and gangsters of middle-class status and background, these films evoked the tragedy of lost dreams. Yet while scholars relate these characters to demobilization or to the paranoia that came with the advent of the atomic bomb and anticommunism in the late forties, that they rose long before these events, in films like *High Sierra* (1941), *Double Indemnity* (1944), and *This Gun for Hire* (1942), suggests a different pattern. The involvement in patriotic causes and new savior institutions created a discontent that had no legitimate channels for expressing itself. These films registered artists' and audiences' loss of freedom after their own equally strong conversion experiences and commitment to winning the war.[39]

Nowhere was that sense of loss for men and women undergoing the conversion narrative more evident than in the most memorable and enduring film of the war, *Casablanca*. Winner of the Academy Award for best picture, the film opens on a map of Europe and Africa. Zeroing in on Casablanca, the camera stops on a courthouse with the words "liberté, egalité, fraternité" gracing its exterior.[40] As in so many war films, that democratic faith is personified in the hero, Rick Blaine, played by Humphrey Bogart. Rick incarnates the independence and much of the subversive élan that wartime films will work to transform. His freedom flows from his ownership of "Rick's Café Americain," a nightclub where diverse peoples mingle apart from state control. Here swing music evokes dreams of erotic love and ecstasy, and when a fellow nightclub owner offers to "buy Sam," the African American piano player, Rick replies, "I don't buy or sell human beings." Further, we learn that Sam and Rick are close friends. Not only do they confide in each other, but Sam owns 25 percent of the café and has helped Rick escape from the Nazis, who had him on a "blacklist" with a "price on his head." In line with these values Rick ran guns to Ethiopia and Spain, supporting the people against fascism and imperialism. At present Rick helps refugees—many of them Jews fleeing the Nazis—while he provides his employees with economic security. In the past he has been in love with an erotic and independent woman, Ilsa, who embodies the dream of a wider public life for both sexes.[41]

Rick is thus the very embodiment of a populist hero aligned with ethnic outsiders and the lower classes in the quest for a fulfilling life. The coming of the war created a great sense of loss. In part this loss focused on Rick's love for Ilsa, who disappeared at the exact moment the Nazis invaded Paris. Though this loss suggests she betrayed him, Ilsa, like the heroines of so many wartime films, turns out to be true to their love. She had thought her resistance-fighter husband was dead, but finding he was alive she had to

Figure 3.13. *Casablanca* (1942). Romantic dreams and wartime realities: Sam plays "As Time Goes By" for Rick and Ilsa. Courtesy of the Academy of Motion Picture Arts and Sciences.

return to him.[42] With this new information Rick goes through a conversion experience that leads him to identify with the patriotic cause and its military institutions. Whereas other wartime films portrayed this change as unequivocally positive, the tragic power of *Casablanca* lies in its ability to evoke the way this choice created loss, a sense that great expectations have been defeated by events.

Rick's new identity as a "patriot" has generated the "blues" more common to black Americans. This sensibility is evoked by the theme song of the film, "As Time Goes By," played and sung by Sam. Symbolic of this sad choice, Rick must sell the Café Americain, which has been the source of his freedom in the civic sphere. At the same time, his commitment to the patriotic cause and savior institutions demands that

93

he and Ilsa give up their dreams of love and a new life. Telling her why she must support her husband, Rick says, "Inside of us we both know you belong to Victor, you're part of his work, the thing that keeps him going. . . . I have a job to do, too. Where I'm going you can't follow. . . . I'm no good at being noble, but it doesn't take much to see that the problems of three little people don't amount to a hill of beans in this crazy world. Some day you'll understand that." As Rick commits to the patriotic cause, as he aligns with the police and the military, he tells Ilsa that she also must shed her dreams and provide the privatized home for her husband. Lazlo reinforces that choice by saying, "Welcome back to the fight. This time I know our side will win." But as these optimistic words fill the soundtrack, they are undercut by somber visuals. The camera penetrates darkness and fog to show a sad Ilsa leaving and Rick standing alienated and alone. They have done their duty, but it has meant a tragic lowering of great expectations.[43]

The theme of conversion and subversion informing World War II films demonstrates that the scholars' view of the uniform "American way" as permeating Hollywood films from the thirties to the sixties is mistaken. Rather, this evidence has shown that the consensus pervading the postwar era had its roots in the historical experience of World War II. There is also tangible evidence that the conversion narrative expressed in World War II films was not isolated on the screen. In real life as in the movies that appealed to popular taste, pollsters found that citizens shed isolationism with a vengeance. In 1937, only 26 percent of the population favored involvement in foreign affairs. But by 1945, 81 percent believed in supporting international bodies like the United Nations.[44] With the rise of the new military state and government bureaucracy to carry on the reformist spirit of the New Deal, there also came a lasting decline in the public's receptiveness to political ideologies hostile to monopoly capitalism. A poll by *Fortune* magazine in 1942 found that 40 percent of respondents were opposed to socialism, 25 percent supported it, and almost 35 percent said they had an open mind. Further, the same polls found high support for labor unions, which were the most radical groups in the New Deal era. By 1949, however, the impact of World War II, coupled with the rise of the cold war and domestic anticommunism, was evident. On the verge of the fifties a Gallup poll found that only 15 percent wanted to "move in the direction of socialism," a large 61 percent wanted to move in the opposite direction, and support for labor unions was in decline. Even if one allows for respondents' possibly vague notions of what unions and socialism meant, it was a remarkable change.[45]

Yet it was no more remarkable than the alteration occurring in family life. The baby boom characterized by lower marriage age and increased family formation that scholars have seen pervading the fifties began *during* the war.[46] Interviews gathered by Studs Terkel in *"The Good War"* suggest that films were implicated. A schoolteacher recalled that during World War II it was "just marvelous" that women went to work in factories. But "even here we were sold a bill of goods. They were hammering away that the woman who went to work did it to help her man, and when he came back, she cheerfully leaped into the home." The first years of the war sparked what another respondent called "excitement in the air." For the first time she worked outside the home, where she met "hundreds of men," but her friends and family insisted that she "get married." Not only was this reinforced by her community, but in the movies of the time "the central theme was girl meets soldier and after a weekend of acquaintance they get married and overcome their difficulties." Still another woman explained that films like *The White Cliffs of Dover* transformed her opinion of the English from hate to love. In this film about a woman who marries a soldier who dies at the front, she found a model for her desire to marry a soldier, long before she was ready. As she looked back on the power of the media in the war, she observed that the idea that "women married soldiers and sent them overseas happy was hammered at us. We had plays on the radio, short stories in magazines, and the movies, which were a tremendous influence in our lives."[47]

As these recollections suggest, the transformation in American culture and politics unfolding in the war did not stop with the conflict. Perhaps the most tangible example of how the consensus forged in the battle against the fascists carried over into the new struggle against communism occurred in the career of Frank Capra. During the thirties he made films that featured populist heroes fighting the moneyed interests. During the war he served as an officer in charge of making government films. To ensure that they reinforced the values of unity at home, he fired writers the FBI accused of subversion. Returning to Hollywood, he found that the antimonopoly themes he had popularized in the thirties were now suspect among producers and anticommunists. As he molded his films to the new order, the protagonists in films like *State of the Union* (1948) were corporate leaders, while the heroines were housewives who supported their men. Explaining why his films were no longer popular, one of his screenwriters noted that once Capra "got into this government stuff, it gave him a new sense of values, and then he was dead. He was working with the people who were the heavies in his own pictures, and it turned him completely around. From that point on, in trying to develop scripts he developed nonsense." Capra himself echoed these views: "Once you get cold feet, once your daring stops, then you worry a little bit. And when you worry about a decision, then you're not going to make the proper films anymore. That is I couldn't. And I think that was the start. When I sold out for money, which is something I had always been against anyhow, and security, I think my conscience told me that I had it. Really. There wasn't anymore of that paladin out there in front fighting for lost causes."[48]

At this point it is possible to see why Eric Johnston understood that movies were part of a major transformation in American liberalism. With the New Deal state creating institutions to forge cooperation among conflicting groups, Hollywood artists identified the war mobilization with the continuation of New Deal aims and goals. Yet given that the new managerial state demanded the displacement of class conflict and autonomous organizations as tools for reform, filmmakers placed on the screen a conversion narrative in which men and women saw that authority lay in savior institutions and patriotic goals. Behind this shift in values lay a reorientation of Americanism itself. Now strong ethnic loyalties and criticism of class and gender arrangements were seen as alien to the American way. With the rise of large corporate organizations, freedom was to be found less in an autonomous civic sphere than in the private domain of leisure and family life. As a result, when men looked to the postwar era they wanted the "new woman" who found her identity in providing nurture for her husband and children within the consumer-oriented home. But as this new liberalism came to flower in the war years, it was also possible to see in films like *Casablanca* that this disruption of past dreams and visions evoked loss and alienation for both sexes. It was this ambivalent American way that leaders like Eric Johnston correctly saw as laying the foundation for the culture of the cold war that flowered in the late forties and fifties.

Notes

1. Archibald MacLeish was director of the Office of Facts and Figures, forerunner of the Office of War Information. Quoted in Stacey

Bredhoff, *Powers of Persuasion: Poster Art from World War II* (Washington, D.C., 1994), 1.

2. Eric Johnston, *America Unlimited* (Garden City, N.J., 1944). Also see "Utopia Is Production," *Screen Actor* 14 (April 1946): 7. The quotation is from Murray Schumach, *The Face on the Cutting Room Floor: The Story of Movie and Television Censorship* (New York, 1964), 129.

3. For the classic liberal view, see Arthur Schlesinger Jr., *The Age of Roosevelt*, 3 vols. (Boston, 1957–60), and Eric Goldman, *Rendezvous with Destiny: A History of Modern American Reform* (New York, 1952). For the New Left view see Barton Bernstein, "The New Deal: The Conservative Achievements of Liberal Reform," in *Towards a New Past: Dissenting Essays in American History,* ed. Barton Bernstein (New York, 1968), 263–88, and Ronald Radosh, "The Myth of the New Deal," in *A New History of Leviathan,* ed. Ronald Radosh and Murray N. Rothbard (New York, 1972), 146–86.

4. The statement that a monolithic Americanism pervaded the thirties can be found in Warren Susman, *Culture as History: The Transformation of American Culture in the Twentieth Century* (New York, 1984), 150–211. See also Alan Trachtenberg, *Reading American Photographs: Images as History, Matthew Brady to Walker Evans* (New York, 1989), 247. Examples of the way historians and media scholars marshal various cultural theories to reinforce this view can be found in Jackson Lears, "Making Fun of Popular Culture," *American Historical Review* 97 (1992): 1418, and Jean Christophe Agnew, "Coming up for Air: Consumer Culture in Historical Perspective," *Intellectual History Newsletter* 12 (1990): 3–21. A fine work that shows how Hollywood filmmakers made movies hostile to established values during the 1930s is Brian Neve, *Film and Politics in America: A Social Tradition* (London, 1992), 1–56.

5. David Bordwell, Janet Staiger, and Kristin Thompson, *The Classical American Cinema: Film Style and Mode of Production to 1960* (New York, 1985); Thomas Schatz, *The Genius of the System: Hollywood Film Making in the Studio Era* (New York, 1988); Dana Polan, *Power and Paranoia: History, Narrative and the American Cinema, 1940–1950* (New York, 1986); Clayton R. Koppes and Gregory D. Black, *Hollywood Goes to War: How Politics and Profits and Propaganda Shaped World War II Movies* (New York, 1987). A brilliant criticism of the apolitical theory and method used by these scholars can be found in Jed Dannenbaum, "Thumbs Down: History and Hollywood in the Forties," *Radical History Review* 44 (1989): 175–84.

6. I am using the concept of the civic sphere as developed by Jürgen Habermas, *The Structural Transformation of the Civic Sphere: An Inquiry into a Category of Bourgeois Society* (Cambridge, Mass., 1989).

7. The sample was derived from the film industry's major trade journal, the *Motion Picture Herald* (MPH). It offered exhibitors a variety of services, including weekly digests of recent releases. These plot synopses served as the basis for the sample and its categories. To ensure consistent coverage over time, and to make sure A and B class films were included in the sample, two plot summaries per month were drawn from even-numbered years. The first and last films of the last week of each month provided the basis for tabulation, generating 24 films per year and 120 per decade.

I thank my research assistants at the University of Minnesota—Chris Lewis, Jonathan Munby, Michael Willard, and Scott Zimmerman—for their invaluable assistance in helping me devise the categories, collate for the computer, and create the graphs that illustrate these themes. When this project is finished our materials, including plots and graphs, will be turned over to the University of Minnesota Research Library, where they can be consulted by future scholars.

8. This view of popular art as engaged in a struggle over power and ideology is close to the views of Antonio Gramsci, *Selections from Cultural Writings,* ed. D. Forgacs and G. Nowell-Smith (London, 1985), 206–11, and Mikhail Bakhtin, *The Dialogic Imagination* (Austin, Tex., 1981). My thinking along these lines also has been influenced by Horace M. Newcombe, "On the Dialogic Aspects of Mass Communications," *Cultural Studies in Mass Communications* 1 (1984): 34–50, and George Lipsitz, *Time Passages* (Minneapolis, 1990).

9. Lizabeth Cohen, *Making a New Deal: Industrial Workers in Chicago, 1919–1939* (New York, 1990); Gary Gerstle, *Working Class Americanism: The Politics of Labor in an Industrial City, 1914–1960* (New York, 1989). On voting by class in the thirties, see Richard Ostreicher, "Urban Working Class Political Behavior and Theories of Electoral Politics, 1879–1940," *Journal of American History* 74 (1988): 1257–86.

10. For political consensus and prosperity as a goal of the war, see John Morton Blum, *V Was for Victory: Politics and American Culture during World War II* (New York, 1976). On labor's cooperation with management and the state, coupled to repeated wildcat strikes, see Nelson Lichtenstein, *Labor's War at Home: The C.I.O. in World War II*

(Cambridge, 1983), and George Lipsitz, *Class and Culture in Cold War America: A Rainbow at Midnight* (New York, 1981).

11. See Lary May, "Movie Star Politics: The Screen Actors' Guild, Cultural Conversion and the Hollywood Red Scare," in *Recasting America: Culture and Politics in the Age of Cold War*, ed. Lary May (Chicago, 1989), 125–53.

12. Dorothy B. Jones, "The Hollywood War Film: 1942–1944," *Hollywood Quarterly* 6 (1945–46): 1–19. See also Clayton R. Koppes and Gregory D. Black, "What to Show the World: The Office of War Information and Hollywood, 1942–1945," *Journal of American History* 64 (1977): 88.

13. On the actions of Hollywood in promoting the war and the profits made, see Editors of *Look, Movie Lot to Beachhead: The Motion Picture Goes to War and Prepares for the Future* (Garden City, N.Y., 1945), 58–69, 82–96, 148–58, 204–15. See also Colin Shindler, *Hollywood Goes to War: Films and American Society 1939–1952* (London, 1979). On the film industry and Jews, see Lary May, *Screening out the Past: The Birth of Mass Culture and the Motion Picture Industry* (Chicago, 1983), chap. 6. On Hollywood, the labor movement, the New Deal, and stars' involvement in the war, see May, "Movie Star Politics." The death of Kaufman is recounted in Otto Friedrich, *City of Nets: A Portrait of Hollywood in the 1940s* (New York, 1976), 49.

14. Editors of *Look, Movie Lot to Beachhead*. "Hollywood Victory Caravan" file, Academy of Motion Picture Arts and Sciences Library, Beverly Hills, Calif. (hereafter AMPAS), has newspaper articles from around the country reporting the stars' parades.

15. Howard Koch, "The Making of *Casablanca*," in *Casablanca: Script and Legend* (New York, 1992), 19. Battleships named in honor of Will Rogers are on display in the Will Rogers Memorial, Claremore, Oklahoma. For the amount of war bonds sold in movie houses, see Editors of *Look, Movie Lot to Beachhead*, 58–69.

16. See May, *Screening*, chaps. 2 and 5, for censorship and the movies.

17. Lester Koenig, "Back from the Wars," *Screenwriter* 1 (1945): 23–25.

18. John Huston, "World Brotherhood Speech," 1955, in Huston file, AMPAS. Robert Andrews, interview by Philip Scheuer, *Los Angeles Times*, 5 December 1943.

19. *New York Times,* 13 January 1944, cited in Shindler, *Hollywood Goes to War,* 76.

20. Examples of this tendency occur in *Bataan, Back to Bataan, Casablanca, The House on 92nd Street, Americans All, December 7,* and many others.

21. The assumptions underlying the cuborealist style of the thirties can be found in Irving Pichel, "Seeing with the Camera," *Hollywood Quarterly* 1 (1945–46): 138–45. The quotations come from Irving Pichel, "Areas of Silence," *Film Quarterly* 3 (1947): 51–55.

22. On the older national identity of Anglo-Saxon exclusion and how it informed World War I, see Philip Gleason, "American Identity and Americanization," in *The Harvard Encyclopedia of American Ethnic Groups* (Cambridge, Mass., 1980), 38–57. John Higham, *Strangers in the Land* (New Brunswick, N.J., 1955), and his *Send These to Me* (Baltimore, 1984), chaps. 8, 9 and 10, are critical for cultural pluralism. That the war was fought in the name of realizing the dream of general abundance is the central theme of Blum, *V Was for Victory.*

23. K. R. M. Short, "Washington's Information Manual for Hollywood, 1942," *Historical Journal of Film, Radio and Television* 3 (1983): 171–80.

24. All the cited films can be found on videotape; see Leonard Maltin, *TV Movies and Video Guide,* 1993 ed. (New York, 1993).

25. Thomas Cripps, "Racial Ambiguities in American Propaganda Movies," in *Film and Radio Propaganda in World War II,* ed. K. R. M. Short (Knoxville, Tenn., 1983), 125–45; the quotation on *Lifeboat* is on page 135. Thomas Cripps, "*Casablanca,* Tennessee Johnson and the Liberal Soldier—Hollywood Liberals and World War II," in *Feature Films as History,* ed. K. R. M. Short (Knoxville, Tenn., 1981), 139–55.

26. This comes from the OWI script review of *For Whom the Bell Tolls* as cited in Koppes and Black, "What to Show the World," 92.

27. See James Narremore, "The Trial: The FBI versus Orson Welles," *Film Comment* 27 (January–February 1991): 22–27. Philip Dunne, *Take Two: A Life in the Movies and Politics* (New York, 1980), 160.

28. Joseph McBride, *Frank Capra: The Catastrophe of Success* (New York, 1992), 356, 451–501. For the revisions of *Why We Fight,* especially the Japanese sections, see John Dower, *War without Mercy: Race and Power in the Pacific War* (New York, 1986), chap. 1.

29. For Huston's recounting of army censorship, see "The Courage

of the Men: An Interview with John Huston," in *Film: Book 2*, ed. Robert Hughes (New York, 1962), 22–35. See also K. R. M. Short, "Hollywood Fights Anti-Semitism," in Short, *Film and Radio Propaganda in World War II*, 147–51. The *Mr. Skeffington* censorship story is recounted on pages 160–62.

30. The quotation about the "spirit of the New Deal" comes from the work by major screenwriter and intellectual for the Communist Party, John Howard Lawson, *Film in the Battle of Ideas* (New York, 1953), 14. The fan's comment comes from John Clellon Holmes, "15 Cents before 6 PM: The Wonderful Movies of the Thirties," *Harper's*, December 1965, 51–55. This is at odds with the scholarly agreement that sees the movies of the thirties as promoting consensus themes. As Clayton R. Koppes and Gregory D. Black phrase it in "What to Show the World," 90, "From the mid 1930's to the eve of World War II the industry was isolated from national intellectual, artistic and political life" because "conservative bankers and businessmen ran the studios." This monolithic view of the industry is overstated.

31. A print of this film is in the National Archives as well as the Library of the Program of American Studies, University of Minnesota.

32. A copy of *Americans All* can be found in the Immigration History Research Archive, University of Minnesota.

33. All of these films are on videotape. See Maltin, *TV Movies and Video Guide*.

34. The quotation is from " 'Sergeant York,' a Sincere Biography of the World War Hero Makes Its Appearance at the Astor," *New York Times*, 3 July 1941. The account of York's visit to the White House is from "President Praises 'Sergeant York' to the Living Hero of the Picture," *News and Feature Service of Warner Brothers Studio*, in Sergeant York File, AMPAS.

35. All the films cited in this paragraph are on videotape. See Maltin, *TV Movies and Video Guide*. The quotation comes from Dudley Nichols, *Airforce*, ed. Lawrence Suid (Madison, Wisc., 1983), 73.

36. All the films cited in this paragraph can be found on videotape; see Maltin, *TV Movies and Video Guide*.

37. See John Rossie, "Hitchcock's *Foreign Correspondent (1940)*," *Film and History* 12 (1982): 25–35. The film is also on videotape; see Maltin, *TV Movies and Video Guide*.

38. A very similar argument concerning the nature of women in war

films can be found in the fine study by Joyce Baker, *Images of Women in Film: The War Years, 1941–1945* (Ann Arbor, Mich., 1980). *Since You Went Away* is on videotape; see Maltin, *TV Movies and Video Guide.*

39. A good summary of these views can be gleaned from Richard Maltby, "*Film Noir:* The Politics of the Maladjusted Text," *Journal of American Studies* 18 (1984): 1, 49–71.

40. These quotations come from the original script as reproduced in Koch, *Casablanca,* 29.

41. Koch, *Casablanca,* 51, 65, 76, 108, 185, 204–5, 163–70.

42. Koch, *Casablanca,* 100–127.

43. Koch, *Casablanca,* 218–28.

44. The changing opinion on United States involvement in world organizations can be found in American Institute of Public Opinion, "World Organization Polls from 1937–1945," *Public Opinion Quarterly,* summer 1945, 253.

45. These polls are cited in Godfrey Hodgson, *America in Our Time: From World War II to Nixon, What Happened and Why* (New York, 1976), 77.

46. See Elaine Tyler May, *Homeward Bound: American Families in the Cold War Era* (New York, 1988), especially 3–15.

47. Dellie Hahn, "Interview," in Studs Terkel, *"The Good War": An Oral History of World War II* (New York, 1984), 117–18.

48. McBride, *Frank Capra,* 504–5, 536–37.

PART
2

Interpreting the "American Way"

FOUR

The Working Class
Goes to War

Most Americans still regard World War II as "the good war." We see ourselves as having fought hard in a noble cause, contributing our manufacturing might, manpower, and dollars to an international crusade to defeat fascism and resuscitate democracy. A spirit of cooperation, unity, and generosity impelled us to work long hours, purchase large numbers of war bonds, and good-naturedly endure sharp restrictions on our freedom to consume and spend. We emerged from the war with a renewed faith in ourselves as a people, convinced that American wizardry in production, combined with the American commitment to fair play, would bring prosperity to our nation and set a shining example for the world.

In quiet and piecemeal ways historians in the 1970s and 1980s were busy prying the "true history" of the war out of the grip of this powerful collective memory. Though John Morton Blum did not intend his 1976 book *V Was for Victory* to be more than mildly revisionist, it did hold up for scholarly reflection a series of unpleasant truths about the war: that in this war for democracy and against racism, the government refused to desegregate the armed forces; that it imprisoned more than 100,000 Japanese Americans; that it awarded the vast majority of military contracts to the largest American corporations, accelerating the monopolization of American industry; and that it promised Americans a cornucopia of consumer goods—everything from nylon stockings to suburban homes—to sustain their slumping patriotism. Other scholars picked up where Blum had left off, and in the space of a decade they published a rash of indictments of 1940s American society and of the government's conduct of the war. These revisionist accounts focused on the racism, anti-Semitism, and sexism that permeated the home front; on the government policies that weakened labor and small business and strengthened corporate control of American life; on the many Americans who, far from committing themselves to a worldwide crusade, quickly grew cynical about the war and "did their part" for the most pragmatic and selfish of reasons.[1]

This assault on the idea of "the good war" was particularly strong in regard to the experience of labor. Many Americans today would not dare think or say that national goodness might somehow be associated with strengthening labor's economic and political power. But this sense of opposition between labor and national well-being is fairly recent. Those of us who can still remember a time when liberalism and the Democratic Party were strong know how integral organized labor was to liberalism's popularity and success. The two were seen as having arisen together in the 1930s, nurtured by a warm, caring president whose affection for ordinary Americans knew few bounds. Their places in American politics were secured in the 1940s when the nation, under the liberal Roosevelt's leadership, gained a great military triumph abroad and economic prosperity at home. The labor movement was thought to have contributed vitally to this double achievement: its full cooperation with industry made possible the manufacturing feats on which America's military victory and economic vigor so clearly rested. The government, in turn, rewarded labor's cooperation by encouraging union growth: union membership nearly doubled (from 8 to 15 million between 1939 and 1945) until it encompassed 35 percent of the nation's workforce. By 1945–46, the American labor movement enjoyed the kind of economic and political power it had never known, power it used to provide unionized workers with job security, high wages, health insurance, pensions, college educations, and homeownership. World War II, in this view, had been more than good; it had been the best of wars for American workers.

The attack on this memory was triggered by Nelson Lichtenstein's influential 1982 book *Labor's War at Home*. Lichtenstein portrayed labor's experience in World War II in far more ambivalent terms: there were pluses, to be sure—full employment, increasing incomes, improved benefits, government support of unionization—but there were also substantial negatives. The government had trumpeted an "equality of sacrifice" policy, by which it meant that no one group would be asked to give more to the war effort than any other; but workers discovered that their wages were often held down while employers' profits were permitted to rise. Workers had given up the right to strike in exchange for the right to bring all workplace grievances to a government agency—the War Labor Board—that would expeditiously process and fairly judge all claims. But grievances accumulated so quickly amid the stresses of war production (around-the-clock-schedules; constant infusion of new workers, often different in race, ethnicity, or religion from those already employed; a shortage of experienced foremen to staff rapidly expanding supervisory ranks) that the War Labor Board could not handle them quickly or judiciously enough. Anger in the ranks of American workers mounted until it exploded in wave after wave of wildcat strikes in 1944 and 1945. More American workers participated in strikes in those two years than in any similar period since 1919—more than in any two consecutive depression years.

Union leaders, according to Lichtenstein, might have sided with this rank-and-file surge, using it to renegotiate the rules of the wartime labor system in a way that increased labor's power and ensured equality of sacrifice in fact as well as in theory. This is what John L. Lewis had accomplished by endorsing the walkout of his United Mine Worker coal miners in 1943. But most labor leaders, in Lichtenstein's view, were too scared of the growing strength of conservatives, too fearful of antagonizing their liberal friends, and too alarmed by rank-and-file rambunctiousness. Rather than side with the wildcat strike movement, they joined hands with government administrators to clamp down on strikers, to refuse their demands, to threaten prosecution if they persisted with their unauthorized protests. In so doing, labor leaders tamed the most vigorously democratic and independent portions of their unions, deepened labor's dependence on the government, and accelerated the flow of union power away from the rank and file (the workers themselves) and toward the encrusted upper echelons of union bureaucracies. In other words, the labor movement (Lichtenstein had in mind the progressive Congress of Industrial Organizations) disarmed itself, made itself weaker than it might have been, and thus found itself with a far more limited role in national life than it might have had. These developments would haunt organized labor during the postwar period and keep it from achieving the national economic and political power it thought it deserved. In short, "the good war" was a lot less good for American labor, Lichtenstein argued, than most people thought.[2]

Lichtenstein's powerful revisionism entailed more than a reassessment of the labor movement. It also raised questions about the engagement of American working people with the war. In Lichtenstein's book the working class did not go to war—if by "going to war" we mean enthusiastically supporting the war effort by volunteering for military service, or working especially hard to support the "boys" overseas, or vocally endorsing the nation's war aims and ideals. Instead, the working class went to work. Support for the war there was, but not in the sense of overriding or supplanting economic concerns or class loyalties. The working class remained apart from the American nation. The war was not really their war, not really a people's war.

Lichtenstein did not offer a sustained argument or marshal evidence for this point of view; rather, it was a perspective threaded through his work, one that seemed to correspond to the high number of wildcat strikes—strikes that interrupted the war effort and could be interpreted as a protest against it—and one informed as well by Lichtenstein's own deep-rooted suspicion that patriotism and nationalism were inimical to working-class solidarity.[3]

In the decade and a half since the publication of his book, Lichtenstein's argument for the 1940s as a critical decade in labor's history has become widely accepted among labor and political historians, whose own research has confirmed Lichtenstein's once provocative findings. But his argument for the separateness of class from nation has fared less well, for the accumulating evidence points to workers' deep patriotic engagement with their identity as Americans and with the welfare of their nation.[4] I shall review some of this evidence and then assess its implications for understanding labor politics in the 1940s.

Some of the strongest evidence for working-class patriotism is also the oldest and most obvious: popular reactions to the Japanese attack on Pearl Harbor. Everyone who was older than ten in 1941 seems to remember exactly when and where they heard the news of the Japanese attack. The powerful antiwar sentiment present in American society in the 1920s and 1930s vanished overnight and did not resurface, though the war carried on for four long years and claimed hundreds of thousands of American lives. No other major war America has fought in this century generated such enthusiastic support and so little public protest.[5] The Korean War never enlisted more than lukewarm support. World War I and the Vietnam War both sparked large, angry, and determined antiwar movements that powerfully influenced domestic and foreign policy for years after the conflagrations had ended.[6]

Recent social history has confirmed, moreover, some standard myths concerning the war's popularity. In the textile city of Lowell, Massachusetts, for example, Marc Scott Miller has uncovered evidence of young working-class men clamoring to join the military. The few who tried to evade the draft or who took advantage of legal deferments were often treated as "wimps." "Girls" whose "boys" had gone overseas were expected to remain romantically faithful for the war's duration. War spirit found its way into schools, comic strips, and children's games. A sudden fascination with warplanes and the romance of flying gripped high-school boys. Among young adults, war bond rallies and dances were wildly popular. War bond administrators, in turn, had little difficulty raising the money required for the war, even as they embarked on their fourth, fifth, and sixth bond drives. Similarly, Red Cross officials easily found enough blood donors to keep an adequate supply of plasma flowing to the war zones.[7] Such evidence seems to corroborate the claim made by another scholar, Mark Leff, that during World War II Americans "gloried in the feeling that they were participating in a noble and successful cause."[8]

The significance of labor unions or of "class-conscious" workers in this war effort is not clear from Miller's study. But in my own work on another New England textile city—Woonsocket, Rhode Island—I found that unions and labor militants contributed essential bonds, blood, and moral support to the war.[9] No single union activity in the years 1941 to 1945 occupied more time or involved more members than war bond drives and servicemen support committees. Many union locals regularly oversubscribed the war bond quotas assigned them. In February 1944 the city's labor movement made Woonsocket the nation's first city to surpass its bond quota in the government's Fourth War Loan Campaign. The next month union members received the news that Woonsocket was the American city with the second highest per capita contribution to the Russian War Relief Society. Servicemen committees in virtually every local raised money through dances or through the profits of plant vending machines and cooperative cafeterias to send checks, gift packages, and letters to their members in the armed forces.

Participation in the war effort was common to all union locals, regardless of their particular ethnic or political orientation.[10] Within Woonsocket, it was as strong among conservative French Canadians—who formed a majority of the workforce—as among radical Belgians; it was equally evident among the Irish, Italian, and Polish workers who belonged to union locals outside the city. Anecdotal testimony adds to the evidence suggesting a profound rank-and-file commitment to the war. Pat Murphy, an Irish lathe operator, impressed his union steward one day by turning out five pieces rather than the assigned four, saying it was a birthday gift to his son in the armed forces. Phillipe Plante, a French Canadian watchman at a spinning mill, achieved union recognition for solemnly saluting the mill's American flag every day before lowering it. A score of French and Belgian union members, many of whom had fought the Germans in World War I, began broadcasting morale-boosting radio messages to the forces of resistance in their native land. Emily Hart, a French Canadian textile worker with a husband in the navy and a brother in the army, donated five pints of blood to the Red Cross plasma drive. And Mary Bednarchuk, an aging Polish textile worker eager to retire from mill work, was determined to "keep going until the war is over" to demonstrate support for her son, a much decorated aerial gunner, and his fellow soldiers.[11]

It is likely that many working-class blood donors, bond purchasers, and care package senders cared less about the nation's official war aims than about getting a loved one home alive. Some grew perturbed at the endless appeals to patriotism that always concluded with a request for more money. Still, the average worker's personal investment in the war, measured in terms of family members or kin serving in the military and risking death, made a skeptical, detached attitude toward the country's war aims difficult to maintain. Mary Bednarchuk, whose stated loyalty was to her son, not her nation, nevertheless lavished great attention on her son's many medals and diligently collected newspaper and magazine clippings describing his heroic acts. In such ways did loyalty to kin merge imperceptibly with patriotic feeling. Similarly, a Lowell, Massachusetts, mother with five sons in the service, her daughter later recalled, followed the war "every which way she could, because of [her] . . . boys being here and there." "She had put a big map in the dining room and, oh, she just followed everything that was going on during the war."[12] In such circumstances, distinctions between personal involvement with the war and ideological commitment to it proved difficult to maintain.

The government, meanwhile, ran sophisticated propaganda campaigns to further mesh national war aims with individual concerns. We still know far too little about these campaigns; those historians (like John Morton Blum) who have studied them have generally not understood the advertising techniques many were based on.[13] Unlike the ham-fisted, overbearing propaganda campaigns of World War I, those of World War II benefited from shrewd advertising innovations in the 1920s and 1930s. The principle of market segmentation, in particular, increased the sophistication and effectiveness of government propaganda. This principle, first adopted by advertising agencies in the 1930s, flowed from the recognition that 130 million Americans did not constitute a single consuming public. Tastes differed, depending on whether those in question were black or white, Yankee or immigrant, male or female, old or young, working class or middle class. Advertisers had to take such differences into account. In some cases this meant identifying the public most interested in a product and constructing an advertising campaign calculated to appeal to its particular tastes. In other cases, especially when a product—such as toothpaste or war bonds—was to be sold to all Americans, advertisers began fashioning several campaigns, each directed at one market segment.[14]

The Treasury Department, under the direction of Secretary Henry Morgenthau, assembled a sophisticated team of advertisers, many "drafted" from Madison Avenue's most successful agencies, to convince Americans to buy war bonds. Morgenthau also hired as consultants individuals with extensive knowledge of European ethnic groups, blacks, and other minority populations to help the advertisers determine how best to tap the patriotic ardor of these particular groups.[15] The Treasury Department, as a consequence of this effort, sent out different appeals to different market segments. Consider two war bond advertisements appearing in Woonsocket in 1944, one in the city's daily newspaper, the *Woonsocket Call,* the other in the city's labor paper, the *ITU News.* The *Call's* success (in terms of subscriptions and advertising) depended on middle-class readers. The *ITU News,* by contrast, was intended for the city's heavily ethnic working class. The war bond advertisements appearing in these two newspapers had strikingly different themes. The *Woonsocket Call* ad, which had been paid for by local Woonsocket industrialists and merchants, stressed that war bonds were a good business investment. "Bonds are safe, they pay a good return, they're easy to buy. When they mature, they mean new machinery and equipment, new conveniences for the house, money for the children's schooling, funds for retirement." These were words intended for businessmen, small and large, whose attention never wavered far from profit and loss, not even (apparently) in a world war.[16] No appeal to financial self-interest appeared in the *ITU News* ad, however; no effort was made to tell workers how war bond purchases would someday bring them savings for a home or desired consumer goods. The labor appeal was couched instead in terms of religious tolerance, racial equality, and cultural pluralism. The advertisement exalted America's time-honored commitment to the inherent equality of all people, of whatever race, creed, or religion. It emphasized how Hitler's doctrines of racial superiority challenged that principle, how Hitler mocked America, depicting it as a weak nation because its blood was "tainted by many strains." Americans had to fight to prove Hitler wrong, to show him that ethnic and racial diversity was a source of strength, not weakness, and to preserve America's historic role as a land of freedom and opportunity for all.[17]

The point of comparing the *Woonsocket Call* and *ITU News* advertisements is not to contrast the self-interestedness of businessmen with the idealism of workers; it is to point out how much the representation of an America made strong by the contribution of different ethnic groups appealed to the personal desires of ethnic workers for inclusion and acceptance in their adopted home. From the start, ethnic workers' attraction to unionism in Woonsocket and elsewhere had been in part a manifestation of their desire to overcome the second-class treatment conferred on them because of their ethnic identity. In the 1930s, unionism was a vehicle not only for gaining economic power but also for overcoming cultural discrimination. Within their own unions, workers attempted to show that individuals from different ethnic groups could work together in an atmosphere of unity, free of bigotry. They imagined reconstructing America along similar lines. They believed that Franklin Roosevelt shared this culturally egalitarian vision and was eager to see it realized.[18]

Building a pro-labor, culturally tolerant America, however, was more easily imagined than accomplished. Millions of workers remained unorganized throughout the 1930s. Those who did belong to unions stayed poor, the continuation of the depression making substantial income gains rare. Meanwhile, opposition to labor and to the New Deal's young welfare state was mounting in corporate boardrooms and in the homes of middle-class Americans who had been scared by labor's militancy and by its association with communism. Father Charles Coughlin, Gerald L. K. Smith, and other hatemongers were reinvigorating the forces of prejudice. For a time Roosevelt's determination to fight these trends wavered. But with the war, and with the need to mobilize for a total fight against Nazi aggression, the prospects of renewing the fight for economic and cultural equality brightened.[19]

The outspoken celebration of America's ethnic diversity that occurred during the war had no precedent in American history. Countless Hollywood war movies built their plots around a multiethnic (and in some cases multiracial) platoon or boat crew whose members' devotion to each other gave them the strength to fight and the will to triumph.[20] A similar theme began appearing in juvenile fiction. John Tunis's *All-American* (1942), for example, tells how a WASP, a Jew, an Irish youth, and a black, who first meet on a ball field, join hands to combat prejudice in their high school and their town.[21] A new liberal journal, *Common Ground,* founded with much fanfare in 1940, conceived of its mission as telling a story "not now being covered by any other magazine": that "of the coming and meeting on this continent of peoples belonging to . . . 60 different national, racial, and religious backgrounds."[22] A 1944 pamphlet of the Congress of Industrial Organizations' Political Action Committee told it this way: "They came from England and from Ireland. . . . They came from Russia and from Germany. They came from Italy and from Poland. They came from Yugoslavia. Africa. . . . They came from all the corners of the earth to share in our way of life."[23] A sense of urgency gripped those intent on telling this story: "Never has it been more important," noted the editors of *Common Ground,* "that we become intelligently aware of the ground Americans of various strains have in common; that we sink our tap roots deep into its rich and varied cultural past and attain rational stability in place of emotional hysteria; that we reawaken the old American Dream, a dream which, in its powerful emphasis on the fundamental worth and dignity of every human being, can be a bond of unity no totalitarian attack can break."[24]

The outpouring of such sentiments cannot be understood simply as war propaganda. The rise of Hitler had genuinely appalled many Americans. It particularly unnerved the nation's liberals and radicals, who had been certain that vicious racial bigotry was characteristic of primitive societies, not advanced ones like Germany. Articles and books, popular and scholarly, on the roots of religious prejudice and on improving intergroup relations began rolling off the presses. The contradiction between America's professed commitment to equality and its discriminatory treatment of its black citizens—"the American dilemma" to use Gunnar Myrdal's 1944 phrase—received the sort of attention it had not been given since the early days of Reconstruction. Social scientists who had been quietly fighting intellectual racism in the United States (such as the anthropologist Franz Boas and his disciples Margaret Mead and Ruth Benedict) suddenly found themselves with large audiences hungry for sociological and psychological explanations of bigotry. Benedict and Mead, among others, were brought into the nation's service to contribute their knowledge and opinions to government war efforts.[25]

The rise of Hitler and America's war against him, in other words, had prompted a serious rethinking of the American liberal agenda.[26] Government propagandists certainly made use of this new liberal focus, but they did not create it. Their job was to work the genuine yearning for racial and religious equality into advertising messages and to transmit them to groups where the effects were likely to be substantial. Little is known about the procedures actually used by government bond sellers and other propagandists to match advertising messages with particular audiences. But there can be no doubt that the message of America as a land of diversity reached and profoundly touched ethnic workers; so too did the idea that the nation—as represented by the federal government—was leading the fight against prejudice. For ethnic workers the war was the historic moment when they felt fully accepted as Americans. They were fighting for America and America was fighting for them. As a group of ethnic unionists in Woonsocket declared in 1944: "We shall protect and amplify . . . democracy in America and in every peace-loving nation of the world, so that the soldiers of every race, creed and color— the Colin Kellys and the Meyer Levins and the Dorie Millers, the black men and the white and the yellow, the Catholic, the Protestant and the Jew, 'SHALL NOT HAVE DIED IN VAIN.' "[27] Here was another instance of the personal—in this case the desire of Catholic unionists to overcome discrimination they had long endured—merging with the political task of delivering to Hitler's Germany (and to its racist propaganda) a knockout blow.

Further evidence of ethnic workers' desire for integration into American society can be found in sharply rising naturalization rates. Though there had been no mass immigration since 1921, the nation still harbored 11.6 million foreign-born, about a third of whom (approximately 4 million) had yet to become citizens.[28] The proportion of aliens was highest among those who had come from eastern and southern Europe in the late nineteenth and early twentieth centuries and from Canada and Mexico. More than 1.5 million of these aliens became citizens in the war years alone (1941–45)—from 35 to 40 percent of the alien population—by far the highest rate of naturalization recorded for any five-year period since the Census Bureau began tracking these statistics in 1907.[29] Contrary to some popular and scholarly impressions, only a small part of these wartime naturalizations—10 percent—occurred as a result of military induction; the rest were voluntary acts by civilians.[30] By 1950 the proportion of naturalized citizens within each of the major European immigrant groups exceeded 70 percent and sometimes reached 80 percent. Moreover, the substantial differential in percentages that had long distinguished "old immigrants" from "new immigrants" had disappeared: by 1950, for example, the percentages of naturalized Poles and naturalized Britons were virtually identical—72 for the former, 75 for the latter.[31]

Because the census did not break down naturalization by occupation, the number of working-class immigrants who became citizens during these years cannot be determined with precision, but it was probably high. The eastern and southern European groups most often seeking citizenship during the war years were those heavily concentrated in working-class occupations. Thus it seems fair to interpret these naturalization patterns as evidence of Euro-American workers' deepening connection to America, reflecting the growing perception that the nation was prepared to welcome those it had long shunned.

The growing enthusiasm for America manifested in rising naturalization rates was propelled by an additional factor, a fully mobilized economy. Unemployment—still 14 percent in 1940—vanished by 1943 as war production triggered an insatiable demand for labor. A tight labor market pushed wages up. In manufacturing, the average weekly earnings grew 65 percent between 1941 and 1944; adjusting for inflation and higher income taxes still leaves a net gain of 27 percent. Fifteen million workers—a full third of the prewar workforce—moved up the occupational ladder during the war's course. Largely as a result of government policies, the poorest paid enjoyed the greatest wage increases. The government added additional value to jobs by requiring employers to offer their workers nonwage benefit packages that included paid vacations and hospitalization insurance.[32]

These gains did not mean that inequities, injustices, and inconveniences in the workplace went unnoticed. On the contrary, the classification of factory work and the wages assigned particular jobs caused conflict between workers and bosses and among different groups of workers who were constantly jockeying for labor market advantage. The influx of new workers to war production centers, meanwhile, everywhere overwhelmed local transportation systems and housing, adding further frustrations to daily life. The resentments and discomforts of wartime living, however, must be set alongside the growing remuneration and security of wartime employment. By itself this economic experience would not have been enough to bring about inclusion of workers who had keenly felt their marginality, but in conjunction with the wartime celebration of the nation's multicultural character it allowed European ethnics to believe that the American dream was finally within their grasp. In this way one very substantial portion of the American working class, its European ethnic component, became deeply engaged with the war. This working-class segment did not just go to work. It went to war. Its commitment to the war may explain why the furious labor strife anticipated by many observers of the time never materialized. "While we have had quite a few strikes," observed Edwin Witte, chair of the Michigan region of the War Labor Board, in July 1943, "the big explosion we have been looking for has never come."[33]

African American workers were far more ambivalent about the war. The ideological assault on Hitler's racism, so prominent in government propaganda, found as receptive an audience among blacks as among European ethnics. The Treasury Department cultivated blacks as assiduously as it hawked its wares to ethnics, and blacks responded by purchasing large numbers of war bonds. Moreover, African Americans found new economic opportunities in war work. Because of labor shortages, industrial jobs from which blacks had long been excluded were now accessible. More than a million responded by leaving southern rural areas, where most of the black population was still concentrated, for factory work in the industrial centers of the South and North. Those who made this journey often experienced a dramatic rise in income, magnified by the poverty-level wages characteristic of the agricultural economy they emerged from.[34]

But few African Americans could embrace the war effort or America with the same enthusiasm evident among Euro-Americans. The government compromised its campaign against racism by refusing to desegregate the military. Throughout the war, black soldiers were trained and fought (when they were allowed to fight) in all-black units.[35] Moreover, white America was plainly nervous about—and often cruelly hostile to— the participation of blacks in the celebration of national diversity. More often than not, they were excluded from cinematic and literary representations of the multicultural platoon. When blacks were included they were often given a subordinate status: they could be seen but not heard, or they could be heard as long as their comments and actions supported, but did not supplant, those of the (white) leading men. Thus in *Guadalcanal Diary*, a 1943 war movie stressing the role of ethnic marines— Irish, "Brooklynese," and Hispanic—in the early assaults on the island, only one black enlisted man (a sailor) is allowed to appear. Materializing on-screen while the marines are still on their troopships, he is asked to identify the battleships and destroyers that have just joined the invasion force. The scene conveys a kind of interracial affection as the black sailor is surrounded, even nuzzled, by a chummy group of whites. But the scene lasts all of ten seconds, during which the black seaman utters a mere half dozen words (all proper nouns). He appears in no other scene; he is permitted no role in the film's main action—the landing on the island and the assault on the Japanese. He thus can take no part in the ordeal by fire that forges the motley marine crew into true Americans.[36]

In their evaluations of the Congress of Industrial Organizations (CIO), African American workers confronted a similar dilemma: whether to celebrate the CIO for the new kind of racial inclusion it seemed to offer or to condemn it for the racist habits it condoned. Specifically, they had to balance their high regard for the antiracist campaigns of the CIO's top brass and communist activists with the racism rampant in the ranks of white workers, South and North. A significant number of the wartime wildcats were "hate strikes," initiated by whites to protest the introduction of blacks to their workplaces. These strikes occurred not only in cities such as Mobile, Alabama, where industrial unionism was new, but also in urban centers such as Detroit where the CIO and progressive politics were thought to be entrenched. In early June 1943, the promotion of three black workers to positions hitherto occupied by whites triggered a vicious strike at a Packard engine factory in Detroit. The rising racial tension prompted an editor of a Catholic labor paper to warn that "there is a growing, subterranean race war going on in the City of Detroit which can have no other ultimate result than an explosion of violence."[37] The explosion came on 20 June in a full-fledged race riot that rocked the city and shocked the nation. In two days of massive violence, 34 people (25 of them black) were killed and 675 were wounded. Property losses totaled $2 million, and a million man-hours of war production were lost. The *Detroit Times* pronounced it "the worst disaster which has befallen Detroit since Pearl Harbor."[38]

It would be tempting to blame Detroit's hostile racial climate on the hundreds of thousands of white, racist southerners who had streamed into the city in the preceding two years, attracted by the promise of good wages in the war plants.[39] But racism was equally apparent among the city's European ethnic populations.[40] These ethnics' embrace of America may well have intensified their prejudice against blacks, for many conceived of Americanization in racial terms: becoming American meant becoming white. Becoming white, of course, acquired meaning and conferred status only in a society that still denigrated blackness. Thus the ethnic workers who freed themselves from racial discrimination during the war years often were anxious to reinforce the racist boundary separating white from black. Only by insisting on that division, it seems, could they enjoy the full fruits of their assimilation. Many refused to work alongside blacks or share neighborhoods with them. Some were eager to participate in rituals that white Americans had long used to intimidate blacks. An Italian American interviewed by Studs Terkel understood this desire all too well: "There were riots in Harlem in '45. I remember standing on a corner, a guy would throw the door open and say, 'Come on down.' They were goin' to Harlem to get in the riot. They'd say, 'Let's beat up some niggers.' It was wonderful. It was new. The Italo-Americans stopped being Italo and started becoming Americans. We joined the group. Now we're like you guys, right?"[41]

Because blacks had to balance their wartime experience of harassment and discrimination against their hopes that the war might erode racism, they approached the war effort with more circumspection and skepticism than did white ethnics. Some could not deny the satisfaction they took in the stunning success of the Japanese attack on Pearl Harbor, a strike that in their eyes dealt a serious blow to the prestige of the white race. "I don't want them [the Japanese] to quite win," admitted one black to another, "but to dish out to these white people all they can dish out to them."[42]

Others had to struggle hard to convince themselves and fellow African Americans that the nation—in spite of its history of slavery and racism—deserved their loyalty and, if necessary, their lives. William Pickens, director of the Inter-racial Section of the Treasury Department's Savings Bond Division, experienced this struggle acutely as he encountered audience after audience of blacks who wanted to be told what and why they should sacrifice for America. The significant volume of war bonds African Americans purchased and the large number of young men they sent to fight suggests that they found a satisfactory rationale, but the struggle to do so was not easy. When Pickens's (white) boss congratulated him in 1945 for his fine work in selling savings bonds, he acknowledged that the job had required "superb patience and Christian fortitude," not just to convince blacks of America's virtues but to help Pickens turn the other cheek to whites—including some in his own agency—who racially insulted him in large and small ways.[43] Bartow Tipper, a steelworker, trade unionist, and civil rights activist in 1940s Aliquippa, Pennsylvania, remembered the red-hot anger that spread among Jones and Laughlin's black steel workers in the summer of 1943 because of their continued exclusion from the most desired jobs—jobs monopolized by Italian and eastern European unionists: "We'd tell everybody: 'We're tired of being pushed in the corner.' We'd done give our lives for this war, we done work hard for this war—-and we can't get no jobs. Can't move up. And so we said, therefore: 'We'll tear this place up. We can't take it no more.' "[44]

Tipper and his fellow black workers, in fact, didn't tear the place up. Federal negotiators, chastened by the racial violence in Detroit, rushed in to mediate the dispute and arranged a compromise settlement that eased African American anger. Black workers could be placated. They understood that the war had offered their people rare economic opportunities, not to be lightly tossed away. In the years immediately following the war, Tipper used to upset his white bosses by declaring: "Goddamit, I wouldn't care if there was a war every week! The only time we ever made a lot money, the only time we'd ever get anything done, was when

the war come."[45] In Tipper's double recollection of rage at racial injustice and appreciation for the new opportunities the war offered blacks,
we can discern the ambivalence that characterized the attitudes of so
many African Americans to the war.

Because of their mixed wartime experience, cultural incorporation into
the nation was slower among African Americans than among European
ethnics. Their patriotism was more subdued, and the nation's claims on
them were fewer. Indeed, one can discern in black workers' attitudes
evidence to bolster the revisionist argument that American workers remained "apart" from the nation during World War II. But black workers
were not sufficiently numerous or well enough accepted by white workers for their wariness to spread throughout the working class.[46] The
African American experience does provide, however, a useful comparative perspective from which to evaluate the effects of war patriotism on
the white working class, and especially its European ethnic majority.

The white ethnic workers who became so devoted to America during
the war did not lose their class consciousness. They continued to skirmish
with their bosses. The massive strike wave in 1946 testifies to their
continuing ability to understand their class interest and act aggressively
in its behalf.[47]

Still, it became harder to act on these class instincts now that they
provoked the wrath—and police power—of a nation that ethnic unionists much admired. This dilemma had not existed for unionists in the
1930s, when the state—or large portions of it, the president included—
endorsed the labor movement's vision of what the country should become and countenanced its militant posture.[48] "The average man once
more confronts the problem that faced the Minute Man," noted Franklin
D. Roosevelt during his 1936 nomination acceptance speech, a moment
when the New Deal was at its most ambitious and the labor movement
was near the zenith of its political power. The average man, Roosevelt
continued, must fight a war against the economic royalists, "take away
their power," and thereby "save a great and precious form of government
for ourselves and for the world."[49] Roosevelt's invocation of the American Revolution offered powerful sanction to a mass movement that had
insistently called attention to the conflict between America's rich and
poor.

But the war prompted Roosevelt to jettison his "economic royalist"
harangues, especially once he decided to rely on corporate America

to direct the economy's war mobilization. Government propagandists, meanwhile, sought to popularize a notion of nationhood that was inclusive and a language of patriotism steeped in metaphors of harmony and mutual respect rather than of antagonism and struggle. If this stress on respect encouraged campaigns for cultural and racial equality, it robbed labor of the leverage needed to increase its power at capital's expense. Patriotism in the 1940s required a different sort of behavior from workers than in the 1930s. Militant protests could not be so easily wrapped in "red, white, and blue"; those packaged this way no longer attracted much sympathy or support beyond the factory gates and union halls. Workers pursuing their economic grievances at all costs risked being stigmatized as un-American—not something that many working-class Americans, especially those ethnics whose allegiance to their nation was quickening, wanted to endure.[50] It may be that many of the wildcat strikes, which tended to involve few workers and to be short, were intended by the wildcatters themselves as a kind of limited protest: here was a way to bring a perceived injustice to light without unduly damaging the nation's military or economic welfare. One piece of evidence to support this view is their timing. As Alan Clive has shrewdly pointed out, the incidence of wildcats rose in months when the news from the war was good, and declined when the outcome of crucial battles was in doubt.[51]

My emphasis on the extent of white working-class patriotism does not negate the central point of Lichtenstein's revisionism, that the 1940s were a time when labor failed to achieve its larger political ambitions. It does suggest, however, that the roots of this failure lie not only in the timidity of union leaders but in the rank and file's affection for "America," in the desire of ordinary ethnic workers for recognition and acceptance as Americans, and in their willingness to believe in the essential goodness of the war and of their nation. Patriotism was a double-edged sword, one that could both help and injure the workers who espoused it. In the 1940s it did both—helping European ethnics feel fully at home in America while simultaneously frustrating the ambition of those who sought to extend popular control over the nation's economic institutions.

If this analysis is correct, it seems that black workers—whose patriotism was more circumspect—preserved in the postwar era a greater freedom of action, a greater readiness to define Americanism in terms that made sense to them rather than in terms set forth by the government. Black workers, in fact, did seem to defy the cold war consensus more easily than white workers. They were more willing than their white counterparts, for instance, to associate with communists. Those who became civil rights activists in the 1950s were more prepared than white unionists to disrupt the narrow political confines that protest movements had been channeled into and to challenge both the moral authority and the police powers of their nation.[52] For African Americans in the 1950s and early 1960s, American patriotism remained a spur to social action rather than to complacency. Their war had yet to be won.

Notes

1. John Morton Blum, *V Was for Victory: Politics and American Culture during World War II* (New York, 1976). A list of revisionist scholarship would include (but would certainly not be limited to) Peter Irons, *Justice at Home* (New York, 1983); John W. Dower, *War without Mercy: Race and Power in the Pacific War* (New York, 1986); Karen Anderson, *Wartime Women: Sex Roles, Family Relations, and the Status of Women during World War II* (Westport, Conn., 1983); Thomas Cripps, "Racial Ambiguities in American Propaganda Movies," in *Film and Radio Propaganda in World War II*, ed. K. R. M. Short (Knoxville, Tenn., 1983), 125–45; Robert B. Westbrook, " 'I Want a Girl, Just Like the Girl That Married Harry James': American Women and the Problem of Political Obligation in World War II," *American Quarterly* 42 (1990): 587–614; David Wyman, *The Abandonment of the Jews: America and the Holocaust* (New York, 1984); Paul Fussell, *Wartime: Understanding and Behavior in the Second World War* (New York, 1989).

2. Nelson Lichtenstein, *Labor's War at Home: The CIO in World War II* (New York, 1982). Lichtenstein and others had begun to sketch out this interpretation in the 1970s. See *Radical America* 9 (July–October 1975), an issue devoted to labor and the home front, and Martin Glaberman, *Wartime Strikes: The Struggle against the No-Strike Pledge in the UAW during World War II* (Detroit, 1980). See also George Lipsitz, *Class and Culture in Cold War America: "A Rainbow at Midnight"* (South Hadley, Mass., 1982), an important revisionist account that received less attention than Lichtenstein's work.

3. On historians' suspicions of patriotism and nationalism, see Joshua Freeman, "Delivering the Goods: Industrial Unionism during World War II," *Labor History* 19 (1978): 581–83, 590–93.

4. Lichtenstein, in fact, has revised his own views on the subject and now attributes far more significance to the role of patriotism in shaping working-class consciousness. See, for example, his "The Making of the Postwar Working Class: Cultural Pluralism and Social Structure in World War II," *History Today* 51 (1988): 42–63, and the volume he coedited with Howell John Harris, *Industrial Democracy in America: The Ambiguous Promise* (New York, 1993), the introduction in particular.

5. I am not including such military actions as the Persian Gulf War in the category "major wars."

6. On the history of antiwar movements, see Charles Chatfield, *The American Peace Movement: Ideals and Activism* (New York, 1992).

7. Marc Scott Miller, *The Irony of Victory: World War II and Lowell, Massachusetts* (Urbana, Ill., 1988).

8. Mark H. Leff, "The Politics of Sacrifice on the American Home Front in World War II," *Journal of American History* 77 (1991): 1296.

9. Gary Gerstle, *Working-Class Americanism: The Politics of Labor in a Textile City, 1914–1960* (New York, 1989), chap. 9.

10. There were virtually no blacks in Woonsocket.

11. Gerstle, *Working-Class Americanism*, 298–301.

12. Miller, *Irony of Victory*, 81.

13. This is also true of Alan Winkler, *The Politics of Propaganda: The Office of War Information, 1942–1945* (New Haven, 1978), and Frank W. Fox, *Madison Avenue Goes to War: The Strange Military Career of American Advertising* (Provo, Utah, 1975). Mark Leff does not address the issue of market segmentation in his article "The Politics of Sacrifice on the Homefront," but his piece is nevertheless a most interesting analysis of how Americans were "sold" on the war. See also Robert Griffith, "The Selling of America: The Advertising Council and American Politics, 1942–1960," *Business History Review* 57 (1983): 388–412.

14. Lizabeth Cohen discusses the introduction of market segmentation principles in her *Making a New Deal: Industrial Workers in Chicago, 1919–1939* (New York, 1990), 329.

15. Thus, for example, William Pickens, NAACP field secretary, was hired by the Treasury Department in 1942 to advise the advertising

experts on selling war bonds in black communities. William Pickens Record Group (hereafter Pickens papers), microfilm, Schomburg Collection of Negro Literature and History, New York Public Library.

16. "I Died Today. . . . What Did You Do?" *Woonsocket Call,* 30 June 1944.

17. *ITU News,* "Whose Blood Killed Private Parkins?" 13 October 1944. For the discussion of other advertisements emphasizing this theme, see Gerstle, *Working-Class Americanism,* 295–301.

18. Gerstle, *Working-Class Americanism,* chaps. 4–6; Cohen, *Making a New Deal,* chap. 8.

19. On the excitement that war mobilization initially unleashed in labor's ranks, see Nelson Lichtenstein, "From Corporatism to Collective Bargaining: Organized Labor and the Eclipse of Social Democracy in the Postwar Era," in *The Rise and Fall of the New Deal Order, 1930–1980,* ed. Steve Fraser and Gary Gerstle (Princeton, 1989), 122–52.

20. See, for example, *Sahara* (1943), with Humphrey Bogart.

21. I am indebted to Russell Kazal for bringing this book to my attention; Kazal, "'There Aren't Any Peasants in This Nation': Class, Pluralism, Nationalism, and Football in John R. Tunis's *All-American,*" unpublished manuscript, University of Pennnsylvania, 1993, in author's possession.

22. *Common Ground* 1 (autumn 1940): 2.

23. CIO-PAC, *This Is Your America* (New York, 1944), published in Joseph Gaer, *The First Round: The Story of the CIO Political Action Committee* (New York, 1944), 20.

24. *Common Ground* 1 (autumn 1940): 103.

25. Gunnar Myrdal, *An American Dilemma: The Negro Problem and Modern Democracy* (New York, 1944), 2 vols.; Walter A. Jackson, *Gunnar Myrdal and America's Conscience: Social Engineering and Racial Liberalism, 1938–1987* (Chapel Hill, N.C., 1990); Robin M. Williams Jr., *The Reduction of Intergroup Tensions: A Survey of Research on Problems of Ethnic, Racial, and Religious Group Relations* (New York, 1947); Carey McWilliams, *Brothers under the Skin* (Boston, 1951); Ruth Benedict, *The Races of Mankind* (New York, 1943); John Dower, *War without Mercy: Race and Power in the Pacific War* (New York, 1986), chap. 6.

26. See Gary Gerstle, "The Protean Character of American Liberalism," *American Historical Review* 99 (October 1994): 1043–73; Philip

Gleason, "Americans All: World War II and the Shaping of American Identity," *Review of Politics* 43 (1981): 483–518; and Richard W. Steele, "The War on Intolerance: The Reformulation of American Nationalism, 1939–1941," *Journal of American Ethnic History* 9 (1989): 11–33.

27. *ITU News*, 26 May 1944.

28. U.S. Department of Commerce, Bureau of the Census, *Historical Statistics of the United States, Colonial Times to 1970* (White Plains, N.Y., 1989), 114–16.

29. The second-highest naturalization rate during an equivalent five-year period, achieved in the years 1936 to 1940, was only 16.8 percent, less than half the wartime total. Ibid.

30. That more women than men were naturalized in these years underscores the civilian character of this process. Ibid.

31. Proportions of naturalized Poles in 1920 and 1930 stood at 28 and 50 percent, respectively, far less than for naturalized English people (63 and 67 percent). By 1950 French Canadians had reached the 70 percent naturalization threshold, but Mexicans, in a strikingly divergent pattern (only 26 percent), had not. Reed Ueda, "Naturalization and Citizenship," in *The Harvard Encyclopedia of American Ethnic Groups*, ed. Stephan Thernstrom (Cambridge, Mass., 1980), 747.

32. Lichtenstein, "Making of the Postwar Working Class"; Geoffrey Perrett, *Days of Sadness, Years of Triumph: The American People, 1939–1945* (Madison, Wisc., 1985), 325–56; Howell John Harris, *The Right to Manage: Industrial Relations Policies of American Business in the 1940s* (Madison, Wisc., 1982), 41–89.

33. Alan Clive, *State of War: Michigan in World War II* (Ann Arbor, Mich., 1979), 77.

34. Richard M. Dalfiume, "The 'Forgotten Years' of the Negro Revolution," *Journal of American History* 56 (1968): 90–106; Joe William Trotter Jr., *Black Milwaukee: The Making of an Industrial Proletariat, 1915–1945* (Urbana, Ill., 1985); William H. Harris, *The Harder We Run: Black Workers since the Civil War* (New York, 1982); "Summary: Activities of William Pickens for 1943," and letter from Pickens to Charles W. Adams, 6 March 1944, reel 3, Pickens papers; Lichtenstein, "Making of the Postwar Working Class."

35. Richard M. Dalfiume, *Desegregation of the U.S. Armed Forces: Fighting on Two Fronts, 1939–1953* (Columbia, Mo., 1969). The government also dragged its heels in desegregating industry, a reluctance that

prompted A. Philip Randolph to threaten a march on Washington in 1941. Randolph called off the march when a worried government established the Fair Employment Practices Commission. See Louis Rucharmes, *Race, Jobs, and Politics: The Story of the FEPC* (New York, 1953), and Herbert Garfinkel, *When Negroes March: The March on Washington Movement in the Organizational Politics of FEPC* (New York, 1959).

36. Richard Slotkin offers some perceptive comments on the multiethnic platoon in his *Gunfighter Nation: The Myth of the Frontier in Twentieth-Century America* (New York, 1992), 318–26.

37. Quoted in August Meier and Elliott Rudwick, *Black Detroit and the Rise of the UAW* (New York, 1979), 192.

38. Robert Shogan and Tom Craig, *Detroit Race Riot: A Study in Violence* (Philadelphia, 1964), 89; Harvard Sitkoff, "The Detroit Race Riot of 1943," *Michigan History* 53 (1969): 183–206; Sitkoff, "Racial Militancy and Interracial Violence in the Second World War," *Journal of American History* 58 (1971): 661–81; Joshua Freeman, "Delivering the Goods."

39. On the white southerners' migration to Detroit, see Clive, *State of War*, 170–85.

40. Blum, *V Was for Victory*, 199–204.

41. Studs Terkel, *"The Good War": An Oral History of World War II* (New York, 1984), 141–42. On Americanizing ethnics' hostility to blacks, see also Arnold R. Hirsch, *Making the Second Ghetto: Race and Housing in Chicago, 1940–1960* (New York, 1983), 171–211, and David R. Roediger, "Whiteness and Ethnicity in the History of 'White Ethnics' in the United States," in his *Toward the Abolition of Whiteness: Essays on Race, Politics, and Working Class History* (London, 1994), 181–98.

42. William Pickens quotes these words of a fellow African American in his essay "The American Negro and His Country in World War," n.d., reel 3, box 6, Pickens papers.

43. Letter from James Houghtelling to William Pickens, 29 October 1945, reel 3, box 6, Pickens papers.

44. Interview with Bartow Tipper, conducted by Charles Lane, 1982; transcript in author's possession. See also Charles Lane, "Honoring Our Commitments: The Role of the United Steel Workers of America in Controlling Rank-and-File Militancy under the World War II No-Strike Pledge" (senior thesis, Harvard University, 1983).

45. Ibid.

46. For a markedly different interpretation, see George Lipsitz's *Class and Culture in Cold War America,* chap. 1, which posits that black-initiated wildcats and public protests in World War II impelled all workers—white and black—to challenge the authority of their employers and their nation and thus intensified working-class militancy. Given the racial and ethnic divisions within the American working class, I find this view too optimistic.

47. See ibid. for a comprehensive account of the postwar strike wave (though one that pays little attention to ethnicity and Americanization).

48. On the close relation between the 1930s labor movement and portions of the New Deal state, see Steve Fraser, "The 'Labor Question,'" in Fraser and Gerstle, *Rise and Fall of the New Deal Order,* 55–84.

49. *The Public Papers and Addresses of Franklin D. Roosevelt* (New York, 1976), 5:230–36.

50. For a more extended discussion of this issue, see Gerstle, *Working-Class Americanism,* chap. 9.

51. Thus Clive writes, "Michigan strikes dropped sharply in the invasion month of June, 1944, and fell again at the turn of 1945 in the wake of the near-disaster at Bastogne." *State of War,* 76.

52. See Michael K. Honey, *Southern Labor and Black Civil Rights: Organizing Memphis Workers* (Urbana, Ill., 1993), 242–44, 288–89.

Elaine Tyler May

FIVE

Rosie the Riveter
Gets Married

*Chicago was just humming, no matter where I went. The
bars were jammed, and unless you were an absolute dog,
you could pick up anyone you wanted to. . . . There were
servicemen of all varieties roaming the streets all the time.
There was never, never a shortage of young, healthy
bucks. . . . We never thought of getting tired. Two, three
hours of sleep was normal. . . . I'd go down to the office
every morning half dead, but with a smile on my face,
and report in for work. There was another girl there who
was having a ball too, and we took turns going into the
back room and taking a nap on the floor behind a desk.*

Young workingwoman during World War II

As the epigraph suggests,[1] World War II opened up all kinds of
opportunities for women. New possibilities for work, play, and sexual
adventure were everywhere. Yet women also faced hardship as fathers,
sons, and husbands left for war, families relocated, and disruption became the norm. Taken together, all the changes, challenges, and difficulties of wartime had a lasting impact on the lives of American women.
But at the time, long-term effects were not on people's minds. The
question was how to respond to the emergency.[2]

Emergency was nothing new to the young adults coming of age at the
time of World War II. They had been reared on the trials and hardships
of the depression. When war broke out they faced a new emergency
calling for strength and sacrifice. Although the war brought an end to
the depression, as prosperity returned it ushered in new challenges for
women and men. Traditional domestic roles were thrown into disarray,
and even the disruption took new forms. In wartime the stigma attached
to employment for married women evaporated. Women not only were
tolerated in the paid labor force, they were actively recruited to take
"men's jobs" as a patriotic duty, to keep the war economy booming while

the men went off to fight. Men were called to war, where their role as soldiers took precedence over their role as breadwinners. Families coped with new realities as men vanished to foreign shores to ward off the enemy, leaving women to fend for themselves.

These readjustments, challenging traditional gender roles and domestic norms, held the potential for long-term changes in public as well as private life. The war emergency opened the way for a restructuring of the economy along gender-neutral lines, bringing an end to sex segregation in the workplace. In addition, wartime dislocation might have led to postponement of marriage and childbearing, continuing the demographic trends of the thirties toward fewer and later marriages. But these possibilities did not materialize. In spite of the many gains women made during the war and their struggles to hold on to those gains, opportunities for them dried up in postwar America. Ironically, the experiences of wartime ultimately reaffirmed a domestic ideal of breadwinner, homemaker, and children. At a time when domesticity faced its greatest challenge, young men and women turned to marriage and childbearing in unexpected numbers. How and why this happened is the subject of this chapter.

Let us first look closely at what some historians consider to be the most substantial change of the 1940s: the entry of unprecedented numbers of female workers into the paid labor force. As a result of the combined incentives of patriotism and good wages, women began streaming into jobs, many for the first time. The fastest-growing group in the workforce was married women, who took jobs during the war in record numbers. In a booming economy responding to the needs of the war effort, the stigma attached to employed wives evaporated.[3]

Yet this entry of women into the paid labor force was not as far reaching as it appeared on the surface. When we look closely at who these women were and what they did—particularly when we consider long-term possibilities—their opportunities appear much more limited. In the first place, at the beginning of the 1940s women entered jobs with tremendous disadvantages. In 1939 the median annual income for women was $568, compared with $962 for men, and for black women it was a mere $246. By 1940 women constituted only 9.4 percent of union members, although they made up 25 percent of the operatives. Women had few levers for improving their working conditions. Considering the strong sentiment that had prevailed in the 1930s against women's holding jobs at all, it is not surprising that even feminist organizations fighting job discrimination stressed women's need to work over their right to employment—a strategy that underscored women's responsibility to their families as their primary concern.[4]

Moreover, when we examine the statistics closely, we find that young married women, those most likely to have small children at home, made the smallest gains in employment during the 1940s—even less than prewar predictions. The reason is demographically as well as culturally interesting. Since single women had provided the largest proportion of the paid female labor force before the war, the demands of production during the forties quickly exhausted the supply. Few young single women were available, for the war almost immediately brought a drop in the marriage age and a rise in the birthrate. Because of these developments, young women who might previously have been expected to work for a few years were marrying and having children instead. Young married women with small children were encouraged to stay home. Although there were some day care centers to accommodate employed mothers, they were generally considered harmful to a child's development. Although only three thousand such centers were established by the federal government, even these were not filled to capacity.[5]

The removal of these younger women from the labor market opened the way for older married women—those without young children at home—to enter the paid labor force. These women were the fastest-growing group among the employed, a trend that would continue after the war. Between 1940 and 1945, the female labor force grew by over 50 percent. The proportion of women employed rose from 28 to 37 percent, and women made up 36 percent of the civilian workforce. Three-fourths of these new female employees were married. By the end of the war fully 25 percent of all married women were employed—a huge gain from 15 percent at the end of the 1930s.[6]

Not everyone was comfortable with this development, however. A writer in *Fortune* magazine lamented: "There are practically no unmarried women left to draw upon. . . . This leaves, as the next potential source of industrial workers, the housewives. . . . We are a kindly, somewhat sentimental people with strong, ingrained ideas about what women should or should not do. Many thoughtful citizens are seriously disturbed over the wisdom of bringing married women into the factories."[7]

In spite of their visibility, women still remained in a fairly small number of occupations. For all the publicity surrounding "Rosie the Riveter," few women took jobs that were previously held exclusively by men, and most of those jobs ended at the conclusion of the war. These developments are typical of a pattern that began during the war and continued during the postwar years: numerical expansion of opportunities flowing into a limited range of occupations. Although more and more women were welcomed into the paid labor force, most of them still ended up in low-paying, sex-segregated jobs.[8]

Women did not accept this situation passively. They recognized their value and fought for better wages and working conditions. The activism of women working at the California Sanitary Canning Company provides one dramatic example. Energetic labor organizers like Luisa Moreno and Dorothy Ray Healy built a powerful union of largely Mexican and Mexican American women who were able to achieve a wage increase and recognition of their union. Family and community networks helped support and strengthen their organization. Although their union could not be sustained after the war in the face of mounting opposition by anticommunist crusaders, its successes during the war demonstrate how much control over their work lives these women were able to achieve.[9]

One reason for the wartime success of these women was the strength of their numbers. Women composed 75 percent of all workers in the California canneries. Because they were in the majority, their segregation from male employees allowed them to develop a female work culture in the plants. In other industries where men were in the majority, the segregation of women was a disadvantage. Automobile manufacturing, for example, remained male dominated. Before the war, women accounted for only 10 percent of all autoworkers, and they were concentrated in relatively few jobs. After an initial shutdown, the industry retooled for war production. When the plant doors reopened in 1942, male workers were in short supply and women were hired in unprecedented numbers. By the end of 1943 one-fourth of the industry's workers were female.

Throughout the war, however, the automobile industry kept women in certain jobs and men in others. The boundaries continued to shift as new definitions of "women's work" were required, but the sex-segregated labor force remained. Despite the dramatic upswing in women's workforce participation, the unions had no fully developed class consciousness that would include women in their concerns, nor was there a strong feminist movement to assert women's needs. As a result, gender division of labor survived the war.[10]

In spite of women's dramatic contributions to the war effort, they were not able to achieve equal pay or working conditions. Their unequal treatment led to a campaign for equal rights. The Republicans in 1940 and the Democrats in 1944 supported the Equal Rights Amendment (ERA), but both the American Federation of Labor (AFL) and the Congress of Industrial Organizations (CIO) opposed it. Even Frances Perkins, secretary of labor, and Eleanor Roosevelt, first lady—two feminist activists—initially refused to support the legislation because they feared loss of the legal protections for women workers that had been enacted in the Progressive Era. In 1945 Congress considered the "Federal Wage Discrimination Act," but even with a fair amount of bipartisan support and some union backing that measure failed. When the ERA finally reached the Senate in 1946, a majority voted for it, but it failed to achieve the two-thirds necessary for passage.[11]

Instead of equal rights women got "protective" legislation, but those laws did not protect them from ill treatment on the job. Sexual harassment was rampant. One female war worker complained:

> At times it gets to be a pain in the neck when the man who is supposed to show you work stops showing it to you because you have nicely but firmly asked him to keep his hands on his own knees; or when you have refused a date with someone and ever since then he has done everything in his power to make your work more difficult. . . . Somehow we'll have to make them understand that we are not very much interested in their strapping virility. That the display of their physique and the lure of their prowess leaves us cold. That although they have certainly convinced us that they are men and we are women, we'd really rather get on with our work.

In spite of such difficulties, women took advantage of every opportunity the war offered. Almira Bondelid was a housewife when her husband left for overseas, but she did not sit home and wait for his return: "I decided to stay in San Diego and went to work in a dime store. That was a terrible place to work, and as soon as I could I got a job at Convair. . . . I worked in the tool department as a draftsman, and by the time I left there two years later I was designing long drill jigs for parts of the wing and a hull of B-24s."[12]

Unfortunately for women like Almira Bondelid, highly skilled, well-paid jobs like the one she finally secured were not likely to last once the war ended. Even before the end was in sight, married women were encouraged to return to their domestic duties when the conflict was over. In addition, single women were expected to relinquish their jobs and find husbands. Although the war offered single women many new opportunities, they also encountered hostility to their newly acquired freedom.

There is no question that wartime offered women new chances to participate in public life and to enjoy a certain amount of sexual freedom, as the epigraph to this chapter suggests. But at the same time, during the wartime emergency, single women were often seen as a threat to stable family life and to the moral fiber of the nation at war. As single women poured into the labor force along with their married sisters, there were fears that they might not be willing to settle down to family life once the emergency ended. Perhaps these anxieties arose because, unlike the 1930s, the war years brought a noticeable number of women out of their homes and traditionally sex-segregated jobs into occupations previously reserved for men. In addition, the war removed men from the home front, demonstrating that women could manage quite well without them. Single women now became targets of campaigns urging them back into their domestic roles, campaigns that continued after the war.

Along with their new economic endeavors, the perceived or potential sexual activity of single women also became a cause for alarm. A typical wartime pamphlet warned: "The war in general has given women new status, new recognition. . . . Women are 'coming into their own' in this war. . . . Yet it is essential that women avoid arrogance and retain their femininity in the face of their own new status. . . . In her new independence she must not lose her humanness as a woman. She may be the woman of the moment, but she must watch her moments."[13] This theme echoed through the prescriptive literature written during the war. One textbook explained why women had to watch their moments so carefully: "The greater social freedom of women has more or less inevitably led to a greater degree of sexual laxity, a freedom which strikes at the heart of family stability. . . . When women work, earn, and spend as much as men do, they are going to ask for equal rights with men. But the right to behave like a man meant [sic] also the right to misbehave as he does.

The decay of established moralities came about as a by-product." In this remarkable passage, the authors state as a scientific fact their opinion that social freedom and employment for women cause "sexual laxity," moral decay, and the destruction of the family.[14]

Women were urged to stay "pure" for the soon to be returning veterans, and men were told to avoid contact with single women for fear of catching venereal diseases. As Allan Brandt has shown, wartime purity crusades marked a revision of the germ theory: germs were not responsible for spreading disease, "promiscuous" women were. Widely distributed posters warned soldiers that even the angelic "girl next door" might carry disease. "She may look clean, but. . ." read the caption next to one picture of everybody's sweetheart. Wartime ushered in a preoccupation with all forms of nonmarital sexuality that had been dormant since the Progressive Era. It ranged from concern about prostitution and "promiscuous" women to fierce campaigns against homosexuals and other "deviants" in military and civilian life.[15]

Those campaigns were not fully effective, however. Young women found tremendous new chances to pursue sexual relationships and forge communities during the war. More young women moved into the city and away from neighborhood and parental supervision. Many now earned their own money and took charge of their own leisure time and behavior. For some young heterosexual women experiencing this new independence, men in uniform held special appeal. "When I was sixteen," recalled a college student a few years later, "I let a sailor pick me up and go all the way with me. I had intercourse with him partly because he had a strong personal appeal for me, but mainly because I had a feeling of high adventure and because I wanted to please a member of the armed forces." With so many girls in this adventurous spirit, one teenage boy described wartime as "a real sex paradise. The plant and the town were just full of working girls on the make. Where I was, a male war worker became the center of loose morality."[16]

Lesbians found similar opportunities, especially in the military. Phyllis Abry quit her job as a lab technician to join the WACs because she "wanted to be with all those women." Homosexuality was not allowed in the military, of course, but lesbians were not easily identified. "I remember being very nervous about them asking me if I had any homosexual feelings or attitudes," she recalled. "I just smiled and was sweet and feminine."[17]

The military establishment was not fully prepared for the impact of large numbers of women, and it took pains to promote a "feminine" image of female recruits. The entry of women into the armed forces during the war marked a major change from the past. They were recruited into every part of military service except combat. As Oveta Culp Hobby, director of the Women's Auxiliary Army Corps, proclaimed, women "are carrying on the glorious tradition of American womanhood. They are making history! . . . This is a war which recognizes no distinctions between men and women." To the female Americans she hoped to recruit, she said, "This is YOUR war." Women of "excellent character" who could pass an intelligence test could enlist, provided they had no children under fourteen. The WAVEs accepted healthy women with no dependents under eighteen if they were unmarried. A WAVE who married could remain in the service as long as she had finished basic training and her husband was not in the service. The birth of a child brought an "honorable discharge."[18]

At first glance it appears as though the armed forces offered dramatic new opportunities for women to shed their domestic roles. Yet on closer examination it is clear that the war emergency gave these endeavors a temporary quality while making it impossible to combine jobs in the service with family life. In addition, every effort was made to dispel prevailing notions that military work would make women "masculine" or ruin their moral character. The military presented the image of the female recruit as very "feminine" as well as domestically inclined. A guidebook for women in the armed services and war industries, for example, included a photograph of a young WAVE with a caption that described her as "pretty as her picture . . . in the trim uniform that enlisted U.S. Navy Waves will wear in winter. . . . smartly-styled, comfortable uniforms . . . with a soft rolled-brim hat." Women were needed for their "delicate hands" and "precision work at which women are so adept," and in hospitals where "there is a need in a man for comfort and attention that only a woman can fill." Women's corps leaders did little to challenge prevailing notions about female domesticity; they assured the public that after the war enlisted women would be "as likely as other women to make marriage their profession."[19]

These publicity measures met with only partial success amid public sentiment suspicious of women in nontraditional roles. In fact, rumors about the supposedly promiscuous sexual behavior and scandalous drunkenness of female recruits were so widespread that the armed forces had to refute the charges publicly. One result was the institutionalizing of the double standard in the military: men were routinely supplied with contraceptives (mainly to prevent the spread of venereal disease), but women were denied access to birth control devices. In addition, in the rare cases when sexual transgressions were discovered, women were punished more severely than men. Lesbianism was another reality of wartime that the military took pains to suppress. The public image they hoped to promote was the military woman whose postwar career would be as a housewife and mother.[20]

We see, then, that women were encouraged to enter the military as a wartime necessity, but were urged to retain their femininity and sexual standards and not abandon their primary responsibility to the next generation. The same themes echoed through the industrial sector. Women taking war jobs were assured that their domestic skills would suit them well for industrial production. Women war workers "have special capacities for work requiring 'feel,' that is minute assembly work and adjustments. Women are especially capable in grinding where fine tolerances are necessary." If they could work a sewing machine, they could handle factory machinery. Automation had reduced the physical strength needed for most jobs, and women's "nimble fingers" were well suited to the tasks at hand. Above all, women were urged to take wartime jobs as a patriotic duty, to support the men at war and contribute to the nation's defense. Propaganda efforts launched by the War Manpower Commission and the Office of War Information presented war work as glamorous and exciting; but the main appeal was to patriotism. Patriotism was a less threatening motive for a woman to take a job because it implied impermanence.[21]

At the same time that women's nontraditional war work was given a domestic aura, their tasks within the home gained new patriotic purpose. Millions of women did volunteer work during the war, and much of it involved traditional skills such as canning, saving fats, and making household goods last longer. Much as homemakers in the depression recognized the importance of their domestic skills for the survival of their families during the economic emergency, so the homemakers of the war years saw their work as contributing to the success of the war emergency.

Wartime, then, encouraged women to enter the workforce and contribute to the war effort, but not at the expense of their domestic duties.

As a result, the potential for a restructuring of the paid labor force that would dismantle the sex-segregated pattern of employment never materialized. In spite of all the changes wrought by the war, in the long run work for women remained limited to certain occupations, with low pay and the expectation of short duration. Traditional marriage, complete with economic dependence on the male breadwinner, was still the norm. It was, in fact, one of the primary reasons given for fighting the war.

Popular culture was filled with many such messages. One example was produced under the sponsorship of the Office of Facts and Figures. It was a series of programs aired on all major radio networks in 1942 in an effort to mobilize support for the war. One highly acclaimed segment, "To the Young," included this exhortation:

> YOUNG MALE VOICE: "That's one of the things this war's about."
> YOUNG FEMALE VOICE: "About us?"
> YOUNG MALE VOICE: "About *all* young people like us. About love and gettin' hitched, and havin' a home and some kids, and breathin' fresh air out in the suburbs . . . about livin' an' workin' *decent*, like free people."

Demographic patterns during the 1940s show that Americans conformed to this expectation. Women may well have entered war production, but they did not give up on reproduction. The war brought a dramatic reversal in patterns of family formation that had characterized the 1930s. Whereas the depression was marked by later marriages and declining marriage rates and birthrates, the trends toward younger marriages and an increasing birthrate normally associated with the postwar era were well under way during the war years. Over one million more families were formed between 1940 and 1943 than would have been expected during normal times. And as soon as Americans entered the war, the birthrate began to climb. Between 1940 and 1945 it jumped from 19.4 to 24.5 per 1,000 population. The marriage rate also accelerated, spurred in part by the possibility of draft deferment for married men in the early war years, and in part by the imminence of departure for foreign shores. We find, then, the curious pattern of widespread disruption in domestic life accompanied by a surge into marriage and parenthood.[22]

We find these same patterns in popular entertainment. Whereas the most popular motion picture of the 1930s was *Gone with the Wind,* a story of survival during hard times focused on a shrewd and tough woman whose domestic life ends up in shambles, the top box office hit of the 1940s was quite different. The 1943 war propaganda film *This Is the Army*, starring Ronald Reagan, was the most successful movie of the decade. In this film the men are center stage as they finish the job their fathers began in World War I. The plot revolves around the efforts of the central character's sweetheart to persuade her reluctant soldier to marry her. Finally she succeeds, and they wed just before the hero leaves to fight on foreign shores. As he marches off with his buddies, she remains at home, providing the vision of what the men are fighting for.[23]

Off the screen as well, images of celebrities shifted. For men, the brave soldier eager to return to hearth and home provided the ideal masculine type. Film heroes, like all able-bodied male Americans, were expected to pull their weight in the war effort. Men who got deferments were resented—all men were urged to do their military duty. It is interesting that the "he-man" was the most popular male image during the 1930s, when the economic depression threatened to undercut the strong and independent male. During the war, however, men had plenty of chances to prove their masculinity in traditionally manly ways. The soldier was the prototypical he-man, after all. Now we find women paying homage to men's gentler qualities. In an item titled "What Should a Girl Expect from a Man?" female stars stressed such qualities as "kindness and tact," "keeping his temper," "courtesy, consideration and sweetness." Instead of references to the tough guy, women now mentioned "manners, fidelity, companionship."[24]

For women we also find a new image portrayed by female stars. Rather than continuing the trend of the 1930s toward more autonomous women as role models, which might be expected in the wartime situation, female celebrities were suddenly featured predominantly as wives and mothers. Ann Sothern, in a 1944 article titled "What Kind of Woman Will Your Man Come Home To?" urged women to fit their lives to their men's. She told her readers to take an interest in their husbands' interests. Read up on

> what he is doing, what we're fighting for, what will come afterward. . . .
> Your plans for your life together afterward are important. . . . We began
> planning our house together—our "perfect house." Then we began to
> think about the nursery . . . and that became the most important room in

the house-to-be, the most important thing in our plans for the future and it made us feel our sense of responsibility to that future. . . . When he comes back it may take a few years for him "to find himself"—it's [your] job—not his—to see that the changes in both of [you] do not affect the fundamental bonds between [you]. . . . I won't bother to remind you of the obvious, to keep up your appearance—to preserve for him the essence of the girl he fell in love with, the girl he longs to come back to. . . . I know that a lot of men are dreaming of coming back not only to those girls who waved good-by to them. They are dreaming of coming back to the mothers of their children!

Sothern herself intended to practice what she preached; she planned to learn to share "outdoor sports and prize-fighting which I've never liked but which he likes. . . . I've made up my mind that I'm going to like them too. . . . The least we can do as women is to try to live up to some of those expectations."[25]

Along with the wifely focus of the 1940s came a move away from flamboyant sexuality, as exhibited by stars of the 1930s like Mae West, toward a more prudent respectability. Young starlets were featured who lived quiet, simple lives with their parents, shunning the fast life of Hollywood. Bette Davis, noted for her strong-minded independence in the 1930s, proclaimed in 1941 that men and women are equals today in business, politics, and sports—they are as brave, intelligent and daring collectively as are men. But it's still "a man's world in spite of the fact that girls have pretty much invaded it." And because it is a man's world, women must protect the most precious thing they have: their reputations. For modern women still want what grandma wanted: "a great love, a happy home, a peaceful old age." Do not be afraid to be termed a "prude," said Davis, "Good sports are dated every night of the week—prudes are saved for special dates. Good sports get plenty of rings on the telephone, but prudes get them on the finger. Men take good sports *out*—they take prudes home—yes, right home to Mother and Dad and all the neighbors."[26]

In keeping with such expressions of enthusiasm for marriage and the family, even men's sexual fantasies were often publicly constructed around images of conjugal bliss. The walls of barracks were decorated with pinups of women in alluring poses reminding the men why they were fighting. Movie star Betty Grable was the most popular pinup, not because she was the most sexy and glamorous, but because she had a rather wholesome look. Grable came to represent the girl back home, and the "American way of life" that inspired the men to fight. As one soldier wrote in a letter to Grable: "There we were out in those damn dirty trenches. Machine guns firing. Bombs dropping all around us. We would be exhausted, frightened, confused and sometimes hopeless about our situation. When suddenly someone would pull your picture out of his wallet. Or we'd see a decal of you on a plane and then we'd know what we were fighting for."

Grable became even more popular when she married bandleader Harry James in 1943 and had a child later that year. It reinforced her image as everyone's sweetheart, future wife, and mother. To be worthy of similar adoration, women sent their husbands and sweethearts photos of themselves in "pinup" poses. Betty Grable herself urged women to send their men photos of themselves in swimsuits, to inspire them to fight on and come home to an erotically charged marriage. Men at war were encouraged to fantasize about sex that awaited them when they returned—not with the "victory girls" who hung around bases, but with their wives. In the words of one GI, "We are not only fighting for the Four Freedoms, we are fighting also for the priceless privilege of making love to American women."[27]

Most soldiers would go home to do just that, and propel the marriage rates and birthrates to new heights. For women, the opportunities that had opened in public life during the war shrank with the return to peace. The War Manpower Commission assumed that "the separation of women from industry should flow in an orderly plan." Frederick Crawford, head of the National Association of Manufacturers, found a point of agreement with his usual adversaries, the union leaders, when he said, "From a humanitarian point of view, too many women should not stay in the labor force. The home is the basic American institution." Many women rejected this idea. As one argued, "War jobs have uncovered unsuspected abilities in American women. Why lose all these abilities because of a belief that 'a woman's place is in the home'? For some it is, for others not." But her words would be drowned in a sea of voices calling on women to prepare to assume their places in the kitchens and bedrooms of returning servicemen.[28]

By the time young adults emerged from the depression and the war, they had been sobered by years of emergency that propelled them toward a vision of "normalcy" focused on traditional family life. The war had extended the state of crisis that characterized the depression and further disrupted domestic gender roles. Yet when the war ended, gone were the positive role models of independent women who offered a viable alternative to marriage, as the nation turned to a reaffirmation of family values and female subordination. There was no positive vision of marriage resting on economic equality; nor was there any trend in the economy toward gender equality. Rather, men and women alike expected to relinquish their emergency roles and settle into domestic life as breadwinners and homemakers. During as well as after the war, all the major institutions in which Americans lived and worked came to foster this vision of a nation finding its ultimate security in the traditional American home.

Notes

1. Quoted in Elaine Tyler May, *Pushing the Limits: American Women, 1940–1961* (New York, 1994), chap. 2.

2. Parts of this chapter are drawn from Elaine Tyler May, *Homeward Bound: American Families in the Cold War Era* (New York, 1988). Whereas *Homeward Bound* examined primarily the experiences of white middle-class women, this essay moves beyond that focus to examine the lives of women from different class and ethnic backgrounds. For an extension of this discussion, see May, *Pushing the Limits*.

3. Susan M. Hartmann, *The Home Front and Beyond: American Women in the 1940s* (Boston, 1982), ix, 4; William Chafe, *The Paradox of Change: American Women in the 20th Century* (New York, 1991).

4. Hartmann, *Home Front*, 19.

5. Hartmann, *Home Front*, 19–21. For an excellent discussion of the wartime problem of working mothers and child care, see William M. Tuttle Jr., *"Daddy's Gone to War": The Second World War in the Lives of America's Children* (New York, 1993), especially chap. 5.

6. Karen Anderson, *Wartime Women: Sex Roles, Family Relations, and the Status of Women during World War II* (Westport, Conn., 1981); Hartmann, *Home Front*, 19–21.

7. *Fortune* magazine, quoted in Sara Evans, *Born for Liberty: A History of Women in America* (New York, 1989), 221.

8. Valerie Kincade Oppenheimer, *The Female Labor Force in the*

United States (Berkeley, Calif., 1970); Winifred D. Wandersee, *Women's Work and Family Values, 1920–1940* (Cambridge, Mass., 1981).

9. Vicki L. Ruiz, *Cannery Women, Cannery Lives: Mexican Women, Unionization, and the California Food Processing Industry, 1930–1950* (Albuquerque, N.M., 1987).

10. Ruth Milkman, *Gender at Work: The Dynamics of Job Segregation by Sex during World War II* (Urbana, Ill., 1987).

11. Evans, *Born for Liberty*, 232.

12. For these and other stories of women during wartime, see May, *Pushing the Limits*.

13. "Boy Meets Girl in Wartime," pamphlet A496, 1943, American Social Hygiene Papers, Social Welfare History Archives, University of Minnesota, box 93.

14. Reuben Hill and Howard Baker, eds., *Marriage and the Family* (Boston, 1942), 567–88.

15. Allan M. Brandt, *No Magic Bullet: A Social History of Venereal Disease in the United States since 1880* (New York, 1985), chap. 5; John D'Emilio, *Sexual Politics, Sexual Communities: The Making of a Homosexual Minority in the United States, 1940–1970* (Chicago, 1983); Allan Bérubé, *Coming out under Fire: Gays and Lesbians in World War II* (New York, 1990).

16. John D'Emilio and Estelle B. Freedman, *Intimate Matters: A History of Sexuality in America* (New York, 1988), 260.

17. See Bérubé, *Coming out under Fire*, for an excellent discussion of lesbians in the military during World War II.

18. Hartmann, *Home Front*, 31–33; Herbert Burstein, *Women in War: A Complete Guide to Service in the Armed Forces and War Industries* (New York, 1943), 1–3, 21–22.

19. Burstein, *Women in War*, 37; Hartmann, *Home Front*, 38–41.

20. See Bérubé, *Coming out under Fire*.

21. Leila Rupp, *Mobilizing Women for War: German and American Propaganda, 1939–1945* (Princeton, 1978); Burstein, *Women in War*, 100.

22. Radio dialogue quoted in John Morton Blum, *V Was for Victory: Politics and American Culture during World War II* (New York, 1976), 28; Andrew J. Cherlin, *Marriage, Divorce, Remarriage* (Cambridge, Mass., 1981), 10–11, 19–21. See also Tuttle, *"Daddy's Gone to War."*

23. *This Is the Army*, Warner Brothers, 1943.

24. "What Should a Girl Expect from a Man?" *Photoplay* 23 (June 1943).

25. Ann Sothern, "What Kind of Woman Will Your Man Come Home To?" *Photoplay* 25 (November 1944): 45, 85–86.

26. Bette Davis, "Is a Girl's Past Ever Her Own?" *Photoplay* 19 (October 1941).

27. Robert Westbrook, " 'I Want a Girl, Just Like the Girl That Married Harry James': American Women and the Problem of Political Obligation in World War II," *American Quarterly* 42 (1990): 587–614.

28. May, *Pushing the Limits,* chap. 2.

Lewis A. Erenberg

SIX

Swing Goes to War: Glenn Miller and the Popular Music of World War II

In September 1942, thirty-eight-year-old Glenn Miller disbanded his successful swing orchestra to enlist in the army. "I, like every patriotic American," he declared, "have an obligation to fulfill. That obligation is to lend as much support as I can to winning the war." Having lived and worked as "a free man," he would use his music to defend "the freedom and the democratic way of life we have that enabled me to make strides in the right direction." In doing so, Miller embodied the wartime ideal of sacrifice for a nation that allowed individuals to succeed and prosper. Besides lifting morale and recruiting GIs, he created a model of patriotic duty and a web of connections between military obligation and an American way of life known by millions of young people.[1]

His sacrifice was real: in giving up the nation's most lucrative band Miller lost millions. The orchestra had broadcast three nights a week on the prestigious Chesterfield Hour, set theater, hotel, and ballroom attendance records, and produced a string of hit records. His Army Air Force (AAF) Orchestra, however, soon surpassed its civilian predecessor. Under Captain (then Major) Miller's command, the AAF Orchestra's forty-two-man marching band, nineteen-person dance unit, radio outfit, string ensemble, and small jazz combo engaged in bond drives, made Victory Discs for the troops, and entertained them at home and abroad. Miller's disappearance in a small plane over the English Channel on 15 December 1944—his ultimate sacrifice—made him a national icon. His story highlights the powerful role that swing played in World War II and helps explain what American soldiers were fighting for.[2]

In going to war, Miller infused the depression's popular music with national purpose. As swing became enmeshed in the conflict, it signified that the defense of popular values nurtured during the depression and imbued with particular conceptions of American life—rather than an ideological or militaristic crusade—would be the basis of the war effort. Indeed, the music played by popular bands was the conflict's music, although the Office of War Information and Tin Pan Alley wanted to produce patriotic songs like those of World War I. Except for "Coming in on a Wing and a Prayer" and "Praise the Lord and Pass the Ammunition," few tunes met the test of popularity. With unity relatively easy to attain because of the unprovoked attack and a clearly defined enemy, it was possible to ideologize the war as a defense of a superior American culture embedded in everyday life. As Miller saw it, GIs wanted "as narrow a chasm as possible between martial and civilian life." Radio, films, records, and big bands made popular music "a great new factor in the American way of life." To the young, listening and dancing to popular bands was "almost as important a part of its daily habits as eating and sleeping," as vital "as food and ammunition." Part of dating, personal freedom, and consumption as well as a measure of ethnic cosmopolitanism, in the minds of young people big band music was firmly associated with the benefits of American life. Hence Miller's proposal to streamline military music and lift morale with swing met with conditional government acceptance.[3]

Big band swing heralded the triumph of modern urban culture during the 1930s as jazz-inflected dance music appealed to a mass audience composed of black and white middle- and working-class college and high-school students. As first played by King of Swing Benny Goodman, the music made the rhythm and soloing of black jazz palatable for whites. Arrangers provided for jazz solos and individual players improvised, but with the power of the group behind them. Audiences did hot jitterbug steps that freed their bodies, and flew through the air transcending earthly reality. Or they listened intently as each soloist acted as an agent of his own fate while the band took them to new levels of ecstatic release from the demands of organized society and of families worried about the depression. In relations between the sexes, swing offered sensuous movements, and the band singers expressed an ironic rather than a sentimental approach to love. As utopian alternatives to the world around them, the bands of Count Basie, Benny Goodman, Artie Shaw, and Charlie Barnet held out a more inclusive vision of American culture. Created largely by urban blacks and the children of immigrants, the bands were exciting examples of big city music and ethnic pluralism. And despite a segregated music business, Goodman pioneered the integration of black musicians in white bands ten years before organized baseball hired African Americans.[4]

Miller's achievement lay in taking the safest parts of this youth culture to the war. His military career lay atop his civilian accomplishments, which had codified swing, polished its jazz elements, and used it to paint an idealized picture of American life. In his person and his art, Miller blended swing with more traditional conceptions of national life and made it acceptable to a vast audience. Unlike most other swing band leaders, Alton Glenn Miller had roots in the "typically American" farms and small towns of the West and Midwest. Born in Clarinda, Iowa, in 1904, he grew up in Fort Morgan, Colorado, where his itinerant handyman father and prohibitionist mother, head of a WCTU chapter, instilled in him values of self-control, persistence, and success. Miller's heroes were Horatio Alger and Theodore Roosevelt, and he hungered for musical and commercial success. He took up the trombone as a youngster, and after two years at the University of Colorado he left to turn professional. Discovering jazz in the 1920s, he played with the best white musicians in the Ben Pollack Orchestra. When his career took him east in 1928, he became an enthusiastic New Yorker. There he played in top bands, freelanced in radio and recording studios, and enjoyed big city life. A midwesterner who achieved his musical identity in New York, Miller fused disparate traditions to create a type of swing that had national appeal.[5]

Miller made swing all-American by merging the two popular music strains of the 1930s—adventurous swing and romantic, more melodic sweet music—into a powerful amalgam. Once he decided he would never outswing Goodman, Shaw, or Count Basie or best Tommy Dorsey on the trombone, Miller went on to his strength—arranging and organizing the talents of others into a more unified, romantic sound. The result was a synthesis: "sweet swing," a clean-cut version of jive suitable for expansion into the nation's heartland via jukeboxes and radio. Tex Beneke, the band's singer-saxophonist, noted that Miller was successful because the public "liked sweet ballads, reminiscent melodies, sentimental words. He found that it liked new pleasant sounds which did not clash." Miller succeeded by taking the standard swing motif—setting brass against reeds over a four-four rhythm section—and using clarinetist Willie Schwartz to play lead melody over the other reeds. These woodwinds smoothed out the sound, giving a "silvery," romantic context to the swing beat. Uniting adventure and security, the Miller style took the edge off the hard-charging Goodman approach and made it comfortable for less experienced dancers.[6]

In his desire to draw large audiences, Miller codified the major elements of big band performance with taste and ingenuity. When all elements worked, the band was a flexible, exciting, and beautiful soloist. "I haven't a great jazz band, and I don't want one," Miller told *Down Beat*. "Our band stresses harmony." Years of legitimate study "finally is enabling me to write arrangements employing unusual, rich harmonies, many never before used in dance bands." At the same time, he organized his band according to a "formula" or, in Gunther Schuller's words, a "sound world." He used his formidable leadership ability and arranging skill to create a totally streamlined sound built on everyone's fitting into an arranged concept. He frowned on long solos, and even hot choruses had to be the same in arrangements imposed from above. He demanded ensemble perfection rather than "one hot soloist jumping up after another to take hot choruses." One critic noted that "the band solos more than any one individual in it." As a result, though, the band suffered from a stiff rhythm section. As trombonist Jimmy Priddy put it, "If you're not going to be a little sloppy, you're bound to be stiff. And that band was stiff!"[7]

Creating a uniform sound required patriarchal authority and discipline. An extremely image-conscious corporate executive, Miller demanded perfect deportment and perfect notes. Musicians had to have everything "just right," recalled trumpeter Billy May, uniform, neckties, socks, handkerchiefs, "or else you'd be fined." This fit the music too. "He would hit on a formula and then he would try to fit everything into it. There was no room for inventiveness. Even the hot choruses were supposed to be the same. [Arranger] Jerry Gray was perfect for the band. He followed the patterns exactly." His insistence on band uniformity and his "sharply disciplined routines bugged many of the musicians." According to singer Chuck Goldstein, Miller "was always the General. Everybody knows what a disciplinarian he was."[8]

Although his commanding style angered some musicians, many players and fans appreciated his authority and patriarchal air, which later enhanced his stature as an air force officer. His aura of fatherly reassurance and authority was heightened by modesty and stoicism that helped him overcome the many problems that plagued traveling bands. He was a confident model of masculinity, capable of meeting any uncertainty. Tall, "bespectacled and scholarly looking," he "was a commanding guy, youthful but mature," according to his press agent, Howard Richmond. As he noted, Miller "looked like security, like all the things I'd never found in a band leader." True, "Mickey Mouse band leaders looked like security. I'm talking about jazz leaders. To me they always looked like they didn't know where they were going to sleep the next night." Seventeen-year-old singer Marion Hutton concurred. As her legal guardian, "he was like a father. . . . He represented a source of strength. . . . He fulfilled the image of what a father ought to be." As a leader and organizer he brought these same traits to jazz, making it clean-cut and respectable, less a challenge to society than one of its commodities.[9]

Similarly, Miller's hits combined big city swing with the currents of a more stable and conservative Midwest. Music critic Irving Kolodin noted that Miller had "a kind of inland sentiment that differed considerably from the 'big town' aura that pulses in Ellington or Goodman." For example, his best-known swing numbers like "In the Mood," "Tuxedo Junction," "String of Pearls," and "Pennsylvania 6-5000" reveled in big city excitement and sophistication. At the same time, the band was known for music about distinctively American regions and symbols: "Dreamsville, Ohio," the folksy "Little Brown Jug," "[I got a gal in] Kalamazoo," and "Boulder Buff." In 1941 "Chattanooga Choo-Choo" became the first song to sell a million records by combining a thrusting train imagery and a "carry me home" theme. In fact, "Chattanooga" was the first popular song hit since 1935 to yearn for the old hometown. "Don't Sit under the Apple Tree" also conjured up a small-town couple hugging in the backyard. In Miller's music, the romantic context and the small-town imagery made freedom less open-ended and more the product of typical American places and settings, found somewhere in a harmonious past. During the war, audiences could defend those real places, not just some abstract ideal.[10]

Besides merging swing and sweet, city and town, Miller consciously sought to build an all-American team that fused the ethnic big city and the Protestant heartland. A New Yorker with a midwestern face, glasses, and a folksy tinge to his voice, he recruited clean-cut all-American musicians and singers like Tex Beneke and Marion Hutton. Initially Miller

Figure 6.1.   Captain Glenn Miller shortly after his enlistment. Courtesy of the Glenn Miller Archives, University of Colorado, Boulder.

introduced Hutton as Sissy Jones, which he felt connoted "apple pie, ice cream and hot dogs better than Marion Hutton did," and dressed her to emphasize her American look. Yet Miller's concept of an orchestra was still a pluralistic vision of an all-American team. The Modernaires, his singing group, included a Jew, a Catholic, a Presbyterian, and a Christian Scientist. This sense of a mixed group applied to the musicians too, whom he stereotyped. "Italian trumpeters," he said, "seldom play good jazz," but they made "great lead men." He also would quote Ben Pollack's remark that "you can't have a good band without at least one Jew in it." Hence the Miller all-American team, like his "sweet swing," included big city ethnics, but in an idealized middle-class depiction of the nation.[11]

Black musicians, however, played no role in this homogenized assemblage. The band used the energy of black jazz but, unlike the harder-swinging Goodman, Shaw, Barnet, or even Jimmy Dorsey, employed no black players. Eddie Durham wrote arrangements for "In the Mood," but Miller never allowed black musicians onstage. His racial conservatism probably derived from his desire to attract the largest possible white audience and his lack of sympathy for rough improvisers and gritty musical expression. Including blacks would have disrupted the band's carefully tended image and total streamlined sound and denied the orchestra bookings at top hotels and ballrooms that were segregated. His personal predilections fit well with army policy, which maintained strict segregation in service bands. In the expanded all-American team, blacks stayed on the bench while a polished black music played a prominent role.

As Miller hoped, the music appealed widely to white teens. Jitterbug dancers loved his medium tempo, which, unlike Goodman's frantic style, allowed them to do lindy hop steps with ease. As a result, jitterbugging spread rapidly in the 1940s. As a reviewer described it, "The frenzy and the ecstasy he created in the auditorium" seemed to be "a case of every emotion for itself and it stirs other emotions as well as other individuals to be up and doing—and shouting." For middle-class youth the music was a romantic backdrop for dating and for establishing independence from one's family. But swing's appeal transcended class lines. As one working-class Polish American noted, his parents did the polka, but "Miller was the music of [his] generation." For him and his ethnic friends swing was the door to new personal and American identities.[12]

The war brought this popular music into the conflict on an unprecedented scale as part of the attempt to define national objectives and create national unity around familiar symbols of everyday life. According to Broadway impresario Billy Rose, show business had to "make us love what is good in America and hate what Hitler and the minor thugs around him stand for," including the Nazi suppression of jazz, popular music, and American films created by "inferior" black and Jewish races. In this context, swing symbolized a war to defend an American way of life under attack.[13]

As central figures in the youth culture of swing, Miller and other big band musicians helped make the music of the home front a vital part of the war. Many enlisted or were drafted, and they were permitted to lead or perform in military musical units. Moreover, the government and the army cooperated with the music industry to bring popular music to the troops. Victory Discs, for example, brought together musicians, singers, music publishers, record companies, the American Federation of Musicians (AFM), and radio executives under armed forces leadership to record and distribute popular music overseas. Despite an AFM strike against the recording industry, union musicians were permitted to record for the sole benefit of the troops. "Wherever there are American soldiers with juke box and jazz tastes," declared music critic Barry Ulanov, "there are V Discs to entertain them." The newly created Armed Forces Radio helped spread the word, just as the enemy attempted to compete for the allegiance of the troops with the swing-laced radio propaganda of Tokyo Rose and Axis Sally.[14]

Of all the popular bandleaders, Miller played an especially important role as he created a military version of his sweet swing, all-American band for battle against the Nazis. Under the leadership of a reassuring father figure who had sacrificed profit for duty, the military band smoothly melded civilian values and military goals in a common cause. Miller's swing was capable of turning the rigidly old-fashioned army marching band into a modernized emblem of cosmopolitan American society. "The interest of our boys lies definitely in modern, popular music, as played by an orchestra such as ours," he declared, rather than in their fathers' music, "much of which is still being played by army bands just as it was in World War days." In a letter to Brigadier General Charles D. Young, Miller offered to "do something concrete in the way of setting up a plan that would enable our music to reach our servicemen here and abroad with some degree of regularity." An army band under his leadership might put "more spring into the feet of our marching men and a little more joy into their hearts."[15]

Yet his most ambitious plans clashed with those of the army. Relying on his arranging and organizing skills, Miller initially proposed to transform the entire army band structure with a fourteen-man arranging staff "to provide music for the Army Air Forces Technical Training Command." When army brass vetoed this plan, Miller instead built a modernized super marching band for the Army Air Force Training Corps. Unveiled at the Yale Bowl during a giant bond rally in July 1943, the forty-man band electrified the cadets. Instead of the usual twelve marching snare and bass drums, the band's rhythm derived from two percussionists using complex swing drum kits and two string bass players, who rode in two jeeps that rolled beside the marching orchestra. When they blared Sousa's "Stars and Stripes Forever"—"in jive tempo," charged *Time*—"sober listeners began to wonder what U.S. brass-band music was coming to. Obviously, there was an Afro-Saxon in the woodpile." Other jazz influences surfaced in the swinging marches created out of blues and swing numbers like "St. Louis Blues," "Blues in the Night," and "Jersey Bounce." Music critic George Simon recalled this fusion of jazz and military music as "the loosest, most swinging marching band we'd ever heard," filled with syncopation. "The horns played with zest and freedom, occasionally bending some notes and anticipating others, the way true jazz musicians do so well."[16] Military brass were aghast at the idea of transforming the military band—and by implication the army itself—into a loose, jazzy organization. As United States Army Bandmaster Franko Goldman put it, "Personally I think it's a disgrace! There isn't any excuse for it. But no one can improve on a Sousa march. . . . My God!" Given official opposition, Miller turned his attention overseas, where his AAF Orchestra raised troop morale with its brand of sweet swing from 1944 to 1946. Although official military march units resisted swing, Miller succeeded in injecting it into the war effort. Few military bands could omit swing entirely, since modern troops demanded the personally freer and more vital music played by cosmopolitan former civilian musicians. As long as they did not threaten military discipline, swing bands were permitted by the army to perform a variety of roles.[17]

At home and abroad, Miller's swing band helped personalize the war for his radio listeners. As early as 1940 his civilian band had broadcast from army camps and dedicated songs to particular units, a practice the

AAF Orchestra continued in England. On a Chesterfield program of 1940, for example, Miller dedicated "Five O'Clock Whistle" to "the boys" in the "New Fighting 69th," from "around New York way," but now at Fort McClellan, Alabama. "They were among the first to leave in service for our country." Other broadcasts featured a "top tune of the week" for soldiers at various bases. Interspersed were references to other aspects of home: Ebbets Field, baseball, and other bandleaders.[18]

His Armed Forces Network broadcasts also included propaganda playlets that dramatized the Four Freedoms, the official goals of the war, and equated American music with free expression and American culture. Just as the AAF Orchestra served as the ethnic platoon writ large underneath the reassuring baton of a good American leader, its novelty tunes hailed America as a cosmopolitan country. "There Are Yanks" (1944) praised the unity of ethnically diverse Americans in the war effort, linking Yanks from "the banks of the Wabash" to "Okies, crackers," and "every color and creed / And they talk the only language the Master race can read." Miller's weekly broadcasts for the Office of War Information's "German Wehrmacht Hour," beamed from England to the German enemy, also equated a cosmopolitan nation and its music. Using "Ilse," a German announcer, Johnny Desmond's vocals, and German dialogue, the show trumpeted the blessings of music and democracy. After the band played the "Volga Boatmen" on one show, for example, Ilse declared that an American could play any music he liked without "barriers," "whether the music is American, German, Russian, Chinese or Jewish." Miller underlined the point: "America means freedom and there's no expression of freedom quite so sincere as music." The band then did a swing tune by Miller, Ellington, or Goodman.[19]

The orchestra became the living embodiment of American culture for troops in the European theater. In England the band endured a grueling schedule to bring American music to GIs away from home. They broadcast thirteen times a week over the Armed Forces Network, flew up and down the British Isles for live concerts, performed for special occasions, and recorded Victory Discs. According to one estimate, the band played seventy-one concerts for 247,500 listeners in England, often on makeshift stages in huge airplane hangars. As drummer Ray McKinley noted, the live performances consisted of a seventy/thirty swing to sweet ratio that included the older hits soldiers demanded and a series of army songs like "Tail-end Charlie," "Snafu Jump," and "G.I. Jive," which

Figure 6.2. Glenn Miller's AAF Orchestra, somewhere in England, performing in an airplane hangar. Note servicemen sitting atop planes and hanging from the rafters. Courtesy of the Glenn Miller Archives, University of Colorado, Boulder.

humorously relieved the pressures of war and reminded GIs that they were defending the nation responsible for such personally liberating music. Audiences wanted familiar music. As Miller put it, "We came here to bring a much-needed touch of home to some lads who have been here a couple of years" and were "starved for real, live American music."[20]

In its ability to recreate familiar and personal ties, Miller's twenty-piece unit became "the most popular band among boys in the service." As a private noted of one concert, "The troops were a cheering mass of swing-hungry GIs. The Joes ate up everything the massive band dished out, most of them in a dream world for an hour or so." But he tired of the repetitious arrangements "that have been played and replayed, all in the same precise, spiritless manner." Miller replied angrily. The musicians might want to experiment, but "we play only the old tunes," because the GIs were away from home and out of touch with current hits, and "know and appreciate only the tunes that were popular before they left the States." Most GIs agreed. One declared that the band pleased millions "who want to hear things that remind them of home, that bring back something of those days when we were all happy and free." The GI wanted "songs he used to know played as he used to hear them played." He looked to music "strictly for its emotional content." Separated from loved ones, facing death, "your pent-up emotions run for just one avenue of escape, an avenue leading to the thing you want most of all, *your home, and all your loved ones and all that they stood, stand and will stand for.*" Perhaps this explains why GIs created their own nightclubs and swing bands, and at "mission parties," guys who used to go to Roseland or the Paramount "now knock themselves out to the music of GI bands with the English lassies jumping with 'em."[21]

The look homeward was often nostalgic in the face of death and military regimentation. If freedom was to be achieved, it would be either in the past or in a future after the army. Miller himself gazed backward as his presentiments of death rose and his frustrations with army red tape grew. His radio director recalled, "I don't know of anyone who was as homesick as Glenn." The day before he died he envisioned the postwar world as a suburban ranch home, Tuxedo Junction, a balsa replica of which he carried with him, where he planned to get away, relax, play golf, and devote time to his family. The preoccupation with family togetherness and security, removed from bureaucracy and public purpose, surfaced increasingly in the sweeter, more romantic songs played in person and on "I Sustain the Wings," his radio program. With their lush chords and wafting clarinet lead they established a dreamy remembrance of romantic togetherness and security to be found back home. One of his hit songs put it well: "When I hear that Serenade in Blue / I'm somewhere in another world alone with you / Sharing all the joys we used to know / Many moons ago."[22]

At the center of the homeward gaze was the American woman, who embodied the virtues of American civilization and the personal obligation to defend them. Pinups, according to Robert Westbrook, reminded servicemen of their personal ties to the home front, occasioning emotions of love, lust, and longing. The Miller band acknowledged this in novelty tunes such as "Paper Doll" (1943), a hit for the Mills Brothers, and "Peggy, the Pin-up Girl" (1944). The former speaks of a lonely soldier looking for solace, while the latter chronicles innocent "Peggy Jones," "with a chassis that made Lassie come home," whose pictures in *Life* and *Look* were carried into battle "all over the world" by American soldiers. The song ends with an explicit statement of obligation: "Pilot to Bombardier, Come on boys, let's drop one here, for Peggy the Pin-up Girl." The band experience itself, moreover, evoked in listeners memories of women and the home front. An RAF pilot remembered the Miller outfit in a smoke-hazed English hangar, crowded "to capacity with uniformed boys and girls swaying gently or 'jiving' wildly," with the vocalist "singing of love not war." As the band wove its spell, they "were conscious of the music. . .the exhilarating rhythm and of course, the girl in our arms. . .she was Alice Faye, Betty Grable, Rita Hayworth or whoever our 'pin up' of that particular week may have been." Perhaps it was sweet-voiced Dinah Shore, on a USO tour with the band, who as a living equivalent of the pinups represented the idealized image of girls left behind.[23]

Women singers and sentimental ballads rose in popularity during the war as they personalized American civilization and the anguish that lay behind the war-enforced separation of the sexes. Women dominated the music audience at home, and they wanted ballads that expressed the pain of waiting for their men to return or the normal life of boys and dating to begin. Under these conditions, love flared intensely, in a race with the relentless march of events. Miller's rendition of Kurt Weill's "Speak Low" conveys passion growing under the pressure of time as the vocalist sings, "Our moment is swift / Like ships adrift, we're swept apart, too soon."

Ostensibly, women waited and thereby symbolized home front faithfulness to the war. The anguish of parting became the subject of "dialogue" songs between soldiers at war and the women back home. Miller's version of "Don't Sit under the Apple Tree" (1942), for example, features a soldier and his girl urging each other to remain true. While he tells her, "Don't go walking down lover's lane with anyone else but me," she demands, "Watch the girls on foreign shores / You'll have to report to me." In Ellington's "Don't Get around Much Anymore," also done by Miller, the singer goes out but finds, "It's so different without you." Often loneliness and frustration led to songs like "No Love, No Nothin' [until my baby comes home]," or "Saturday Night Is the Loneliest Night in the Week." Separation and loneliness also produced pledges of faithfulness by women aimed at soldiers far away, as in "I'll Walk Alone," and "I Don't Want to Walk without You," top hits of 1944. These and many other such songs conveyed the gender disjunctures as girls stayed home and boys went off to war. Both felt the anguish of separation and suspended personal lives.

Sweeter bands and singers able to express the pain of separation and the dream of future togetherness increased in popularity. Harry James's Orchestra, for example, shot to the top in 1942 with a string section, a syrupy trumpet style, and beautiful ballads. One reviewer caught the appeal to an unhappy seventeen-year-old out with a soldier: "Tomorrow he will have gone back to duty and you to the dull, lonely routine of your life without him—waiting, waiting for the day of his return." While James played, "her innermost feelings were taking shape and finding expression, almost as if she had never thought them until that moment." Helen Forrest helped James's rise with increasingly romantic songs of loss and parting. They both had "the same feeling for a song," and her longing for James meshed with the feelings of millions of women. As Forrest put it, her songs "aimed at wives and lovers separated by the war from their men in the service." In a war that set the sexes apart for long periods, women vowed to wait, as in "If That's the Way You Want It Baby," and be the idealization of stability and civilization that men were fighting for. Male singers idealized the "true" woman, as in the Ink Spots' "I'll Get By [as long as I have you]" and the Mills Brothers' "Please wait for me / Till then." In the face of death, both sexes sought peace and security in small pleasures: "I'll Buy That Dream" and when daddy returns, "Shoo, Shoo, Baby" asserts, "we'll live a life of ease."[24]

Under the surface, however, songs of home front devotion and unity contained deep anxieties about sexuality. "Don't Sit under the Apple Tree" and "Everybody Loves My Baby" expressed jealousy and fears about women's sexual activity at home and the lack of home front support for the war. Frank Sinatra brought these concerns to a head as a bobby-soxers' idol who made adolescent girls scream and swoon with sexual fervor. "I looked around at the faces of the girls," noted the narrator of Frederick Wakeman's *Shore Leave.* "It was mass hysteria, all right. Those kids were having a mass affair with Sinatra." In an era of loneliness he gave young girls a vulnerable, dark boy next door as a sex object who expressed their desires. Ballads like "I'll Never Smile Again" and "All or Nothing at All," sung in bel canto style, stretched the emotions to the breaking point and made girls think of clinging forever to their partners. At the same time, as a figure of female desire with a medical exemption from service, Sinatra challenged wartime images of male toughness. He was narrow shouldered and frail, but his appeal to women of all ages was strong. As one girl told *Time,* "My sister saw him twice and she was afraid to go again because she's engaged." Sinatra's songs expressed the hopes of a generation for pure love in a mad world, but his strong sex appeal for women of all ages underscored the fragility of those dreams of home. Moreover, at the USOs and canteens where true women served the cause, they danced with strange men and tested the limits of their faithfulness.[25]

Although sexual tensions remained an undercurrent, it was in the area of race that musical tensions reached their height. Miller's orchestra fed both government purpose and popular desire for unity between home front and war effort, but it was undeniable that for most listeners his home front was white. As part of the goal of including blacks in a unified war effort, the orchestra continued to incorporate elements of black swing, and even particular songs—doses of Ellington, Basie, Fats Waller—into its national musical repertoire. Yet Miller's musical preferences for a clean-cut version of American jive and a sanitized conception of American culture worked with the government policy of military segregation and its desire not to disturb deeply held racial values. As a result, the AAF Orchestra was all-white rather than all-American. Black players remained excluded, relegated to performing in second-class military bands under segregated conditions. By playing black music, however, Miller brought race to the surface of national musical identity.

During the war racial tensions increased in the music world over the meaning of American "home" values. At its simplest, black musicians encountered increasing racial conflict as southern white soldiers and civilians hassled black musicians and entertainers for "race mixing" in the clubs and ballrooms where they played. Black bands, moreover, had problems getting buses, gas, and tires for their tours. Dependent on endless one-night engagements in the South, black bands were forced to abandon their buses and ride segregated trains in which they encountered an endless series of racial humiliations. They no longer reacted quietly. Increasingly, they viewed American society, engaged in a war for democracy, as a hypocritical white supremacist nation. Having ridden the segregated trains and heard tales of black soldiers on leave from fighting for their country who also had had to face discrimination, trumpeter Dizzy Gillespie forcefully expressed his hostility toward white society at his draft hearing and was exempted as psychologically unfit. He refused to accept "racism, poverty, or economic exploitation."[26]

At the same time, the conflicts engendered by a segregated society fighting against a white supremacist enemy heightened the elements in swing that were favorable to racial integration. Black and white radicals and many swing musicians and fans believed that swing carried a vision of democratic community rooted in ethnic and racial pluralism. The war sent conflicting messages to black and white jazz fans about the meaning of American culture. For example, although USO canteens and entertainment units generally were segregated as a matter of government policy, civil rights organizations and white and black progressives in the music and entertainment community established racially integrated Hollywood and Broadway canteens where top bands, among them Benny Goodman's and Count Basie's, entertained free and couples could dance together regardless of race. According to Margaret Halsey, the racially liberal manager of the Stage Door Canteen, the policy was designed "to close the unseemly gap between our democratic protestations and our actual behavior." As a result, she employed black and white hostesses who were instructed to dance with GIs regardless of color. Whereas southern whites often protested, black GIs wrote to her that "we had given them hope for the first time in their lives." Some white servicemen also wrote that "we were the kind of people they were glad to go overseas and fight for."[27]

The discrepancy between defending democracy and the racial realities of American life intensified black attacks on segregation at home. As the *Pittsburgh Courier* put it when Ellington's orchestra was denied hotel accommodations, "It didn't happen in Tokio or Berlin, but right here in the good American city of Moline, Illinois, U.S.A." Music magazines joined the black press in a campaign to recognize Ellington as America's top bandleader and composer and pointed out that he was denied his own radio show and lucrative bookings because of racism. Indeed, the jazz, black, and Left press now protested segregated music venues and audiences as officially un-American.[28]

The black press and African American entertainers did the most to challenge the definition of the home Americans were defending. The *Pittsburgh Courier,* for instance, launched the Double V Campaign for Victory Abroad and Victory at Home and, as part of their efforts, focused on how black entertainers fared at home and abroad in the face of segregation. Black entertainers participated by actively supporting the war effort and openly protesting the segregation and discrimination they encountered. They toured segregated army bases in separate USO troupes, for instance, but objected to performing before segregated audiences. Black bands also appeared in benefits for black soldiers victimized by violence and discrimination. Singer Lena Horne played a special role. Because black troops could not have white pinups, she became the unofficial African American pinup queen, who represented what they were fighting for. As part of that mutual obligation, she vociferously refused to perform before segregated army audiences and objected strongly to the army's policy of giving German POWs front-row seats at shows for black soldiers. In many ways, then, black activists, white radicals, and sympathetic black entertainers saw themselves in a fight for a new national identity. It was in this spirit that Duke Ellington launched his Carnegie Hall concerts with "Black, Brown, and Beige," which memorialized black military contributions in the past, and in "New World a'Comin'" held out hope for cultural pluralism and racial democracy as the definition of American freedom in the near future. As the *Amsterdam News* declared, "To accept half a loaf as better than none is silly in the light of what a war is being fought over."[29]

As the realities of war undercut the perfect dreams of racial and gender unity on the home front, the epitome of American culture, the swing band, began to lose its energy. Sweet music enjoyed an upsurge, and the highly organized war effort altered swing. In a total war dominated by large-scale bureaucracy and rigid military hierarchy, swing was no longer an outsider to the establishment. Following Miller's lead, other bands became more organized, arranged, and sentimental, adding string sections to play sweet songs. Miller became an officer, his band a military unit, and his style even more arranged, laid out from on high with less room for invention. The result was a subtle taming of the musical and utopian vision of swing. Ironically, Miller himself resented the struggle he waged with the military brass over the type of band he wanted, and many of his players felt alienated from him as a rigid authority figure who demanded full military discipline. Wary of military distrust of jazz musicians, he wanted his men to conform to military standards. His demand that they shave off mustaches proved the last straw, especially for horn players, who considered this hard on their embouchures. Many other musicians found the military intolerable and turned to more spontaneous traditional jazz as the voice of improvisatory individualism and organic music making. As one observed, "The individuality of a hot musician became a liability when orchestrators, who are the draftsmen of the music business, started to devise arrangements of popular music for bands of twenty or thirty men." In jazz, fans and creators were on the verge of revolt. Hence, although Glenn Miller and his AAF Orchestra conveyed important conceptions about the American way of life, that vision of the home front was a matter of much contention and debate.[30]

Yet Miller's music lived on, rooted in the personal memories of wartime experiences and the collective memory of sacrifice and national unity. Conveying hopes of personal freedom, ethnic assimilation, and security, his band symbolized an American dream of freer lives made possible by American culture. Moreover, his death elevated his personal sacrifice to mythic status. Given the mystery surrounding it, his death became a metaphor for the lost lives and interrupted careers of all GIs. In fact, a year after he disappeared many theaters observed "Glenn Miller Day," the first such tribute accorded a bandleader. Swing remained a symbol of victory too. After his death the orchestra performed a concert for 40,000 allied troops in Nuremberg Stadium on 1 July 1945, marking a victory over Hitler's belief that jazz was a decadent example of a "mongrelized" society and making a statement of the personal and musical freedom accorded by a nation devoted to cultural pluralism. At the National Press Club in Washington, moreover, the country's highest political and military leaders saluted Miller. After the opening bars of "Moonlight Serenade," President Truman and Generals Dwight Eisenhower and Hap Arnold led the assembled dignitaries in a standing ovation for a man who "felt an intense obligation to serve his country" and "made the supreme sacrifice."[31]

Critic George Simon declared that Miller's band was "the greatest gift from home" GIs had "known in all their Army days, a living symbol of what America meant to them, of what they were fighting for." A GI correspondent agreed. Listening to a Miller memorial in an army recreation center in Britain, he "saw men openly crying." The music was "tied up with individual memories, girls, hopes, schools. It's a tangible tie to what we are fighting to get back to." But the message was ambiguous. "We haven't forgotten, nor can we ever. You owe these guys when they get back, not so much money or gadgets, but a shot at the way of life that many of them have been dreaming about." Given a war fought for personal obligation, many soldiers expected a national commitment to their own personal enjoyment of that life in the future. For soldier boys and the girls they left behind, the attempt to capture and define the American way of life would dominate the late 1940s. For many it represented personal dreams and family security removed from public life and bureaucracy; for others it meant opportunities for young ethnic boys and girls to have a place in American life; for many blacks it meant "victory at home" or rejection of that way of life as racially restrictive. These conflicting themes would shape the postwar jazz scene, which became a battle for America's musical soul at the very time the nation embarked on "a sentimental journey home."[32]

Notes

1. Miller quoted in Frank Stacy, "Glenn Miller Day Boosts Bond Sale," *Down Beat*, 15 May 1945, 14.

2. George Simon, *Glenn Miller and His Orchestra* (New York, 1974), covers Miller's career. See also *Current Biography*, 1942, 597–99. On his music, see Gunther Schuller, *The Swing Era* (New York, 1989), 661–77. On political obligation linked to personal ties and consumption, see Robert B. Westbrook, "'I Want a Girl, Just Like the Girl That Married Harry James': American Women and the Problem of Political Obligation in World War II," *American Quarterly* 42 (1990): 587–614. For the strongest statement of this, see John Morton Blum, *V Was for Victory* (New York, 1976).

3. Glenn Miller, "Travel's Tough but the Jazzmen Hit the Road for Army Camps," *Daily Worker*, 3 July 1942, 7. On the Office of War Information's campaign for "war songs," see John Costello, *Virtue under Fire* (Boston, 1985), 120–21. For Tin Pan Alley, see *Variety*, 5 January 1944, 187.

4. James Lincoln Collier, *Benny Goodman and the Swing Era* (New York, 1989), and Benny Goodman with Irving Kolodin, *The Kingdom of Swing* (New York, 1939), cover Goodman's career. Lewis A. Erenberg, "Things to Come: Swing Bands, Bebop, and the Rise of a Postwar Jazz Scene," in *Recasting America*, ed. Lary May (Chicago, 1989), 221–45, examines the utopian side of swing in greater depth.

5. The phrase "typically American" is in "Glenn Miller," *Current Biography*, 1942, 597.

6. "New King," *Time,* 27 November 1939, 56; Barry Ulanov, "The Jukes Take over Swing," *American Mercury,* October 1940, 172–77, details the jukebox's role in Miller's rise. Tex Beneke, "Swing Was Never Really King," *Metronome,* February 1947, 20–21.

7. For "King of Swing," see "Room at the Top," *Time,* 8 January 1945, 76; Dave Dexter Jr. " 'I Don't Want a Jazz Band,' " *Down Beat,* 1 February 1940, 8; Irving Kolodin, "A Tonefile of Glenn Miller," *Saturday Review of Literature,* 1953, 63, in Miller file, Institute of Jazz Studies, Rutgers, Newark. *Current Biography,* 1942, 597, and Simon, *Glenn Miller,* 238, 246, for discipline. Priddy is quoted in Simon, 219.

8. Billy May quoted in Simon, *Glenn Miller,* 232; Chuck Goldstein quoted in Simon, 245-46. Tommy Mace, in Mort Good, liner notes to *The Complete Glenn Miller,* 3 (1939–40) (RCA-Bluebird Records, 1976), recalled that musicians considered Miller "a boy-scout leader" and noted Glenn's desire to be called " 'Skipper' or 'Captain' or something like that. And that was before the war. Discipline was terrible in that outfit. Rough." See Schuller, *Swing Era,* 671–73, for more on the Miller sound world.

9. For Richmond, see Simon, *Glenn Miller,* 135; for Hutton, Simon, 139.

10. Kolodin, "Tonefile of Glenn Miller," 63. "Choo Chugs to Million Mark," *Metronome,* February 1942, 11. Norman Charles, "Social Values in American Popular Song" (Ph.D. diss., University of Pennsylvania, 1958), 77–78, notes the homeward direction of songs of the 1940s.

11. Simon, *Glenn Miller,* 184.

12. For Cleveland theater, W. Ward Marsh, *Cleveland Plain Dealer,* 10 January 1942, n.p., as quoted in John Flowers, *Moonlight Serenade, a Bio-discography of the Glenn Miller Civilian Band* (New Rochelle, N.Y., 1972), 404. Interviews with Theodore Karamanski, "Big Ray" Murray, Trudy Faso, Lawrence McCaffrey, all in author's possession.

13. Billy Rose, " 'Escapology' Not the Answer, Showmen Must Sell Americanism to Everybody," *Variety,* 7 November 1942, 28.

14. "Pacific Tour for Bob," *Metronome,* October 1944, 9; Barry Ulanov, "The Air Force Jumps!" *Metronome,* May 1944, 15. See also Harry Jaeger, "Buzz Bombs and Boogie Woogie," *Metronome,* May 1945, 11, for bands in England. Frank Mathias, *G.I. Jive: An Army Bandsmen in World War II* (Louisville, Ky., 1982), for a swing musician in the army. Barry Ulanov, "V Discs," *Metronome,* May 1944, 20–21. Bob Klein, who

soldiered in New Guinea, told me about Tokyo Rose. For Axis Sally see Robert and Jane Easton, *Love and War* (Norman, Okla., 1991), 243.

15. Miller to Brigadier General Charles D. Young, 12 August 1942, quoted in Simon, *Glenn Miller,* 311–12.

16. Miller to Jerry Gray, quoted in Simon, 324; for the marching band, 311–12; Simon's reaction, 337–38, 349–52. *Time,* 6 September 1943, 48–49.

17. Goldman quoted in "Sousa with a Floy Floy," *Time,* 6 September 1943, 48–49. See also "Letters," *Time,* 27 September 1943, 4.

18. For broadcasts, see Edward Polic, *The Glenn Miller Army Air Force Band, Sustineo Alas/I Sustain the Wings* (Metuchen, N.J., 1989), 1:3, 714.

19. Polic, *Glenn Miller Army Air Force Band,* 1:51; 2:1027. Examples of the "Wehrmacht Hour" can be heard at the Glenn Miller Archives, University of Colorado, Boulder.

20. For number of performances, Simon, *Glenn Miller,* 369. Miller to Simon, quoted in Simon, 361. On the repertoire, Ray McKinley, "Ooh, What You Said Tex!" *Metronome,* March 1947, 19, 39–41.

21. Pfc. David B. Bittan, "Miller over There," *Metronome,* September 1944, 26–27; Miller to Simon, September 1944, quoted in Simon, 384–87; a GI, "Miller a Killer," *Metronome,* November 1944, 15. Pvt. William Piatt to *Metronome,* April 1945, 4–5, also extolled Miller's ties to home. Jaeger, "Buzz Bombs and Boogie Woogie," 11, for mission parties. For nightclubs on North African bases, see *Depot Dope,* 29 September 1945, 1.

22. Don Haynes, *Diary,* quoted in Simon, 406–7; discussion of Tuxedo Junction, 375–76. For radio repertoire, Polic, *Glenn Miller Army Air Force Band.*

23. RAF pilot quoted in Costello, *Virtue under Fire,* 130–31. Westbrook, "I Want a Girl."

24. Helen Forrest with Bill Libby, *I Had the Craziest Dream* (New York, 1982), 128–37. Richard Lingeman, *Don't You Know There's a War On?* (New York, 1970), 210–21, for World War II songs.

25. David Ewen, *All the Years of American Popular Music* (Englewood Cliffs, N.J., 1977), 430–65, for ballads and singers during the war. Gene Lees, "The Sinatra Effect," in *Singers and the Song* (New York, 1987), 101–15, analyzes Sinatra. Dana Polan, *Power and Paranoia* (New York, 1986), 124–127, explores the sexual tensions around Sinatra. "That

Old Sweet Song," *Time*, 5 July 1943, quoted in Polan, 126–27; Frederick Wakeman, *Shore Leave*, quoted in Polan, 125. For more on sexual conflicts, see Elaine T. May, *Homeward Bound* (New York, 1988), and her chapter in this volume.

26. Dizzy Gillespie, *To Be, or Not . . . to Bop* (Garden City, N.Y., 1979), 119–20.

27. Margaret Halsey, *Color Blind: A White Woman Looks at the Negro* (New York, 1946), 11–13, 31, 33–34. For USO policy, *Amsterdam News*, 22 May 1943, 14. For more on this, see Bruce Tyler, *From Harlem to Hollywood* (New York, 1992), 137–70.

28. "It Happened to the Duke," *Pittsburgh Courier*, 18 April 1942, 21; " 'Hurricane' Target for Welter of Criticism," *Pittsburgh Courier*, 12 June 1943, 21; and "To Help Woodard," *Pittsburgh Courier*, 17 August 1946, 18, offer examples of the black press's growing militance and the role of entertainment. For the music press, see editorials "Why?" *Metronome*, March 1943, 34; "Because," *Metronome*, April 1943, 5; and "Bouquets," *Metronome*, July 1943, 5.

29. For "half a loaf," see "Billie Holiday and the 'St. Louis Incident,' " *Amsterdam News*, 23 December 1944, 9. See also Tyler, *From Harlem to Hollywood*, 171–98.

30. Rogers E. M. Whitaker, "Eddie Condon," *New Yorker*, 28 April 1945, 30.

31. On Nuremberg, Simon, *Glenn Miller*, 423; Press Club, 427–31.

32. Simon, "Glenn Miller Lives On," *Metronome*, March 1946, 14–15; Mike Levin, "When Johnny Comes Marching Home," *Down Beat*, 15 June 1945, 1, 4.

The Challenge of Race and
Resistance to Change

John W. Dower

SEVEN

Race, Language, and War in Two Cultures: World War II in Asia

For most Americans, World War II always has involved selective consciousness. The hypocrisy of fighting with a segregated army and navy under the banner of freedom, democracy, and justice never was frankly acknowledged and now is all but forgotten. In Asia, Japan was castigated for subjugating the native peoples of the Dutch East Indies (Indonesia), British Hong Kong, Malaya, Burma, the American Philippines, and French Indochina—and neither then nor later did the anomaly of such condemnation sink in. Consciousness and memory have been deceptive in other ways as well. If one asks Americans today in what ways World War II was atrocious and racist, they will point overwhelmingly to the Nazi genocide of the Jews. When the war was being fought, however, the enemy Americans perceived as most atrocious was not the Germans but the Japanese; and the racial issues that provoked their greatest emotion were associated with the war in Asia.

With few exceptions, Americans were obsessed with the uniquely evil nature of the Japanese. Allan Nevins, who twice won the Pulitzer Prize in history, observed immediately after the war that "probably in all our history, no foe has been so detested as were the Japanese." Ernie Pyle, the most admired of American war correspondents, conveyed the same sentiment unapologetically. In February 1945, a few weeks after being posted to the Pacific following years of covering the war in Europe, Pyle told his millions of readers that "in Europe we felt that our enemies,

---

An earlier version of this essay, without the present illustrations, is included in *Japan in War and Peace* by John W. Dower, copyright 1993 by John W. Dower. Reprinted by permission of The New Press.

horrible and deadly as they were, were still people. But out here I soon gathered that the Japanese were looked upon as something subhuman and repulsive, the way some people feel about cockroaches or mice." Pyle went on to describe his response on seeing Japanese prisoners for the first time. "They were wrestling and laughing and talking just like normal human beings," he wrote. "And yet they gave me the creeps, and I wanted a mental bath after looking at them." Sober magazines like *Science Digest* ran articles titled "Why Americans Hate Japs More Than Nazis." By incarcerating Japanese Americans, but not German Americans or Italian Americans, the United States government—eventually with Supreme Court backing—gave its official imprimatur to the designation of the Japanese as a racial enemy. It did so, of course, in the most formal and judicious language.

It is not really surprising that the Japanese, rather than the Germans and their decimation of the Jews, dominated American racial thinking. In the United States, as well as Britain and most of Europe, anti-Semitism was strong and—as David Wyman among others has documented so well—the Holocaust was wittingly neglected or a matter of indifference. Japan's aggression, on the other hand, stirred the deepest recesses of white supremacism and provoked a response bordering on the apocalyptic. As the Hearst papers took care to editorialize, the war in Europe, however terrible, was still a "family fight" that did not threaten the very essence of occidental civilization. One Hearst paper bluntly identified the war in the Pacific as "the War of Oriental Races against Occidental Races for the Domination of the World."

There was almost visceral agreement on this. Thus Hollywood formulaically introduced good Germans as well as Nazis but almost never showed a "good Japanese." In depicting the Axis triumvirate, political cartoonists routinely gave the German enemy Hitler's face and the Italian enemy Mussolini's, but they rendered the Japanese as plain, homogeneous "Japanese" caricatures: short, round-faced, bucktoothed, slant-eyed, frequently myopic behind horn-rimmed glasses. In a similar way, phrasemakers fell unreflectively into the idiom seen in the *Science Digest* headline: Nazis and Japs. Indeed, whereas the German enemy was conflated to bad Germans (Nazis), the Japanese enemy was inflated to a supra-Japanese foe—not just the Japanese militarists, not just all the Japanese people, not just ethnic Japanese everywhere, but the Japanese as Orientals. Tin Pan Alley, as so often, immediately placed its finger on the American pulse. One of the many popular songs inspired by Pearl Harbor was titled "There'll Be No Adolph Hitler nor Yellow Japs to Fear." Pearl Harbor and the stunning Japanese victories over the colonial powers that followed so quickly in Southeast Asia seemed to confirm the worst Yellow Peril nightmares.

World War II in Asia was, of course, not simply or even primarily a race war. Alliances cut across race on both the Allied and Axis sides, and fundamental issues of power and ideology were at stake. Where the Japanese and the Anglo-American antagonists were concerned, however, an almost Manichaean racial cast overlay these other issues of contention. This was true on both sides. The Japanese were racist too— toward the white enemy, and in conspicuously different ways toward the other Asians who fell within their "Co-Prosperity Sphere." Thus the war in Asia offers an unusually vivid case study through which to examine the tangled skein of race, language, and violence from a comparative perspective—not only with the luxury of retrospect, moreover, but also at a time when United States–Japan relations are very different and yet still riven with racial tension.

The war exposed core patterns of racist perception in many forms: formulaic expressions, code words, everyday metaphors, visual stereotypes. Such ways of thinking, speaking, and seeing were often vulgar, but their crudeness was by no means peculiar to any social class, educational level, political ideology, or place or circumstance (such as the battlefield as opposed to the home front as opposed to the corridors of power and policymaking). On the other hand, in many instances the racist patterns of perception and expression were just the opposite: subtle, nuanced, garbed in the language of empiricism and intellectuality. This too was typical. Ostensibly objective observations often are laced with prejudice.

That racist perceptions shape behavior may seem obvious, but the war experience calls attention to how subtly this occurs, and at how many different levels. Myths, in this case race myths, almost always override conclusions drawn from sober, rational, empirical observation—until cataclysmic events occur to dispel or discredit them. It took Pearl Harbor and Singapore to destroy the myth cherished by Caucasians that the Japanese were poor navigators and inept pilots and unimaginative strategists, for example, and it required a long, murderous struggle to rid the Japanese of their conceit that the Anglo-Americans were too degenerate

Figure 7.1. As this popular song title reveals, Americans routinely regarded the German enemy as but one part of the German populace ("Hitler," "the Nazis"), while at the same time identifying the "Japs" as a whole with an even larger Yellow Peril.

and individualistic to gird for a long battle against a faraway foe. We have become so mesmerized by the contemporary cult of military intelligence gathering that we often fail to recognize how extensively unadulterated prejudice colors intelligence estimates, causing both overestimation and underestimation of the other side. Beyond this, in its most extreme form racism sanctions extermination—the genocide of the Jews, of course, but also the plain but patterned rhetoric of exterminating beasts, vermin, or demons that unquestionably helped raise tolerance for slaughter in Asia.

o   o   o

*F*ive categories subsume the racist perceptions of the Japanese that dominated Anglo-American thinking during World War II. The Japanese were subhuman. They were little men, inferior to white Westerners in every physical, moral, and intellectual way. They were collectively primitive, childish, and mad—overlapping concepts that could be crudely expressed but also received "empirical" endorsement from social scientists and old Japan hands. At the same time, the Japanese also were portrayed as supermen. This was particularly true in the aftermath of their stunning early victories, and it is characteristic of this thinking that the despised enemy could be little men and supermen simultaneously. Finally, the Japanese in World War II became the nightmare come true of the Yellow Peril. This apocalyptic image embraced all others and made unmistakably clear that race hates, and not merely war hates or responses to Japanese behavior alone, were at issue.

Dehumanization of the enemy is desirable among men in combat. It eliminates scruples and hesitation from killing, the reasoning goes, and this contributes to self-preservation; the enemy, after all, is simultaneously dehumanizing and trying to kill you. Among Allied fighting men in the Pacific, this attitude emerged naturally in the ubiquitous metaphor of the hunt. Fighting Japanese in the jungle was like going after "small game in the woods back home" or tracking down a predatory animal. Killing them was compared to shooting down running quail, picking off rabbits, bringing a rabid and desperate beast to bay and finishing it off. The former sportsman was now simply "getting *bigger* game." One put the crosshairs on the crouching Jap, just as in deer hunting back home.

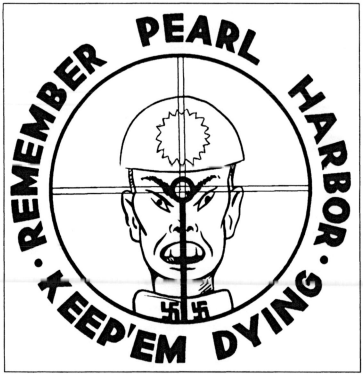

Figure 7.2. The notion that "the only good Jap is a dead Jap" was an American cliché during the entire course of the war. Undiluted rage at the surprise attack on Pearl Harbor greatly reinforced this sentiment, as seen in this graphic that appeared in a monthly magazine for marines early in 1942.

The kill did not remain confined to the combat zones, however, nor did the metaphors of dehumanization remain fixed at this general, almost casual level. In the United States, signs appeared in store windows declaring "Open Season on Japs," and "Jap hunting licenses" were distributed amid the hysteria that accompanied the incarceration of Japanese Americans. The psychology of the hunt became indistinguishable from a broader psychology of extermination that came to mean not merely taking no prisoners on the battlefield, but also having no qualms about extending the kill to the civilian population in Japan. Here the more precise language and imagery of the race war became apparent. The Japanese were vermin. More pervasive yet, they were apes, monkeys, "jaundiced baboons." The war in Asia popularized these dehumanizing epithets to a degree that still can be shocking in retrospect, but the war did not spawn them. These were classic tropes of racist denigration, deeply embedded in European and American consciousness. War simply pried them loose.

Vermin was the archetypal metaphor Nazis attached to the Jews, and the appalling consequences of that dehumanization have obscured the currency of this imagery in the war in Asia. On Iwo Jima, the press found amusement in noting that some marines went into battle with "Rodent Exterminator" stenciled on their helmets. Incinerating Japanese in caves with flamethrowers was referred to as "clearing out a rats' nest." Soon after Pearl Harbor, the prospect of exterminating the Japanese vermin in their nest at home was widely applauded. The most popular float in a day-long victory parade in New York in mid-1942 was titled "Tokyo: We Are Coming," and depicted bombs falling on a frantic pack of yellow rats. A cartoon in the March 1945 issue of *Leatherneck*, the monthly magazine for marines, portrayed the insect "Louseous Japanicas" and explained that though this epidemic of lice was being exterminated in the Pacific, "before a complete cure may be effected the origin of the plague, the breeding grounds around the Tokyo area, must be completely annihilated." "Louseous Japanicas" appeared almost simultaneously with initiation of the policy of systematically firebombing Japanese cities and accurately reflected a detached tolerance for annihilationist and exterminationist rhetoric at all levels of United States society. As the British embassy in Washington noted in a weekly report, Americans perceived the Japanese as "a nameless mass of vermin."

Perception of the Japanese as apes and monkeys similarly was not confined to any particular group or place. Even before Pearl Harbor, Sir Alexander Cadogan, the permanent undersecretary of the British Foreign Office, routinely referred to the Japanese as "beastly little monkeys" and the like in his diary. Following Japan's capitulation, United States General Robert Eichelberger, alluding to the Japanese mission en route to the Philippines to arrange the surrender procedures, wrote to his wife that "first, monkeys will come to Manila." Among Western political cartoonists, the simian figure was surely the most popular caricature for the Japanese. David Low, the brilliant antifascist cartoonist working out of London, was fond of this. The *New York Times* routinely reproduced such graphics in its Sunday edition, at one point adding its own commentary that it might be more accurate to identify the Japanese as the "missing link." On the eve of the British debacle at Singapore, the British humor magazine *Punch* depicted Japanese soldiers in full-page splendor as chimpanzees with helmets and guns swinging from tree to tree. *Time* used the same image on its cover for 26 January 1942, contrasting the monkey invaders with the dignified Dutch military in Indonesia. The urbane *New Yorker* magazine also found the monkeymen in trees conceit witty. The *Washington Post* compared Japanese atrocities in the Philippines and German atrocities in Czechoslovakia in a 1942 cartoon pairing a gorilla labeled "Japs" and a Hitler figure labeled simply "Hitler." In well-received Hollywood combat films such as *Bataan* and *Guadalcanal Diary*, GIs routinely referred to the Japanese as monkeys.

The ubiquitous simian idiom of dehumanization came out of a rich tradition of bigoted Western iconography and graphically revealed the ease with which demeaning racist stereotypes could be floated from one target of prejudice to another. Only a short while before they put the Japanese in trees, for example, *Punch*'s artists had been rendering the Irish as apes. Generations of white cartoonists also had previously refined the simian caricature in their depictions of Negroes and various Central American and Caribbean peoples. The popular illustrators, in turn, were merely replicating a basic tenet in the pseudoscience of white supremacism—the argument that the "Mongoloid" and "Negroid" races (and for Englishmen, the Irish) represented a lower stage of evolution. Nineteenth-century Western scientists and social scientists had offered almost unanimous support to this thesis, and such ideas persisted into the mid-twentieth century. President Franklin D. Roosevelt, for example, was informed by a physical anthropologist at the Smithsonian Institution that Japanese skulls were "some 2,000 years less developed than ours."

In the world outside the monkey house, the Japanese commonly were referred to as "the little men." Their relatively short stature contributed to this, but again the phrase was essentially metaphorical. The Japanese, it was argued, were small in accomplishments compared with Westerners. No great "universal" achievements were to be found in their traditional civilization; they were latecomers to the modern challenges of science and technology, imitators rather than innovators, ritualists rather than rationalists. Again, the cartoonists provided a good gauge of this conceit. More often than not, in any ensemble of nationalities the Japanese figures were dwarfish.

TIME

THE WEEKLY NEWSMAGAZINE

TER POORTEN OF THE INDIES

Figure 7.3. *Time* magazine's cover for 26 January 1942 conveyed the virtually ubiquitous Anglo-American perception of the war as a conflict between Japanese "monkeymen" and civilized Caucasians—in this instance, the Dutch commander of the Netherlands East Indies. © 1942 Time Inc. Reprinted by permission.

Figure 7.4. Dehumanizing the Japanese enemies made killing them easier. This cartoon from the *Chicago Tribune* typifies the prevailing American sense of a just war of retribution against a subhuman foe. Copyrighted Chicago Tribune Company. All rights reserved. Used with permission.

Arizona war worker writes her Navy boyfriend a thank-you note for the Jap skull he sent her

35

Figure 7.5. In this famous photograph from the 22 May 1944 issue of *Life* magazine, a young woman sweetly contemplates a "Jap skull" sent by her boyfriend. Although it was well known that American fighting men collected such grisly battlefield trophies in the Pacific theater, such practices would have caused an uproar had they involved desecration of the German and Italian war dead. Ralph Crane, *Life* magazine. © Time Inc.

Such contempt led, among other things, to a pervasive underestimation of Japanese intentions and capabilities by British and American observers at even the highest levels. Before Pearl Harbor, it was common wisdom among Westerners that the Japanese could not shoot, sail, or fly very well. Nor could they think imaginatively; as a British intelligence report carefully explained, this was because the enormous energy required to memorize the ideographic writing system dulled their brains and killed the spark of creativity. There can be few better examples of the power of myth and stereotype over the weight of objective analysis than the unpreparedness of the Westerners when Japan attacked. Almost everything was a shock: the audacity of the Pearl Harbor attack and the ability of the Japanese to bring it off, the effectiveness of the Zero aircraft (which had been in operation in China for over a year), the superb skills of the Japanese pilots, the esprit and discipline of the Japanese ground forces, the lightning multipronged assault against the European and American colonial enclaves. Equally shocking, of course, was the Western side of the coin: the unpreparedness in Hawaii, the debacle at Singapore, the humiliation in the Philippines. In the long view, despite Japan's eventual defeat, the events of 1941–42 exposed the dry rot of the old empires and irreparably shattered the mystique of white superiority among the native peoples of Asia.

These Japanese victories—coupled with the spectacle of Japanese brutality and atrocity—set whole new worlds of racial thinking in motion. The little men suddenly became supermen; and at the same time, more elaborate versions of the little-men thesis were developed. A remarkable intelligence report circulated by psychological warfare experts within General Douglas MacArthur's command in mid-1944, for example, masticated the old thesis with excruciating thoroughness:

> And yet in every sense of the word the Japanese are *little people*. Some observers claim there would have been no Pearl Harbor had the Japanese been three inches taller. The archipelago itself is a land of diminutive distances. Japanese houses are artistic but flimsy and cramped. The people, tiny in stature, seem to play at living. To a Westerner they and their country possess the strange charm of toyland. Centuries of isolation have accentuated the restrictive characteristics of their outlook on life.
>
> Being *little people*, the Japanese dreamed of power and glory, but lacked a realistic concept of the material requirements for a successful

world war. Moreover, they were totally unable to envisage the massive scale of operations in which the United States is now able to indulge.[1]

At the same time, the little-men thesis also was elaborated on in ways that shed harsh light on racist bias in the academic disciplines by revealing how Western social sciences could be used to support popular prejudices. The war years witnessed the emergence of anthropologists, sociologists, psychologists, and psychiatrists as the new mandarins of theories of "national character," and on the whole they performed a valuable service in repudiating the old theories of biological determinism. What the social scientists did not dispel, however, were the racial stereotypes that had been associated with biological determinism. On the contrary, they essentially reaffirmed these stereotypes by offering new cultural or sociopsychological explanations for them.

This is seen most clearly in three of the most influential themes that American and British social scientists introduced to explain Japanese behavior. The Japanese, they argued, were still essentially a primitive or tribal people, governed by ritualistic and particularistic values. The influence of cultural anthropologists was particularly apparent here. Furthermore, it was emphasized that Japanese behavior could be analyzed effectively using Western theories of child or adolescent behavior. Here the Anglo-American intellectuals turned to Freudian-influenced theories concerning toilet training and psychic blockage at various stages of immaturity (the British social anthropologist Geoffrey Gorer was extremely influential on this theme) and also extolled the value of applying insights gained from American studies "of individual adolescent psychology and of the behavior of adolescents in gangs in our society, as a systematic approach to better understanding of the Japanese" (the quotation is from the minutes of a large 1944 symposium involving, among others, Margaret Mead and Talcott Parsons). Finally, in the third great preoccupation of the new intellectual mandarins, it was argued that the Japanese as a collectivity were mentally and emotionally unstable—neurotic, schizophrenic, psychotic, or simply hysterical.

In the final analysis, the "national character" studies amounted to a new way of explaining what the presumedly discredited biological determinists had concluded long ago: that the Japanese as a people displayed arrested development. Although this was not inherent in their genes, it was the inevitable consequence of their peculiar history and culture. All this was expressed with considerable erudition, and many of the insights of wartime social scientists concerning societal pressures and situational ethics remain influential today. For the proverbial man from Mars given access only to such wartime writings, however, it would be reasonable to conclude that imperialism, war, and atrocity had been invented in Asia during the twentieth century by developmentally retarded Japanese. They were unique, sui generis, and very peculiar indeed.

When all was said and done, however, these designations of Japanese peculiarity possessed a universal quality. They were formulaic and rested in considerable part on code words that transcended Japan and even transcended racial and cultural discourse in general. In suggestive ways, these code words also overlapped with vocabularies associated with discrimination based on gender and class. The central image of arrested growth, or "childishness," for example, was and remains one of the most basic constructs used by white Euro-Americans to characterize nonwhite peoples. This could be buttressed with pseudoscientific explanations (nonwhites being lower on the evolutionary scale, and thus biologically equivalent to children or adolescents vis-à-vis the "mature" Caucasian races) or meretricious social scientific equations (the "less developed" peoples of "less developed" nations, for example, or peoples alleged to be collectively blocked at a primitive or immature state psychologically by indigenous cultural practices or mores). In the milieu of war, the image of the Japanese as children conveyed utter contempt (as in *Newsweek*'s wartime reference to "the child mind of the Jap conscript"), but in less harsh circumstances it also was capable of evoking a condescending paternalism (as reflected in the depiction of Japanese after the surrender as "MacArthur's children" or as the beneficiaries of a student-teacher relationship with Americans). This same metaphor also is integral to the rationale of male domination and rule by elites. Thus, to describe women as childish or childlike is one of the most familiar ways men traditionally have signified both the inherent inferiority of women and their own obligation to protect or at least humor them. Similarly, dominant social and political classes commonly affirm their privileged status and inherent right to rule by dismissing the masses as irrational, irresponsible, and immature. In its softer guise, the elite sense of noblesse oblige masks class inequalities with a paradigm of parent-to-child obligations.

The resonances of this broader conceptual world also help clarify how Japan's attack on the West revitalized other fantasies. It is characteristic of the paranoia of self-designated master groups that even while dismissing others as inferior and "less developed," they attribute special powers to them. The lower classes may be immature to the elites, but they also are seen as possessing a fearsome potential for violence. Women may be irrational in male eyes, but they also are said to have special intuitive powers and the Jezebel potential of becoming castrators. Where Western perceptions of the Japanese and Asians in general are concerned, there is in fact a provocative congruence between the female and oriental mystiques as expressed by white male elites. Thus, even in the war years, the "femininity" of Japanese culture was indirectly if not directly emphasized. Traits attributed to the Japanese often were almost identical to those assigned to women in general: childishness, irrationality, emotional instability and "hysteria"—and also intuition, a sixth sense, and a talent for nondiscursive communication. It even was said that the Japanese, like women generally, possessed an exceptional capacity to endure suffering. Put negatively, these latter intuitive and emotional qualities could be equated with nonrationality and simply integrated into the argument of arrested development. Positively framed, they became suprarational powers—impossible to explain, but all the more alarming to contemplate.

Because nothing in the "rational" mind-set of Western leaders prepared them for either the audacity and skill of Japan's attack or the debacle of British, Dutch, and American capitulations to numerically inferior Japanese forces that followed in Southeast Asia, it was natural to look to nonrational explanations. Scapegoating helped obfuscate the situation—the United States commanders at Pearl Harbor were cashiered, and the West Coast Japanese Americans were locked up—but this was not enough. It also became useful to think of the Japanese as supermen. Graphic artists now drew the Japanese as giants on the horizon. Rhetorically, the new image usually emerged in a more serpentine or backhanded fashion. Thus the United States print media from 1941 to the end of the war featured a veritable "between the lines" subgenre debunking the new myth of the supermen. Battle A proved they could be beaten at sea, battle B that they could be beaten in the jungle, battle C that they were not unbeatable at night fighting, battle D that the myth of the "invincibility of the Zero" was finally being destroyed. The *New York Times Magazine* took it upon itself to address the issue head-on with a feature article titled "Japanese Superman: That Too Is a Fallacy."

Admiral William Halsey, the most blatantly racist officer in the United States high command, later claimed that he deliberately belittled the Japanese as "monkeymen" and the like in order to discredit "the new myth of Japanese invincibility" and boost the morale of his men.

The myth of the superman was never completely dispelled. To the end of the war—even after most of the Japanese navy and merchant marine had been sunk; after Japanese soldiers in the field, cut off from support, had begun starving to death and were being killed by the tens and hundreds of thousands; after the urban centers of the home islands had come under regular bombardment—Allied planners continued to overestimate the will and capacity of the Japanese to keep fighting. There are surely many explanations for this, but prominent among them is a plainly racial consideration: the superman image was especially compelling because it meshed with the greatest of all the racist bogeys of the white men—the specter of the Yellow Peril.

Hatred toward the Japanese derived not simply from the reports of Japanese atrocities, but also from the deeper wellsprings of antiorientalism. *Time* magazine's coverage of the American response to Pearl Harbor, for example, opened on this very note. What did Americans say when they heard of the attack, *Time* asked rhetorically. And the answer it quoted approvingly as representative was, "Why, the yellow bastards!" *Time*'s cover portrait for 22 December 1941, depicting Admiral Yamamoto Isoroku, who planned the Pearl Harbor attack, was colored a single shade: bright yellow. At one time or another almost every mainstream newspaper and magazine fell into the color idiom, and yellow was by far the dominant color in anti-Japanese propaganda art. Among the music makers, we already have encountered Tin Pan Alley's revealing counterpoint of Hitler and the "Yellow Japs." Other song titles included "We're Gonna Find a Fellow Who Is Yellow and Beat Him Red, White, and Blue" and "Oh, You Little Son of an Oriental." In some American pronouncements, the Japanese were simply dismissed as "LYBs," a well-comprehended acronym for the double entendre "little yellow bellies."

Spokesmen for Asian Allies such as China were aghast at such insensitivity, and the war years as a whole became an agonizing revelation of the breadth and depth of anti-Asian prejudice in the United States. In the very midst of the war these revelations prompted a year-long congressional hearing to consider revision of the notorious "Oriental Exclusion Laws"—the capstone of formal discrimination against all people of Asian origin. What the Japanese attack brought to the surface, however, was something more elusive and interesting than the formal structures of discrimination: the concrete fears that underlay the perception of a menacing Orient.

Since the late nineteenth century, when the Yellow Peril idea was first expressed in the West, white people had been unnerved by a triple apprehension—recognition that the "hordes" of Asia outnumbered the population of the West, fear that these alien masses might gain possession of the science and technology that made Western domination possible, and the belief that Orientals possessed occult powers unfathomable to Western rationalists. By trumpeting the cause of Pan-Asianism and proclaiming the creation of a Greater East Asia Co-Prosperity Sphere, Japan raised the prospect that the Asian hordes might at last become united. With their Zero planes and big battleships and carriers, the Japanese gave notice that the technological and scientific gap had narrowed dramatically. And with the aura of invincibility that blossomed in the heat of the early victories, the Japanese "supermen" evoked the old fantasies of occult oriental powers. All this would be smashed in August 1945, when Japan capitulated. And it would all resurface three decades later when Japan burst on the scene as an economic superpower and other Asian countries began to emulate this "miracle."

o   o   o

*R*acism also shaped the Japanese perception of self and other—again in patterned ways, but patterns different from those of the West. History accounts for much of this difference. Over centuries, Japan had borrowed extensively from India, China, and more recently the West and had been greatly enriched thereby; and it acknowledged these debts. And over the course of the preceding century, the Japanese had felt the sting of Western condescension. Even when applauded by the Europeans and Americans for their accomplishments in industrializing and "Westernizing," the Japanese were painfully aware that they were still regarded as immature and unimaginative and unstable—good in the small things, as the saying went among the old Japan hands, and small in the great things.

Thus Japanese racial thinking was riven by an ambivalence that had no clear counterpart in white supremacist thinking. Like the white Westerners, they assumed a hierarchical world; but unlike the Westerners, they lacked the unambiguous power that would enable them to place themselves unequivocally at the top of the racial hierarchy. Toward Europeans and Americans, and the science and civilization they exemplified, the national response was one of admiration as well as fear, mistrust, and hatred. Toward all others—that is, toward nonwhites including Asians other than themselves, their attitude was less complicated. By the twentieth century Japan's success in resisting Western colonialism or neocolonialism and emerging as one of the so-called Great Powers had instilled among the Japanese an attitude toward weaker peoples and nations that was as arrogant and contemptuous as the racism of the Westerners. The Koreans and Chinese began to learn this in the 1890s and early 1900s; the peoples of Southeast Asia learned it quickly after 7 December 1941.

For Japan, the crisis of identity came to a head in the 1930s and early 1940s, taking several dramatic forms. Behind the joy and fury of the initial attacks in 1941–42, and indeed behind many of the atrocities against white men and women in Asia, was an unmistakable sense of racial revenge. At the same time, the Japanese began to emphasize their own destiny as a "leading race" (*shidō minzoku*). If one were to venture a single broad observation concerning the difference between the preoccupations of white supremacism and Japanese racism, it might be this: that whereas white racism devoted inordinate energy to the denigration of the other, Japanese racial thinking concentrated on elevating the self. In Japanese war films produced between 1937 and 1945, for example, the enemy was rarely depicted. Frequently it was not even made clear who the antagonist was. The films concentrated almost exclusively on the admirable "Japanese" qualities of the protagonists. The focus of the broader gamut of propaganda for domestic consumption was similar. In its language and imagery, Japanese prejudice thus appeared to be more benign than its white counterpart—by comparison, a soft racism—but this was misleading. The insularity of such introversion tended to depersonalize and, in its own peculiar way, dehumanize all non-Japanese "outsiders." In practice, such intense fixation on the self contributed to a wartime record of extremely callous and brutal behavior toward non-Japanese.

The central concept in this racial thinking was that most tantalizing of cultural fixations: the notion of purity. In Japan as elsewhere, this has a deep history not merely in religious ritual, but also in social practice and the delineation of insider and outsider (pure and impure) groups. By turning purity into a racial ideology for modern times, the Japanese were in effect nationalizing a concept traditionally associated with differentiation within their society. Purity was Japanized and made the signifier of homogeneity, of "one hundred million hearts beating as one," of a unique "Yamato soul" (*Yamato damashii,* from the ancient capital of the legendary first emperor). Non-Japanese became by definition impure. Whether powerful or relatively powerless, all were beyond the pale.

The ambiguity of the concept enhanced its effectiveness as a vehicle for promoting internal cohesion. At a superficial level, this fixation on the special purity or "sincerity" of the Japanese resembles the mystique of American "innocence." Whereas the latter is a subtheme in the American myth, however, the former was cultivated as the very essence of a powerful racial ideology. Like esoteric mantras, a variety of evocative (and often archaic) words and phrases were introduced to convey the special racial and moral qualities of the Japanese; and like esoteric mandalas, certain visual images (sun, sword, cherry blossom, snowcapped Mount Fuji, an abstract "brightness") and auspicious colors (white and red) were elevated as particularistic symbols of the purity of the Japanese spirit.

Where Westerners had turned eventually to pseudoscience and dubious social science to bolster theories of the inherent inferiority of non-white and non-Western peoples, the Japanese turned to mythohistory, where they found the origins of their superiority in the divine descent of their sovereign and the racial and cultural homogeneity of the sovereign's loyal subjects. Deity, monarch, and populace were made one, and no words captured this more effectively than the transcendent old phrase resurrected to supersede plain reference to "the Japanese": *Yamato minzoku,* the "Yamato race." "Yamato"—the name of the place where Jimmu, grandson of the grandson of the sun goddess, was alleged to have founded the imperial line in 660 B.C.—was redolent with the archaic mystique of celestial genetics that made Japan the divine land and the Japanese the chosen people. In *Yamato minzoku,* the association became explicitly racial and exclusionary. The race had no identity apart from

the throne and the traditions that had grown up around it, and no outsider could hope to penetrate this community. This was blood nationalism of an exceptionally potent sort.

Many of these themes were elaborated in the ideological writings of
the 1930s and early 1940s, and the cause of blood nationalism was elevated when 1940 became the occasion for massive ceremony and festivity
in celebration of the 2,600 year anniversary of the "national foundation
day." At the same time, the racial ideologues took care to emphasize
that purity was not merely an original state, but also an ongoing process
for each Japanese. Purity entailed virtues that needed to be cultivated,
and preeminent among these were two moral ideals originally brought
to Japan from China: loyalty and filial piety (*chūkō*). Why these became
a higher expression of morality in Japan than elsewhere, higher even
than in China, was explained by their ultimate focus in the divine sovereign. Purity lay in transcendence of ego and identification with a greater
truth or cause; and in the crisis years of the 1930s and early 1940s this
greater truth was equated with the militarized imperial state. War itself,
with all the sacrifice it demanded, became an act of purification. And
death in war, the ultimate expression of selflessness, became the supreme attainment of this innate Japanese purity. We know now that
most Japanese fighting men who died slowly did not pass away with the
emperor's name on their lips, as propaganda claimed they did. Most
often they called (as GIs did also) for their mothers. Still, they fought
and died with fervor and bravery, enveloped in the propaganda of being
the divine soldiers of the divine land, and this contributed to the aura
of a people possessed of special powers.

Both the Western myth of the superman and the bogey of the Yellow
Peril had their analogue in this emphasis the Japanese themselves placed
on their unique suprarational spiritual qualities. In Western eyes, however, this same spectacle of fanatical mass behavior also reinforced the
image of the little men, of the Japanese as a homogeneous, undifferen-
tiated mass. There is no small irony in this, for what we see here is the
coalescence of Japanese indoctrination with the grossest anti-Japanese
stereotypes of the Westerners. In the crudest of Anglo-American collo-
quialisms, it was argued that "a Jap is a Jap" (the famous quotation of
General John DeWitt, who directed the incarceration of the Japanese
Americans). In the 1945 propaganda film *Know Your Enemy—Japan*,
produced by Frank Capra for the United States Army, the Japanese

were similarly described as "photographic prints off the same negative"—a line now frequently cited as the classic expression of racist American contempt for the Japanese. Yet in essence this "seen one seen them all" attitude was not greatly different from the "one hundred million hearts beating as one" indoctrination that the Japanese leaders themselves promoted. Homogeneity and separateness *were* essential parts of what the Japanese ideologues said about themselves. In their idiom, this was integral to the superiority of the Yamato race. To non-Japanese, it was further cause for derision.

The rhetoric of the pure self also calls attention to the potency of implicit as opposed to explicit denigration. In proclaiming their own purity, the Japanese cast others as inferior because they did not, and could not, share in the grace of the divine land. Non-Japanese were, by the very logic of the ideology, impure, foul, polluted. Such sentiments usually flowed like an underground stream beneath the ornate paeans to the "pure and cloudless heart" of the Japanese, but occasionally they burst to the surface with extraordinary vehemence. Thus, in a book of war reportage titled *Bataan,* Hino Ashihei, one of the best-known Japanese wartime writers, described American POWs as "people whose arrogant nation once tried to unlawfully treat our motherland with contempt." "As I watch large numbers of the surrendered soldiers," he continued, "I feel like I am watching filthy water running from the sewage of a nation which derives from impure origins and has lost its pride of race. Japanese soldiers look particularly beautiful, and I feel exceedingly proud of being Japanese."[2] These were the American prisoners, of course, whom Japanese soldiers brutalized in the Bataan death march. Hino's contempt for the "impure" American prisoners provides an almost perfect counterpoint to Ernie Pyle's revulsion on seeing his first "subhuman" Japanese POWs.

As a rule, however, the Japanese turned to one particular negative image when referring directly to the Anglo-American enemy: the demon or devil. "Devilish Anglo-Americans" (*kichiku Ei-Bei*) was the most familiar epithet for the white foe. In the graphic arts the most common depiction of Americans or British was a horned Roosevelt or Churchill, drawn exactly like the demons (*oni, akuma*) found in Japanese folklore and folk religion. As a metaphor of dehumanization, the demonic white man was the counterpart of the Japanese monkeyman in Western thinking, but the parallel was by no means exact. The demon was a more

impressive and ambiguous figure than the ape, and certainly of a different category entirely from vermin. In Japanese folk renderings, the
demon was immensely powerful; it was often intelligent, or at least exceedingly crafty; and it possessed talents and powers beyond those of
ordinary Japanese. Not all demons had to be killed; some could be won
over and turned from menaces into guardians. Indeed, Japanese soldiers
killed in battle often were spoken of as having become "demons pro-
tecting the country" (*gokoku no oni*)—easy to imagine when one recalls
the statues of ferocious deities that often guard Buddhist temples. Here
again, like the flexible Western metaphor of the child, was an intriguingly
malleable stereotype—one that would be turned about dramatically after
the war, when the Americans became the military "protectors" of Japan.

During the war years, however, this more benign potential of the
demonic other was buried. For the Japanese at war, the demon worked
as a metaphor for the enemy in ways that plain subhuman or bestial
images could not. It conveyed a sense of the adversary's great power
and special abilities, and in this respect it captured some of the ambivalence that had always marked Japan's modern relationship with the West.
At the same time, the demonic other played to deep feelings of insecurity
by evoking the image of an ever-present outside threat. Unlike apes or
vermin, the demon did not signify a random presence. In Japanese folklore, these figures always lurked just beyond the boundaries of the community or the borders of the country—in forests and mountains outside
the village, on islands off the coast. In origin, they exemplified not a
racial fear, but a far more basic fear of outsiders in general.

Contrary to the myth of being homogeneous, Japanese society was
honeycombed with groups suspicious of one another, and the blue-eyed
barbarians from across the seas became absorbed into patterns of thinking that had emerged centuries earlier as a response to these tense and
threatening insider/outsider relationships. The Westerners who suddenly
appeared on Japan's horizon in the mid-nineteenth century were the
most formidable of all outsiders, and the response to them mobilized
nationalist and racist sentiments in unprecedented ways. Symbolically
the demonic other was already present to be racialized. There was, moreover, a further dimension to this complicated play of symbolic representation, for it was but a short step from the perception of an ever-present
threat to the consciousness of being an eternal victim. This too is a

sentiment that recurs frequently in the Japanese tradition, and in the modern world this "victim consciousness" (*higaisha ishiki*) became inextricably entangled with the perception of foreign threats. From this perspective, modern Japanese racism as exemplified in the demonic other reflected an abiding sense of being always the threatened, the victim, the aggrieved—and never the threat, the victimizer, the giver of grief.

Where images and actions came together most decisively, however, demon, ape, and vermin functioned similarly. All made killing easier by dehumanizing the enemy. The rhetoric of "kill the American demons" and "kill the British demons" became commonplace not only in combat, but also on the home front. A popular magazine published in late 1944 conveyed the fury of this rhetoric. Under the title "Devilish Americans and English," the magazine ran a two-page drawing of Roosevelt and Churchill as debauched ogres carousing with fellow demons in sight of Mount Fuji and urged all Japanese, "Beat and kill these animals that have lost their human nature! That is the great mission that Heaven has given to the Yamato race, for the eternal peace of the world!" Another magazine, reporting on the decisive battle in the Philippines, declared that the more American beasts and demons "are sent to hell, the cleaner the world will be." Iwo Jima, where United States marines called themselves "rodent exterminators," was described in official Japanese newsreels as "a suitable place to slaughter the American devils."

Demonization was by no means an essential precondition for killing, however. The most numerous victims of Japanese aggression and atrocity were other Asians, who were rarely depicted this way. Toward them the Japanese attitude was a mixture of "Pan-Asian" propaganda for public consumption, elaborate theories of racial hierarchy and Japanese hegemony at official and academic levels, and condescension and contempt in practice. Apart from a small number of idealistic military officers and civilian officials, few Japanese appear to have taken seriously the egalitarian rhetoric of Pan-Asian solidarity and genuine liberation of colonized Asian peoples. Never for a moment did the Japanese consider liberating their own Korean and Formosan colonies, and policy toward Southeast Asia—even when "independence" was granted—was always framed in terms that made Japan's preeminence as the "leading race" absolutely clear. The purity so integral to Japanese thinking was peculiar to the Japanese as a race and culture—not to "oriental" peoples in general—

Figure 7.6. Titled "The Cruel Nature of Americans," this two-page spread appeared in the November 1944 issue of a popular Japanese magazine. Read from right to left, the top portion illustrates American viciousness with scenes of boxing matches, white people stoning a drowning Negro (a reference to the Detroit race riots), Negroes being humiliated as carnival targets, a black man being lynched, and an American pilot bombing a Japanese hospital ship. The

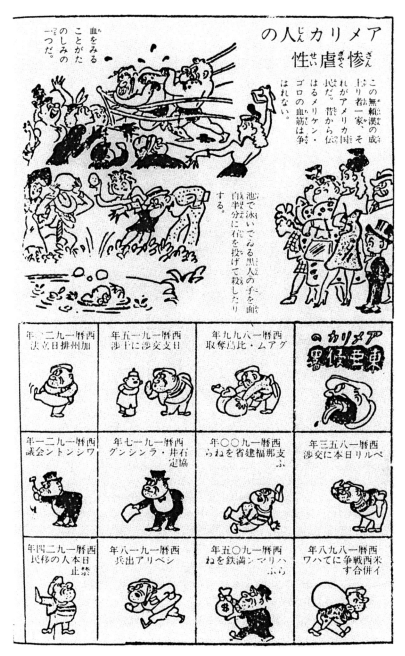

bottom panels offer a chronological cartoon history of "American Aggression in East Asia," beginning with the arrival of Commodore Matthew Perry in Japan in 1853 and ending with the encirclement of Japan by the "ABCD" (American, British, Chinese, and Dutch) powers on the eve of Pearl Harbor, and gangster America's final ultimatum to Japan. From *Hinode*, November 1944.

Figure 7.7.   In the most common Japanese rendering, the Anglo-American enemy was demonized. This illustration, which appeared immediately after Pearl Harbor, accompanied a discussion of the road to war and depicts innocent Japan extending the hand of friendship while the United States and Britain (President Roosevelt and Prime Minister Churchill) feign amity and clandestinely extend their demonic claws (marked "conspiracy") to seize the Orient. From *Osaka Puck,* January 1942.

and consequently there emerged no real notion of "Asian supremacism" that could be regarded as a close counterpart to the white supremacism of the Anglo-Americans.

Before the 1930s, the Japanese did not have a clearly articulated position toward other Asians. The rush of events thereafter, including the invasion of China and the decision to push south into Southeast Asia, forced military planners and their academic supporters to codify and clarify existing opinions on these matters. The result was a small outpouring of studies, reports, and pronouncements—many of a confidential nature—that explicitly addressed the characteristics of the various

Figure 7.8.   The Japanese counterpart to the Anglo-American exterminationist imagery of killing beasts entailed annihilating demons. In this poster from 1942, the bayonet of Japanese righteousness skewers the Anglo-American demons. The caption reads, "The death of these wretches will be the birthday of world peace." From *Osaka Puck*, February and December 1942.

peoples of Asia and the appropriate policy toward them. That these were not casual undertakings was made amply clear in 1981, when a hitherto unknown secret study dating from 1943 was discovered in Tokyo. Prepared by a team of some forty researchers associated with the Population and Race Section of the Research Bureau of the Ministry of Health and Welfare, this work devoted over three thousand pages to analysis of race theory in general and the different races of Asia in particular. The title of the report gives an inkling of its contents: *An Investigation of Global Policy with the Yamato Race as Nucleus.*

The *Investigation* was a serious intelligence report, and its style was academic. In its way it was a counterpart to the "national character" writings of the Anglo-American social scientists who mobilized in support of the Allied war effort. The Japanese researchers called attention to Western theories of race and, while attentive to Nazi ideas, surveyed the gamut of racial thinking beginning with Plato and Aristotle. In the modern world, they noted, racism, nationalism, and capitalist imperialism had become inseparably intertwined. And though modern scholarship had repudiated the notion of biologically pure races, blood still mattered greatly in contributing to psychological unity. In this regard, as Karl Haushofer had observed, Japan was fortunate in having become a uniform racial state (Haushofer, the geopolitician whose writings influenced the Nazis, had done his doctoral work on Japan). At the same time, overseas expansion should be seen as essential not merely for the attainment of military and strategic security, but also for preserving and revitalizing racial consciousness and vigor. On this point the Japanese again quoted Western experts, including not merely the Germans but also the British. Looking ahead, it was predictable that the second and third generations of overseas Japanese might face problems of identity, and thus it was imperative to develop settlement policies that would thwart their assimilation and ensure that they "remain aware of the superiority of the Japanese people and proud of being a member of the leading race."

The focus of this massive report was on Asian rather than Western peoples, and its dry language provides insight into how racial inequality in Asia was rationalized. The central metaphor was the family. The critical phrase was "proper place"—a term that had roots in Confucian prescriptions for domestic relationships but was carefully extended to cover international relations beginning in the late 1930s. The family idiom is another example of the malleable social construct, for it suggests harmony and reciprocity on the one hand, but clear-cut hierarchy and division of authority and responsibility on the other; and it was the latter that really mattered to the Japanese. The authors of the *Investigation* were emphatic in condemning false consciousness concerning equality. "To view those who are in essence unequal as if they were equal is itself inequitable," they observed. And it followed from this that "to treat those who are unequal unequally is to realize equality." The family exemplified such equitable inequality, and the Japanese writers made clear that Japan was not merely the head of the family in Asia, but also destined to maintain that position "eternally." Whether the Yamato race also was destined to become the head of the global family of races and nations was left unanswered, although passing comments suggested that this was the ultimate goal. The opening pages of the study flatly declared that the war would continue "until Anglo-American imperialistic democracy has been completely vanquished and a new world order erected in its place." And as the *Investigation* made amply clear, the Japanese-led imperium in Asia would assume a leading role in this new world order.

Despite their Confucian overtones, the family metaphor and proper-place philosophy bore close resemblance to Western thinking on issues of race and power. The Japanese took as much pleasure as any white Westerner in categorizing the weaker peoples of Asia as "children." In their private reports and directives, they made clear that "proper place" meant a division of labor in Asia in which the Yamato race would control the economic, financial, and strategic reins of power within an autarkic bloc and thereby "hold the key to the very existence of all the races of East Asia." A secret policy guideline issued in Singapore at the outset of the war was equally frank. "Japanese subjects shall be afforded opportunities for development everywhere," it stated, "and after establishing firm footholds they shall exalt their temperament as the leading race with the basic doctrine of planning the long-term expansion of the Yamato race." Despite their detailed country-by-country, race-by-race summaries, the Japanese were interested in other Asians only as subordinate members of the family who could be manipulated to play roles assigned by Japan. For other Asians the real meaning of Japan's racial rhetoric was obvious. "Leading race" meant master race, "proper place" meant inferior place, "family" meant patriarchal oppression.

o   o   o

Given the virulence of the race hate that permeated the Pacific war, at first it seems astonishing that Americans and Japanese were able to move so quickly toward cordial relations after Japan's surrender. Intimate face-to-face contact for purposes other than mutual slaughter enabled each side to rehumanize the other in the highly structured milieu of the Allied Occupation of Japan, which lasted from 1945 to 1952. Although the United States–dominated Occupation was ethnocentric and overbearing in many respects, it also was infused with goodwill and—in its early stages—a commitment to "demilitarization and democratization" that struck a responsive chord among most of the defeated Japanese. Contrary to the wartime stereotypes of propagandists in both the Allied and Japanese camps, most Japanese were sick of regimentation, indoctrination, and militarism. At the same time, the cold war facilitated a quick diversion of enmity, and anticommunism became a new crusade uniting the two former antagonists at the state level. Enemies changed, enmity did not.

On both sides, the abrupt metamorphosis from war to peace was cushioned by the malleability of racial, cultural, and ideological stereotypes. With only a small twist, patterns of perception that had abetted mass slaughter now proved conducive to paternalistic patronage on the American side—and to acquiescence to such paternalism by many Japanese. Racism did not disappear from the United States–Japan relationship, but it was softened and transmogrified. For the Americans, the vermin disappeared but the monkeymen lingered for a while as charming pets. The September 1945 cover of *Leatherneck,* for example—the first issue of the marine monthly to appear after Japan's capitulation—featured a cheery cartoon of a GI holding a vexed but thoroughly domesticated monkey wearing the cap, shirt, and leggings of the Imperial Army. *Newsweek,* in its feature article on what sort of people the Americans might expect to find in Japan when the Occupation commenced, ran "Curious Simians" as one subheading.

Other racist stereotypes traveled from war to peace in comparable ways. Although defeat temporarily extinguished the superman mystique, it reinforced the perception of the Japanese as little men or lesser men. Stated conversely, victory over Japan reinforced the conceit of inherent white and Western superiority. The more precise associations of Japan's "lesser" stature, however—the primitive social relations and attitudes, the childishness of the populace both psychologically and politically, the collective neurosis—all now provoked a paternalistic response. The American overseers of Occupied Japan thought in terms of a civilizing mission that would eliminate what was primitive, tribal, and ritualistic—an old but idealistic colonial attitude indeed. They would guide an immature people with backward institutions toward maturity. The Japanese "children" now became pupils in General MacArthur's school of democracy, learners and borrowers of advanced United States technology, followers of United States cold war policies. Where the Japanese psyche was tortured, the Americans would be healers.

These were not frivolous attitudes, any more than paternalism itself is necessarily frivolous. At the individual level, moreover, countless Japanese and Americans collaborated equitably in pursuit of common goals. Neither democratization and demilitarization nor—later—economic reconstruction and remilitarization were ethnocentric American goals forced on unwilling Japanese. The overall relationship, however, was inherently unequal and patronizing on the part of the Americans, and it is here that racist attitudes survived. United States policymakers at the highest level also were not above cynically manipulating Japanese racism to serve their own purposes. In 1951, when Japan's allegiance in the cold war was still not entirely certain, for example, John Foster Dulles recommended that the Americans and British take advantage of Japanese feelings of "superiority as against the Asiatic mainland masses" and play up the "social prestige" of being associated with the Western alliance. (In a fine example of a truly free-floating stereotype, Dulles and other American leaders also liked to emphasize that the Soviet menace could be better understood if one remembered that the Russians were an Asiatic people.)

On the Japanese side, defeat was bitter but peace was sweet, and certain attitudes associated with wartime racial thinking also proved adaptable to the postsurrender milieu. Proper-place thinking facilitated acceptance of a subordinate status vis-à-vis the victorious Allies, at least for the time being. In this regard it is helpful to recall that the "leading race" rhetoric of the war years was a relatively new ideology in Japan, and that for most of their modern history the Japanese had played a subordinate role in the world order. The militarism of the 1930s and early 1940s arose out of a desire to alter that insecure status, and it ended in disaster. To seek a new place in new ways after 1945 was in fact the continuation of a familiar quest.

In fascinating ways, the wartime fixation on purity and purification proved adaptable to this commitment to a new path of development. Individuals who had been exhorted to purge self and society of decadent Western influences before the surrender now found themselves exhorted to purge the society of militarism and feudalistic legacies. This sense of "cleansing" Japan of foul and reactionary influences was truly phenomenal in the early postwar years, and while this tapped popular aspirations for liberation, it also politicized the militarists' ideology of the pure self in undreamed-of ways. Universal "democratic" values now became the touchstone of purity. And the guardians at the gates, to cap these astounding transmogrifications, were the erstwhile American demons. The United States assumption of a military role as protector of postwar Japan was a hard-nosed, rational policy, but from the Japanese perspective it had a subtle, almost subconscious logic. The fearsome demons of Japanese folklore, after all, were often won over and put to use by the ostensibly weaker folk.

The transitional adaptations of proper place, purity, and the demon more or less deracialized the wartime fixations. They did not, however, eliminate racial tensions latent in the structure of institutionalized inequality that characterized postwar United States–Japan relations until recently. So long as Japan remained conspicuously inferior to the United States in power and influence, the structure and psychology of what is known in Japan as "subordinate independence" could be maintained. When relations of power and influence changed, neither side could be expected to rethink these fundamental relationships without trauma. The great change came in the 1970s, when it became apparent—abruptly and shockingly for almost everyone concerned—that Japan had become an economic superpower while America was in relative decline. In this situation, war talk became fashionable again: talk of trade wars; ruminations on who really won the Pacific war; doomsday warnings of a new yen bloc, a seriously rearmed Japan, a "financial Pearl Harbor." In American rhetoric, the simian subhumans were resurrected as "predatory economic animals," the old wartime supermen returned as menacing "miraclemen," garbed in Western business suits but practicing sumo capitalism. Japanese, in turn, often in high government positions, decried America's demonic "Japan bashing" and at the same time attributed their country's accomplishments to a "Yamato race" homogeneity and purity that "mongrelized" America could never hope to emulate.[3]

As times change, the malleable idioms of race and culture, power and status, change with them. They never completely disappear.

Notes

This chapter summarizes some of the themes developed at length in my *War without Mercy: Race and Power in the Pacific War* (New York, 1986), where extensive annotations can be found. Here I have focused in particular on racial language in comparative perspective.

1. "Answer to Japan," 20. This report appears in several archival collections at the Hoover Institution, Stanford University. Cf. "Bonner Frank Fellers Collection," boxes 1 and 15; also "U.S. Army Forces in the Pacific, Psychological Warfare Branch," box 1.

2. From Hino's 1942 book *Bātān Hantō Kōjōki,* as quoted in Haruko Taya Cook, "Voices from the Front: Japanese War Literature, 1937–1945" (M.A. thesis in Asian Studies, University of California, Berkeley, 1984), 59–60.

3. I have addressed these themes in contemporary United States–Japan relations in greater detail in *Japan in War and Peace* (New York, 1993), 279–335.

EIGHT

The Changing Path to Citizenship: Ethnicity and Naturalization during World War II

In modern societies war can act as a force that redefines the social boundaries and qualities of citizenship.[1] During the years the United States was engaged in World War II, new concerns arose over the citizenship and nationality of immigrants as the unpredictable exigencies of wartime brought important changes in their status. World War II was the peak period of naturalization in American history, and the internment of Japanese Americans represented the culmination of policymakers' historical reluctance to recognize the citizenship of Asians. The repeal of Chinese exclusion, however, marked a new willingness to accept Asians as fellow citizens. During World War II, American citizenship was reformulated by the inclusion and exclusion of groups on the social margins.

From 1941 to 1945 naturalization became a major social movement in the United States.[2] More immigrants became naturalized citizens than in any previous five-year period.[3] One of every four aliens who were naturalized from 1907 to 1945 became a citizen during World War II. More than 112,000 were naturalized during their wartime service in the armed forces, but the vast bulk of naturalized citizens, over 1,539,000, came from the civilian population. Nine of every ten aliens becoming American citizens during the war were civilians.

This massive infusion to the citizenry was a social movement of the most recent arrivals who came from the principal nations of the two opposing wartime alliances. Three out of five aliens naturalized during World War II had arrived in the United States since 1920. The largest numbers of naturalized newcomers came from the British Empire, Italy, Germany, Poland, and the Soviet Union. Aliens from these principal belligerent powers were probably prompted to naturalize by an acute need to verify and clarify their status. The passage of the Smith Act in 1940, which required all aliens to be registered and fingerprinted and widened the grounds for deportation, may well have raised their concern over their status.[4] Most of the new citizens had started families: three out of four were married. These demographic patterns suggest that wartime naturalization was a social movement of those recently arrived and newly invested in American families, who sought the security of American nationality during a crisis where their loyalty was a volatile political question.

During the war, the pattern in which men seeking naturalization annually outnumbered women was reversed dramatically. For the first time in history, immigrant women naturalized at a higher rate than immigrant men. In 1936, 39 percent of those naturalized had been females, but by 1942 females made up 59 percent. From the first to the final year of the war, slightly over half of all naturalized citizens were females. The data indicate that most naturalized women were married, and a higher proportion were married than was true for naturalized men. This is a clue that there was a time lag between the naturalization of husbands and of wives. The rise in female naturalization during World War II may have been related to a two-step process after restrictionist policies in the 1920s cut down mass immigration: first, beginning in 1920 the pool of male aliens shrank as they naturalized; meanwhile, their wives had a greater tendency to maintain alien status, especially after a 1922 law ended the tradition of permitting alien wives to derive citizenship from their relation to a citizen husband and required them to file separately for naturalization.[5] By World War II, alien wives constituted a larger pool of potential applicants for naturalization than alien husbands. The number of adult male aliens was cut in half from 1920 to 1940, dwindling from 3,740,000 to 1,890,000, while the number of adult female aliens decreased by only one-fifth, falling from 2,720,000 in 1920 to 2,240,000 in 1940, so that they outnumbered male aliens in that year.[6]

Although citizenship through naturalization became a powerful force in the assimilation of European aliens and women during World War II, it was a political impasse for Asian Americans. The war in Asia and the Pacific brought the issue of their citizenship and nationality into a new light. The policy of excluding Asian immigrants from the right to naturalized citizenship lay at the heart of this issue. The exclusion had a long and complex history, developing cumulatively from federal law and court decisions. In 1790 Congress had specified that only "free white" persons were eligible for naturalized citizenship, but this rule left open the question of who would be considered white. After Reconstruction, lawmakers believed naturalization policy lacked sufficient discrimination and rigor. From 1882 to 1924 Congress and the courts tightened access to naturalization and the administrative procedure of qualifying for it. Under this process, Asian immigrants became "aliens ineligible for citizenship."[7]

The ineligibility of the Chinese as nonwhites was first implied by a congressional act passed in 1870 granting naturalization rights to African immigrants but to no other colored races.[8] The Chinese Exclusion Act of 1882 prohibited Chinese immigrants from naturalizing.[9] This law established a racial standard for courts to use in excluding from citizenship the Japanese, Koreans, Filipinos, and Hindus entering the country in growing numbers after the turn of the century.[10] The courts also ruled that the small numbers of Burmese, Malaysian, and Thai applicants were ineligible nonwhite aliens.[11] In 1922 the United States Supreme Court in *Ozawa v. United States* affirmed that Japanese aliens were not white and hence were ineligible for American citizenship.[12] The next year, in *U.S. v. Thind*, the Supreme Court found a high-caste Hindu ineligible.[13]

The conception of the civic unassimilability of Asians originally had grown out of the negative reaction to the first Asian immigrants to the United States, the Chinese, who began to arrive after 1849 in California and other western states. Nativists looked on the Chinese as a competitive economic threat and supported municipal laws that restricted their opportunities in commerce and industrial occupations. A consensus grew that the Chinese were too alien in race and culture to be assimilated like European immigrants. An official lamented, "Our institutions have made no impression on them during the more than thirty years they have been in the country. . . . They do not and will not assimilate with our people." The historian Charles Price has concluded that exclusion was rationalized on the grounds that "the continued presence of the Chinese was a serious obstacle to the orderly process of nation-building and that continued Chinese immigration transformed this obstacle into a grave immediate danger."[14]

Americans of European ancestry regarded Asians as the most culturally distant of peoples. William Graham Sumner in *Folkways* (1906) elaborated on the bifurcation that separated Westerners from Asians:

"The two great cultural divisions of the human race are the oriental and the occidental. Each is consistent throughout; each has its own philosophy and spirit; they are separated from top to bottom by different mores, different standpoints, different ways, and different notions of what societal arrangements are advantageous."[15] Even a sympathetic American missionary to Japan affirmed the opposite polarities of East and West. In 1915 Sydney L. Gulick wrote, "Japanese are always and everywhere Japanese, loyal to their emperor for generations untold. American and Asiatic civilizations are based on postulates fundamentally different and antagonistic."[16]

Assumptions about the alien identity of Asians were coupled with notions about their separatism and cultural inertia. Henry George, the economic reformer, believed the Chinese were hopelessly unassimilable. He explained his reasoning by juxtaposing Chinese and blacks. He argued that the Chinese were fatally loaded down with cultural baggage, whereas blacks had no culture. George contrasted blacks "with nothing to unlearn" to Chinese "with everything to forget and everything to learn."[17] Charles M. Thompson's textbook *A History of the United States*, published during World War I, revealed similar views nearly two generations after Henry George made his observations. It expounded, "The Chinese and Japanese have neither demanded, nor have they been asked, to become a real part of American life. They are separated from the mass of the people by racial and religious differences. At the present time a 'Chinaman,' in the mind of the typical American, is a foreigner and must remain so." Thompson went on to make an invidious comparison stressing that the Chinese were changelessly alien: "Unlike the Chinese . . . , negroes have, with the bulk of the population, many points in common—religion, language, customs, manners, habits. In spite of its handicaps, the negroes have made notable progress during their half century of freedom. Without education, training, or property at the time of their emancipation, they have come to be, if not prosperous, at least self-supporting as a people."[18] Filipinos, too, were so culturally removed that they could not be expected to become American citizens. President William Howard Taft, who served as the first civil governor of the Philippines, explained that an indefinite period of tutelage was required before peoples like the Filipinos would be ready to participate in a republican and democratic polity: "The principle which our anti-imperialists seek to apply, that people must acquire knowledge of self-government by independence, is not applicable to a tropical people. We cannot set them going in a decade and look to their future progress as certain. We must have them for a generation or two generations, or perhaps even three, in order that . . . our guiding hand, in teaching them common sense views of government, shall give the needed direction."[19]

Naturalization policy became a key legal expression of these deeply ingrained views of Asian unassimilability. Naturalization was available to blacks, American Indians, mestizo Mexicans, and other racial groups.[20] Denying it to Asian immigrants marked the limit of American nationality. The Immigration Act of 1924 represented the fullest and clearest definition of this situation. This law establishing sharp restrictions on immigration from outside northern and western Europe defined admission to the United States in terms of the capacity for naturalized citizenship. According to its provisions, aliens ineligible for citizenship—immigrants from Asia—were henceforth inadmissible.[21]

From the end of the nineteenth century, access to citizenship became increasingly important, because naturalization became a stronger determinant of status with the growth of antialien municipal laws that derogated aliens' rights with respect to employment, property, and the franchise. (Aliens lost political rights when alien suffrage was struck down in several states.) As the erosion of aliens' status compared with that of citizens spread, those who were not naturalized saw their rights and opportunities shrink. Asian aliens were permanently denied the right to naturalization just when it was growing increasingly desirable.

The importance of access to naturalization was reflected in its differential effects on European and Asian immigrant communities. Naturalization was a social normalization for European aliens. It gradually and incrementally relieved immigrant communities of the stigma and disabilities of identification with a foreign nation. For individual European aliens, naturalization ceremonies provided a public theater for dramatizing and proclaiming their Americanism—a voluntary patriotic act in the tradition of republican citizenship—particularly important for aliens of German and Italian ancestry during World War II.[22]

Being "aliens ineligible for citizenship" created a uniquely inferior status for Asian immigrants that impeded their assimilation and social mobility. Denying naturalization to Asians also denied them a device for political adaptation, for achieving personal legal security, and for a useful symbolic declaration of Americanism. The Asian community was slow to mobilize politically because the entire first generation was deprived of a place and an identity in the democratic politics of industrial society.

The compartmentalization of the first generation in permanent alienage politically subdivided the Asian population in a unique way, creating two wholly different communities of allegiance: the perpetually alien first generation and a second generation consisting of those who were citizens by virtue of their birth in the United States. Although they were obviously of the same disqualified race as their parents, American-born Asians qualified for citizenship by the *jus soli* principle of the Fourteenth Amendment.[23]

During World War II naturalization policy created distinctive political problems for Japanese Americans, who were associated with an enemy nation. The leaders of the community, the first-generation Issei, were all aliens. None could speak in self-defense as patriotic citizens. They could not petition political representatives as advocates of their interests. They could not escape external distrust of their loyalty. Their influence over their community was suspect. As a consequence their children, the Nisei, also were stigmatized as a potentially disloyal element because they had been reared under the influence of their permanently foreign parents.

The ultimate consequences of naturalization policies that created a category of aliens ineligible for citizenship unfolded during World War II in fears and anxieties over national security. The rationale for interning Japanese Americans derived from the axiomatic foundation of restrictionist naturalization policy: Asians could not be included in the tradition of volitional citizenship—they did not have the capacity to transfer their allegiance—because of their profoundly alien race and culture. The allegiance of even American-born Nisei citizens to the United States was denied when they were interned in relocation camps during the war. Their Japanese racial ancestry was seen as an overriding factor that disqualified them from American citizenship and the civil rights it provided.

The assumption of the profound alienage of Asians—the historic grounds of restrictive naturalization policy—appeared in justifications for denying civil rights to Japanese American citizens enunciated during the prosecution of internment. Earl Warren, attorney general of California in 1942, argued that Nisei citizens were the most dangerous group of all. The loyalty of Germans and Italians could be ascertained, he announced, but because of the alien character of the Japanese race no loyalty tests administered to them could be reliable. Warren cautioned: "We believe that when we are dealing with the Caucasian race we have methods that will test the loyalty of them, and we believe that we can, in dealing with the Germans and Italians, arrive at some fairly sound conclusions because of our knowledge of the way they live in the community and have lived for many years. But when we deal with the Japanese we are in an entirely different field and we cannot form any opinion."[24]

General John J. DeWitt, commanding general of the Western Defense Command, who officially supervised the relocation and internment, also sought justification in the notion of the perpetual alienage of Asians. DeWitt declared: "In the war in which we are now engaged, racial affinities are not severed by migration. The Japanese race is an enemy race and while many second- and third-generation Japanese born on United States soil, possessed of United States citizenship, have become 'Americanized' the racial strains are undiluted."[25]

Whereas Japanese Americans fell victim to the traditional presumption of perpetual Asian alienage, Chinese Americans were aided by new tendencies to view them as a positive ethnic group. A comparison of the position of the Chinese with that of the Japanese reveals that World War II heralded a change in American policy toward Asians. Ironically, Japanese Americans were victimized by an anti-Asian ideology that had largely been fashioned in response to the Chinese. The Chinese, by contrast, became the beneficiaries of pragmatic changes in policy dictated by the United States' need to exercise its global military leadership. These changes were reflected in the repeal of Chinese exclusion during the war. In December 1943 Congress rescinded the exclusions on Chinese admissions and naturalization in force since 1882.[26] In the hearings and debates on the repeal of exclusion, new ways of thinking were being charted about the place of the Chinese in the American nation. The new views emerged gradually from the old, and the two coexisted in an odd tension.

Most lawmakers in Congress in 1943 did not believe in social equality between white Americans and the Chinese. Many southern lawmakers resisted repeal for fear its passage would endanger racial segregation in the South by validating racial equality. Representative Ed Gossett from Texas remarked that "the boys down below the Mason-Dixon line do not like the idea of trying to tie this thing up with social equality and racial equality."[27] Their views were forcefully presented in congressional discussion, especially during the hearings of the House Committee on

Immigration and Naturalization. On the committee, Representative A. Leonard Allen of Louisiana was the most vigorous opponent of the principle of racial equality. He spearheaded a bloc of southerners opposed to repeal that included Representatives Dan R. McGehee of Mississippi, O. Clark Fisher of Texas, and Lex Green of Florida.[28]

Even those who favored repeal took care to point out that their position did not endorse racial equality. During the floor debate in the House, Representative John R. Murdock of Arizona favorably cited the precedent set by Abraham Lincoln when he supported equal rights for the races but disavowed their social equality. Representative John R. Vorys of Ohio reassured fellow lawmakers that even the Chinese did not desire social equality with whites. "They have a pride of race," he explained, "similar to the pride of race that you and I have; they have a pride of color. . . . They . . . do not go in for intermarriage between races."[29]

Lawmakers argued that the Chinese were racially and culturally separate, which Representative Thomas A. Jenkins of Ohio believed made Chinese exclusion a just and necessary policy.[30] Senator Rufus C. Holman reminded his colleagues that the Chinese are "incompatible in that their civilization and their racial characteristics are entirely divergent from our own."[31] Representative Compton I. White of Idaho, a leading opponent of the repeal bill, despaired, "I do not think we can take the Chinese with their habits and mentalities in this year and time into our great American melting pot and in ten years or a hundred years bring them up to our standards of civilization."[32] Even strong supporters of repeal such as Representative Walter H. Judd of Minnesota assumed Chinese immigrants had unique qualities that set them apart from other races. He alluded particularly to their putative ability to live and work on less food than white Americans.[33]

The most compelling arguments mounted against repeal, however, focused on a "domino theory" of Chinese exclusion rather than on racial or cultural unassimilability. Many lawmakers saw the policy of Chinese exclusion as the linchpin holding together the discriminatory national origins quota system in which nations outside northern and western Europe received very small token admissions quotas or none at all. In the event of repeal, Representative William P. Elmer of Missouri predicted, "The copious tears shed for the Chinese are only a few drops compared to the dramatic climax of The Rains Came that is to follow."

Hubert S. Ellis of West Virginia summarized, "It is one of a succession of attempts to punch the first hole in the immigration dike."[34]

Despite the continuing power of belief in the inequality of races, Chinese alienage, and the integrity of restrictive admissions laws, the war had placed new practical realities in the foreground. The United States needed to consolidate the military alliance with China against Japan, and the policy of Chinese exclusion was an obstacle to American and Chinese collaboration. Congressional lawmakers were concerned that the Japanese would turn the Chinese exclusion law into a propaganda tool. Representative Carl T. Curtis of Nebraska feared the Japanese would use Chinese exclusion to promote "Asia for Asiatics" and ultimately unite all the "yellow and brown men of Asia to turn against us." Curtis vividly evoked the vulnerability of the Chinese to this racial appeal: "[For] five long years the Chinese have resisted invasion. With disease, hunger, and military defeat staring them in the face day after day, the Japanese say to them why are you people such saps? The United States is against you. There is not one of you that can lawfully enter the United States." Curtis asserted that "voting to allow 105 Chinese to enter the United States lawfully" could "remove or lessen" this "danger."[35] The pragmatic requirements of war diplomacy forced American lawmakers to rethink the desirability of Chinese exclusion; they realized its repeal was necessary to the United States' credibility as a world leader.

Another practical issue, the postwar economic relationship with China, also persuaded lawmakers of the advantages of repealing Chinese exclusion. Lawmakers concerned with China's role in postwar economic adjustment felt that continuing exclusionary policies would needlessly offend the Chinese. Representative Noah M. Mason of Illinois pointed out that it would not pay to insult consumers in the largest potential market for American goods.[36] Just before the vote on repeal, Senator Elbert D. Thomas of Utah reminded his colleagues, "Let us be sordidly economic for just one minute. I wonder if anyone else has ever estimated the buying power of 400,000,000 people?"[37]

Military and economic internationalism galvanized the broadest sentiment for repeal, but a minor insurgency grew out of idealistic and moral concerns. A handful of congressmen proposed that the unfair and discriminatory character of Chinese exclusion was sufficient to warrant repeal. Representative Martin J. Kennedy of New York criticized exclusion as unjust and "impossible to explain logically to a Chinese person."[38]

Representative John McCormack of Massachusetts declared that the repeal motion would be "a denial of the false doctrine of racism and a reiteration of the American principles of equality of opportunity for life, liberty, and happiness for all mankind."[39]

The small group who advocated repeal on the principle of racial justice were joined by many who were moderate supporters of repeal. These lawmakers downplayed the racial issue. On the one hand, they explained that they endorsed repeal out of a pragmatic concern with gaining a diplomatic and economic advantage in relations with China. On the other hand, they made it known that their cautious approach did not stem from racial animus. The moderates emphasized that their concern lay with the cultural assimilation of the Chinese, not racial differences. Representative Elmer of Missouri even avowed his objective neutrality: "Personally I never had any particular feeling for them and nothing against them."[40] Indeed, an important factor militating for repeal was growing popular sentiment that the resistance of the Chinese to Japanese aggression demonstrated their positive, even American, national character. Many Americans saw the Chinese war effort as a kind of war of independence, akin to the American Revolution, in which the people were proving their capacity for democracy and citizenship. The public received Madame Chiang Kai-shek on her tour in 1943 as personifying the new image of a modern and progressive China.

The popular portrayal of the Chinese as heroic freedom fighters unleashed a flood of idealized characterizations of the Chinese. Representative McCormack of Massachusetts gave a stirring speech during the House debate that extolled the Americanism of the Chinese people:

> China is more to America than an ally. She is our friend, united in her sentiment of friendship for the people of the United States. Our constitution has been her governmental inspiration. Her children quote with pride our constitutional guarantees of liberty and equality. They are taught to believe that America believes that all men are created equal, with rights and privileges which the State did not create, but which the State is bound to safeguard and protect. The Stars and Stripes to the Children of China is the flag of a generous nation protecting human rights from tyrannical intolerance.[41]

In his message to Congress urging repeal President Roosevelt declared that "their great contribution to the cause of decency and freedom" entitled them to "a preferred status over certain other oriental people."[42] In the world of journalistic opinion, editorialists of big city and small town newspapers argued that the Chinese were proving their loyalty to America in their heroic fight against the Japanese. The *Saint Louis Post-Dispatch* urged repeal "to prove our good faith" toward "China's epic resistance in her war—and our war—against Japan." The *Columbus (Georgia) Enquirer* supported repeal as "a gesture of friendship to the Chinese, who are fighting so courageously against the Japs."[43] The popular opinion grew that the Chinese were proving their fitness for American citizenship by fighting against an enemy of America and its democratic heritage. Written into the final Senate report on the repeal bill was a salute: "Above all, the tenacity and courage of the Chinese in their terrible ordeal of the last seven years has impelled a respect that we are proud to acknowledge."[44]

The repeal bill passed smoothly from committee to the floor of Congress to the signature of the president. The House Committee on Immigration and Naturalization gave a favorable report on the repeal bill on 7 October 1943, the majority concluding, "It is fitting that the incongruity of discriminatory legislation, inconsistent with the dignity of both our peoples, should be eliminated."[45] A week later the House passed the bill by a voice vote, so great was consensus in its favor; the Senate concurred without requiring a recorded vote the following month. The president signed it into law on 17 December 1943. The passage of repeal was truly anticlimactic.

On its face, repeal represented a small alteration in the fortress of restrictionism. An annual quota of 105 admissions was allotted to members of the Chinese race, with a preference for natives of China, thus recognizing race rather than nativity alone as a determinant in qualifying for admission. The quota clearly symbolized the principle of admissibility rather than providing any real opportunity for Chinese people to immigrate to the United States.

Nevertheless, repeal marked a turning point in the idea of American nationality. It established the right of Chinese not only to admission but also to naturalization. It marked the unprecedented legal recognition by the federal government that members of an Asian nation could become American citizens. It made the whole structure of Asian exclusion from admission and naturalization increasingly anachronistic. In the wake of the repeal of Chinese exclusion, Congress discussed ways to undo anti-

Asian policies case by case. Lawmakers decided to move ahead and give the right to admission and naturalization to two other Asian groups. On 2 July 1946 Asian Indians were permitted a small quota, and they as well as Filipinos were made eligible for naturalized citizenship.[46] Finally, in 1952 Congress rescinded all anti-Asian exclusionary provisions in immigration and naturalization policy.[47] The racial conservatives who prophesied that revoking Chinese exclusion would produce a legal domino effect proved prescient.

The pressures generated by World War II to reexamine and affirm American citizenship in an international crisis profoundly affected alien and marginal ethnic populations. Naturalization reached its most active point in American history and served as a mechanism for European immigrants to secure their legal status and political identity. For them World War II brought the culmination of the tradition of patriotic naturalization. The internment of Japanese Americans, by contrast, was the most radical expression of the legal and ideological tendencies to exclude Asians from American citizenship—the ultimate consummation of that historical trend. The repeal of Chinese exclusion to promote American international leadership initiated the gradual reformulation of American nationality to include Asian peoples. Once started, its momentum was not halted and led to the eventual abandonment of discriminatory immigration and naturalization policy against Asians. It was a turning point in the changing path to citizenship during World War II.

Notes

1. Morris Janowitz, *The Reconstruction of Patriotism: Education for Civic Consciousness* (Chicago, 1983), 14–16.

2. Arthur M. Schlesinger, *Paths to the Present* (New York, 1949), 72; Richard Polenberg, *One Nation Divisible: Class, Race, and Ethnicity in the United States since 1938* (New York, 1980), 57.

3. Data were compiled from the U.S. Immigration and Naturalization Service, *Annual Report*, 1945 (Washington, D.C., 1945), tables 38, 39, 40, 41, 43, 45.

4. Robert A. Divine, *American Immigration Policy: 1924–1952* (New Haven, 1957), 106.

5. Luella Gettys, *The Law of Citizenship in the United States* (Chicago, 1934), 111–24.

6. U.S. Bureau of the Census, *Historical Statistics of the United States, Colonial Times to 1970* (Washington, D.C., 1975), 116.

7. Reed Ueda, "Naturalization and Citizenship," in *Harvard Encyclopedia of American Ethnic Groups*, ed. Stephan Thernstorm (Cambridge, Mass., 1980), 741–42.

8. Charles A. Price, *The Great White Walls Are Built: Restrictive Immigration to North America and Australasia, 1836–1888* (Canberra, Australia, 1974), 128–29; Alexander Saxton, *The Indispensable Enemy: Labor and the Anti-Chinese Movement in California* (Berkeley, Calif., 1971), 36–37.

9. 22 Stat. 58 (1882).

10. Milton Konvitz, *The Alien and the Asiatic in American Law* (New York, 1946), 80–96; Paul S. Rundquist, "A Uniform Rule: The Congress and the Courts in American Naturalization, 1865–1952" (Ph.D. diss., University of Chicago, 1975), chap. 7.

11. In re San C. Po, 7 Misc. 471, 28 N.Y. Supp. 383 (1894); Petition of Easurk Emsen Charr (D.C. Mo. 1921) 273 F. 207; Wadia v. U.S.C.C.A., N.Y. 1939, 101 F 2d. 7 (1939).

12. *Toyota v. United States*, 268 U.S. 408 (1925); *Ozawa v. United States*, 260 U. S. 178 (1922); *Yamashita v. Hinkle*, 260 U.S. 198 (1922).

13. *U.S. v. Bhagat Singh Thind*, 261 U.S. 204 (1923).

14. Stanford M. Lyman, *Chinese Americans* (New York, 1974), 81–82; Price, *Great White Walls*, 257, 269–70.

15. Quoted in Akira Iriye, "Introduction," in Norris Hundley Jr., *The Asian American: The Historical Experience* (Santa Barbara, Calif., 1976), ix.

16. Quoted in Lawrence H. Fuchs, *Hawaii Pono: A Social History* (New York, 1961), 132.

17. From "The Chinese on the Pacific Coast," New York *Tribune*, 1 May 1869, quoted in Glenn C. Altschuler, *Race, Ethnicity, and Class in American Social Thought, 1865–1919* (Arlington Heights, Ill., 1982), 29.

18. Charles M. Thompson, *A History of the United States: Political, Industrial, Social* (Chicago, 1917), 366–67.

19. William Howard Taft, *Four Aspects of Civic Duty* (New York, 1906), 88–89.

20. See Konvitz, *Alien and Asiatic*, chap. 3; Rundquist, "Uniform Rule," chaps. 2, 3, 4.

21. 43 Stat. 153 (1924).

22. Edith Abbott, *Immigration: Select Documents and Case Records* (Chicago, 1924), 568–70; James H. Kettner, "The Development of American Citizenship in the Revolutionary Era: The Idea of Volitional Allegiance," *American Journal of Legal History* 18 (1974): 208–42.

23. In the case of *U.S. v. Wong Kim Ark* in 1898, the United States Supreme Court affirmed the citizenship of the second generation of Chinese Americans. The ruling brought the Constitution squarely into conflict with the federal law of naturalization making race, not nativity, the touchstone of naturalization. See 169 U.S. 649; Norman Alexander, *Rights of Aliens under the Federal Constitution* (Montpelier, Vt., 1931), 46.

24. Quoted in Bill Hosokawa, *Nisei: The Quiet Americans* (New York, 1969), 287–88, from Warren's statements in Select Committee Investigating National Defense Migration, *Hearings,* 77th Cong., 2d sess., 1942.

25. U.S. War Department, Chief of Staff, *Final Reports: Japanese Evacuation from the West Coast, 1942* (Washington, D.C., 1943), 39.

26. Fred W. Riggs, *Pressures on Congress: A Study of the Repeal of Chinese Exclusion* (New York, 1950), 195–96; David M. Reimers, *Still the Golden Door: The Third World Comes to America* (New York, 1985), 13–15.

27. House Committee on Immigration and Naturalization, *Hearings: Bills to Repeal the Chinese Exclusion Acts,* 78th Cong., 1st sess., 1943, 65, 72, 73. Edward Foster and Xin Zhao, graduate students at Tufts University, provided research on the text of the debates cited here and in the following notes.

28. Riggs, *Pressures on Congress,* 178.

29. *Congressional Record,* 78th Cong., 1st sess., 1943, 8600.

30. Ibid., 8599.

31. Ibid., 9989.

32. Ibid., 8593.

33. Ibid., 8633.

34. Divine, *American Immigration Policy,* 152–53.

35. *Congressional Record,* 78th Cong., 1st sess., 1943, 5745, 5746, 8573, 9990.

36. House Committee on Immigration and Naturalization, *Hearings,* 173.

37. *Congressional Record,* 78th Cong., 1st sess., 1943, 9993.

38. Ibid., 8576.

39. Ibid., 8579.

40. Ibid., 8626, 8593.

41. Ibid., 8580.

42. *Congressional Record*, 78th Cong., 1st sess., 1943, House Doc. 333, 8293.

43. *Congressional Record*, 78th Cong., 1st sess., 1943, appendix 3, A4408–A4409.

44. Senate, *Report Number 535*, 78th Cong., 1st sess., 1943, 6.

45. House, *Report Number 732*, 78th Cong., 1st sess., 1943, 4.

46. 60 Stat. 416 (1946).

47. 66 Stat. 50 (1952).

NINE

Native Sons and the Good War: Retelling the Myth of American Indian Assimilation

Shortly after the end of World War II, an Ojibwe-Oneida family appeared in a human interest photograph published in the *Milwaukee Journal*. The family—father in dress navy uniform, mother, and seven children ages three to fourteen—was that of George B. "Artishaw" (the reporter got the name wrong; it was actually Artishon) and his wife Grace. The nine faces in the photo are dark-eyed and serious, the children dressed up and carefully groomed as any family might be for a newspaper picture. The caption relates that Artishon, a recently discharged chief electrician's mate in the navy, and his family are looking for a place to live. Since June Mrs. Artishon and her children had been living in Milwaukee with her brother's family, also including seven children, in a six-room apartment. The family is appealing for help, readers are told, since "with seven children, landlords are reluctant to rent." Rose Artishon, the seven-year-old in the photo, remembers that the family was eventually offered a garage in Hilbert, Wisconsin. "We took it because the landlords in Milwaukee did not rent to families of our size, particularly Indians. I remember the row of beds along one wall for us kids to sleep in, and I can also see my mother cooking on a stove made from stones outside the garage."[1]

During George Artishon's naval service from 1941 to 1945, the family had relocated from reservation life in rural Minnesota and Wisconsin to several urban settings, including Brooklyn, New York. After the war, according to Rose, they never really settled down again.

> I do remember when he would wake up during the night shouting that the planes were coming and to duck down. My father never expected to be in a place very long because we didn't have money, or there were

no places for us to live. He never had a job for very long. It would only last until he felt he had enough money to travel to another town. After the war, he would move from one small town to another as he was an electrician, and his work would be wherever he could find it. . . . I believe to this day that we could not find a real home so that we could claim it as our own. Either Dad was frantic with needing to find some roots or he was tired of having to put up with himself because he never seemed to have a job.[2]

The experience of George Artishon and his family is in several ways a microcosm of the problems of World War II for American Indians. From the official federal perspective, and certainly for some Indian groups and individuals as well, the war provided an extraordinary stimulus toward assimilation, a goal some welcomed as inevitable and desirable. But for many others the war also engendered a cultural subversion resulting not in emancipation and inclusion but in exile and disillusion. This is the war story powerfully and consistently presented by N. Scott Momaday and by Leslie Marmon Silko in two narratives, *House Made of Dawn* (1968) and *Ceremony* (1977), whose publication initiated a reflowering of American Indian oral tradition in the talking leaves of contemporary literature.

Within the body of published work by American Indian writers that has emerged over the past twenty-five years, the consequences of "white people's wars" for American Indians have been a recurring and powerful theme of both poetry and fiction.[3] Momaday's and Silko's narratives on one level corroborate recent assessments by historians Gerald Nash and Alison Bernstein that cast World War II as profoundly transformative of American Indian affairs. But significantly, Momaday and Silko, in their echoing stories of the dysfunction that wrenches the lives of Indian veterans trying to reenter their traditional communities after the war, provide persuasive counters to the tendency of dominant culture analysis to rationalize the negative impact on American Indian individuals and communities caused by the war's push toward accelerated acculturation. At the same time that they present their case to white audiences, both narratives launch an internally directed contention. The books remind Indian readers of the war's unkept promise of a new American pluralism and argue for a restoration of individual and communal Native American identity vested in the functionality of traditional cultural patterns. They do so from positions informed by historical distance and an ideological climate quite different from that surrounding World War II. By dramatizing and interrogating the connection between American Indians' participation in the war and the myth of successful assimilation both abroad and at home, Momaday and Silko quite deliberately complicate the attitudes of many American Indian people about military service and national loyalties.

It is certainly true, as Nash has noted, that Native American response to the initial call to arms was enthusiastic.[4] This historically consistent response was perhaps the result, at least in part, of the veneration of the warrior tradition among many groups. One has only to attend any contemporary powwow with its flag entries and honor songs for military veterans to observe how potent this tradition still is. Military service has also, of course, represented one of only a few avenues of economic and social opportunity. This seemed especially so in the circumstances of America's entry into World War II, when patriotism and opposition to fascism offered clear-cut opportunities for Indian people to invest fully in "American" interests and to demonstrate their eagerness to be full shareholders in the risks—and rewards—of democracy. From the perspective of Anglo-America, the war, for all its human cost, suggested potentially positive ways to expand American interests internationally. On idealistic grounds—the contest between democracy and fascism as social philosophies—the war was supposed to demonstrate and stimulate a new pluralism, to reconstruct public consensus, and to rejuvenate the principles of political and social equality and opportunity in ways that would advance the democratic agenda here at home. On the international stage, Henry Luce and others argued that America's participation in the war would thrust the country fully and irrevocably into the position of dominant world power. But Luce's privileged position influenced his vision of the glories of an American century in which freedom, equality of opportunity, and the other "great principles of Western civilization" were to be exported worldwide and led him to ignore the domestic inequities that argued a core of hypocrisy within that vision.[5]

A summary of the status quo for American Indians before and after the war gives evidence of how fully they were excluded from the full benefits of American democracy that Luce was promulgating. The Indian Reorganization Act, passed in 1934, was the latest pendulum swing of federal Indian policy. In the decade before the war, the Indian New

Deal, despite its benevolent intentions, essentially bartered the promise of economic development and some measure of self-management for an agreement to impose white political organization on traditional tribal structures of government and leadership. Such a trade-off was met with ambivalence and resistance by many groups, but the economic circumstances of most Indian people were so desperate that any other considerations had to be secondary. In 1939 the median income for all Indian males living on reservations was $500, less than one-fourth the median for all United States males, and the 1940 census reported that one-third of all Indian males living off reservation were unemployed.[6] The average life expectancy for Indians in 1940 was less than thirty-five years, compared with sixty to sixty-four years for the country at large.[7] The war provided a rationale for extensive co-optation of already limited Indian resources, as in the development of mineral reserves by commercial operators on reservation lands. Although John Collier, Roosevelt's commissioner of Indian affairs, pursued a policy throughout the 1930s of building Indian holdings by purchase of additional lands, Indians controlled almost a million fewer acres by 1945 because of government use and sale.[8]

American Indians had officially been given the status of citizens by Congress in 1924, but at the outbreak of World War II they were still ineligible to vote in three states, including Arizona and New Mexico, which, with Oklahoma, had the largest Native American populations. Despite the irony that they were frequently disfranchised in the country they were called on to defend, more than 25,000 served in some branch of the military. According to Alison Bernstein in *American Indians and World War II: Toward a New Era in Indian Affairs,* by the end of the war one-third of all able-bodied Indian men between ages eighteen and fifty had served (and in some groups as many as 70 percent); about 5 percent had been killed or wounded in action. Among those, a disproportionate number of casualties from Plains Indian groups leads Bernstein to wonder whether "these Indians were more courageous in battle or whether their non-Indian commanders assumed that the Indians had a 'warrior' instinct and sent them into combat more frequently."[9] In general, however, few Native voices are allowed to speak for themselves in Bernstein's text, and her interpretation of American Indian wartime experience frequently seems Eurocentric, as when she writes that the involvement of Indians in the war effort represented "an unparalleled opportunity to compete in the white world in an arena where their talents and reputation as fighters inspired respect. Small wonder that the Indian fighting man, regardless of his rank, was indiscriminately called 'Chief' by his white buddies."[10] Bigotry and stereotyping, as we shall see in *House Made of Dawn,* might also account for American Indian soldiers' being indiscriminately called chief, and the "unparalleled opportunity" to compete in the potentially deadly arena of combat rather than in more benign social or political spheres might more aptly be viewed as exploitation.

In addition to the immediate cost in injury and loss of life, the war precipitated other damaging consequences to the cultural stability of Native people. Military service and relocation to urban areas were supposed to hasten assimilation by weakening tribal ties, and that is precisely what happened. The short-term windfall of GI pay and boom employment led people out of their communities and away from their cultural bases. By war's end, one-half of all able-bodied Indian men who were not in the services and one-fifth of the women had left reservations and home communities for war-related jobs.[11] But for Native Americans the boom economy and the extra money ended with the war. Fewer than 10 percent of the two thousand Indians who relocated to Minneapolis and Saint Paul in the years following the war found permanent employment, and this situation was replicated in every major urban area where Indians sought work.[12] The postwar circumstances of southwestern groups were especially desperate. Oliver LaFarge reported that in 1947 the average income per person among the Navajos was $1.25 a week, and many were in danger of starving. Thirty-six hundred Navajos had served in the military, but when the war was over they still could not vote, were denied by the state the Social Security benefits allotted to them by the federal government, and were too poorly educated to be able to take advantage of the GI Bill to secure admission to high schools and colleges.[13] Having been allowed during the war a temporary taste of the opportunities available to other Americans, many Indian families, like the Artishons, found themselves unable to make a permanent living afterward either in Indian communities or in urban centers. Thus began a debilitating cycle of movement that continues to this day.

The now well known example of the Pima Ira Hayes is perhaps more typical of the experience of the returning Indian serviceman than Gerald Nash credits in his account of Hayes's postwar experience. Having the good or bad fortune to be in the right place at the right time to have his image frozen in the most celebrated photograph of wartime heroism, Hayes was immediately catapulted to national fame and put on tour to publicize the War Loan Drive. But he was tragically unprepared for such an alien public role. Unable either to subsist on his family's hardscrabble farm on the Pima reservation in Arizona or to adjust to the life of a relocation Indian in Chicago or Los Angeles, within ten years of the war's end Hayes was dead of alcoholism at age thirty-three.

At least some elements of Hayes's story are loosely paralleled in both *House Made of Dawn* and *Ceremony*, whose Indian veteran protagonists—Abel in Momaday's story and Tayo in Silko's—bring personal and communal dysfunction home with them from World War II like some modern strain of the alien diseases that decimated Indian populations over centuries of exposure. Both Momaday and Silko position the war as a particularly virulent source of dislocation and cultural denigration, identified by Ashcroft and his coauthors as major features of the "special post-colonial crisis of identity" that must be addressed by "recovery of an effective identifying relationship of self and place."[14] Other circumstances related to cultural contention, including the dissolution of traditional stabilizing family structures, also contribute to Abel's and Tayo's individual sense of alienated identity: neither Momaday nor Silko is naive or self-serving enough to view the war machine as the singular spoiler in the garden. But in Native American epistemologies all things are interdependent, including calamity. World War II is represented as a catalyst bringing about separation, exploitation, and loss, and in both narratives recovery at individual and communal levels depends on crucial reintegration of self and place.

House Made of Dawn's author, Scott Momaday, of mixed Kiowa and Cherokee descent, was only seven when America entered the war, but he has spoken directly about the specific significance of World War II to the generation of Native people embodied by his protagonist Abel, who "represents such a dislocation of the psyche in our time. Almost no Indian of my generation or of Abel's generation escaped that dislocation, that sense of having to deal immediately with, not only with the traditional world, but with the other world which was placed over the traditional world so abruptly and with great violence."[15] For Momaday, the tragedy that results from this dislocation is the true outcome, regardless of whether the war "set a new agenda" for economic betterment and social mobility.[16]

The description of place that begins Momaday's telling uses ceremonial language to portray an undisrupted traditional world in which terrain and time are unified and then bound to human presence: "Dypaloh. There was a house made of dawn. It was made of pollen and of rain, and the land was very old and everlasting. . . . The land was still and strong. It was beautiful all around."[17] In the anachronous landscape of Momaday's prologue, Abel is running, his arms and shoulders ritually marked with ashes, appearing, "in the long, light landscape of the valley at dawn, almost to be standing still" (2). The reader's first and last views of Abel are identical, but Abel's experience in the war, his failure to reconnect with his community, and his equally failed relocation in Los Angeles, come in between—and meaning must wait until that last view is completed.

In Abel's traditional homeland, Momaday writes later in the narrative, there is a "tenure" held by the coyotes, eagles, lizards—the wildest creatures who have lived upon it for immemorial time. The "latecoming" things, beasts of burden, domesticated animals—and by implication whites, the latest comers—"have an alien and inferior aspect, a poverty of vision and instinct, by which they are estranged from the wild land, and made tentative. . . . Man, too, has tenure in the land; he dwelt upon the land twenty-five thousand years ago, and his gods before him" (57–58). Invasion and change have disturbed this tenure, but in this story the war is portrayed as the immediate literal event of dislocation and chaos. *House Made of Dawn* follows Abel's disintegration as he first leaves his home community for induction and is psychologically unable to rejoin it upon his return. His efforts to reclaim a functional existence are complicated by an affair with a wealthy white woman and conflict with a mysterious "albino," an ageless, ambiguously malevolent figure who appears to seek Abel out and whom Abel eventually kills in equally mysterious circumstances. Released from prison several years later, he drifts into the community of relocation Indians in Los Angeles and there meets Tosamah, the trickster/con man priest of the sun, and the friendly but equally directionless Benally, two characters whose important narrative voices add to Momaday's evocation of the postwar disillusion of Native people. After being beaten almost to death by a sadistic policeman, Abel returns home for the final time and, in an ambiguous ending, reconnects himself to his community's traditional ceremonial life.

Throughout much of both "tellings," Abel in *House Made of Dawn* and Tayo in *Ceremony* are physically and psychologically adrift. It is in fact only through a process of restored ceremonial sentience that the protagonists—and their cultures—have any chance for recovery. *House Made of Dawn*'s first section, "The Longhair," is set in a particular time and place, Walatowa, Canon San Diego, 1945, and begins on the day Abel returns home from the service. But the present-tense description that begins the section suggests a changeless continuum binding present and past—this is the way it is and always has been in Canon San Diego. Abel's grandfather, Francisco, is also initially presented in a ceremonial context. He is setting a snare to catch a blue or yellow bird whose tail feathers will make a suitable prayer plume. He practices both Catholicism and the ancient religion of his people. In his wagon on the way to meet Abel's bus, Francisco sings both in his native language and in Spanish. From the beginning, he is presented as one who has reconciled cultures and created a functional space within them. He is, literally and figuratively, at home. Abel, by contrast, stumbles off the bus drunk, falling against his grandfather without recognizing him.

Abel has learned loss and estrangement early. His father is unknown; his mother and brother have died of tuberculosis. In a society where kinship determines identity, Francisco is his only family. From the beginning, then, Abel has reason to be uncertain of his selfhood and his "place"—even more so because, like his grandfather but much more tenuously, he is essentially a long hair, immersed in a disrupted traditional world in which the old beliefs vie with the new in mysterious convergences. Francisco has been reared in the Catholic Church, but he has also been one of the black runners, the runners after evil, whose role in Pueblo spiritual life is ancient and powerful. Abel himself has seen eagles catch snakes in their talons in midair, "an awful, holy sight, full of magic and meaning" (15). His vision leads him to accompany the Bahkyush eagle watchers on their sacred hunt, but he feels so much shame and disgust at the helplessness and ungainliness of the captured bird that "he took hold of its throat in the darkness and cut off its breath" (22). His action is emblematic of his confused perception of how to make meaning of traditional belief.

Having established the instability of Abel's prewar relation to his home

NATIVE SONS AND THE GOOD WAR

culture, Momaday then abruptly sends him off to combat. His careful description of Abel's lonely leave-taking as the first motor vehicle he has ever ridden in takes him out of the valley reproduces the radical estrangement this creates: "There was no one to wish him well or to tell him how it would be. . . . And suddenly he had the sense of being all alone, as if he were already miles and months away. . . . There was a lot of speed and sound then, and he tried desperately to take it into account, to know what it meant. Only when it was too late did he remember to look back in the direction of the fields" (23).

For Abel, the bus is not only the literal vehicle of his leaving home; it is a metaphorically powerful machine as well, evoking all the other "machinery" of Western civilization. By the time he returns, Abel's physical dislocation has expanded to the devastating psychological dislocation that Momaday sees as the war's tragic result. Though Abel can remember with clarity everything before his going, "It was the recent past, the intervention of days and years without meaning, of awful calm and collision, time always immediate and confused, that he could not put together in his mind" (23).

The one incident he remembers distinctly and recurringly is his encounter with another of the machines of war, a tank that comes crashing down almost upon him as he lies on a battlefield among the dead and wounded. This is a crucial experience not merely because of its intrinsic violence and terror: Indian soldiers were obviously not the only ones who endured wartime trauma. It is more important for its context in the narrative, its relation to the immediately subsequent scene, which begins, "And now the silent land bore in upon him" (25). Terror inspired by individual helplessness in the face of a crushing alien force is a familiar motif in minority literatures, as in Richard Wright's use of it to describe Bigger Thomas's hopelessness in the "Flight" section of *Native Son*. But on his return Abel feels similarly threatened by the land itself— Momaday's signal of how far out of balance, how separated he is from coherent tribal identity.

The tank experience is also important because of the significance of the difference between Abel's memory of what happened and the version recounted by his white GI "buddies." What Abel remembers is paralyzing fear as the machine bears down on him, comes close, then passes by. But the witnesses' version begins, "He was not afraid, no sir," and goes on to describe "the chief . . . giving it the finger and whooping it up and doing a goddam war dance, sir. . . . There he was, hopping around with his finger up in the air and giving it to that tank in Sioux or Algonquin or something, for chrissake" (116–17). Whatever actually happened, even in their admiration his fellow soldiers don't see or know Abel. They neither call him by his name nor know what tribe he comes from. Momaday's point undercuts the interpretation that the war broke down the barriers of difference between whites and Indians in the ranks. To his fellow soldiers Abel is still the chief, the brave, the savage—the dehumanized stereotype of popular culture.

In the aftermath of war, Abel is actually *dis*abled—fitting in nowhere, unable to speak to his grandfather, to pray or to sing in the old language. "His return to the town had been a failure, for all his looking forward. . . . Had he been able to say . . . anything of his own language . . . [it] would once again have shown him whole to himself; but he was dumb" (58). His attempts to take up his traditional place with his grandfather and enter into the communal life of the town are thwarted by his own alienation and also by the presence and enmity of the albino Juan Reyes, whose symbolic potency derives from his unnatural whiteness, his age-lessness and power, and Momaday's clear indications that he is precisely what Abel believes him to be—evil incarnate. The meaning of his myste-rious identity in the narrative may be interpreted variously, but Abel's belief that he is a serpent in the form of a man—that one kills such an enemy when he can—and the trial that sends Abel to prison certainly illustrate the irony and error implicit in the idea that assimilation would be an inevitable product of wartime service. John Collier had written in 1943 that "never before have Indians been so well prepared to take their place among the general citizenry and become assimilated into the white population."[18] But the character Tosamah, part trickster but also the closest thing to an authorial voice in the narrative, presents a sardonic counter to that simplistic misjudgment, noting that despite the "advan-tages" of free haircuts and letting him fight on their side, Abel " 'was too damn dumb to be civilized. So what happened? They let him alone at last. They thought he was harmless. . . . But it didn't turn out that way. He turned out to be a real primitive sonuvabitch, and the first time he got hold of a knife he killed a man. . . . They put that cat away, man. They *had* to. It's part of the Jesus scheme. *They,* man. They put all of us renegades, us diehards, away sooner or later. They've got the right idea. They put us away before we're born' " (148–49).

Out of prison in Los Angeles, Abel appears to have even less chance of attaining some functional integration of self and place. A relocation officer helps him find a factory line job, and Momady uses "The Night Chanter" section narrated by Abel's friend Benally to demonstrate that Abel's situation is hardly unique. Postwar relocation means the dead-end of hopeless subsistence rather than the opportunity to make a better life. There is the cycle of deadening work, minimal pay, rented rooms, and drinking to numbness with others in the same circumstances. Benally too is drifting, displaced. He has his own sweet memories of home, of his previous life at the core of the world, when "you were little and right there in the center of everything, the sacred mountains, the snow-covered mountains and hills, the gullies and the flats, the sundown and the night, everything—where you were little, where you were and had to be" (157). He is envious of those who "have plans" but almost resigned to his permanent place in white society's underclass. In a critically eloquent passage, he speaks for himself and many others when he tries to describe why Abel is dysfunctional in the face of the contradictory processes of assimilation:

> You have to get *used* to everything, you know; it's like starting out some-
> place where you've never been before, and you don't know where you're
> going or why or when you have to get there, and everybody's looking at
> you, waiting for you, wondering why you don't hurry up. . . . And you
> *want* to do it, because you can see how good it is. It's better than any-
> thing you've ever had; it's money and clothes and having plans and going
> someplace fast. . . . You've got to get used to it first, and it's hard. . . .
> You've got to take it easy and get drunk once in a while and just forget
> about who you are. . . . You think about getting out and going home. You
> want to think that you belong someplace, I guess. . . . But the next day,
> you know it's no use; you know that if you went home there would be
> nothing there, just the empty land and a lot of old people, going noplace
> and dying off. And you've got to forget about that too. (158–59)

In the character of the good-hearted and lonely Milly, a white woman with an impoverished past and her own poignant story of loss, Momaday injects at least tangentially the mutual inequities of class and gender as well as race. Milly's story—her father's sacrifice, the death of her child, her compassion for Abel—is important. Yet Abel in his self-absorbed misery is incapable of treating her well. His initial lovemaking is brutal;

later, he exploits her and denigrates her to Benally. Abel's treatment of her demonstrates the now familiar ripple effect that extends cycles of victimization and provides evidence that powerlessness breeds abuse. This is an important theme throughout American Indian narrative, not only here but for Leslie Silko, Louise Erdrich, and Simon Ortiz and elsewhere in minority literatures (e g , Bigger Thomas's victimization of Bessie). Momaday reinforces it subtly in the detail that the sadistic cop whose beating of Abel precipitates his lowest descent is named Martinez. As in Ortiz's short story "The Killing of a State Cop," the violence of oppressed groups and individuals is frequently directed at targets equally oppressed.[19] But beaten almost to death by the cop, delirious, Abel has a vision of ceremonial runners that prefigures the means of his recovery of balance and function:

> The runners after evil ran as water runs, deep in the channel, in the way of least resistance, no resistance. . . . They were whole and indispensable in what they did; everything in creation referred to them. Because of them, perspective, design in the universe. Meaning because of them. They ran with great dignity and calm, not in the hope of anything, but hopelessly; neither in fear nor hatred nor despair of evil, but simply in recognition and with respect. (103–4)

When he returns for the last time, sick and injured, to Canon San Diego, he is in time to hear his grandfather's words during the six dawns of the old man's leaving. The narrative ends as it began, in an elemental unification of past and present, time and space, with Abel ready to take a place among the runners. In that act, rather than in whether Abel lives or dies, is Momaday's resolution. Running, Abel surrenders resistance and is finally able to sing in the old language. He has recovered himself by recovering his human voice and his place in his world's ordered design.

o   o   o

*L*eslie Marmon Silko's influential 1977 novel *Ceremony* also deliberately rejects the assimilation fable but moves on to confront more global threats to the fragile interdependence of the natural world and human well-being. Writing within the very recent and resonant aftermath of the Vietnam War, Silko, a mixed-blood Laguna Pueblo who was not even born until 1948, chooses to take the ideological risk of setting her narrative in World War II instead of Vietnam, positioning "the good war" as a critical piece in an escalating global pattern of destructiveness and violence. Silko has consistently spoken of the healing capacity of storytelling, of its power to unify past and present, word and act, "so that there wasn't anything lost, nothing was dead, nobody was gone, that in the stories everything was held together, regardless of time."[20] Elsewhere, she has said, "I'm interested in certain convergences and configurations," and one such convergence is that America's development and use of the atomic bomb were dependent on uranium mined on tribal lands.[21]

Like Abel, Silko's protagonist Tayo also returns from the war traumatized by his experience. Alcoholic, ill, he cannot be helped by the traditional medicine man's cures because they are powerless against the impersonality and huge scope of white warfare: "It was all too alien to comprehend, the mortars and the big guns . . .; the old man would not have believed anything so monstrous. Ku'oosh would have looked at the dismembered corpses and the atomic heat-flash outlines, where human bodies had evaporated, and the old man would have said something close and terrible had killed these people. Not even oldtime witches killed like that."[22] In *Ceremony*, the war is one reason why the whole traditional Pueblo world is out of balance and drought-stricken, but Silko's unfolding point is that there is only one world, and the war has unleashed a previously inconceivable inhumanity that poses a universal threat to its tenuous interconnectedness.

The first image of the novel is a cacophony that introduces the major elements of Tayo's alienation. His mind is assaulted by the acute disharmonies of Spanish and Laguna voices merging into those of his angry Japanese captors. He hears as well the particular voice of his uncle Josiah calling to him, the words of his mother, which he cannot interpret, "fever" voices whirling around him, drowned out by the loud music of a jukebox with flashing red and blue lights—an icon of the pop-materialist, postwar culture he and the other veterans, Emo, Pinky, Harley, and Leroy, have returned to. Like Abel's, Tayo's memory is tangled by the jarring associations of his experience in the war: his being ordered to kill unarmed Japanese POWs and seeing in their brown faces his uncle's face, then subsequently his own captivity and his inability to prevent the death of his cousin Rocky.

"Even white men were darker after death," he realizes. "There was no difference when they were swollen and covered with flies" (7). In war, he perceives that death establishes a universal kinship. This idea is particularized in his identification with the Japanese who are supposed to be his enemies. When he sees his uncle in the faces of the men he is ordered to kill, he is sickened by the illogic of it. "Rocky had reasoned it out with him; it was impossible for the dead man to be Josiah, because Josiah was an old Laguna man, thousands of miles from the Philippine jungles and the Japanese armies. . . . 'Hey, I know you're homesick. But, Tayo, we're *supposed* to be here. This is what we're supposed to do' " (8).

Silko's argument is that Tayo's dysfunction is related to a similar imbalance manifested in the natural world, and that both are exacerbated by the sanctioned inhumanity and violence of world war. "The drought years had returned again," she writes, "as they had after the First World War and in the twenties" (10). Tayo believes he has caused the drought by cursing the jungle rain—so different from the life-giving rain of Laguna—that is making Rocky's wound fester and bringing on his death. "So he had prayed the rain away, and for the sixth year it was dry; the grass turned yellow and it did not grow" (14). The narrative's design is to weave around Tayo's central predicament of guilt and separation a fuller and fuller explanation of the ways cultural impositions have fractured the shared Pueblo consciousness, the "simple certainty of the world they saw, how everything should be" (68). European language has been one of those impositions, as has Christianity with its substitution of individual guilt and redemption for the kinship and reciprocity imaged in the Mother's care for her children. Tayo's mother's promiscuity and alcoholism are a part of this pattern of dividedness and loss, as are Auntie's shame and cruelty. Silko and Momaday are arguing to both white and Indian readers the same point: the war poses a particular danger to Native peoples because it foments chaos, straining the fabric of community and kinship by moving people outside, by changing them injuriously and then breaking the promises that lured them in the first place. Rocky wanted to enlist, for example, because, from his mother and his teachers he had already internalized the desire to succeed on white terms. "Anyone can fight for America, . . . even you boys. In a time of need anyone can fight for her," the recruiter has told them (64). "We can do real good," Rocky coaxes Tayo, "Go all over the world" (72). Rocky's aspirations are a second-generational manifestation of his mother's fear of being trapped in the old ways. He wants to be a pilot—that option is part of the recruiter's cynical spiel—but of course what Rocky inevitably becomes is a foot soldier, fodder for the machinery of war.

In the veterans' hospital after his discharge, Tayo cannot be made whole by white medicine. In effect, he makes himself invisible, speaks of himself in the third person, turns himself into white smoke, and restructures the material world within one-dimensional lines. His nonexistence in the hospital is a refuge of protective nonidentity. A new doctor seeks to break down this defense by sending him home, and in the Los Angeles railroad depot on the way, he is helped by a group of Japanese women accompanied by a child. Silko's contrivance here affirms the ideological association of Native Americans and Japanese Americans as related peoples, sharing a kinship created by their otherness and experience of bigotry and exploitation. When the little boy's face changes into Rocky's, "He [Tayo] couldn't vomit anymore, and the little face was still there, so he cried at how the world had come undone, how thousands of miles, high ocean waves and green jungles could not hold people in their place" (18).

Back at home, Tayo's friend Harley represents another version of American Indian veteran experience. Harley and the malignant Emo had won Purple Hearts on Wake Island. Initially, Tayo reflects that Harley has not been changed—still a little fat, joking and clowning. But Harley *has* changed. From being a boy who didn't like beer, he has returned from the army an alcoholic. He is irresponsible, self-destructive—according to Tayo, seemingly unable to feel anything, even when his deserting his family's sheep to go on a binge results in the death of the sheep dog and the loss of half the herd. Alcohol use may have been for American Indian veterans, as Bernstein suggests, a marker of wartime social acceptance, but more realistically it is, as Tayo asserts in a vitriolic explosion, anesthesia for the bitter disillusion that Harley, Emo, and the others feel at the bait-and-switch disappointments of their postwar situations.

> "See these dumb Indians thought these good times would last. . . . They were America the Beautiful too, this was the land of the free just like teachers said in school. . . . Here they were, trying to bring back the old feeling, that feeling they belonged to America the way they felt during the war. They blamed themselves for losing the new feeling . . . just like they blamed themselves for losing the land the white people took. . . .

They never saw that it was the white people who gave them that feeling and it was white people who took it away again when the war was over." (42–43)

In Emo, Silko delineates another version of cultural dissolution. Emo is a sadist—literally, in Silko's parlance, a destroyer. The war has validated and encouraged the worst in him. "Look what is here for us. Here's the Indians' mother earth! Old dried-up thing!" (25). He carries the teeth of men he has killed in a bag around his neck. In the white people's war, his skill and pleasure in destroying are rewarded: "He understood them right away; he knew what they wanted. He was the best, they told him; some men didn't like to feel the quiver of the man they were killing; some men got sick when they smelled the blood. But he was the best; he was one of them. The best. United States Army" (62).

The natural enmity between Tayo and Emo increasingly marks polarities as the constructed world of the narrative unfolds. When Tayo stabs Emo in the bar, one is reminded of Abel's killing of the albino because in both scenes violence assumes similar mythic dimensions. As we have seen, Abel believes during the struggle and afterward that the being he kills is an entity of evil rather than a man, and Momaday provides evidence in the narrative to support his belief. Less overtly and within the moment at least, Tayo's assault on Emo is similarly described: "He moved suddenly, with speed which was effortless and floating like a mountain lion. He got stronger with every jerk that Emo made, and he felt that he would get well if he killed him" (63). The image of the mountain lion is significant: the lion appears later as a benevolent spirit helper whose presence saves Tayo when he is threatened by white ranchers.

An eye for an eye is complex in its translation within Native cultures. In the Lakota camp life described by Ella Cara Deloria in *Waterlily* (1988), for example, it was a frequent practice to "punish" one who had killed another by adopting the offender into the dead man's family, by forcing him essentially to take the dead man's place.[23] The carrying out of this extraordinary kinship obligation was a matter of function—a means of honoring the lost life and meeting the dead man's family responsibilities while the killer was at once profoundly shamed and offered the opportunity of redemption. Both *House Made of Dawn* and *Ceremony* likewise defy conventional patterns of conflict/resolution that drive much of the Western canon. The lack of resolution resulting from the death of the albino and, especially, the surprising bend of *Ceremony's* conclusion attest that the ideal of individual and communal balance on which harmonious social function depends is not attained through unsanctioned confrontations of physical violence. Maintaining and, in the context of its disruption, restoring that balance require an ongoing ceremonial process crucially concerning the entire group, not an isolated event or singular individual act. As we have seen, Ku'oosh can counsel Tayo, but he cannot heal him by traditional means because modern warfare has involved Tayo in a sort of destruction far more complicated than the straightforward killing of an enemy in battle. But cured he must be: "It is important to all of us," the traditional healer Ku'oosh tells him. "Not only for your sake but for this fragile world" (36).

The narrative's first half, then, is a presentation of what has gone wrong not only for Tayo but for his original world. The second half, beginning with Josiah's decision to buy the spotted cattle—representing independence, endurance, and faith in the future and the mysterious knowledge possessed by the Night Swan and passed on to Tayo— recounts an increasingly complex but coherent ceremonial process created out of tradition but also responding to the changing circumstances of contemporary life. This process encompasses more and more of Tayo's internal and external environment and culminates in his growing realization of the critical part he is playing in a profoundly larger story of personal and universal survival. From the mixed-blood medicine man Betonie and the woman/spirit Ts'eh, he comes to understand that a pattern of destruction has been building since long before his birth, a pattern engendered at the most elemental level by white greed and the powerlessness of Native Americans in the face of it, translated into shame and self-hatred. Within this pattern, his mother's stories and his aunt's, Emo's and Harley's, and his own are related and clarified. "This has been going on for a long long time now. It's up to you. Don't let them stop you. Don't let them finish off this world," warns Betonie, enlarging Ku'oosh's caution that Tayo's situation and fate are inextricably intertwined with everyone's (152). In this narrative and even more radically in *The Almanac of the Dead* (1991), Silko's vision transcends ideologies of red and white: old-time cures and ceremonies, unmitigated by change, cannot break the pattern laid out by the "rocks with veins of green and yellow and black," the uranium whose discovery and use in World War

II charges the story's particular time and place (137). The war then is presented as both a major event and a mere opening salvo within this pattern, an escalation building toward a global destruction prefigured by Hiroshima and Nagasaki.

Silko contends that a restoration of functional tribal life must first reconstruct responsibility and agency: the white world is mere tool, not source. The mixed-blood medicine man Betonie says, "That is the trickery of the witchcraft. They want us to believe all evil resides with white people. Then we will look no further to see what is really happening. They want us to separate ourselves from white people, to be ignorant and helpless as we watch our own destruction. But white people are only tools that the witchery manipulates; and I tell you that we can deal with white people, with their machines and their beliefs" (132). Tayo's personal reclamation of agency and responsibility, self-knowledge and control, evolves through an incremental series of encounters and events. He is first strengthened by Betonie's blending of cultural wisdom and ritual. Next, his decision to recover Josiah's cattle leads him to Ts'eh, whose first and last names associate her with the sacred mountain and illuminate her identity as spirit guide. Through her he is reconnected to the mother, the land, and given access to the understanding and acceptance necessary to play out his part in the ongoing mythic-historical story that Silko and the Pueblo deity Thought Woman are telling simultaneously. Warned by Ts'eh of what is to come, hunted by Emo and the others in the mountains one hundred miles from Los Alamos,

> He had arrived at the point of convergence where the fate of all living things, and even the earth, had been laid. From the jungles of his dreaming, he recognized why the Japanese voices had merged with Laguna voices, with Josiah's voice and Rocky's voice; the lines of cultures and worlds were drawn in flat dark lines on fine sand, converging in the middle of witchery's final ceremonial sand painting. From that time on, human beings were one clan again, united by the fate the destroyers planned for all of them, for all living things. . . . He had only to complete this night, to keep the story out of reach of the destroyers for a few more hours, and their witchery would turn, upon itself, upon them. (246–47)

The mystical dimension of this passage translates into specific human behavior. To "complete the night"—to preserve himself and his human clan—Tayo must finally do nothing, resisting the temptation to meet Emo's violence with violence. He must further renounce guilt and shame, not only for his refusal to act violently in the present, which keeps him from avenging Emo's murder of Harley. He must also let go of his guilt for what has happened in the past—holding himself responsible for Rocky's and Josiah's deaths—and for his people's subjugation. Otherwise, as he comes to understand, he would simply become another Indian victim unable to survive in a white man's world. And among his own people, "the blame on the whites would never match the vehemence the people would keep in their own bellies, reserving the greatest bitterness and blame for themselves, for one of themselves they could not save" (253). At the climactic moment in *Ceremony*, there is no climax, no Ramboesque face-off between Tayo and Emo, no screwdriver through the brain to provide the conventional resolution. Instead, at sunrise, Tayo simply follows the railroad tracks back to the pueblo, apparently to take up a personally and communally functional life herding and breeding the spotted cattle, tending the medicine plants as Ts'eh has shown him, and significantly, adding his story to the cultural wisdom of the group by telling it to the elders in the kiva. The other veterans get their assorted just deserts, especially Emo, who ends up in California—ironically, "a good place for him" (260). As does Momaday's, Silko's telling circles back in the way of the oral tradition to its beginning—to sunrise, prayer, and acknowledgment of the ongoingness and interdependence of time, place, and people. The conclusion suggests only temporary respite, but at least for the moment, for this American Indian young man reconnected to his significant postwar time and place, the damage of the war and the larger cultural threat the war represents are diminished by a restoration of internal balance within the traditions of home culture.

By telling the stories as they do, Momaday and Silko create an ideological counternarrative of the consequences of "American" wars for American Indian people very different from the story told from the dominant perspective. Their versions display the problematic unreality of an equitably plural, inclusive wartime and postwar society. In these books and in the real lives of hundreds of individuals and families like the Artishons—including two of my own uncles who returned from the war but never really came home—assimilation was never an attainable American dream. Importantly, though, a fair scrutiny will reveal in these lives and stories of lives more than new chapters of exploitation. The Ojibwe writer Ignatia Broker, for example, describing wartime urban relocation, speaks of overcrowding and discrimination, but she also refuses the role of victim by recasting the experience as an affirmation of her own values as a Native person: "This was how we got a toehold in urban areas—by helping each other. Perhaps this is the way nonmaterialistic people do. We were a sharing people and our tribal traits were still with us. . . . I think now that maybe it was a good thing, the migration of our people to the urban areas during the war years because there, amongst the millions of people, we were brought to a brotherhood."[24]

More than two decades after the war, in narratives that attempt a seamless bonding of past and present social realities, Momaday and Silko reconstruct the consequences of World War II to argue for internal agency and cultural renewal. Choctaw critic Louis Owens asserts the falsity for American Indian narrative of Bakhtin's conception that in literature the tragic hero is powerless to transcend the destiny he has been assigned by fate.[25] Acknowledging intersections of tragedy and convergence, American Indians have long experience in sometimes living out, sometimes reshaping, the destinies constructed for them by white people's wars.

Notes

1. My thanks to Rose Artishon Scott and her family for allowing me to tell part of the story she relates in "Claiming My Anishinabe," a senior report submitted to Native American Educational Services College, Minneapolis, Minnesota (1993).

2. Ibid., 8.

3. See, for example, Silko's "Tony's Story," in *Storyteller* (New York, 1981), 123–29; Simon Ortiz's "The Killing of a State Cop," in *The Man to Send Rain Clouds: Contemporary Stories by American Indians*, ed. Kenneth Rosen (New York, 1975), 101–8; Louise Erdrich's treatment of Russell Kashpaw in *The Beet Queen* (New York, 1986) and Henry Lamartine in *Love Medicine* (New York, 1984); most recently, see Jim Northrup's *Walking the Rez Road* (Stillwater, Minn., 1993).

4. Gerald Nash, *The American West Transformed* (Lincoln, Neb., 1985), 129.

5. Henry Luce, *The American Century* (New York, 1941), 38–39.

6. Alan Sorkin, *American Indians and Federal Aid* (Washington, D.C., 1971).

7. J. G. Townsend, "Indian Health—Past, Present, and Future," in *The Changing Indian,* ed. Oliver LaFarge (Norman, Okla., 1942), 28–41.

8. *Annual Report of the Secretary for the Interior* (Washington, D.C., 1945), 229.

9. Alison R. Bernstein, *American Indians In World War II: Toward a New Era in Indian Affairs* (Norman, Okla., 1991), 40, 61.

10. Ibid., 40.

11. *Annual Report of the Secretary for the Interior* (Washington, D.C., 1944), 237.

12. Bernstein, *American Indians in World War II,* 150.

13. Oliver LaFarge, "They Were Good Enough for the Army," *Harper's,* November 1947, 444–49.

14. Bill Ashcroft et al., *The Empire Writes Back: Theory and Practice in Post-colonial Empires* (New York, 1989), 8–9.

15. Laura Coltelli, *Winged Words: American Indian Writers Speak* (Lincoln, Neb., 1990), 94.

16. Nash, *American West Transformed,* 147.

17. N. Scott Momaday, *House Made of Dawn* (New York, 1969), 7. Succeeding page references are given in the text.

18. *Annual Report of the Secretary for the Interior* (Washington, D.C., 1943), 294.

19. Simon Ortiz, "The Killing of a State Cop," 101–8.

20. Per Seyersted, "Two Interviews with Leslie Marmon Silko," *American Studies in Scandinavia,* 13 (1981): 28.

21. Coltelli, *Winged Words,* 140.

22. Leslie Marmon Silko, *Ceremony* (New York, 1977), 36–37. Succeeding page references are given in the text.

23. Ella Cara Deloria, *Waterlily* (Lincoln, Neb., 1988).

24. Ignatia Broker, *Night Flying Woman* (Saint Paul, Minn., 1983), 5.

25. Louis Owens, *Other Destinies: Understanding the American Indian Novel* (Norman, Okla., 1992), 18.

PART

4

Mobilization for Change

Susan E. Hirsch

TEN

No Victory at the Workplace: Women and Minorities at Pullman during World War II

For years this company had utilized every known and conceivable method to defeat any attempt of the workers to organize—they had pitted nationality against nationality—race against race—divide and rule, that was it! As long as they could maintain disunity and racial strife, they could continue to print the rules and regulations governing employment in their plants.

The *Keel*

Exulting that the "Pullman Dynasty Falls" in 1944 when the United Steelworkers of America won a representation election at the Pullman Car Works,[1] workers pinpointed the key to this company's anti-union strategy. For fifty years since the famous Pullman Strike of 1894, the company had employed divide and conquer tactics, differing from other corporations only in the greater sophistication and success of its efforts. The Pullman Company, like many others, however, found World War II to be a turning point. Building on the unity of races and ethnic groups achieved in the late 1930s, unions made great gains during World War II, when government oversight forced employers to hold open and honest elections and to bargain with representatives of the workers' choosing. On the home front, the war made many workers' dreams of greater power at the workplace seem within reach.

The union gains of the war period brought a new prosperity and security to millions of American workers, black and white, female and male. The divisions and inequities of the past did not disappear, however. Workers continued to view victory at the workplace in different terms. As the unemployment of the depression years faded and America entered the war, African American men and women called for the Double V, victory over racism at home and abroad. They wanted not only more jobs, but also equal access to the good jobs through an end to discrimination. The rhetoric of a war against racism encouraged the black activism that had begun in the New Deal to flower into the first mass movement for civil rights. Although there was no comparable women's movement for greater rights or equality, individual women also looked forward to new opportunities during the war to get jobs that paid men's wages instead of the 40 percent less they usually received for "women's work."

By 1943 the war-induced labor shortage and the power of the federal government together had compelled corporations to hire women and minorities in semiskilled and skilled blue-collar jobs that previously had been the preserve of white men. White women also found entry into clerical jobs that had been "men's work." Yet many of these new opportunities did not outlast the war, and none brought true equality. The forces for change were not strong enough to overcome traditional patterns of employment or beliefs about the proper place of women and minorities. Minority men, especially black men, made some permanent gains in semiskilled and skilled industrial work during the war, but Rosie the Riveter was sent home again in 1945 and 1946. White women retained their new clerical jobs, but companies continued to discriminate against qualified minority men and women in the office.[2]

Workers' aspirations for change foundered on the rock of corporate decision making. Hiring and promotion patterns in American corporations had been shaped by prejudice and the struggle between management and labor for control of the workplace. These factors continued to influence management decision making during the war. The resulting stalemate redirected black activism toward targets other than fair employment and contained female aspirations within the "pink-collar ghetto." Workers experienced similar situations at workplaces nationwide, but centers of African American employment like the Pullman Company were particularly important to the outcome of the conflict.

The Pullman Company was both a microcosm of the employment possibilities for Americans during the war and a key site of black activism.[3] Pullman was a multinational corporation that manufactured railcars and ran the sleeping car service on American, Mexican, and Canadian railroads. Because of its diverse activities, the company hired an exceptionally wide variety of employees. Its offices needed clerical workers of all types, while its repair shops hired skilled craftsmen from blacksmiths and electricians to painters and upholsterers. Its manufacturing plants hired thousands of steelworkers, and service workers such as porters and car cleaners maintained the trains themselves. Because it had offices, train yards, repair shops, and manufacturing plants all over the United States, the company had the opportunity to hire workers from virtually every ethnic and racial group in the country.

At the beginning of the war, the Pullman workforce was highly segmented by race and gender, reflecting patterns that predominated in other major American corporations. Pullman's white male managers shared the prejudices of other white middle-class men. They hired only whites for office or supervisory positions; they believed that blacks and other racial minorities made good servants, and they hired them preferentially in service positions. Thus all Pullman conductors were white, but all the porters who worked under them were black. Pullman managers also believed that women had no mechanical or leadership abilities. They preferred men for skilled repair shop work and hired women in Pullman offices only in dead-end jobs. The clerical jobs that led upward to management were reserved for men.[4]

Prejudice was not the only factor that determined who got what job, however. Management also had made its decisions as part of a strategy to retain control of the workplace. The company continually looked for ways to impede unionization by its employees. Under government supervision of the railroads during World War I, the American Federation of Labor railroad unions had organized Pullman shopcraft workers and conductors. Pullman porters and manufacturing workers also tried to unionize. In breaking the railroad shopcraft strike of 1922, the Pullman Company decided to hire black and other minority men in new jobs to undercut labor organizing among white workers. Whereas most corporations hired minority men only in unskilled blue-collar jobs, the strength of unions in the railroad industry induced Pullman management to go further. It integrated its repair shops, hiring hundreds of black men and training them for every skilled job from blacksmith to upholsterer. In 1927 Pullman's management made it clear that this reflected no change of heart toward equality for the races. According to Sterling Spero and Abram Harris, "In spite of the fact that it finds this labor perfectly satisfactory, the executives of the company stated they would continue to use Negro labor only as long as it was unorganized."[5]

If the Pullman Company was like other corporations in many ways, in one way it was unique. It was the largest single employer of black labor for much of the twentieth century, and its manipulation of African American workers was a key spur to black labor activism. In the 1920s the company gave hundreds of black workers in its repair shops opportunities unparalleled in American industry, but it treated its thousands of black porters like second-class citizens. Whereas the black shopworkers toiled in integrated settings and received the same wages as white workers, the porters were stigmatized by race, treated as separate and unequal. The porters' job was dead-end, since only white men could become conductors. Their base pay was not a living wage, and they had to rely on tips from customers to survive.

During the 1920s the company's antiunion racial strategy worked; Pullman's black shopworkers supported the company-dominated employee representation plan. Although they were grateful for the opportunities they received, however, African American shopworkers also came to expect to be treated according to the rules in the contracts that the plan established: wage rates set by job classifications rather than prejudice, and layoffs, recalls, and promotions based on seniority, not skin color. The strategy of segregation began to backfire as Pullman porters started to challenge the company to overcome their second-class status. In 1925 a group of porters along with socialist organizer A. Philip Randolph founded the Brotherhood of Sleeping Car Porters. The Brotherhood's strategy of self-organization and black empowerment reflected the increasing militancy found in African American communities in the North and the growing belief among black workers that they had to organize themselves and could not rely on white unions. It also reflected the segregationist policies of the Pullman Company, which confined most of its black workers to separate and unequal jobs. The militantly racial and class-conscious stance of the Brotherhood made it the center of black activism in the American labor movement. It achieved success in the first union representation election held under New Deal auspices in 1935, when it won a vast majority of the votes of Pullman's porters and maids. That the first Pullman workers to successfully challenge the company's nonunion status after 1922 were black did not go unnoticed by management.[6]

During World War II the Pullman Company found that its black workers continued to be the best organized and most militant of its employees, challenging not only the company's policies but those of the federal government. In 1940 when the Roosevelt administration asked for a peacetime draft, A. Philip Randolph, president of the Brotherhood of Sleeping Car Porters, opposed it. He believed that in a wartime buildup "minority groups [would] be helpless to prosecute and fight for democratic rights and privileges" and that it would "paralyze and break up the trade union movement, because it [would] sweep away all the safeguards of collective bargaining."[7] When the draft seemed certain of passage, Randolph and the union changed tactics and demanded an end to segregation in the armed forces and equal access to defense jobs. Randolph used Brotherhood locals, composed primarily of Pullman workers, to create the base of the March on Washington Movement that organized African Americans nationwide to press for equal employment in the defense industry. To get Randolph to cancel the planned march of 100,000 people, President Roosevelt issued the first executive order mandating that federal contractors like Pullman hire without discrimination. Roosevelt also established the President's Committee on Fair Employment Practice (FEPC) to monitor the situation and handle complaints. Significantly, Milton P. Webster, president of the Brotherhood's Chicago local, was a member of the committee. Moreover, the FEPC chose the railroad industry, including the Pullman Company, as one of its major targets.[8] As the United States entered World War II, the Pullman Company's long history of manipulating and exploiting black workers was bearing some very strange fruit indeed.

Within the company, black workers began to protest the deviations from true equality that they had previously accepted. In 1940 a black upholsterer in the repair shops, who had been among the first hired after the 1922 strike, accused his foreman of discrimination in assigning overtime. The shop manager threatened the upholsterer with a thirty-day suspension for insubordination unless he retracted the charge. The man refused and took the suspension.[9] Black workers did not have to fight all their battles alone, however. White workers began to support their complaints. During the war, for example, when the United Steelworkers of America first organized Pullman manufacturing plants in the Chicago area, white union leaders protested management discrimination against "colored" workers in calculating seniority.[10]

The limitations of a black movement for equality that had few allies outside the labor movement and focused on workplace issues were evident even during the war, however. The issue that created the most sustained discussions between representatives of Pullman employees and management about what equality should mean was that of reduced-rate passes for train travel for workers and their families. This was a traditional fringe benefit for workers in railroad operations. Although the company paid equal wages to white and black shopworkers, it had denied this benefit to black workers. This saved the company money, but more important, it allowed the company to respect the Jim Crow practices of the South. Since most of Pullman's black workers and their families would have used such passes to visit relatives there, the company itself would have been integrating its sleeping cars in defiance of southern law and custom. David Knox, the black representative from the Saint Louis repair shop workers, first raised this issue during negotiations between management and the company union for the repair shops in 1937. He demanded that black shopmen get the same transportation benefits as whites for travel through states that did not have legal segregation.[11]

The military buildup in 1941 brought to a head the restiveness of the black shopmen and the porters on this issue and extended the demand for equality in new directions. Because of Jim Crow laws, large numbers of porters who transported troops to southern bases were denied sleeping berths and had to sit up all night in coaches on the return trip North. Black shopmen demanded the Pullman Company take "Americanism" seriously and stop discriminating. As Knox said, "It is quite a thing in our shops for a man to be working right alongside another fellow and he is granted one thing and by reason of your color, you are denied the same thing."[12] A white representative from Buffalo, Stanley Meyer, seconded those sentiments: "There are men there that have boys in the service whom they would like to visit. They wonder if they do visit a son in camp, and they are told they have to stay in the day coach all night because they are denied the privilege of riding in the Pullman car, how the son who is in service will feel toward the country he is being trained to defend."[13] Management insisted, however, that the company could not change unless the country did, and neither the company union for the repair shops nor the Brotherhood of Sleeping Car Porters was strong enough to force the company to integrate its sleeping cars. Only the Civil Rights Act of 1964 would bring an end to Jim Crow laws and the segregation of Pullman cars.

In the midst of demands by black workers for equity, World War II placed great pressures on Pullman's employment strategies. The Pullman Company played a vital role in the war effort by transporting troops throughout North America. The demands of troop travel swelled employment; in only one year, from 1942 to 1943, the workforce in Pullman's railroad operations expanded from 24,000 to 31,000 employees, an increase of 29 percent.[14] The war created a demand for new workers of all types, beginning with porters and car cleaners. As the company hired more African American workers in these traditionally black jobs, it estimated that 51 percent of the employees in its railroad operating division were "colored." The company also lost many white skilled workers from its repair shops. They left for jobs in defense plants that paid higher wages than Pullman or other railroad companies. In addition, the company experienced a wholesale loss of white male clerical workers to the draft. Although the federal government exempted skilled workers in defense industries from the draft, it deemed male clerical workers replaceable. As its manufacturing plants converted to defense production, the company needed even more workers. The company's recruitment problems mirrored those of other firms, being most severe in areas of great labor shortage—those with the highest concentration of defense industries.[15]

Despite the level of black militancy, the company continued to reserve porter positions for black men. Officials still believed that "the Negro race" had "excellent adaptability" to the servant role.[16] They became, however, much more selective about which black workers they hired. A 1941 company memo decreed that no West Indians were to be considered for new porter positions, perhaps because several of the earliest Brotherhood leaders were West Indian.[17] Men who had attended college were no longer desirable, nor was "a light complexioned man" to be hired. In the 1920s Pullman's white managers and white passengers might well have felt superior to any "colored" man. Now Pullman's management had been challenged by those men and had lost, and black demands for equality were insistent. Thus the company drew the color line more carefully and reinforced it by selecting for lesser educational attainment in hopes that these men would be more docile.

In other jobs, the company had less interest in hiring minorities or women during the war than it had in the past. The militancy of the Brotherhood of Sleeping Car Porters and the cooperation between white and black workers destroyed any hope of using black workers to undercut unionization. Furthermore, the company could not use women or minorities as cheap labor in blue-collar jobs in its yards and repair shops. Management had signed contracts with company unions on wages, benefits, and job descriptions in order to weaken organizing drives by AFL and CIO unions among Pullman workers. When women and minorities held no special attraction, the company sought to retain the hiring patterns that favored white males. In its repair shops, for instance, Pullman management dropped its bar on hiring employees over age forty-five. At the Richmond, California, repair shop, where the labor shortage was most severe, management turned to sixteen- and seventeen-year-old white boys to fill the gap.[18] There were never enough white men, however, and 90 percent of the teenagers quit the shop before the war ended to take jobs elsewhere.

The Pullman Company was not alone in hesitating to hire more black workers; most American corporations attempted to hold the line. Progress was slow, and the Fair Employment Practice Committee had little power to force change. But as labor shortages became critical, minority men at last began to leave the unskilled industrial jobs they had held since World War I for better-paying semiskilled and skilled positions. When all the men were taken, corporations began to hire women. For the Pullman Company the critical point came in late 1943; then, like other firms, it was forced to open new positions to women and minorities.[19]

At this point black men made more inroads into the ranks of skilled repair shop workers. Management designed a training program to produce skilled workers from helpers in one month, and current helpers were given the first chance of applying. In this way helpers, white or black, who had been stymied in their upward mobility in the 1930s became skilled shopmen.[20] Management did not throw all jobs open to new groups of workers, however, but continued to define as many jobs as possible in racial or gender terms. In the repair shop storerooms, where parts, tools, and materials were stockpiled, the company allowed black men into the jobs of packer and stockkeeper, but it continued to deny them other clerical positions.[21]

By 1946, 25 percent of the Pullman shop force was "nonwhite," and virtually all of these workers were black. Nonwhites held the greatest number of jobs in the South and the fewest in California, which in general accorded with their proportion of the local population (table

Table 10.1
Repair Shop Employees, 1946

Shop	Excepted[a]		Clerical		Mechanical		Total	
	N	% NW[b]	N	% NW	N	% NW	N	% NW
Atlanta	40	0.0	49	10.2	493	42.0	582	36.4
Buffalo	68	1.5	74	4.1	1,023	19.0	1,165	17.0
Chicago	88	0.0	120	2.5	1,061	14.0	1,269	12.0
Richmond	41	0.0	51	3.9	536	13.6	628	11.9
Saint Louis	58	10.3	66	0.0	600	57.8	724	48.8
Wilmington	37	0.0	46	4.3	568	22.4	651	19.8
Total	332	2.1	406	4.0	4,281	25.2	5,019	22.3

Source: Table, "Breakdown of Repair Shops Employees as of June 21, 1946," from Office of Assistant Vice President, in file "1946 Representation Dispute," Pullman Archives, Newberry Library.
[a]Excepted = supervisory employees from foremen to managers.
[b]NW = nonwhite.

10.1). Only in Saint Louis and Buffalo were the proportions of nonwhites employed at Pullman shops much greater than their proportion of the general population.[22] And only in these cities did any nonwhites become supervisors. Virtually all clerical workers remained white also, since management opened new opportunities only when there was no alternative.

Many corporations blamed their discriminatory racial practices on their workers. Corporate executives argued that they were deferring to the wishes of white workers, who resented working with blacks, and there is certainly evidence of this resentment. In some of the best-known incidents during World War II white autoworkers in Detroit staged "hate strikes" against new black workers.[23] According to one management report, there were no serious problems of race relations between Pullman's white and black workers in the railroad operations. This calm may well have been kept, however, only because toilets, dressing rooms, and the like were segregated at the southern shops and yards.[24] Where the company violated Jim Crow norms, white workers did react. At the Pullman manufacturing plant in Birmingham, Alabama, white machinists walked off the job when a black man was put on a boring machine, previously a "white" job.[25]

Nevertheless, the pressure of white workers was not the major source of discriminatory practices at Pullman. Although the number of black shopworkers increased at Pullman from 885 in 1941 to 1,097 in 1946, this 24 percent increase pales beside the inroads blacks made in the

1920s.[26] When management used black men to undercut unions in the 1920s, hundreds more were hired. Although Pullman officials stated that black workers produced just as well as white workers, they were not eager to hire them now that they were no longer a bulwark against unionism.[27]

Despite their hesitancy about black men, Pullman managers, like those elsewhere, looked to women last when they needed more workers in blue-collar jobs, because they doubted women's ability to do the work. Management defined skilled work in both racial and gender terms, as most appropriate for white men, but gender was the fundamental criterion. As the memo announcing the trainee program declared: "We cannot expect Trainees to turn out the same quantity or quality of work as a mechanic of long experience. This is especially true of women, outside of certain jobs which require dexterity."[28] In the view of Pullman officials, women had nimble fingers and hence could sew or type, but management doubted their ability to master anything else. Managers viewed women workers as qualitatively different from men. For instance, they expected greater absenteeism from women than men and believed women would need special attention from supervisors. The company instituted "an increasingly progressive handling of relations with women employees" in 1944, appointing two women to the new jobs of women's counselor and women's consultant.[29] These positions were analogous to the black welfare workers hired in the 1920s when the company first brought black men into its repair shops and still regarded them as needing significantly different supervision than white men.

Pullman management might have been interested in women as cheap labor, but the contracts with the company unions in the repair shops and yards specifying the rates for jobs irrespective of who held them made it impossible to save on blue-collar wages there. The only inequality in wages in the shops and yards dated back to the nineteenth century, when the company set the wage rate for the sole woman's job—seamstress—well below that of the comparably skilled man's job of upholsterer. Every year beginning in 1937 the company union demanded that the seamstresses be paid the same rate as the upholsterers and that the seamstresses' female leaders be paid monthly salaries equal to male work leaders'.[30] Although company negotiators sometimes rejected equal pay for the seamstresses by questioning their skill, the reason most often cited was the financial one. As long as seamstresses' pay in other companies was low, Pullman would not pay them more.

Where not hampered by unions, the Pullman Company, like many other employers, refused to pay women wages equal to men's. The National War Labor Board did not mandate equal pay for women, but merely permitted employers to raise women's wages to equalize them with men's if they so desired. Few employers did. Nationally the gap between men's and women's wages actually widened during the war, although sometimes unions were able to force equality. The United Steelworkers of America forced the Pullman Company to pay equal wages at its armaments plants in the first union contract in 1944. According to the union negotiator, this was one of the two demands that the company resisted most strongly.[31]

Given management prejudice and the inability to use them as cheap labor, only in late 1943 did Pullman begin to bring women into the craft trainee program in the repair shops. Where labor shortages were most severe, women became a large percentage of those hired during the war. Like the new men hired for mechanical work, women began as laborers and then were promoted to the helper level. Women rarely became mechanics, however, because the older employees had been given the first opportunities for upgrading.[32] In the repair shops, women's opportunities were greatest in Richmond, California, where the labor shortage was most acute. In Pullman Standard manufacturing plants, where the labor shortage also was critical, women made more inroads, especially in welding, as they did at other defense plants.[33]

The management prejudices and strategies that created employment patterns had their most negative impact on black women. Nationally white women had access to much better jobs than minority women did, and the war did little to change this. White women got the best of the new opportunities, while minority women had a very difficult time leaving service jobs for even unskilled industrial work. Pullman management also maintained its preference for white women. Black women got work that previously had been black men's, as car cleaners, janitors, and train porterettes.[34] They found some jobs at Pullman's Calumet Harbor shipyard, but they were not hired into the craft trainee program in the repair shops despite the large number of black men who were already craftsmen.

Although management prejudice was the major obstacle to new jobs for women, male workers were at best ambivalent toward greater equity. The union contract in the Pullman repair shops and yards assured women equal pay for their work, but the company union did not fight for their right to long-term employment. In general, government, industry, and male-dominated unions sought to maintain the customary roles of men and women in the labor market. Women were hired in blue-collar jobs that previously had been reserved for men, but only for the duration of the emergency; they had to sign away their rights to accumulate seniority and hence to future employment.[35] Women hired as "emergency employees" at Pullman could accumulate seniority, but it counted only for the duration of the conflict. Any man hired during the war was a regular employee, governed by the usual union rules.

The limited gains women made in blue-collar jobs, however, did not mean the war had little impact on their employment. When the federal government refused to exempt male clerks from the draft, companies across the nation turned to women to fill the void. From 1920 to 1940 the clerical workforce nationally had remained evenly divided, almost half male and half female. It was the war that made clerical work a predominantly female occupation.[36] Women became clerical workers in Pullman storerooms for the first time and increased their numbers in accounting and managerial offices. Although women got new jobs in the office during the war, male managers continued to resist hiring women in supervisory positions.[37]

The relative ease with which women filtered into new office jobs was caused at least in part by management's ability to use them as cheap labor. Unlike its shopworkers and porters, Pullman clerical workers did not have a contract providing a set wage rate for each job irrespective of who held it. As they replaced men with women, Pullman management began paying "office boys" and "junior clerks" less than before. A management representative explained that as long as "we can get plenty of girls to come to work for the Pullman Company in beginning jobs, such as sorting tickets, diagrams, and so forth at $86 a month" they would do so.[38] Very few clerical workers were unionized, and most employers took advantage of the labor shortage to hire more women in the office at lower wages.

If white women found new opportunities in offices across the country, those offices generally maintained their color bars throughout the war.

The Pullman Company, for instance, had refused to hire black men or women for office work, even though it had been pressured to do so as early as the 1910s.[39] Gender may have been the fundamental criterion for blue-collar work at Pullman, but race was the key factor in the office. By 1946 only 4 percent of the clerical workers in its repair shops were nonwhite (table 10.1), and the company worked actively to keep minorities out of its other offices regardless of their qualifications. One of the first charges against the company for violation of fair employment practice, for example, was brought in 1943 by a man of Filipino background who applied to be a clerk in the central office accounting department in Chicago. The employment agent admitted to him that the company needed "male clerks" but referred him to the commissary department, the Filipino ghetto in the Pullman Company. An internal company memo on this case suggests the validity of his charge of discrimination: "I think it rather dangerous to say that [X] did not possess the necessary qualifications, particularly in view of his educational background. His application states that he is a graduate of Loyola University."[40] Pullman officials realized that if the FEPC were successful in prosecuting such cases things would change, and that "we will have colored girls, and probably men, in our clerical forces."[41]

Just as black women found fewer opportunities than white women in blue-collar work, they also faced greater discrimination in the office.[42] Another of the complaints to the FEPC in 1943 involved two black women who answered newspaper advertisements for jobs as checkers (a clerical position) in Pullman's commissary department. They were informed that the company did not hire Negroes in those positions and were referred to jobs as car washers.[43] Internal company memos support their charge of discrimination. Executive Vice President Champ Carry wrote, "It is a fact that we have had applications from colored girls for checkers, and there is no question that they are qualified as far as education is concerned." He then revealed the underlying causes for this policy: "Personally, I have no great feeling about whether we should hire colored commissary checkers, but the difficulty comes in the fact that once we do hire them they immediately acquire seniority in the clerks' organization, and there is no telling where they will eventually end up in the organization . . . so we might as well face the fact squarely that they could appear in almost any office in the Company."[44] If black workers could be kept in low-level, dead-end jobs, as they had been as porters and maids, they would be hired. A structure of internal promotion and seniority in the office had developed decades earlier, however. A complete color bar was the only way to keep minority men or women from rising in the clerical ranks and hence to protect top management or white customers from having to interact with minority employees in nonmenial positions. In most companies the combination of management preference and concern for the feelings of white customers kept the color bars up.

When the war ended, some black men found that the gains they had made in semiskilled and skilled work were permanent.[45] At Pullman, black men kept their new positions in the storerooms of the shops and yards, and the company announced in July 1945 that "even if all the Pullman shop employees now in the armed services were rehired, the Company still would need additional workers."[46] The need for troop transport would continue throughout demobilization, and the Pullman Company did not have to cut back. At other companies, some minority men did not have enough seniority to maintain their positions when layoffs and cutbacks hit during reconversion. In 1946 and 1947, when the Pullman Company was still hiring new workers, many black men came to the company as opportunities elsewhere again disappeared.[47] After 1948, however, Pullman, along with other passenger railroads, went into steep decline and provided few opportunities for workers white or black. The biggest problem for minority men after the war was the lack of continued progress at other firms because of the death of the FEPC.[48]

Women who had entered men's jobs in the shops and yards at Pullman, like women who took defense jobs elsewhere, did not fare so well. Across the country, management pushed women out of the factories, sometimes with the acquiescence of male unionists, sometimes without. Most women shopworkers had been hired as "emergency employees" at Pullman, and their seniority counted only for the duration of the war. Although the Pullman Company was actively recruiting new workers for its repair shops, the head of the Brotherhood of Railway Carmen noted that "female employees are being laid off wherever the company can employ males to take their places."[49] Furthermore, although the company continued to hire women for clerical jobs it did not hire them anew into helper or mechanic positions. By 1947 there were only four women electricians in all the Pullman shops and none in the yards, although this had been one of the most common uses for women workers during the war.[50] Some Pullman women wanted to stay in their new jobs. One black woman train porterette told her union newspaper she felt that "this avenue of employment should remain open not on the basis of sex, but on the basis of the ability to do the job."[51]

For the company to make an exception in hiring, a woman had to be an outstanding worker and to have the backing of the union representative. When workers were needed at the Chicago repair shop in 1947, the union shop committeeman requested that the company rehire one of the women war workers, although "we understand the management attitude toward hiring women for mechanical work."[52] When asked, her foreman recommended her highly, but he had not requested her reemployment of his own accord. In another case a manager noted that a specific woman mechanic "can produce as much work as a man."[53] These few individual instances did not change the company's preference for men in mechanical tasks, however, nor did the war experience change its policy toward paying women workers as little as possible. In 1946 Pullman shops were having difficulty securing enough seamstresses, but the company continued to refuse to raise their wage rate. Instead managers requested that they be allowed to hire women over age forty-five, since no young women were applying for this difficult and strenuous job that paid so little.[54]

The place where women made permanent gains, both at Pullman and at other companies, was in the office, not the factory. The postwar increase in labor force participation by white married women, which changed the historical pattern of women's employment outside the home, was predicated on the expansion of opportunities in clerical work.[55] Rosie the Riveter might have been laid off, but she and her sisters often went right back to work in offices. On the other hand, the continued discrimination against black men and women in the office contributed to the relative lack of economic progress for black families after the war. Neither black men nor black women had access to the new growth areas for jobs—managerial and clerical employment.

The progress toward equality for women and minorities that was made during the war could be sustained only with continued pressure from government and labor unions. When the war ended government support was withdrawn. A coalition of Republicans and white southern Democrats scuttled war labor boards and the FEPC as quickly as possible. In addition, after 1947 the unions were on the defensive because of the attempt by major manufacturers to roll back wartime gains, the anticommunist crusade, and the destructive competition between the AFL and the CIO.[56] Only the more broadly based Civil Rights movement of the 1950s and the women's movement of the 1960s would again bring change.

Yet if there was no victory at the workplace, World War II did have a great impact on women and minorities, though one that analysts searching for female electricians and black office workers overlook. The black men who retained semiskilled and skilled jobs—usually unionized jobs—became the core of a stable working class in postwar African American communities. Their experiences of discrimination and of success made them active participants in keeping alive the demand for equality of opportunity and expanded civil rights in the difficult years of the cold war. These men also played a critical role in providing support for a generation of urban black youth, who could take advantage of the educational and job opportunities eventually opened under the pressure of the Civil Rights movement. The unique role of this generation of black industrial workers has become clearer since the 1970s. The decimation of the industries in which they worked has left urban African American communities without a solid base for either a political movement to address economic needs or the physical resources to support a new generation of black youth.

The impact of the economic opportunities that World War II opened for white women was equally significant, if even more elusive to cursory analysis. The white women who left home for the office belied the stereotype of the feminine mystique. Their families came to see working mothers in a more positive light as their income made possible a more affluent lifestyle, including college educations for both daughters and sons. These women's criticism of their low-wage, dead-end jobs did not lead them to make public demands or to unionize. They voiced their discontent in private, where it powerfully influenced their daughters to prepare for and demand more for themselves.

Notes

Research for this chapter was funded by the National Endowment for the Humanities and the National Science Foundation as part of a larger project examining job segregation by ethnicity, race, and sex in the Pullman repair shops. I thank Janice Reiff, my collaborator on that project, for her part in collecting and analyzing the quantitative data this analysis is based on. Support from the Newberry Library and Loyola University of Chicago also aided me in writing this essay.

Since the research for this project was completed, the Newberry Library has cataloged the Pullman Archives. No box numbers are given in these notes, since all have been changed during cataloging.

1. "Pullman Dynasty Falls," *Keel* (CIO News for and by workers at the Calumet Harbor Shipyards), 28 January 1944, 1–2. This article is the source of the chapter epigraph.

2. Major works on women and minorities in wartime employment include Karen Anderson, *Wartime Women: Sex Roles, Family Relations, and the Status of Women during World War II* (Westport, Conn., 1981); Alice Kessler-Harris, *Out to Work: A History of Wage-Earning Women in the U.S.* (New York, 1982); Ruth Milkman, *Gender at Work: The Dynamics of Job Segregation by Sex during World War II* (Urbana, Ill., 1987); Herbert Northrup et al., *Negro Employment in Land and Air Transport* (Philadelphia, 1971); Robert Ozanne, *The Negro in the Farm Equipment and Construction Machinery Industries* (Philadelphia, 1972).

3. In 1940 the legal name of the corporation was Pullman, Inc. This was a holding company for the Pullman Company, which ran the railroad operating service, and the Pullman Standard Car Manufacturing Company, which built railcars. In both the popular press and historical literature, however, these distinctions are rarely made, and I will refer to the entire enterprise as the Pullman Company.

4. Susan E. Hirsch, "Rethinking the Sexual Division of Labor: Pullman Repair Shops, 1900–1969," *Radical History Review* 35 (1986): 26–48.

5. Sterling Spero and Abram Harris, *The Black Worker: The Negro and the Labor Movement* (New York, 1931), 309.

6. William H. Harris, *Keeping the Faith: A. Philip Randolph, Milton P. Webster, and the Brotherhood of Sleeping Car Porters, 1925–37* (Urbana, Ill., 1977); Susan E. Hirsch, "Job Segregation and Labor Relations in the Pullman Company, 1890–1970," unpublished manuscript, chap. 4.

7. "Sleeping Car Porters' Head Opposed to Peace-time Draft," *Federation News* (Chicago Federation of Labor), 2 September 1940.

8. Howard W. Risher, "The Negro in the Railroad Industry," in

Northrup et al., *Negro Employment in Land and Air Transport*, 59–64; Jervis Anderson, A. *Philip Randolph: A Biographical Portrait* (New York, 1972), 5–6, 243–48; Herbert Garfinkel, *When Negroes March: The March on Washington Movement in the Organizational Politics for FEPC* (New York, 1959).

9. Letter from Charles Gartelman to C. W. Pflager, 11 April 1940, in employee records of number 101, Calumet Shop, Pullman Archives, Newberry Library (hereafter PANL).

10. Proceedings before Arbitrator, Pullman Standard Car Manufacturing Company and United Steelworkers of America Local 2534, re Lester Thaden and Joseph Dunning, 297–98, United Steel Workers of America Papers, 108–11, Chicago Historical Society (hereafter USWA-CHS).

11. Proceedings, Meeting of Representatives of the Pullman Car Employes Association of the Repair Shops and the Pullman Company, 1937, 275–76; Proceedings, 1940, 205–6, PANL.

12. Proceedings, 1941, 219, PANL.

13. Ibid., 222.

14. "Statement 1—Pullman Company Payrolls, May 21, 1943," in file "1943 Increase"; Proceedings, 1941, 81; Confidential Inquiry for the benefit of the Personnel Officers Working Group, prepared by H. Guilbert, 27 November 1943, in file "Fair Employment Practice Act," PANL.

15. Pullman experienced its greatest problem with labor turnover in its Richmond, California, repair shop. Richmond, whose Kaiser-Bechtel shipyards hired 90,000 workers in one year, was the country's premier example of a defense boomtown with an insatiable demand for more workers. Minute Book F, Board of Directors meeting 17 June 1942, 895–96; memo from H. R. Lary to Champ Carry, 20 October 1942, 2, in file "1943 Increase"; letter from H. R. Lary, M. R. Wendt, and C. H. Poole Jr. to Champ Carry, 16 March 1943, in file "Rates of Pay—Shop Employes"; memo of L. R. Hyry, 3 May 1948, in employment records of numbers 102 and 103, Calumet Shop; Proceedings, 1940, 136, 153; Proceedings, 1941, 22–23, 44, 82, PANL. Joseph Whitnah, *A History of Richmond, California* (Richmond, Calif., 1944), 118–23.

16. Letter from L. M. Greenlaw to Hotterman Rauch, Director, Fair Employment Division, Wisconsin Industrial Commission, 1 August 1946, in file "Fair Employment Practice Act," PANL.

17. "Memorandum of features to be considered in the employment

of new porters," 27 January 1941, in file "Fair Employment Practice Act," PANL.

18. File, "Employment—Overage Reports"; memo from C. Gartelman to C. W. Pflager, 26 February 1943, in employee records of number 104, Calumet Shop, PANL. Twenty-one percent of wartime hires at the Calumet Shop in Chicago were forty-five or over; 35 percent of the wartime hires at the Richmond Shop were under eighteen. At Richmond and at the Wilmington, Delaware, shop, all new hires under eighteen were white; at Calumet, 83 percent were white. Statistics for workers at three shops—Richmond, California; Wilmington, Delaware; and Chicago, Illinois (Calumet)—from samples of employee records at the Newberry Library. For information on the samples see Susan Hirsch and Janice Reiff, "Job Segregation and the Replication of Local Social Hierarchies," in *Essays from the Lowell Conference on Industrial History, 1982 and 1983,* ed. Robert Wieble (North Andover, Mass., 1985).

19. Risher, "Negro in the Railroad Industry," 74, notes that this increase in black and female employment was common on the railroads despite discrimination. At the Calumet Shop 30 percent of new men hired during the war were black compared with 20 percent before the war. At the Wilmington Shop, where the company had less need for new workers, black hiring remained stationary at 18 percent.

20. General Letter to All Repair Shops, from C. W. Pflager, 9 September 1943, PANL.

21. These were the only clerical jobs for which black men were hired at Calumet, and they had never been hired in these positions before the war.

22. In those cities the proportion of nonwhites at Pullman was almost three times the proportion of nonwhites in the local population. What accounts for these variations is not clear.

23. Philip Foner, *Organized Labor and the Black Worker, 1619–1981* (New York, 1981), 254–59.

24. Confidential Inquiry for the Benefit of the Personnel Officers Working Group, by H. Guilbert, 27 November 1943, PANL.

25. Copy Memo to George Johnson, Assistant Executive Secretary, Committee on Fair Employment Practice from John Beecher, Field Representative, 15 April 1942, 2, Brotherhood of Sleeping Car Porters papers, box 21–22, Chicago Historical Society (hereafter BSCP-CHS).

26. Table, "Breakdown of Repair Shops Employes as of June 21,

1946," from Office of Assistant Vice President, in file "1946 Representation Dispute"; Proceedings, 1941, 221, PANL.

27. Confidential Inquiry, H. Guilbert, 27 November 1943, PANL.

28. General Letter to All Repair Shops from C. W. Pflager, 9 September 1943, 2, PANL.

29. *Pullman News,* January 1944, 103; letter of C. Gartelman to C. W. Pflager, 20 April 1945, in employee records of number 105, Calumet Shop, PANL.

30. Proceedings, 1937, 200–202; Proceedings, 1941, 173; "Employees Proposals to the Company, 1944," in file "Repair Shops, Vacation Agreement," 1–2, PANL.

31. Official Report of Proceedings, National War Labor Board, Case 111-5948-D, 22 February 1944, 12, 160–29, USWA-CHS. Ruth Milkman, "Female Factory Labor and Industrial Structure," *Politics and Society* 12 (1983): 180–81; Anderson, *Wartime Women,* 56; Kessler-Harris, *Out to Work,* 289.

32. Women were 41 percent of wartime hires at Calumet, 22 percent at Richmond, but only 7 percent at Wilmington, which was not experiencing a severe labor shortage. Only 1 percent of the women hired at Calumet rose to the mechanic level, but 17 percent of those at Richmond did.

33. See numerous pictures and articles in the *Pullman Standard Log* or the *Carbuilder* during the war, and Radio Script, USWA CIO Station KJOB Hammond, 19 January 1944, 184–83, USWA-CHS.

34. Karen Anderson, "Last Hired, First Fired: Black Women Workers during World War II," *Journal of American History* 69 (1982): 82–97; "Sister Maggie Hudson," *Black Worker* 10 (October 1944): 5; various pictures and articles, *Pullman Standard Log.* Martha Dennis vs. the Pullman Company and R. Bucherati, General Foreman, Case CSF-12682-66, State of New York, State Commission for Human Rights, in file "Boston Discrimination File," PANL. According to our samples, virtually no black women were hired during the war at any of the repair shops.

35. Kessler-Harris, *Out to Work,* 289; Hirsch, "Rethinking the Sexual Division of Labor," 38; Michael Nash, "Women and the Pennsylvania Railroad: The World War II Years," *Labor History* 30 (1989): 608–21.

36. U.S. Bureau of the Census, *Historical Statistics of the United States,* part 1 (Washington, D.C., 1975), 139–40.

37. A Pullman shop manager even replaced the one traditionally female supervisor, the forewoman of the seamstresses, with a part-time male leader, despite outcries by the workers and a protest by the company union. Proceedings, 1938, 14, PANL. New jobs for women at Calumet were office boy, stockkeeper, packer, stock record clerk, messenger, and junior clerk.

38. Proceedings, 1942, 20, PANL.

39. "Julius Avendorph, Who Is Doing Things for His Race," *Chicago Defender*, 22 January 1921.

40. Memo from M. R. Wendt to L. M. Greenlaw, 19 June 1943, in file "Fair Employment Practice Act," PANL.

41. Letter from Champ Carry to David Crawford, 15 October 1943, in file "Fair Employment Practice Act," PANL.

42. Anderson, "Last Hired, First Fired," 84–89.

43. Letter from Elmer A. Henderson, regional director, President's Committee on Fair Employment Practice to Louis Taylor, Vice President, Pullman Company, 20 October 1943, and letter from Champ Carry to David Crawford, 15 October 1943 in file "Fair Employment Practice Act," PANL.

44. Letter from Champ Carry to D. A. Crawford, 27 October 1943, in file "Fair Employment Practice Act," PANL.

45. Risher, "Negro in the Railroad Industry," 74. Black men may have made more permanent gains on the railroads than in other industries such as steel. See Edward Greer, *Big Steel: Black Politics and Corporate Power in Gary, Indiana* (New York, 1979), 94.

46. *Pullman News*, July 1945, 21.

47. There were virtually no layoffs before 1948 at Pullman shops. At Richmond the proportion of new hires who were black rose to 23 percent; at Wilmington to 35 percent; at Calumet to 49 percent.

48. See especially Risher, "Negro in the Railroad Industry," and Michael Reich, *Racial Inequality: A Political-Economic Analysis* (Princeton, 1981).

49. Letter from Felix Knight, General President, Brotherhood of Railway Carmen of America, to "Pullman Crew," 27 July 1945, box 8, AFL Railway Employes Department, Records 1917–70, Labor-Management Documentation Center, Cornell University.

50. "Summary of Discussions . . . IBEW . . . Dec. 1947," 56, PANL. Nancy Gabin, *Feminism in the Labor Movement: Women and the United*

Auto Workers, 1935–1975 (Ithaca, N.Y., 1990), chap. 3. At Calumet, 55 percent of women hired during the war left during it and another 28 percent left during reconversion. The comparable statistics for men were 14 percent and 7 percent. Most of these were voluntary quits, but during reconversion when no men were laid off, 25 percent of women who left the shop were laid off or discharged. Women's percentage of new hires during reconversion at Calumet was down to 16 percent, and 61 percent of these were hired in clerical jobs. At Richmond, women were 5 percent of new hires after the war; at Wilmington, they were 2 percent.

51. "Sister Maggie Hudson," *Black Worker*, 10 (October 1944): 5. Sherrie Kassoudji and Laura Dresser argue that it was older housewives, African American women, and those who had been service workers who most wanted to keep their wartime jobs in "Working Class Rosies: Women Industrial Workers during World War II," *Journal of Economic History* 52 (1992): 431–46.

52. Letter from E. A. Iles to C. Gartelman, 7 January 1947, in employee records of number 106, Calumet Shop, PANL.

53. Letter from D. M. Cohee, Manager, to L. F. Munson, 30 October 1953, attached to general file card of number 107, Wilmington Shop, PANL.

54. Memos from C. Gartelman to C. W. Pflager, 4 September 1946 and 10 September 1946, in employment records of number 108, Calumet Shop, PANL.

55. Valerie K. Oppenheimer, *The Female Labor Force in the United States* (Westport, Conn., 1970), chap. 5. Only the post office and some other government bodies hired any sizable number of black clerical workers before the 1960s.

56. The bitter fight between AFL and CIO unions for railroad workers weakened the Brotherhood of Sleeping Car Porters and is documented in the volumes of the *Black Worker* throughout the 1940s. For the decline of a working-class civil rights movement within the CIO see Robert Korstad and Nelson Lichtenstein, "Opportunities Found and Lost: Labor, Radicals, and the Early Civil Rights Movement," *Journal of American History* 75 (1988): 786–811.

Shirley Ann Wilson Moore

ELEVEN

Traditions from Home: African Americans in Wartime Richmond, California

Before the tumultuous events of 7 December 1941 thrust the United States into World War II, Richmond, California, was a sleepy coastal city of 23,000 people on the east side of the San Francisco Bay. Although Richmond's prewar population consisted largely of native-born whites who controlled the city's political and commercial life, European immigrants also made up a substantial percentage of the population. People of color, including Japanese Americans, Chinese Americans, Mexican Americans, and Native Americans, numbered fewer than 500 in 1940. The African American population in Richmond climbed from 29 in 1910 to 270 in 1940.[1]

Before World War II Richmond was no more than a dot on the map. Since its incorporation in 1905, the city had languished in the shadow of cosmopolitan San Francisco, fifteen miles across the bay, and Oakland, the major East Bay city some twenty miles to the south. Richmond's mild climate, deep harbor, and vast tracts of unused land, however, made it ripe for commercial and industrial exploitation. Thus city founders pursued a dream of becoming the industrial giant of the Pacific Coast. By its first decade the city seemed well on the way toward its goal, as important businesses including Standard Oil, the Santa Fe Railroad, and the Pullman Company located there and Richmond's industrial base became a powerful labor magnet attracting workers from all over the Bay Area. Early on, Richmond gained a reputation as a "workingman's town" and boasted that its "mechanics and laborers are not transient" but stable, dependable, and productive.[2] African Americans also were drawn by Richmond's employment possibilities and joined their white counterparts in seeking work in the "Pittsburgh of the West."

However, they and other "nonwhites" encountered workplace discrimination and segregation that consigned them to the lowest, most menial occupations. An editorial in the *Richmond Record* of 7 July 1900 described the racial hierarchy that existed in the city's businesses and industries: "There are no Japanese at work for the Santa Fe about Point Richmond [the original industrial center of Richmond]. The Chinese are limited to cooks at the boarding camps. White men have full sway here." Such attitudes and practices also plagued African Americans within and outside the workplace. The city's largest industry, Standard Oil, did not employ black workers at all. Those who found industrial employment performed the most arduous jobs with little chance for advancement. One black prewar resident recalled that "if you were just brute strength, they would hire you for lifting pieces of steel, but if you had a little bit of education, they would not hire you." Many would be paid "whatever they thought you was worth." African American women fared no better. Before the war most black women who "weren't too old" worked as domestic day workers in the homes of affluent whites in Oakland, San Francisco, and other Bay Area cities, earning two to five dollars a week. Those black women not engaged in domestic work sometimes found employment in Richmond's numerous produce and fish canneries, which relied heavily on female labor but provided only seasonal, low-paying work. They often worked alongside Filipina, Mexican, Portuguese, and Italian women sorting, pitting, and canning fruits, vegetables, fish, or other produce. Frequently black women seeking cannery work had to look outside the city, since Richmond's largest cannery, Filice and Perrelli, employed no black workers before the war.[3]

Black Richmondites also encountered racial barriers in other areas. Before the war African Americans generally lived scattered throughout the city and in rural North Richmond (an area lying partially outside the city limits, with inadequate lighting, few paved streets, and scant police and fire protection), where their neighbors included Italians, Portuguese, Mexicans, Chinese, and Japanese. A high proportion (about 50 percent) of Richmond's prewar population consisted of the foreign-born or first-generation citizens, and black children usually attended the same schools as whites. Therefore black Richmondites were part of a multicultural milieu that to a great extent shaped their social experiences before World War II. For example, in the 1910s and 1920s Walter Freeman Jr. recalled teaching English to the parents of his Italian playmates in North Richmond and learning to speak Italian from them. Similarly, Ivy Reid Lewis, whose family moved to Richmond from Oakland in the early 1930s, noted that she became bilingual in Spanish because she "played with the Mexican kids" and wanted to learn the language so she could join in their celebrations. She recalled that had it not been for the war bringing in more black people, she might "have married a Mexican or something" because there were few black men her age in North Richmond.[4]

This multicultural living environment was rapidly being limited, however, by race prejudice, avaricious land developers, and restrictive covenants. Within the first decades of the city's incorporation, Richmond real estate developers had begun inserting into property deeds and bills of sale clauses that excluded blacks from buying or inhabiting dwellings in certain areas of the city. In 1927 the Oakland-based black-owned *Western American* newspaper reported: "A realty firm subdividing outlying districts of Richmond, California, are broadcasting circulars stating that the property will not be sold [to] or occupied by Negroes nor Asiatics. The sponsors of this movement seem very earnest in their desires to create as much hatred and strife between the races as possible. They will probably argue that their plan is a stroke of good business."

Even before the war brought thousands of black newcomers to North Richmond, therefore, blacks were being concentrated. Blacks learned to accommodate to racial boundaries that were often invisible but nonetheless real. Stanley Nystrom, a white prewar resident, explained the physical divisions that separated blacks from whites before World War II: "In high school there was a handful of colored kids my age, but we were all one. They lived on their side of town, and we lived on our side. But that was because they wanted to live there."[5] However, Walter Freeman Jr., whose family moved to Richmond in 1915, recalled that those boundaries frequently bristled with racial tension: "I saw there's a [white] boy who [lived] between Lincoln and Sixth Street. They lived right around the corner from us. We was on this side of the track and he was on the other side. Every time we'd go that way to Peres [elementary] school, he'd come out and start something. . . . So him and my brother would go to fighting. . . . He just wanted to whip a white boy."[6]

Black accommodation to the racial status quo may have appeared as acceptance to most whites, but it was reinforced by the threat of physical violence and intimidation that lurked just beneath the surface of the city's seemingly placid race relations. For instance, as early as 1917 the

Ku Klux Klan was openly participating in Richmond's civic celebrations, parading down the main thoroughfares in full regalia and staging rallies and cross burnings in the hills and parks surrounding the city. In 1922 the powerful *Richmond Independent* went so far as to editorially endorse "freedom of association" for the Ku Klux Klan, proclaiming that "every free-born American citizen" had the right to "join a secret society every day of the year" because Americans as a people are "jiners."[7]

Despite these visible and covert constraints, however, black Richmondites, who numbered fewer than 300 in 1940, were able to establish a thriving and optimistic community in the years before the war. In 1918 their efforts created the first black church in all of Contra Costa County, North Richmond Missionary Baptist Church. By 1922 African Americans in the city had organized the Ashler Elks Lodge, which like the church, became a focal point for social, cultural, and political activities. These institutions and others provided a meeting place for black worship and for black mutual aid, benevolent, and charitable activities. Musical "entertainments" also became a mainstay of Richmond's black churches and social institutions, providing a welcoming and supportive environment for church choirs, solo performers, and professionally trained black musicians who derived a good deal of their livelihood from performing for black audiences.

Well before the war brought thousands of black newcomers, the Bay Area had become home to a community of accomplished African American musicians. Black instrumentalists, composers, and singers performed and taught virtually every genre from European classical music to opera, spirituals, gospel, jazz, and popular musical fare. Local black institutions often were the only places these artists could perform, although some won wider acclaim. For example, the great African American tenor Roland Hayes was discovered by the influential black East Bay women's organization, the Fannie Jackson Coppin Club, which had an active Richmond membership. Before becoming a popular stage and radio performer as the nationally renowned director of the WPA's Northern California "Colored Chorus," William Elmer Keeton did turnaway business at his Oakland music studio offering "instruction in piano, organ playing, courses in music, theory, harmony, counterpoint, form, analysis, history, composition and instrumentation" to Bay Area African Americans. Like Roland Hayes, he frequently performed in black churches in Richmond and throughout the Bay Area.[8]

Richmond's multicultural currents influenced African American secular musical traditions before the war and resulted in an eclectic musical environment. For example, blacks, whites, Mexicans, Italians, Portuguese, and Asians sometimes attended "polka dances" in the small taverns that had been established in North Richmond in the 1920s and 1930s. When not listening or dancing to music from the jukebox, black Richmondites often joined with their nonblack neighbors in providing the music in these taverns. Residents recall one such "shoestring operation" existing in North Richmond before World War II that was owned by a Mexican man. Local residents went there to socialize, listen to music, and dance. Ivy Reid Lewis recalls that as a child she learned to dance the polka by peeking into the tavern and watching the patrons dance. Thus, before the war the African American community in Richmond had developed a tradition of nurturing and showcasing black music and musicians—a tradition that was enriched by Richmond's diverse ethnic and racial population. Mildred Slocum, a resident of Richmond since the 1930s, noted that for many black Richmondites these cross-cultural currents were valuable aspects of "that California lifestyle."[9]

Everything changed, however, when Richmond developers persuaded industrialist Henry Kaiser to locate four shipyards in the city. Early in 1940 Kaiser won a lucrative government contract to construct British merchant ships for President Roosevelt's "arsenal of democracy," transforming Richmond, California, from a sleepy little town to a bustling and bulging city of over 120,000 at the center of America's war production industry.

Kaiser constructed four massive shipyards in Richmond, which boasted California's second-largest port. The Kaiser shipyards became omnipresent as the most important wartime industry in the Bay Area. Innovative shipyard assembly-line techniques and state-of-the-art mechanization allowed the shipyards to operate twenty-four hours a day and to turn out "liberty ships" at an astounding rate. Even those with few industrial skills became experts in performing one small job in the total shipbuilding process.

The Kaiser yards employed over 150,000 workers, 25 to 30 percent of whom were African American. Despite the persistence of racial tension and the discrimination black workers faced from fellow employees, Kaiser management, and racially restrictive unions, they streamed into

Richmond's shipyards, attracted by the pay, health and safety benefits, and the promise of greater freedom. As a result, Richmond's prewar black population of 270 increased by 5,000 percent by mid-1943.

Kaiser workers earned as much as $1.25 an hour on an eight-hour shift. These wages, however, generally were reserved for white workers, who were allowed to advance more readily from the unskilled labor category to the skilled and higher-paying shipyard occupations. Black workers encountered blatant discrimination from the powerful shipyard unions (most notably the Boilermakers' Union), which fiercely resisted admitting blacks. Black shipyard workers routinely were assigned to the lower-paying unskilled jobs, making about ninety cents an hour on an eight-hour shift. Approximately 80 percent of Kaiser's black workers were employed as unskilled or semiskilled trainees. Still, entry into this urban industrial labor force represented a significant economic shift upward for most African Americans.[10]

Black people who migrated to Richmond during these boom years generally came from the South (most commonly Texas, Arkansas, Mississippi, Louisiana, and Oklahoma), were young (23.13 years on average), included more women than men (53 percent to 47 percent), and usually were married.[11] Although most of the black migrants came from the South and Southwest as agricultural workers, many had worked in southern industrial positions and had attained considerable industrial skills. Thus some black workers who entered the Kaiser shipyards in Richmond were experienced as carpenters, machine operators, welders, and stonecutters, and others had some college or professional training. Their employment as unskilled workers represented a "downward thrust" in occupational status but usually meant a substantial boost in pay.[12]

Black migration to Richmond was motivated by a number of complex and interrelated economic, political, and social factors. The migration was accomplished through overlapping networks of friendship, kinship, and social and employment ties. Charles Henry Thurston, a newcomer from Jackson, Mississippi, had been a teacher and school principal in his home state, but he concluded that Richmond offered more promise than Mississippi. He and his brother arrived in Richmond in 1943 and went to work in the Ford Motor Company making military vehicles for "fifty or sixty dollars" a week, "vastly more" than his principal's salary. Similarly, a former lumber mill worker from Georgia was persuaded to move to Richmond by a co-worker who had already migrated there. His friend "wrote to me to come out here and get one of these defense jobs." Twenty-two-year-old Wilbur Wheat left his barbershop in Port Arthur, Texas, after a visit from an old acquaintance who cut an impressive figure with his "fine clothes, money and new car." Moreover, Wheat hoped that a move to Richmond shipyard work would keep him from the military draft: "I was a barber before the war and they was grabbing those guys left and right. I didn't want no part of that. . . . I could get me a defense job and make good money." So Wilbur and his wife, Vesper, headed out to Richmond, where he landed a job "picking up scraps" in Kaiser shipyard 2. Another Texan recalled that she set out for Richmond at the age of forty-two because "colored women don't have a chance for any kind of job" in Texas "except in somebody's kitchen working for two or three dollars a week." Shipyard employment, she believed, would improve her life. She joined thousands of other black migrants who resolved to break free of old ways and start life over in the Golden State. A former black sharecropper explained: "It looked like just about everybody was going into the army or doing war work [so] I sold my tools and mules and come out to Richmond."[13]

World War II encouraged the evolution of African Americans from a largely rural, agrarian population to an urban, industrial one. The war not only dispersed African Americans throughout the United States, but it also disseminated African American culture in the larger society. African American migrants from the South brought with them a strong desire for economic advancement and high hopes for a freer political and social life in California. However, although they hoped to leave behind the oppressive laws and customs of the Jim Crow South, few were willing to abandon the cultural and social traditions that had been nurtured in the southern, agrarian matrix. These "traditions from home" were firmly based in an African and African American ethos that valued communality, spontaneity, and emotional freedom. Blues music, a cultural expression of the black working class born out of this matrix, was one tradition they transported. Black migrants to Richmond brought along their love of this music and transplanted it into the new urban industrial environment. In the process they helped transform African American culture and society in Richmond and were themselves transformed.[14]

Their music came to symbolize much of Richmond's African American cultural character and provided channels of power for a people with little access to power. In the music and in the blues clubs of North Richmond, black working-class people found reassurance and sustenance in their new urban industrial environment. North Richmond's blues clubs of the 1940s and 1950s were less multicultural than the taverns and drinking establishments that had operated before the war. The new clubs attempted to cater to the cultural preferences of the wartime black newcomers and were less "sophisticated" than most of the popular "middle-class" nightclubs and cafés that sprang up on Oakland's Seventh Street and in San Francisco's Fillmore district. Eschewing the more subdued "cocktail piano" styles of these "uptown clubs," the blues establishments of North Richmond were "rough places which catered to a hard-drinking, fast-living black clientele." Unlike the clientele of the polished supper clubs of Oakland and San Francisco, North Richmond blues club patrons demanded music closer to their southern traditions, such as the blues of Muddy Waters, John Lee Hooker, and Howling Wolf. One observer noted that this music had a "slow draggier beat and a kinda mournful sound." The urban blues phrasing of electric guitars and "crying harps" proved to be the music of choice of the transplanted black southerners who lived and worked in Richmond. Thus, as more and more blacks moved in and whites increasingly left the city for the segregated housing developments that were springing up around the Bay Area, Richmond's cultural character became indelibly imprinted with black working-class musical tastes.[15]

Many Bay Area blacks referred to North Richmond's blues establishments as "honky-tonks," "juke joints," and "buckets of blood." The Savoy Club, on Chesley Street in North Richmond, was one of the city's most popular blues spots. Oklahoma-born blues guitarist Lowell Fulson did "extensive residency" at the Savoy Club in the late 1940s after moving to the Bay Area. He recalled that the club was a "one-room country shack," but it could accommodate about three hundred people at one time. The Savoy Club was owned and operated by Willie Mae "Granny" Johnson, an Arkansas migrant and the sister-in-law of Missouri blues pianist and singer Jimmy McCracklin. The Savoy hosted blues greats like Fulson, L. C. "Good Rocking" Robinson, and Jimmy McCracklin. Its decor resembled an old roadhouse, with oilcloth tablecloths on wooden tables. It had a room-length bar that sold beer and wine; patrons could buy Granny Johnson's home-cooked meals of greens, ribs, and chicken. Johnson was firmly in charge, doing all the cooking, bookkeeping, and hiring and firing. Lowell Fulson recalled that Johnson's husband, Deacon, worked a "day job. . .and didn't have anything to do with it." A house band, composed of Bay Area–based musicians like Fulson and Robinson, alternated with touring blues entertainers such as B. B. King, Charles Brown, and Jimmy McCracklin. In addition to the food and music, patrons could take their chances with the card and crap games that were familiar fixtures in the Savoy Club.[16] Jimmy McCracklin paid musical homage to the club in his postwar hit recording:

> Now Richmond, California, is a great little town
> And I live there and, Jack, I gets around.
> If you ever go there and you want to jump for joy,
> I'll tell you where to go—that's the Club Savoy. . . .
> Now everybody goes there to have some fun
> 'Cause the joint really jumps from nine to one.
> Around midnight everybody's higher than the moon
> 'Cause the band starts playing them dirty blues.[17]

Minnie Lue Nichols's club, "Minnie Lue's," also became a blues staple in North Richmond. A native of Atlanta, Georgia, Nichols moved to New York, where she worked as a cook in various restaurants in the early 1940s and perfected her culinary skills. She became acquainted with Richmond after frequent visits to relatives living in North Richmond during the war. Nichols moved there permanently in 1948 when she leased a restaurant and filled it with "customers [who] kept the jukebox going day and night." She opened her own place shortly afterward, and it was an immediate hit with Bay Area residents, newcomers and longtime residents alike. Her club became a showcase for local blues musicians and national celebrities like B. B. King, Bobby "Blue" Bland, Ray Charles, and James Brown. In addition to these musicians, Charles Brown, Sugar Pie DeSanto, and Jimmy McCracklin frequently played at Minnie Lue's. Minnie Lue's club became the first black establishment in the city of Richmond to obtain a full liquor license in 1958.[18]

Although Minnie Lue's club remained a community fixture until her death in 1983, Tappers Inn was the most popular night spot in North Richmond during the war years until its demise in the mid-1950s. Tappers Inn was owned by East Indian entrepreneur George Bally, known to local residents as "the Hindu." Tappers Inn offered black shipyard workers and others a variety of services including round-the-clock barber and beauty shops, a service station that operated all night, and a restaurant that served "southern style" food. Patrons recall that Tappers Inn was a "very lavish place." The highly polished rectangular bar was twenty-five feet long and sat in front of a tall mirror that reflected multi-colored lights. Red leather booths and tables spread with white linen cloths ringed the dance floor, which at times held over six hundred people. One patron recalled that "it got so crowded on weekends that we had to take the bar stools out and the people just stood three and four deep at the bar." Patrons jitterbugged and "slow dragged" out on the dance floor to the well-stocked jukebox or to live music played by people like Charles Brown, Jimmy Witherspoon, B. B. King, Mabel Scott, and Ivory Joe Hunter. Others engaged in card games like "tonk" poker and craps or played the illegal slot machines that were set up in the back room.[19]

These clubs and the more clandestine "after hours" clubs that proliferated in North Richmond were the secular equivalent of the numerous black storefront churches that mushroomed in wartime Richmond. Both institutions attracted black newcomers who insisted on retaining their southern cultural roots, with the devout preferring the uninhibited expressiveness found in the Pentecostal and "Holiness" churches and the less pious finding similar comfort in the music of the blues clubs. The clubs provided working-class African Americans with cultural channels through which they could interpret, comprehend, and cope with their surroundings and offered them a way to gain power even as the urban industrial setting tried to limit their access to it. Composer Olly Wilson has suggested that black Americans have managed to "retain some semblance of a unique identity" despite countervailing historical and sociological pressure by continually tapping into a basic store of African ways of creating music. These creative resources lie "buried deep in [the African American] collective psyche."[20] This revitalizing process has sustained waves of black migrants from 1619 to those who arrived in Richmond, California, during World War II. Like millions of European immigrants who streamed into American cities during the nineteenth and early twentieth centuries, the black newcomers pouring into Richmond from the rural and urban areas of the South in the 1940s used their traditions as a means to both transmit and sustain themselves within an environment that remained at best indifferent and at worst hostile to their being.[21]

The blues clubs represented a special place in the urban arena where African American newcomers could interact with others as both performers and patrons on a basis of equality.[22] Margaret Starks, an Arkansas migrant and former shipyard worker who served as a talent-booking agent for Tappers Inn and other clubs in North Richmond, explained the refuge these clubs provided: "Those people didn't have too much, so they weren't about to let go of the music and good times they were used to. It made them feel better. I remember one lady from Louisiana, had gold all in her mouth, told me that she loved to hear that music because listening to that music in Tappers made her forget all that stuff in the shipyards. She always felt better when she left."[23] Richmond's blues clubs, a few of which were owned or operated by black women, seemed to offer black working-class people psychological sustenance and cultural affirmation.

Blues musicians in Richmond, in the tradition of their southern predecessors, served as secular priests to the newcomers, inspiring admiration and loyalty. One Louisiana migrant and blues devotee declared: "I would follow a guitar player to hell!" Although the performers aroused passion among African American migrants and were the "symbols of their hopes and ambitions in the North," blues musicians in North Richmond clubs were never removed or aloof from their audiences. In keeping with African American musical and cultural tradition, the audience and performers engaged in spontaneous, improvisational give-and-take. Audience members might "sit in with the band" and frequently responded to the musical messages with cries of "Sing your song!" or "Tell it!" Minnie Lue Nichols described the camaraderie that developed in the clubs: "Well, if you've never felt the blues, I can't hardly explain. You know how it *feels!* It was a blues crowd, a beautiful crowd. When the house is full and they're rocking with members of the band, you just enjoy it!"[24]

North Richmond's blues clubs also provided many working-class African Americans with a social oasis where, in contrast to the outside world, the rules were straightforward and consistent. Blues club egalitarianism countered the inequality of "auxiliary" unions that kept black workers from higher-paying shipyard jobs, housing discrimination that confined them to cramped, substandard living conditions, and the blatant racism of "Negro Patrons Not Wanted" signs that greeted them in many of Richmond's downtown stores.[25]

The clubs also blunted some of the intraracial class conflict that pitted black newcomers against black longtime residents, who often characterized the migrants as "low-class," unsophisticated, uncouth troublemakers. Longtime black residents considered the blues clubs of North Richmond unsavory and devoid of middle-class respectability. Bill Thurston, son of a former school principal, was a teenager when he arrived in Richmond in 1944. He observed: "If someone of some kind of stature went out there, they'd generally have to sneak to go out there." During a surreptitious visit to Tappers Inn young Bill, an innocent bystander, was shot in the leg when gunplay erupted in the club that night. Firearms were so commonplace at Tappers Inn and other establishments in North Richmond, Margaret Starks observed, that "we used to have to check the guns and knives just like we did hats and coats." Patrons tended to subscribe to if not scrupulously honor the culture of egalitarianism that prevailed in North Richmond's blues clubs. Etiquette dictated that "it didn't matter what you did outside on your job or who you were. If you acted right, nobody was better than anybody else."[26] Even though the rough-and-tumble atmosphere of the North Richmond clubs implied lower-class status, many middle-class black people from surrounding Bay Area communities were drawn to them and interacted with black newcomers. A former Oakland resident from a prominent black Bay Area family noted, "That's where you went if you wanted to hear good music. Tappers Inn, that's where I went. Everybody came to Tappers Inn."

Aside from psychological sustenance, these establishments sometimes provided more pragmatic assistance to black migrants who, through their workplace and other experiences in Richmond, had become astute and assertive critics of the racial barriers that kept them economically and politically marginal. A few of North Richmond's blues clubs provided a place where African Americans could meet and plan how to breach these barriers. For example, in November 1944 the West Coast Regional Office of the National Association for the Advancement of Colored People (NAACP) opened its doors in San Francisco. That same year black newcomers William McKinney and Margaret Starks joined prewar Richmond resident and labor activist Cleophus Brown and other black Kaiser shipyard employees in founding the Richmond NAACP branch and locating its first office in the Harbor Gate housing project for shipyard workers. As secretary of the Richmond branch from 1944 through 1947, Margaret Starks conducted much of the chapter's business from the blues clubs she managed in North Richmond, because "everyone knew where to find me if they needed something or had something to tell me. Everyone came through those clubs. We plotted many strategies there." Starks noted that many of the NAACP-led store desegregation campaigns of the late 1940s and early 1950s were planned in her office at Tappers Inn. The Richmond NAACP became the fastest-growing branch in the western region, with newcomers taking leadership positions. The organization's first priority became breaking down the Jim Crow policies of the shipyard unions and dismantling housing discrimination.[27]

In addition to providing a springboard for attacks on Jim Crow, Richmond's blues clubs appear to have been one area where black men and women could exercise authority and achieve some economic and social autonomy in their lives by regulating white access to their community. The clubs attracted a significant white clientele, drawn by the music and the "exotic" atmosphere of the area, including illicit activities like gambling and prostitution.[28] As a result, black club owners and operators established the rules by which whites could gain entry into their world. Margaret Starks, who earned a reputation as the "mayor of North Richmond," explained how white club patrons were handled: "Well, the whites were scared to come out here. The blacks didn't allow them just to come out here anytime. If they came out, they said they were Mexicans. A taxi couldn't bring them. I didn't allow a white taxi cab company out here because they were prejudiced. . . . When whites came, I told them to come 'round through the back."

Some black Richmondites also operated more clandestine and transitory "after hours" clubs that catered to black and white clientele and commonly operated out of private homes. Here blues "jams" featured musicians from all over the Bay Area. Patrons could purchase home cooked meals, liquor flowed, and gambling and prostitution were often featured attractions in these establishments. Although most served a racially mixed clientele, a few catered to whites only and arranged sexual liaisons with prostitutes of various races.

As the shipyards and other wartime industries began to pull out of Richmond by 1946 and a thousand workers a day were thrown out of jobs, most blacks could not sustain the economic rise they had enjoyed during the war. Although Richmond's white power structure hoped that most black residents would now "go back where they came from," blacks had no intention of leaving. Therefore the economic function of North

Richmond's blues and after hours clubs became even more crucial for the African American community. Unemployed black shipyard workers turned to club owners for economic assistance and employment. The clubs often served as informal employment agencies. Although this effort could not begin to meet the need in the community, on a small scale the clubs provided employment for a cross section of African Americans, from musicians, bartenders, and cooks to bookkeepers and security guards. Minnie Lue's and Tappers Inn "kept some fellows with money in their pocket[s]," by providing them with "little sweeping up jobs and things like that." Even in the relatively hard economic times of the postwar years, Richmond's black population continued to grow as the white population shrank, and African American music became one of Richmond's most prominent cultural expressions.[29]

The winds of change were blowing, however, and would touch every facet of African American life, including black musical expression and the blues clubs in Richmond. Participation in the war effort had heightened blacks' awareness of their economic and political potential as first-class citizens. The Supreme Court's 1954 ruling that overturned the Jim Crow doctrine of "separate but equal" appeared to signal a significant fissure in the seemingly impregnable wall of legal segregation. Moreover, the movement of such large numbers of black people from the South to the urban centers of the North and West enlarged economic, political, and social possibilities for African Americans. In the urban industrial arena, however difficult the conditions, the sheer mass of new people seen every day and the speed of events brought an ever-changing face to the world black people now lived in. All this contributed to the feeling that "the past was falling away" and life's fundamentals had indeed been altered. No matter how frustrating the realities might be, migration and wartime participation convinced many blacks that "where there was change there was hope." Black Richmondites along with their counterparts across the country had begun to mount aggressive legal attacks on all facets of racial discrimination and segregation. As early as 1943 black Kaiser shipyard workers had established an ad hoc committee, Shipyard Workers against Discrimination, which led to the Supreme Court decision outlawing auxiliary unions in *James v. Marinship* in 1945. Richmond's NAACP had become a vital community focal point, serving as an articulate and aggressive advocate for black newcomers and longtime residents alike. One black Richmondite reflected on the changes: "It was exciting, fun to be with all different types of people. I really felt free." Finally, by the mid-1950s almost 5 percent of Richmond's black population of 13,374 were under age twenty-five (the percentage was even higher in other black communities in the Bay Area) and thus too young to have had any direct experience with the South. Therefore by the late 1940s and 1950s, as black newcomers started to establish themselves in Richmond, new attitudes began to emerge in the African American community there and elsewhere.[30]

These changes also affected the musical expressions of African Americans as blues music gave way to rhythm and blues (R&B). Blues, with its southern agrarian base, now seemed anachronistic in the fast-paced, industrialized cities of postwar America. The quickened beat, amplified volume, and more commercial lyrics of R&B seemed to point to the future. The blues musicians who had become staples in Richmond's clubs during the war years either adapted to the new sensibilities and "cleaned up their act" or waned in popularity. Bobby Bland and B. B. King symbolized that postwar transition, as one African American observer noted: "They're mellow, man. . . . Well, B. B.'s cleaned up the blues; they've refined it, so it's smooth and easy—no harps, moaning, or shit like that. Those guys have brought the blues up to date—made it modern."[31]

The rhythm and blues musicians who emerged in the postwar period were younger and urban born, and with their flamboyant attire, polished stage presentation, and amplified instruments, they seemed to reflect and confirm the new hopefulness and assertiveness in their music. They employed "honking" saxophones to augment the traditional piano, drums, and guitars. Guitarists like Aaron "T-Bone" Walker and Bo Diddley often would play their electric guitars behind their backs, over their heads, or with their teeth as if to proclaim their fearlessness of and mastery over the new technology of the postwar era. What remained, however, was the communal nature and function of the music and clubs in Richmond. For example, even if R&B entertainers performed separated from their audience by the stage, costumes, lighting, and other show business trappings, they attempted to bridge the distance by shaking hands, hurling pieces of clothing into the crowd, or leaping into the audience from the stage. These R&B rituals made the performance more intimate and linked performer and audience, in keeping with African ways of making music.

By the early 1960s, however, the popularity of blues and R&B began to wane both in Richmond and throughout the country. As the Civil Rights movement evolved into more militant articulations of black power and black pride, African American musical expressions also evolved. The southern, agrarian communal experience implicit in blues and R&B gave way as African Americans, now solidly "urbanized," began to formulate a broader definition of community. Their wartime experiences had made them a part of a national and international community of "people of color" with similar goals and aspirations. The global impact of World War II and the cold war political maneuvering that propelled Third World countries onto the world stage began to enlarge the perceptions of African Americans. Musically, the urban experiences and aspirations of black America found a voice in the polished, sophisticated sounds being turned out by black performers recording for the Motown label, for example. These performers, with their costumes and meticulous choreography, spoke to the hopes and dreams of an urban, upwardly mobile black population. By the early 1960s only a few North Richmond blues clubs remained. A postwar law-enforcement crackdown on gambling and vice shut down many clubs, but more important, the changes in the political and social mood of black America eroded the significance of blues and R&B in Richmond. The cross-cultural popularity and wide commercial dissemination of soul artists and soul music by record companies and television undercut the importance of blues clubs as cultural refuges. Soul music became accepted in the mass popular culture. Ollie Freeman, a resident of North Richmond since 1929 and owner of Jazzland, a popular record store in North Richmond in the 1950s, explained the decline of blues in Richmond: "People are seeking a little different class of night life. . . . Today there has come a different trend in music. People watch TV and accept a different class of entertainment. If they can't go out and find this type of excitement for themselves, they don't want this other thing. They label it lowbrow. 'I don't want my kid to listen to that crud,' they will say. 'That blues sickens me. I don't want no blues.'"[32]

By the early 1960s blacks who had come to work in Richmond's war industries over a decade before were no longer newcomers. Their determination to realize the "California dream" had helped to revitalize Richmond's black community and initiated the dismantling of the racial barriers that stood in the way. The pursuits of these black working-class people underscored how profoundly World War II migration had transformed their personal and collective lives. The cultural traditions that they transported were themselves transformed to reflect the realities of the new urban industrial environment that most African Americans now called home.

Notes

1. United States Department of Commerce, Bureau of the Census, *Thirteenth Census of the United States (1910), Statistics for California Supplement* (Washington, D.C., 1913), 118, 614; United States Department of Commerce, Bureau of the Census, *Fourteenth Census of the United States, 1920,* "Population," 3 (Washington, D.C., 1923), 118–19; United States Department of Commerce, Bureau of the Census, *Fifteenth Census of the United States, 1930,* "Population," 3, part 1 (Washington, D.C., 1933); United States Department of Commerce, Bureau of the Census, *Sixteenth Census of the United States, 1940,* "Population," 2 (Washington, D.C., 1943), 610.

2. Joseph C. Whitnah, *A History of Richmond, California: The City That Grew from a Rancho* (Richmond, Calif., 1944), 8, 18–31, 46–48, 78; Susan D. Cole, *Richmond: Windows to the Past* (Richmond, Calif., 1980), 51–52; *Richmond Independent,* "Woman's Edition," Richmond Historical Association, 1910, 8, 15, 17, 21; Evan Griffins, *Early History of Richmond, Contra Costa County, California,* unpublished manuscript, Richmond Museum, December 1938, suppl., December 1939, 5–6.

3. Irene Batchan, Richmond resident since 1926, interview by author, 14 September 1985; Lawrence P. Crouchett, Lonnie G. Bunchy III, and Martha Kendall Winnacker, *Visions toward Tomorrow: The History of the East Bay Afro-American Community, 1852–1977* (Oakland, Calif., 1989), 17–19.

4. *Thirteenth Census,* "Statistics for California Supplement," 582–614; *Fourteenth Census,* "Population," 3, 118–19; *Fifteenth Census,* "Population," 3, part 1; *Sixteenth Census,* "Population," 2, 610; Walter Freeman Jr., interview by author, 28 November 1987; Ivy Reid Lewis, interview by author, 29 July 1987; also see Robert Wenkert, *An Historical Digest of Negro-White Relations in Richmond, California* (Berkeley, Calif., 1967), 11–16.

5. *Colored Directory of the Leading Cities of Northern California*

(Oakland, Calif., 1916), 70; *Oakland Western American,* 29 April 1927, 1; *West [Contra Costa] Times,* 20 January 1986; Franklin N. Williams, "Keepers of the Wall," *Frontier,* April 1960: 9–10; Stanley Nystrom, interview by author, 31 July 1986.

6. Walter Freeman Jr., Richmond resident since 1915, interview by author, 28 November 1987.

7. *Richmond Independent,* 16 June 1922, 1; Whitnah, *History of Richmond,* 67–68; Dr. Lawrence Crouchett, former director, Northern California Center for Afro-American History and Life, Oakland, California interview by author, September 1987; Walter Freeman Jr., interview by author, 28 November 1987.

8. See the University of California, Bancroft Library collection, YMCA, Oakland, California, Linden Branch, Miscellaneous Publications, pamphlets 1–3, especially the program "The House Committee of the Linden Street Y.M.C.A. Presents Roena Eloise Mucklely soprano assisted by Eugene Anderson, Tenor, with Elmer Keeton accompanist, June 24, 1926." The selections included pieces by Handel, Verdi, Schubert, and Burleigh and an original work, "Weep No More, Sad Fountain," by Elmer Keeton. The program was presented in Oakland's Fifteenth Street African Methodist Episcopal Church. See also Michael Fried, "Sing It, When You Can't Tell It," unpublished manuscript, Michael Fried/Public Interest Films, 1994, 7, 10, 14–22, 36–39; and "There Was Real Jazz at Tenth and MacDonald," *Richmond Terminal,* 14 January 1921, which describes black jazz musicians from West Oakland performing for the white Elk lodge in Richmond: "Those colored folks from West Oakland can beat all comers in dispensing this modern article so popular now with the musical (and non-musical) public."

9. Walter Freeman Jr., interview by author, 28 November 1987; Ivy Reid Lewis, interview by author, 29 July 1987; Mildred Slocum, interview by author, 17 November 1987.

10. Shirley Ann Moore, "Getting There, Being There: African American Migration to Richmond, California, 1910–1945," in *The Great Migration in Historical Perspective: New Dimensions of Race, Class, and Gender,* ed. Joe William Trotter (Bloomington, Ind., 1991), 111, 118–20.

11. Charles S. Johnson, *The Negro War Worker in San Francisco* (San Francisco, 1944), 5–7.

12. Cy W. Record, "Characteristics of Some Unemployed Negro Shipyard Workers in Richmond, California," unpublished manuscript,

Library of Economic Research, University of California, September 1947, 19–21, 26, 32.

13. William Thurston, son of Charles Henry Thurston, interview by author, 19 September 1983; Wilbur Wheat, interview by author, 24 January 1987; Record, "Characteristics of Some Unemployed Negro Shipyard Workers," 9, 30, 31.

14. Burton W. Peretti, *The Creation of Jazz: Music, Race, and Culture in Urban America* (Urbana, Ill., 1992), 15–17; George Lipsitz, *Time Passages: Collective Memory and American Popular Culture* (Minneapolis, Minn., 1994), 116–18; Olly Wilson, "The Significance of the Relationship between Afro-American Music and West African Music," *Black Perspective in Music* 2 (1974): 3–22. See especially page 19. Also see Olly Wilson, "Black Music as an Art Form," *Black Music Research Journal* 4 (1983): 2–3; LeRoi Jones [Amiri Baraka], *Blues People: The Negro Experience in White America and the Music That Developed from It* (New York, 1963), 95–140.

15. Robert W. Stephen, "Soul: A Historical Reconstruction of Continuity and Change in Black Popular Music," *Black Perspective in Music* 12 (1984): 25; Robert Springer, "The Regulatory Function of the Blues," *Black Perspective in Music* 4 (1977): 278–87; William Ferris Jr., "Racial Repertoires among Blues Performers," *Ethnomusicology* 14 (1970): 439–49. Virginia Rose, black Oakland resident since the 1920s, interview by author, 2 January 1984; Lee Hildebrand, "Oakland Blues," n.d., 3 (article in the personal collection of Bob Geddins, Oakland, California).

16. Hildebrand, "Oakland Blues," 3; Lee Hildebrand, "North Richmond Blues," *East Bay Express,* 9 February 1979, 1; Bill Thurston, interview by author, 8 September 1983; Margaret Starks, interview by author, 29 June 1988; Tilghman Press, *We Also Serve* (Berkeley, Calif., 1945), 59, 61, 66; Tilghman Press, *We Also Serve: Armed Forces Edition* (Berkeley, Calif., 1945), 38; Joseph Malbrough, Richmond resident since 1926, interview by author, 18 August 1985; Sheldon Harris, *Blues Who's Who: A Biographical Dictionary of Blues Singers* (New Rochelle, N.Y., 1979), 188–90; Lowell Fulson, interview by author, 21 January 1993.

17. Lyric quoted in Hildebrand, "North Richmond Blues," 1.

18. Eldreadge Wright, "An Interview with Minnie Lue," unpublished paper, 24 March 1972; Hildebrand, "North Richmond Blues," 1; Minnie Lue Nichols, interview by author, 6 January 1980.

19. Tilghman Press, *We Also Serve: Armed Forces Edition*, 38; Joseph

Malbrough, interview by author, 18 August 1985; Margaret Starks, interview by author, 2 April 1988.

20. Olly Wilson, "The Significance of the Relationship between Afro-American Music and West African Music," 3–22, and Wilson, "Black Music as an Art Form," 2–3.

21. Roy Rosenzweig, *Eight Hours for What We Will: Workers and Leisure in an Industrial City, 1870–1920* (New York, 1983), 35–64; Perry R. Duis, *The Saloon: Public Drinking in Chicago and Boston, 1880–1920* (Urbana, Ill., 1983). I am indebted to Madelon Powers for her discussion of immigrant saloons. See Madelon Mae Powers, "Faces along the Bar: Lore and Order in the Workingman's Saloon, 1870–1920" (Ph.D. diss., University of California, Berkeley, 1991), especially 23–36.

22. Charles Keil, *Urban Blues* (Chicago, 1969), 157–58; Hildebrand, "Oakland Blues," 3–4; Lipsitz, *Time Passages,* 110–13; Peretti, *Creation of Jazz,* 50–55.

23. Margaret Starks, interview by author, 2 April 1988.

24. Keil, *Urban Blues,* 157–58; Peretti, *Creation of Jazz,* 53; Minnie Lue Nichols, interview by author, 6 January 1980.

25. Moore, "Getting There, Being There," 115–19.

26. Bill Thurston, interview by author, 8 September 1983; Margaret Starks, interview by author, 2 April 1988; Ivy Reid Lewis, interview by author, 29 July 1987.

27. West Coast Regional Office of the National Association for the Advancement of Colored People (NAACP), carton 16 (ca. 1946–70) (hereafter NAACP papers): Margaret Starks letter to Noah W. Griffin, 4 May 1945; [Noah Griffin] Memo to file, 9 November 1945; Noah Griffin to Margaret Starks, 13 April 1945; Noah W. Griffin to Margaret Starks, letter 14 April 1945. See also NAACP papers, Miscellaneous Papers (ca. 1944–59): Gloster B. Current to Noah Griffin, 1 December 1947; Noah W. Griffin to Gloster B. Current, 19 November 1947. Margaret Starks, interview by, author, 2 April 1988; Cleophus Brown, interview by author, 18 October 1987; Ursula Brown, interview by author, 11 September 1993.

28. *Oakland Tribune,* "Vice Is Held Rampant in North Richmond Area," 12 October 1949; Bill Thurston, interview by author, 8 September 1983; Ivy Reid Lewis, interview by author, 29 July 1987; Margaret Starks, interview by author, 2 April 1988.

29. Walter White, Executive Secretary, NAACP, letter to Noah W.

Griffin, 16 July 1945, NAACP papers, carton 16, Miscellaneous Papers, four folders (1944–59); Minnie Lue Nichols, interview by author, 6 January 1980; Wright, "An Interview with Minnie Lue," 3–5; Joseph Malbrough, interview by author, 18 August 1985; Margaret Starks, interview by author, 2 April 1988.

30. Moore, "Getting There, Being There," 119; City of Richmond Planning Department and Model Cities Programs, *Richmond Facts* (Richmond, Calif., 1974), "Total Population, Ethnic, Sex and Age Distribution for 1950–1970," 2. NAACP papers, carton 16, miscellaneous papers, four folders (1944–59); Robert Wenkert, *Historical Digest of Negro-White Relations*, 87; Minnie Lue Nichols, interview by author, 6 January 1980; Margaret Starks, interview by author, 2 April 1988.

31. Keil, *Urban Blues,* 145, 157; Arnold Shaw, *Honkers and Shouters: The Golden Years of Rhythm and Blues* (New York, 1978), 116–17; Jonathan Kamin, "Taking the Roll out of Rock and Roll: Reverse Acculturation," *Popular Music and Society* 2 (1972): 3.

32. Quoted in Lee Hildebrand, "North Richmond Blues," 5.

Edward J. Escobar

TWELVE

Zoot-Suiters and Cops: Chicano Youth and the Los Angeles Police Department during World War II

Between 3 and 10 June 1943 the city of Los Angeles was rocked by the worst rioting it had seen to that point in the twentieth century. For eight days scores of American servicemen, sometimes joined by civilians and even police officers, roamed the streets of the city in search of Mexican American youths wearing a distinctive style of dress called a zoot suit. When they found the zoot-suiters, the servicemen attacked and beat them, tearing off their clothes and leaving them naked and bleeding in gutters. As the riots progressed, the level of violence escalated, with servicemen entering bars, theaters, dance halls, restaurants, and even private homes in search of victims. Toward the end of the rioting, the servicemen expanded their attacks to include all Mexican Americans, whether they wore zoot suits or not, as well as African Americans. The rioting did not subside until the War Department made Los Angeles out of bounds to military personnel.[1]

An illuminating aspect of the riots was the role of the Los Angeles Police Department (LAPD). Rather than enforcing the law impartially, police officers handled the rioting in a biased manner. They allowed the servicemen to beat and strip the zoot-suiters, and after the servicemen had left the scene, they moved in and arrested the Mexican American youths for disturbing the peace. Police, in fact, detained only a handful of servicemen but arrested over six hundred Mexican Americans during the riots.[2]

The LAPD actions in the zoot suit riots highlight a startling conclusion reached by local law enforcement agencies. Police, along with local civic leaders, believed that Mexican American youths, especially young males, were inclined toward violent crime and constituted a severe social problem. This belief merged with police officers' frustration over their inability to crack down on the alleged lawbreakers and led to their allowing servicemen to beat and humiliate the zoot-suiters.[3]

The view that young minority males were a dangerous social element may not be novel in the late twentieth century, but before World War II the LAPD, like other big city police departments, had not yet linked race and crime in any systematic manner. More important, they had not yet developed any specific set of policies or practices for addressing crime by a racial minority group. The zoot suit riots and the anti-Mexican hysteria that preceded them changed all that, convincing the LAPD that Mexican Americans constituted a serious crime problem and that the department needed to develop training, deployment, and general policing strategies for dealing with Mexican American crime. Moreover, within a few years after the war the LAPD gained a reputation as the most modern and professional police department in the nation, and law enforcement agencies throughout the country emulated much of what it did. Thus the assumptions reached and the strategies developed by the LAPD regarding the inherent criminality of racial minorities would have profound consequences for policing during the second half of the twentieth century.[4]

A variety of factors during the war years contributed to the conclusion that Mexican American youths were criminally inclined and that stern measures had to be taken to control them. These included the misinterpretation of arrest statistics; the LAPD's adoption of the police professionalism model; general wartime anxieties; and the sensational press coverage of Mexican American crime that led to public hysteria over an alleged Mexican-American crime wave. More important, however, were the rise of the zoot suit fad among Mexican American youth and a corresponding belief among local civic leaders that the zoot suit represented a severe social problem and even reflected criminality within the Mexican American community.

The first thing to be said about the zoot suit hysteria is that it had little basis in fact. Since the mid-1920s the LAPD had kept detailed statistics on arrests, cross-referenced by charge and race. These statistics show that the LAPD consistently arrested Mexican Americans at a rate higher than the best estimates of their representation within the general population. During the war years, however, the LAPD began arresting significantly higher numbers of Mexican Americans, especially youths, and the department claimed that these increased arrests demonstrated that Mexican American crime was getting out of control and that Mexican Americans were criminally inclined.[5]

By equating arrests with the actual rate of crime, however, police officials misinterpreted their own statistics. Reported crime, which is a more accurate measure of the crime rate, actually fell during 1942 and 1943, the years of the alleged crime wave. The increases in arrests resulted more from changes in the law and in police practices than from changes in Mexican Americans' behavior. Specifically, the enactment and enforcement of new statutes, such as immigration and draft laws for adults and curfew ordinances for juveniles, created new classes of laws that Mexican Americans violated, thus swelling the arrest statistics. The LAPD also engaged in selective enforcement, enforcing laws such as the curfew ordinance more vigorously in the barrios than in white sections of the city. Finally, the LAPD simply overarrested people during the 1940s. Although arrests of Mexican Americans rose, only a fraction of them resulted in criminal prosecutions.[6]

To a great extent the LAPD's excessive arrests of Mexican American youths resulted from the "war on crime" orientation that was part of the professional reform model the LAPD began adopting in 1938. An unforeseen but significant outcome of professionalism was a different relationship between the police and the community, as police changed from a responsive to a preventive force. Throughout the nineteenth and early twentieth centuries, police made arrests and performed other duties primarily in response to calls from citizens. If police were to be on the front line of the war against crime, however, they needed to take a much more active role. They needed to prevent crime by confronting the potential "criminal elements" in society with a show of force designed to convince them that violating the law brought swift and severe punishment. Henceforth officers aggressively patrolled neighborhoods that arrest statistics had identified as "high-crime areas." The more they patrolled the area the more arrests they made, which of course led to even more intensive patrolling.[7]

Probably the most important factor in the growing popular fear of Mexican Americans was the development of a decidedly rebellious and potentially hostile Mexican American youth culture. The symbols of this youthful rebellion were the zoot suits worn by many Mexican American youths, the distinctive argot they spoke, and a general attitude of both hostility and scorn toward white society. Whites, however, interpreted this rebelliousness not merely as a sign of youthful rambunctiousness but as evidence of the inherently pathological, antisocial, and even criminal nature of Mexican Americans.

The zoot suit phenomenon resulted primarily from the racism, discrimination, and extreme poverty that people of Mexican descent faced in the United States. Economic and social indicators confirmed that Mexican Americans constituted the most destitute racial group in the Los Angeles area during the early 1940s. Because of discrimination by employers and unions, they found employment only in the lowest-paying, most menial jobs. Thus in 1941 Mexican Americans had a yearly median family income of only $790, or more than 29 percent below "the minimum required for decent food and housing for the average family of five persons."[8]

This poverty produced a variety of social conditions that made life very difficult for Mexican American youth. Mexicans, for example, lived in the most dilapidated housing in Los Angeles. They also suffered from poor health. According to the Los Angeles County Tuberculosis Association, the death rate from tuberculosis for "Latin Americans" was double that for whites, and the infant mortality rate for Los Angeles Mexican Americans was more than 12 percent higher than for whites.[9]

Mexican American youth suffered from blatant educational discrimination. Los Angeles city school officials placed Mexican American children into segregated "Mexican schools." In addition, whether in the Mexican schools or in mainstream schools, these children had to endure the racist attitudes and actions of school officials, from superintendents to classroom teachers. One school official, for example, stated that Mexican Americans were "lazy, have no ambition and won't take advantage of opportunities offered them." Another superintendent claimed he found "lower moral standards" among Mexican American children than among whites. One teacher returning from a workshop titled "The Education of Mexican and Spanish-Speaking Pupils" summed up the prevailing attitudes toward Mexican American children: "I've had a very entertaining experience," she said, "but as far as I am concerned, they are still dirty, stupid and dumb."[10]

Mexican American children also encountered these attitudes in the classroom. School officials, for example, generally prohibited them from speaking Spanish. The penalties for violating this rule were often severe, including corporal punishment. Other teachers had extremely low expectations. "You can't force these children into the Anglo-Saxon mold or pattern of schooling," one teacher stated. "They are different—they are elemental in their conception of things. They have different temperaments."[11]

Such attitudes led directly to the undereducating of Mexican American children. "If you teach them attitudes and responses and how to be good citizens, how to wash and iron and scrub and bake, that's all you need to do," an elementary-school principal explained. "Why teach them to read and write and spell? Why worry about it . . . they'll only pick beets anyway." Other educators developed more callous methods for dealing with overachieving Mexican American students. The head of a high-school business department, for example, stated: "I have no problems with the Mexicans. I take care that the first few days' work is so difficult and involved that they become discouraged and quit."[12]

These practices proved disastrous for Mexican American children. Many, but especially those from poorer families, performed so badly that school officials placed them in special continuation schools where, according to sociologist Joan Moore, "they could enjoy themselves without being bothered too much by academic requirements." Many others, frustrated and angry, simply dropped out before finishing their education.[13]

Mexican American youths also suffered from other forms of discrimination, especially in public places. Local officials, for example, prohibited them from using particular parks and public pools except for certain days of the week or month. Typically, a sign at a pool read: "Tuesdays Reserved for Negroes and Mexicans"—Tuesday being the day before workers drained and cleaned the pool. Some theaters seated Mexican Americans only in certain sections, and some restaurants, dance halls, and other amusements refused them admittance.[14]

Even social service agencies designed to help citizens and promote the war effort discriminated against Mexican Americans. According to War Manpower Commission representative Guy Nunn, the activities of the Civilian Defense, the Red Cross, the War Bonds program, the Office of Price Administration Consumer Division, and the Office of Defense Health and Welfare Service "have persistently been characterized by discrimination and neglect in Spanish-speaking districts." "Only the draft," Nunn concluded, "has to date shown no bias against Mexicans."[15]

Although these forms of public humiliation served to remind Mexican American youths of their inferior position in American society and to embitter many, perhaps no other form of discrimination created more anger in the community than the mistreatment they received from police. Probably the most common type of police misconduct was verbal abuse, in particular racial slurs. Former congressman Edward R. Roybal, who grew up in East Los Angeles, states that police officers regularly referred to Mexican Americans as "dirty Mexicans" or "cholos." Sexual harassment occurred as male officers hand-searched women's bodies, allegedly looking for weapons or drugs. The LAPD had such a bad reputation regarding treatment of young women that Mexican American parents told their daughters that if stranded or in trouble they should walk home rather than seek assistance from a police officer.[16]

The practice of arbitrary "field interrogations" of Mexican Americans also angered the community. In a typical field interrogation officers would stop a car with Mexican American passengers, order everyone out, then search the car and the people for contraband. Anyone of Mexican descent was subject to these searches, but the police seem to have focused on youths. Congressman Roybal remembers that in 1940, while driving home from a dance with his date, he was pulled over by an LAPD squad car. The officers ordered him to stand spread-eagled over the car while they searched him. During the search the officers stuck their hands in his pockets and made a series of racial slurs. Roybal recalls that he felt "degraded" and that he was sure he was not a "hit" with his date. Evidently he was wrong at least on the last count, for about a year later he married the girl.[17]

Many Mexican American youths found themselves arrested for no reason other than being of Mexican descent. Police, for example, regularly arrested whole groups of Mexican American juveniles who congregated on street corners or home lawns and charged them with vagrancy, curfew violation, or suspicion of some crime. As Pete Vásquez, a young Mexican American of draft age, explained: "If the cops catch you on the street after 8 o'clock, usually they run you in—or rough you up, anyway. If you look like a Mexican you just better stay off the street, that's all." As noted earlier, only a small fraction of these arrests resulted in prosecutions.[18]

The police practice that most angered the Mexican American community was the excessive use of force or police brutality. Typically, if police officers felt young men failed to show proper deference and respect for authority, they could expect a violent reaction; but just about any response, from a look to a question, could be interpreted as lack of respect and result in a beating. A Mexican American army private home on leave and on his way to the store, for example, was stopped by two officers, one of them a Mexican American, who questioned him and demanded to see his papers. Despite his protest that only the military police had authority over him, the young serviceman complied. As he returned from the store the same two officers again stopped him and demanded his papers. This time the private refused, and for his insolence he received such a savage beating at the hands of the Mexican American officer that he suffered a fractured skull and had to be discharged from the army. People continually saw or heard of police abuse, and many came to fear and even hate LAPD officers.[19]

The extreme poverty, the pervasive discrimination, and the constant police abuse and brutality led to rebellion and to alienation from American society by a significant segment of Mexican American youths. This rebellion generally did not manifest itself through direct challenges to constituted authority, however. Rather, Mexican American youth engaged in what sociologist Joan Moore calls a "symbolic challenge to the world" through the zoot-suiter.[20]

The zoot suit or "drapes" represented an exercise in excess. It consisted of very baggy pants that fit high on the waist (in extreme cases all the way to the armpits), deep "reet" pleats, and narrow pegged cuffs. The coat had wide lapels and shoulder pads that resembled epaulets; it was sometimes so long that it extended to the knees. Accessories included a broad-brimmed "pancake" hat, long watch chain, and thick-soled shoes. The female equivalent of the zoot-suiter, the "cholita," also wore distinctive clothes, if not as outlandish. Her outfit, which many found sexually provocative, consisted of either a flared or a tight short skirt, tight sweater, and distinctive earrings and makeup. Boys wore long hair combed in a ducktail, while girls stacked their hair high on their heads in a pompadour. In addition to the way they dressed, some Mexican American youths spoke a special argot called Caló. The use of Caló, a derivative of a fifteenth-century Iberian Gypsy dialect, made them incomprehensible to Spanish-speaking elders and to white English-speaking authority figures, and it intensified their sense of uniqueness and generational solidarity. The youths who most completely adopted the zoot suit lifestyle were called pachucos.[21]

With the zoot suit, Mexican American youths reciprocated the rejection they experienced from white society. Especially during the war years, when Americans prized the neat, trim look of the servicemen, when they placed high value on conserving basic materials such as cloth, and when they expected unity and conformity in order to defeat the common foe, these youths knew the zoot suit offended whites. As historian Mauricio Mazón has noted, adult society met the zoot-suiter "with anger, shock, and undoubtedly envy." The youths knew this, and they reveled in the knowledge.[22]

Zoot-suiters flaunted their outlandish clothes, and both boys and girls gained a measure of satisfaction and a sense of unity from the looks of ridicule and disgust they received from "squares" when they walked down the street. United Farm Workers leader César Chávez remembers that as a teenager he wore a zoot suit and that he and others "needed a lot of guts to wear those pants, and we had to be rebellious to do it, because the police and a few of the older people would harass us." While only a handful were hard-core pachucos, as many as two-thirds of all Mexican American youths in Los Angeles judged wearing some version of the zoot suit worth the harassment, for it gave them a sense of belonging to at least one group in a society from which they generally felt alienated.[23]

In Los Angeles, according to sociologist Joan Moore, the quintessential pachucos came from the barrio of El Hoyo Maravilla, one of the most destitute Mexican American neighborhoods in southern California. At Jackson, the continuation high school, Hoyo Maravilla youths learned to distinguish themselves from Mexican American youngsters from other barrios. These distinctions often led to rivalries, and though they most often worked themselves out on the basketball court or the baseball field, fights also broke out.[24]

Moore reports that the youths from El Hoyo Maravilla "were deeply caught up in the Pachuco fad and *la vida loca* [the wild life]" that, at least for these youngsters, went with the clothes. In addition to their drapes and ducktail haircuts, "chucos" from El Hoyo smoked marijuana and had tattoos with various symbols designating allegiance to girlfriends, barrio, or race. In fact these youths took special pride in their Mexican

Figure 12.1. The zoot-suiter (*Life*, 21 June 1943, 30). AP/Wide World Photos.

heritage and rejected any thought of assimilation into American culture. They spoke primarily in Caló or Spanish and ridiculed any Mexican American who spoke Gabacho (English). According to Moore, although the zoot-suiters from El Hoyo Maravilla may have fought with youths from other barrios, their "enmity for Anglos and their system was paramount."[25]

The extreme alienation of some zoot-suiters went beyond symbolic rebellion and led them into much more aggressive and often even violent behavior. These youths, however, directed much of their hostility inward within the Mexican American community. Almost all the violence the press reported with such great alarm during the war years consisted of Mexican American youths fighting and often killing other Mexican American youths. On the other hand, zoot-suiters also sometimes consciously attacked, albeit spontaneously, the obvious sources of racial discrimination. One example occurred at a downtown movie theater when management ejected three Mexican American youths for making noise during the movie. Twenty-five to thirty others sitting in the balcony objected, and the management called the police. Apparently the officers threw out the protesters, and a fight erupted outside the theater. According to newspaper accounts, as many as two hundred people fought with police, but officers managed to make only one arrest. It also seems that zoot-suiters engaged in more organized and planned actions against the police. One source states that they often retaliated for police harassment and brutality "by 'pantsing' the cops [accosting an officer, pulling down his pants, and running off] and generally making life miserable for them." These kinds of interactions heightened tension between police and the community.[26]

Finally, although zoot-suiters never developed a political movement, at least some pachucos had a political consciousness. On at least two occasions during the war years Mexican American youths burned the American flag and tore down posters promoting the war effort. The vice principal of Garfield high school accused Mexican American students who formed their own organization of having "pro-Nazi designs," and police officials became extremely alarmed when a convicted German spy waiting to be transferred to a federal penitentiary began telling his Mexican American jail mates that they were victims of racial discrimination. In fact, during the war years Los Angeles community leaders, both white and Mexican American, believed the pachuco fad was a scheme of an extreme right-wing and possibly pro-Axis Mexican movement known as the Sinarquistas that allegedly hoped to disrupt the war effort by sowing disunity between Mexican Americans and Anglo-Americans.[27]

We should remember, however, that although most Mexican American youths wore some part of the zoot suit costume, the overwhelming majority did not engage in illegal acts, politically motivated or otherwise. Nevertheless, Mexican American youths had plenty of reason to be rebellious. These young people had grown up indoctrinated in the American dream only to discover that simply because they were Mexican they could never fully partake of America's riches. Attorney Manuel Ruiz says that Mexican American youths began wearing the zoot suit to "articulate their dissatisfaction" with the discrimination they endured daily. Congressman Roybal remembers that the zoot-suiters often ran afoul of the law because they demanded respect. Mexican American youths, Roybal recalls, got into trouble because they insisted on defending themselves even if it meant fighting with police officers.[28]

Perhaps it is this last point that is the most insightful, for it seems that above all the zoot-suiters wanted respect. Despite their outlandish clothes and sometimes outlandish behavior, what the pachucos really wanted—indeed what they demanded—was to be treated like all other members of their age group. They wanted to get the same kinds of jobs, to be treated fairly in school, to frequent the same entertainment spots, to be treated fairly by the police, and above all, they wanted in all these interactions to be treated with respect.

White society, however, was unwilling to respect Mexican Americans, especially zoot-suiters. Whites were repelled by the zoot suit precisely because of what it represented: rebellion against traditional forms of discrimination and subordination. Mexicans were not supposed to have as good jobs as whites, they were not supposed to get an equal education, they were not supposed to go to the same dances or sit in the same section of theaters—and the role of the police was to keep them in their place. Moreover, Mexicans were supposed to be humble and meek and generally invisible, and youths were supposed to obey authority figures. That Mexican American youth chose to attack these norms of behavior not directly through political action, but symbolically through actions that showed their defiance and hostility toward white society made it easier for whites to dismiss their protests and label them as deviant, criminal, and even pathological.

Los Angeles white society thus interpreted the zoot suit phenomenon as a sign of inherent criminality among Mexican Americans and especially among youths. This idea of Mexican Americans' innate criminality contributed to a growing hysteria during the war years that a Mexican American crime wave was sweeping the city. Official pronouncements and newspaper stories fed the hysteria, reinforcing in the public's mind and in the minds of LAPD officials the idea that people of Mexican descent were criminally inclined. As might be expected of a police force that was quickly transforming itself into the shock troops of the war against crime, the LAPD's acceptance of Mexican Americans' inherent criminality resulted in extremely harsh and repressive police practices.

To a certain extent, the popular belief that Mexican American juvenile delinquency was sweeping Los Angeles was a an outgrowth of wartime. Los Angeles became the West Coast center for war-related production, which resulted in rapid population increases and concomitant social dislocations. In addition, public officials across the nation expected a significant rise in juvenile delinquency once the United States entered the war. Such an increase had occurred in the United States during World War I and in Great Britain earlier in the current war.[29]

The United States' actual entry into the war raised fears of internal enemy conspiracies and demands for total conformity. Even before the United States entered the war, the Los Angeles Police Commission recommended that the City Council pass an ordinance ordering all noncitizens to register with the chief of police. Once the war started, the expulsion of Japanese nationals and Japanese Americans from the West Coast and their "internment" in concentration camps was the most obvious consequence of this paranoia and demand for conformity. After the removal of the Japanese, municipal officials, the press, and much of the public transferred their anxiety to the city's largest minority group, Mexican Americans. That fear eventually led to public hysteria over an alleged Mexican American crime wave.[30]

Los Angeles newspapers helped create the hysteria with a campaign of sensational headlines and lurid news stories depicting the latest depredations of so-called Mexican American youth gangs. Beginning in the spring of 1942, six months after Pearl Harbor and only weeks after the internment of the Japanese and Japanese Americans, newspapers featured stories on Mexican American juvenile delinquency. These stories continued through the summer, growing in intensity and reaching a peak in August 1942. Because of protests from the federal government that the stories hurt the war effort, newspapers cut back on their sensational coverage for a time. They resumed in early 1943, however, and continued throughout the spring until they peaked again in May. The coverage of Mexican American crime and the frenzy it created culminated with the zoot suit riots of 3–10 June 1943.[31]

To a certain extent, the World War II era news stories resembled earlier newspaper accounts of Mexican crime. Headlines such as "11 Mexican Youths Indicted in Gas Station Robbery" and "2 Mexicans Held as Molesters" paralleled headlines on Mexican crime from earlier in the century in explicitly stating that Mexicans committed the crimes.[32] Nevertheless, World War II coverage of Mexican American crimes differed from previous accounts in some fundamental and highly significant ways. Unlike earlier periods when newspapers reported only the most sensational crimes committed by Mexicans, during the zoot suit hysteria the press seemed to cover every Mexican American arrest. Alerted by the police, the press reported on and distorted the importance of relatively minor crimes and even trivial incidents. For example, a story on a gas station robbery, not to mention the indictment of the alleged assailants, would never have been printed during the twenties or thirties. Similarly, the story behind the provocative headline regarding the Mexican "molesters" was really about the arrest of two Mexican American boys for disturbing the peace by verbally harassing a woman on the street.[33]

Local newspapers also created an impression that Mexican Americans were a dangerous element in society through headlines and articles that implied significant increases in crimes committed by Mexican American youths. Headlines such as "New Zoot Gangster Attacks Result in Arrest of 100," "Gang Attacks Spread," "Zoot Suiters Blamed in New Killing," and "Six More Mexicans Charged with Weapon Assault" all gave the impression that Mexican Americans were committing crimes at an ever increasing rate. To add to this fear, headlines also suggested that the crime wave was well organized. One headline, for example, spoke of a "Zoot Suit Revolution." Others, such as "Zoot Network over L.A.," "Nab Boy Gang 'General,'" and "Zoot Arsenal," implied that zoot-suiters were organized into citywide gangs, were well armed, and had leadership.[34]

Sometimes the newspapers turned positively vicious. In November 1942 a small weekly, the *Los Angeles Equalizer*, complained about taxing citizens so that "certain people can raise their kids by charity, go to the public schools, snatch purses, slug old folks [and] defie [sic] authority." The *Equalizer* proposed that "when these young Mexican hoodlums raise the hell they are raising in wartime, we should put them in a stockade and try them after the war." All the publicity and the provocative rhetoric seemed to have had an effect on the public. One letter to the *Times* called on police to treat the zoot-suiters as they treated their victims. If this meant that "officers might kill or seriously injure some young hoodlum," the writer concluded, "Well, why not!"[35]

From mid-1942 onward, the theme that dominated the Los Angeles press's treatment of Mexican American youth was that of the gang, and local newspapers consistently assumed that any Mexican who committed a crime must belong to a gang. Even when newspapers did not write about "gangs," the way the local press used the terms Mexican, zoot-suiter, and pachuco interchangeably, and almost always in association with some crime, implied that all Mexican American youths wore zoot suits and that anyone who wore a zoot suit was certainly a criminal. The effect was an ever growing public apprehension that eventually turned into hysteria.

The incident that fixed the public's attention on Mexican American crime was the infamous Sleepy Lagoon case. The general facts regarding Sleepy Lagoon are well known and have been recounted in a variety of sources. On the morning of Sunday, 2 August 1942, José Díaz was found severely injured next to a dirt road close to a gravel pit called Sleepy Lagoon. He was taken to a local hospital, where he died of head injuries later that day. The next day Los Angeles newspapers attributed his death to "Mexican Boy Gangs," and over the next several weeks and months the local press repeatedly charged that a "Boy Gang Terror Wave" was sweeping the city.[36]

The actual circumstances surrounding Díaz's death never were determined. He was inebriated when he died, and no one testified about how he received his injuries. An autopsy reported that the injuries could have been caused by repeated falls to the ground or by an automobile accident. There was no proof that anyone actually killed Díaz. Nevertheless, prosecutors filed first-degree murder charges against twenty-two Mexican American boys from the Thirty-eighth Street neighborhood on the grounds that they had been in a fight at a party that Díaz also attended.[37]

The trial was a mockery of justice and demonstrated the prevailing attitudes of government officials and the press toward Mexican American youths. Throughout the trial local newspapers ran sensational stories on Mexican American crime, and one newspaper even referred to the "Goon" or "Gooner Trial" and described the defendants as "the goons of Sleepy Lagoon." The prosecuting attorney repeatedly referred to the defendants' heritage and once said that Mexicans always made good suspects. For his part, Judge Charles W. Fricke refused to allow the defendants to sit next to their attorneys or to get haircuts or a change of clothes, in order to maintain their "distinctive" appearance for the jury. Not surprisingly, the jury found the defendants guilty of charges ranging from assault to first-degree murder. Thanks to the efforts of a citizens' group called the Sleepy Lagoon Defense Committee, however, the verdicts were overturned on appeal.[38]

The LAPD used the death of José Díaz and the fears it raised as an excuse to repress the growing rebelliousness of Mexican American youth. On the weekend following Díaz's death, police conducted a massive three-day sweep of the barrios, apprehending over six hundred youths. Officers stationed themselves at strategic intersections and stopped every passing car containing young Mexican Americans. Although they could not link any of them to a specific crime, police arrested anyone who looked as if he or she could have committed a crime sometime in the past. Police charged the youths with "suspicion," usually of robbery or assault with a deadly weapon. To connect them with specific offenses, LAPD officials announced a "show-up" in which the arrested youths were paraded before the public to make identifications.[39]

In the midst of this crisis atmosphere, the Los Angeles County Grand Jury initiated hearings into the extent, nature, and causes of Mexican American juvenile delinquency. The hearings and the debate they sparked among government officials and community leaders were the clearest articulation ever of law enforcement's attitude toward the Mexican American community. They also revealed the unanimity with which the various segments of Los Angeles society—conservative police officers, liberal social activists, and even the Mexican consul—viewed the growing rebelliousness of Mexican American youth with alarm and labeled that rebelliousness deviant, antisocial, and criminal. These "experts" on crime and on Mexican Americans might have differed about the causes, extent, and cures for the phenomenon, but they agreed that the zoot-suiters and the pachuco lifestyle represented a grave social ill that must be repressed.

The grand jury hearings were held in two phases. In the first phase, which began two days after Díaz's death, the jury heard primarily from law enforcement officials. Using arrest statistics, police officials argued that Mexican American juvenile delinquency was increasing at an alarming rate. On the causes of Mexican American crime, police officials differed in emphasis. For example, only Captain Edward Duran Ayres of the Los Angeles County Sheriff's Department addressed the issue of discrimination as a factor in causing crime. Other police officials offered different explanations, including the inability of Mexican immigrants to adapt to their new environment; the establishment of neighborhood recreational facilities that led to greater neighborhood identification and eventually to neighborhood gangs; the weakening of the patriarchal structure of the Mexican family; and finally, the proverbial leniency of the courts.[40]

The testimony that caused the most controversy and most closely reflected the thinking of the Los Angeles law enforcement community came from the Sheriff Department's Captain Ayres. Although he acknowledged that discrimination was a factor, Ayres believed the main cause for Mexican American criminality was biological. He attributed this "biological basis" to the Los Angeles Mexican Americans' descent from the inherently violent Indians of Mexico. After all, the Aztecs were known for sacrificing 30,000 Indians in one day, he maintained, and "this total disregard for human life has always been universal throughout the Americas among the Indian population, which of course is well known to everyone." Ayres also believed that, unlike whites, who fought as individuals using only their fists, Mexican Americans fought in gangs using knives and were not satisfied until their biological blood lust was satisfied. According to Ayres, all a Mexican "knows and feels is a desire to use a knife or some lethal weapon. In other words, his desire is to kill, or at least let blood." To dramatize the difference between whites and Mexican Americans, Ayres used the analogy of a house cat and a wild cat. A house cat could be domesticated and treated leniently; a wild cat, Ayres argued, would always be wild and must therefore be caged.[41]

Ayres's racial theories had significant implications for society's response to Mexican American juvenile delinquency; he did not flinch from expressing those implications. Since he believed in the inherent criminality of Mexican Americans, Ayres called for harsh and repressive measures against that community. He proposed that all Mexican American men over age eighteen be forced into the armed services. Those under eighteen should be forced to attend school or go to work. He also thought it essential that all gang members, whether they had committed a crime or not, be incarcerated. Finally, Ayres warned that if these "drastic measures are not taken to put an end to gangsterism[,] it will increase, with resultant murders, and that which none of us want to see—race riots."[42]

The Los Angeles police establishment fully supported the Ayres report. Sheriff Eugene Biscailuz stated that Ayres and the other police officers who testified before the grand jury presented a thorough analysis of Mexican American juvenile delinquency. LAPD Chief of Police Horrall also praised the Ayres report for its "intelligent statement of the psychology of the Mexican people, particularly, the youths."[43]

Ayres and the other officers who testified before the grand jury thus developed a broad strategy for dealing with Mexican American youth. They recommended prosecuting all juveniles suspected of lawbreaking or simply belonging to a gang and called for filing charges of contributing to the delinquency of a minor against any adult gang members. Another part of the law enforcement plan called for an increase in arrests and "field investigations" of Mexican American youth and the creation of a central juvenile delinquency file of information on all potential juvenile delinquents—that is, anyone who was arrested and put on probation as well as students who got into trouble in school.[44]

Police officials thus saw Mexican American youths as a criminal and dangerous element within society that must be suppressed even at the cost of violating their civil liberties. As one LAPD official asserted, the Sleepy Lagoon killing showed that the Mexican American juvenile delinquency problem had "reached a stage where it must be dealt with firmly and without sympathy for the individuals." Even the moderate and usually sympathetic chief county probation officer, Karl Holton, joined in the hysterical condemnation of Mexican American youth. Matching Captain Ayres's rhetoric, he demanded that Mexican American boys either work or be drafted. "If these fighting boys don't enlist or go to work," he warned, "we will take them out of circulation." Within a few days, police made good on Holton's threat with their mass arrests of Mexican American youths and the "show-ups" that followed.[45]

On 8 October 1942 the grand jury held a second set of hearings into Mexican American juvenile delinquency. This time testimony came from liberal activists, government officials, and academicians, and the newly arrived consul general from Mexico, Manuel Aguilar, also was asked to give testimony. Although each speaker condemned Captain Ayres's racist explanation for Mexican American criminality as scientifically unsound and the police's repressive measures as counterproductive, they generally agreed that zoot-suiters constituted a serious crime problem that had to be addressed. Most liberals believed that discrimination and poor living conditions contributed to the rise of juvenile delinquency in the Mexican American community. Some also argued that culture conflict and "the second generation problem" contributed to juvenile delinquency.[46]

UCLA anthropologist Harry Hoijer, however, best synthesized the economic and behavioral science approaches and articulated the liberal position most clearly. Hoijer argued that "a scientific analysis" of the problem made it evident that Mexican Americans were a suppressed minority and that such groups "inevitably" engaged in "cult activities" or "sporadic acts of senselessly violent behavior." According to Hoijer, these problems and tendencies were exacerbated in the case of Mexican American youths, who had grown alienated from their parents' culture but were scorned by American society precisely because of their Mexicanness. "Individuals misunderstood at home and regarded as inferior abroad can express their resentments only by violence against those they believe to be their enemies." Mexican American youths thus joined gangs that "quite inevitably . . . engage in hostilities with one another and in depredations against society at large." But, Hoijer concluded, these "gangsters" should not be regarded as common criminals; rather, he believed, "they are. . .individuals driven to excesses of misbehavior by circumstances beyond their control."[47]

Despite the liberals' critique of police tactics, their basic assumptions about the extent of Mexican American crime and, more important, their explanation for its causes in fact supported the harsh tactics of the police. The liberals accepted the notion that the zoot suit and pachucismo were synonymous with delinquency, that this delinquency constituted a grave social problem, and finally, that the root cause of this problem was discrimination. The irony is that their analysis was every bit as deterministic as Captain Ayres's racial explanation for Mexican American juvenile delinquency and led just as "inevitably" to the same conclusion: that Mexican Americans were criminally inclined.

Given the pervasiveness of that discrimination, most Mexican American youths could be expected to become alienated from American society. Moreover, as long as they suffered from racial discrimination, they would continue their delinquent behavior. Although the liberals railed against law enforcement's repressive tactics, their deterministic analysis in fact supported law enforcement's harsh measures. Since the function of the police was to fight crime and since Mexican Americans were either biologically or environmentally inclined toward criminality, the police had to do everything in their power to suppress this evident social danger. Anything else would have been an unprofessional dereliction of duty.

In the short term, however, despite the consensus regarding the seriousness of "the Mexican problem," law enforcement could not implement the most repressive aspects of its proposed campaign against Mexican American youth. After the initial police actions in the wake of Sleepy Lagoon, the need for the United States to maintain good relations with its Latin American allies and the effectiveness of German propaganda in that part of the world precluded any more mass arrests or other wholesale repression. For the duration of the war, at least, the LAPD would have to satisfy itself with piecemeal responses to pachuco rebelliousness and to passing along to the newspapers information about the latest instance of Mexican American juvenile delinquency. Officers' complicity during the zoot suit riots shows the frustration they must have felt over their inability to take more vigorous action.

In the long term, the consensus regarding Mexican American criminality changed the way the LAPD policed the Mexican American community. It accepted the environmental interpretation and began training officers, both formally and informally, to expect more crime from Mexican Americans than from the white population. In addition, since theories of scientific management and other aspects of police professionalism directed that police be aggressively deployed in high-crime areas, the concentration of officers became much greater in the Mexican American community than in other areas of the city. The combination of these two factors and the department's more aggressive posture toward fighting crime resulted in chronic overarresting of Mexicans in Los Angeles. Since the police used arrest statistics to determine the crime rate within a given population, the idea that Mexican Americans were criminally inclined became a self-fulfilling prophecy. Not only did the officers arrest more Mexican Americans because they considered them potential criminals, but the increased police presence and more aggressive policing methods further alienated a significant portion of Mexican American youth. Police methods may therefore have contributed to the emergence of the truly pathological youth gangs that plague the Mexican American community today. Similarly, officers who were trained to expect violent behavior from Mexican Americans were more likely to resort to violence themselves when they perceived a threatening situation. Thus the years beginning immediately after World War II saw a dramatic rise in the number of police brutality complaints made by Mexican Americans against the LAPD.[48]

The war years thus saw the LAPD adopt a theory of criminality that linked crime with race. After the war that theory was increasingly institutionalized in police policies and practices. Moreover, the LAPD transferred both the theory and the policies and practices regarding Mexican American criminality to African Americans when that community began to grow in Los Angeles after the war. Aggressive police tactics against the black and Chicano communities continued and intensified, and so did allegations of police abuse from minorities. The 1960s saw the eruption of the resultant hostilities into the Watts rebellion of 1965 and the violence associated with Chicano Moratorium demonstrations of 1970 and 1971. During the relatively quieter seventies and eighties the idea that minority males are criminally inclined became, if anything, even more ingrained in the work habits of police officers. One need only see the videotape of the 1991 beating of Rodney King by Los Angeles police officers, recall the nationwide debate it generated, and remember the massive violence that erupted when a jury acquitted the accused officers to understand the long-term consequences of those events.

Notes

1. The zoot suit riots are fully described in Solomon James Jones, *The Government Riots of Los Angeles, June, 1943* (San Francisco, 1973); Carey McWilliams, *North from Mexico: The Spanish-Speaking People of*

the United States (New York, 1968); Mauricio Mazón, *The Zoot-Suit Riots: The Psychology of Symbolic Annihilation* (Austin, Tex., 1984); Rodolfo Acuña, *Occupied America: A History of Chicanos* (New York, 1988).

2. *Time,* 21 June 1943, quoted in Jones, *Government Riots,* 29; Citizens' Committee for Latin American Youth, *Minutes,* 7 June 1943, Manuel Ruiz Jr. papers, Stanford University Libraries, Department of Special Collections, Stanford, California, box 3; *Los Angeles Times* (hereafter *Times*), 7 June 1943; *Los Angeles Daily News* (hereafter *Daily News*), 7 June 1943.

3. On Mexican Americans fighting back see *Daily News,* 8 June 1943; *Los Angeles Herald and Express,* 8 June 1943; *People's World,* 10 June 1943; *Times,* 9 May 1978; also see Beatrice Griffith, *American Me* (Westport, Conn., 1973), 11–12, for a vivid description of a fight in a home.

4. On the development of police professionalism see Robert M. Fogelson, *Big City Police* (Cambridge, Mass., 1977); for the police professionalism movement in Los Angeles see Joseph Gerald Woods, "The Progressives and the Police: Urban Reform and the Professionalization of the Los Angeles Police" (Ph.D. diss., University of California, Los Angeles, 1973).

5. LAPD arrest statistics can be found in Los Angeles Police Department, *Annual Reports,* 1939–46.

6. Arrest statistics are inherently inferior to reported crime statistics, since an arrest does not guarantee guilt or even necessarily mean there has been a crime, whereas the report of a crime implies that at least someone believes one has been committed. Even reported crime statistics do not accurately reflect the crime rate, however, since not all crime is reported. For a discussion on the use of criminal statistics see Edwin H. Sutherland and Donald R. Cressey, *Criminology,* 9th ed. (Philadelphia, 1974), 25; Richard Quinney, *Criminology,* 2d ed. (Boston, 1979), 56 and 63–64; for the selective enforcement of the curfew ordinance see Horrall to All Officers, 29 October 1942; Horrall to Police Commission, 9 October 1944, Chief of Police, General Files, Los Angeles City Record Center, box 35288. The LAPD's penchant for making baseless arrests is best demonstrated by two examples. The LAPD *Annual Reports* show that only once during 1939–46 did more than 30 percent of LAPD arrests for violent crimes result in prosecutions. In 1944 only a little more than 7 percent of arrests for this category of crimes actually reached the

courts. Second, the statistics show that the LAPD arrested close to a thousand more Mexican American youths in 1943 than they had in 1942 but gained only sixty-six additional prosecutions.

7. This model sought to raise the status of policing by making crime fighting the primary function of police and by arguing that like other professions this function required special skills and training, which only the police themselves could define, develop, and implement. Police professionalism thus also sought to make police autonomous from the control of elected officials. Although the LAPD did not fully adopt police professionalism until the 1950s, the reform movement that began in 1938 and continued through the forties contained many aspects of the full-blown professionalism model. See Fogelson, *Big City Police,* and Woods, "Progressives and the Police."

8. Guy T. Nunn, Testimony before the Los Angeles County Grand Jury, 8 October 1942, Carey McWilliams papers, Special Collections Room, University Research Library, University of California, Los Angeles (hereafter McWilliams papers); Special Services Division, Bureau of Intelligence, United States Office of War Information, "Spanish-Americans in the Southwest and the War Effort," Report no. 24, 18 August 1942, Research Group 228, Division of Review and Analysis of the Fair Employment Practice Committee, National Archives, Washington, D.C. Special thanks go to Ruth Needleman for this source; Edward Duran Ayres, "Statistics" (henceforth "Ayres report"), in Jones, *Government Riots,* 85; Los Angeles County Coordinating Council, "Notes on the Mexican Population in Los Angeles County," December 1942, McWilliams papers.

9. Los Angeles County Coordinating Council, "Notes on the Mexican Population in Los Angeles County"; Louise Harvey, "The Delinquent Mexican Boy in an Urban Area, 1945" (master's thesis, University of California, Los Angeles, 1947), 53; also see Griffith, *American Me,* 131–33, 137, and 142. For a detailed report on the status of housing in a Mexican colonia see "A Tabulation of Facts on Conditions Existent at Hicks Camp," 8 October 1942, Sleepy Lagoon Defense Committee Papers (hereafter SLDC papers), reel 2, University of California, Los Angeles, Special Collections, University Research Library, and Robin Fitzgerald Scott, "The Mexican-American in the Los Angeles Area, 1920–1950: From Acquiescence to Activity" (Ph.D. diss., University of Southern California, 1971), 197. In 1945 the community newspaper the

Belvedere Citizen noted the severe nature of the health problem when it reported that Mexican Americans still had the city's highest death rate from tuberculosis. *Belvedere Citizen,* 17 August 1945, quoted in Rodolfo Acuña, *A Community under Siege: A Chronicle of Chicanos East of the Los Angeles River, 1945–1975* (Los Angeles, 1984), 417.

10. Mario T. Garcia, "Americans All: The Mexican American Generation and the Politics of Wartime Los Angeles, 1941–1945," in *The Mexican American Experience: An Interdisciplinary Anthology,* ed. Rodolfo O. de la Garza et al. (Austin, Tex., 1985), 204–5; quoted in Manuel Ruiz, "Latin-American Juvenile Delinquency in Los Angeles: Bomb or Bubble!" *Crime Prevention Digest* 1 (December 1942): 492–94; quoted in McWilliams, *North from Mexico,* 281–82; quoted in Griffith, *American Me,* 156. Griffith reported that one school checked Mexican American girls' hair for lice or nits before allowing them to walk across the auditorium stage and receive their diplomas.

11. Nunn, Testimony; quoted in Griffith, *American Me,* 158.

12. Quoted in Griffith, *American Me,* 167.

13. Joan W. Moore, *Homeboys: Gangs, Drugs and Prison in the Barrios of Los Angeles* (Philadelphia, 1978), 56–57; Los Angeles County Coordinating Council, "Notes on the Mexican Population."

14. Ayres report.

15. Guy T. Nunn, Testimony.

16. Interview with Congressman Edward R. Roybal, 5 January 1988; interview with Manuel Ruiz Jr., 14 January 1988. Also see García, *Mexican Americans,* 161.

17. Roybal interview.

18. Griffith, *American Me,* 203–4; Stephen J. Keating to Karl Holton, 29 June 1942, John Anson Ford papers, Huntington Library, San Marino, California (hereafter Ford Collection), box 65; Citizens' Committee for the Defense of Mexican-American Youth (hereafter CCDMAY), *The Sleepy Lagoon Case* (Los Angeles, 1942), 1. Griffith tells the story of one eighteen-year-old boy who "had been arrested on suspicion seventeen times, and beaten up nine times . . . and yet had never had a conviction or even appeared in court."

19. Later the young soldier recalled that "the one [white] cop wasn't so bad. He told him to let me alone—it was the Mexican cop that did the beating." Quoted in Griffith, *American Me,* 209.

20. Moore, *Homeboys,* 36–37; Mazón in *Zoot Suit Riots* discusses the symbolic nature of the zoot suit phenomenon in great detail.

21. For a picture of a ducktail haircut see "Hair Style Used in identification of Hoodlums," *Los Angeles Examiner* (hereafter *Examiner*), 27 October 1942; Douglas Henry Daniels, "Depression Children: The Zoot Suiter, the Pachuco, and the Hipster," paper presented at the seventy-second meeting of the Pacific Coast Branch of the American Historical Association, 9–12 August 1979, 3 and 15; Mazón, *Zoot Suit Riots*, 2–3.

22. Mazón, *Zoot Suit Riots*, 7–9.

23. Daniels, "Depression Children," 21; Griffith, *American Me*, 45 and 47; Chávez quoted in Daniels, "Depression Children," 31.

24. Moore, *Homeboys*, 56–57.

25. Ibid., 57–59.

26. *Daily News*, 26 October 1942. Most of the other Los Angeles daily newspapers also carried the story. *Times* 5 August and 7 October 1942; *Daily News*, 27 February 1943; *Examiner*, 28 February 1943; anonymous untitled typescript, n.d., SLDC papers, reel 2. In addition, zoot-suiters in Oxnard, about sixty miles north of Los Angeles, were in the habit of stoning police cars that cruised the barrio. *Oxnard Press Courier*, 22 March 1942.

27. Anonymous (but probably by Carey McWilliams) typescript, n.d., McWilliams papers; Mexicans of the Industrial Union Council (CIO), Resolution, 18 September 1942, SLDC papers, reel 2; *Belvedere Citizen*, 23 March 1945, quoted in Acuña, *Community under Siege*, 417; Los Angeles County Coordinating Council, "Notes on the Mexican Population in Los Angeles County," typescript, December 1941, SLDC papers, reel 2, also available in the Ford Collection; Los Angeles County, Coordinating Council for Mexican American Youth, *Minutes*, 7 June 1943; *Examiner*, September 1942; *Bell Industrial Post*, 17 December 1942; for contemporary analyses of sinarquismo see Enrique Prado "Sinarquism in the United States," *New Republic* 109 (26 July 1943): 97–102, and Heinz Eulau, "Sinarquismo in the United States," *Inter-American* 3 (March 1944): 25–27 and 48; for the Mexican American interpretation of Sinarquista activities in southern California see Spanish Speaking People's Congress, "Statement on Youth Activities," n.d., and Spanish Speaking People's Congress, typescript, 14 October 1942, SLDC papers, reel 2; for a historical analysis of the pachuco-Sinarquista connection see Mazón, *Zoot Suit Riots*, passim.

28. Ruiz interview; Roybal interview.

29. For the effects of the war on the western United States see Gerald D. Nash, *The American West Transformed: The Impact of the Second*

World War (Bloomington, Ind., 1985). For the fear of juvenile delinquency during the war see James Gilbert, *A Cycle of Outrage: America's Reaction to the Juvenile Delinquent in the 1950s* (New York, 1986), 24–41; for the local reaction see Karl Holton, "Delinquency in Wartime," n.d., quoted in Jones, *Government Riots*, 89.

30. Los Angeles Police Department Police Commission, *Minutes*, 4 June 1940; for civilian hysteria during wartime see Mazón, *Zoot-Suit Riots*, 15–19 and 31; for the transference of anxiety from Japanese Americans to Mexican Americans see McWilliams, *North from Mexico*, 227.

31. McWilliams, *North from Mexico*, 227.

32. *Daily News*, 9 August 1942; *San Pedro News-Pilot*, 26 October 1942.

33. Ibid.

34. *Times*, 27 October 1942; *Wilshire Press*, 29 October 1942; *Examiner*, 23 February 1943; *Daily News*, 11 November 1942; *Times*, 20 April 1943; *Los Angeles Herald and Express* (hereafter *Herald and Express*), 7 October 1942; *Examiner*, 30 April 1943; also see *Hollywood Citizen News*, 30 April 1943.

35. *Los Angeles Equalizer*, November 1942; *Times*, 8 October 1942.

36. *Times*, 6 October 1942. For accounts of the case see, for example, Acuña, *Occupied America*, 253–56; McWilliams, *North from Mexico*, 228–33; Jones, *Government Riots*, 13–19. For a psychohistorical interpretation see Mazón, *Zoot-Suit Riots*, 15–30; for a contemporary account see CCDMAY, *Sleepy Lagoon Case*.

37. McWilliams, *North from Mexico*, 228–29; Rita Michaels, untitled typescript, 30 April 1943, SLDC papers, reel 1; *Times*, 5 August 1942.

38. *Herald and Express*, 5 October 1942; *Examiner*, 30 October 1942; *Times*, 5 November 1942; untitled newspaper clipping, January 1943, SLDC papers, reel 2; *Herald and Express*, 27 October 30, 4–5 November 1942, and 9, 11, 18 January 1943; McWilliams, *North from Mexico*, 230–31; CCDMAY, *Sleepy Lagoon Case*, 21; Shibley quoted in Michaels, manuscript, 30 April 1943; *Herald and Express*, clipping, n.d., McWilliams papers; *Daily News*, 27 October 1942; "A Statement on the Sleepy Lagoon Case," n.d., Stanford University Libraries, Department of Special Collections, Stanford, California (hereafter Corona papers), box 20. CCDMAY, typed statement, n.d., SLDC papers, reel 2; Michaels, manuscript, 30 April 1943.

39. Reed to Horrall, 12 August 1942, McWilliams papers; of the ninety-seven arrests of Mexican American youths made by the Reserve Division of the LAPD on 8 August all but twelve were for suspicion of robbery or suspicion of assault with a deadly weapon, LAPD Reserve Division Report, 10 August 1942, SLDC papers, reel 2; *Times,* 10 August 1942; also *Daily News,* 11 August 1942.

40. Ayres report. E. W. Lester, "Information for the 1942 Los Angeles County Grand Jury," 11 August 1942; Rasmussen to Ernest W. Oliver, 12 August 1942; Horrall to Ernest W. Oliver, 13 August 1942, McWilliams papers.

41. Ayres report.

42. Ayres also proposed that everyone stopped by the police be fingerprinted whether they were arrested or not. Ibid.

43. Biscailuz to Oliver, 20 August 1942, SLDC Papers, reel 2; Horrall to Oliver, 13 August 1942, McWilliams papers.

44. Lester, "Information," 11 August 1942, McWilliams papers.

45. Rasmussen to Oliver, 12 August 1942, McWilliams papers; Holton quoted in *Times,* 5 August 1942.

46. *Daily News,* 9 October 1942, McWilliams, *North from Mexico,* 237; only those specifically invited by Harry Henderson, chairman of the Special Mexican Relations Committee of the grand jury, could give testimony. Henderson to "Those Interested in Youth," 2 October 1942, McWilliams papers; Guy T. Nunn, "Testimony of Guy T. Nunn," 8 October 1942, McWilliams papers; Oscar Fuss, transcript of testimony before the Los Angeles County Grand Jury, 8 October 1942, SLDC papers, reel 2; also see Manuel Aguilar, "Paper Presented by Consul Aguilar," 8 October 1942, McWilliams papers.

47. Harry Hoijer, "The Problem of Crime among the Mexican Youth of Los Angeles," 8 October 1942, McWilliams papers.

48. On the development of police professionalism see Fogelson, *Big City Police;* for the professionalism movement in Los Angeles see Woods, "Progressives and the Police." On police practices in the Los Angeles Mexican American community during the 1950s and 1960s see Armando Morales, *Ando Sangrando (I Am Bleeding): A Study of Mexican American–Police Conflict* (La Puente, Calif., 1972), and Edward J. Escobar, "The Dialectics of Repression: The Los Angeles Police Department and the Chicano Movement, 1968–1971," *Journal of American History* 79 (1993): 1483–1514.

PART

5 The New Political Paradigm

Alan Brinkley

THIRTEEN
World War II
and American Liberalism

rchibald MacLeish is not much remembered for his poetry, although he considered himself a poet above all else. Even during his life his public reputation—which was considerable—stemmed as much from his official positions (librarian of Congress, deputy director of the Office of War Information, assistant secretary of state) and the essays he often wrote for liberal political journals as from his poems and plays. But there were moments when MacLeish the poet and MacLeish the liberal political activist seemed to converge, when he tried to fuse his own poetic language and imagination with the discussion of public issues. One such moment was in the spring of 1943, when MacLeish was invited to deliver the Charter Day address at the University of California at Berkeley, an address he titled "The Unimagined America."

In 1943 MacLeish was working in the Office of War Information, the government's principal wartime propaganda agency. In World War I the equivalent agency, the Committee on Public Information, had devoted much of its energy to creating lurid images of the enemy (the "barbarian Huns," the "Prussian cur"), discrediting dissenters, and exhorting Americans to be alert for signs of disloyalty.[1] The Office of War Information (or at least MacLeish's area of it, the propaganda division) conceived its task differently—in self-consciously liberal terms. MacLeish sought to keep the public's gaze fastened on the future beyond the war. He hoped to persuade Americans that out of this struggle would come a new and better world in which the liberal promise of the New Deal could be realized and expanded both in America and in other societies.[2] In his speech at Berkeley he spoke in poetic (if somewhat mawkish) terms about the importance of "imagining" that future, of seizing it and harnessing it to some great purpose:

> The great majority of the American people understand very well that this war is not a war only, but an end and a beginning—an end to things known and a beginning of things unknown. We have smelled the wind in the streets that changes weather. We know that whatever the world will be when the war ends, the world will be different. . . . There is a deep, unreasoning conviction in the minds of people here, as in the minds of people elsewhere, that this war, whatever was true of wars before, *must* have consequences—that anything that costs in life and suffering what this war is costing *must* purchase, not merely an end to itself, but something else, something admirable, something of human worth and human significance.[3]

Few would disagree that World War II changed the world as profoundly as any event of this century, perhaps any century. What is less readily apparent, perhaps, is how profoundly the war changed America—its society, its politics, and (as Archibald MacLeish hoped) its image of itself. Except for the combatants themselves, Americans experienced the war at a remove of several thousand miles. They endured no bombing, no invasion, no massive dislocations, no serious material privations. Veterans returning home in 1945 and 1946 found a country that looked very much like the one they had left—something that clearly could not be said of veterans returning home to Britain, France, Germany, Russia, or Japan.[4]

But World War II did transform America in profound, if not immediately visible, ways. Not the least important of those transformations was in the nature of American liberalism, a force that would play a central role in shaping the nation's postwar political and cultural life. Liberalism in America rests on several consistent and enduring philosophical assumptions: the high value liberals believe society should attribute to individual rights and freedoms and the importance of avoiding rigid and immutable norms and institutions. But in the half century since the New Deal, liberalism in America has also meant a prescription for public policy and political action; and in the 1940s this "New Deal liberalism" was in a state of considerable uncertainty and was undergoing significant changes.[5] Several broad developments of the war years helped lay the foundations for the new liberal order that followed the war.

∘   ∘   ∘

Among those developments was a series of important shifts in the size, distribution, and character of the American population. Not all the demographic changes of the 1940s were a result of the war, nor were their effects on liberal assumptions entirely apparent until well after 1945. But they were a crucial part of the process that would transform American society and the way liberals viewed their mission in that society.

Perhaps the most conspicuous demographic change was the single biggest ethnic migration in American history: the massive movement of African Americans from the rural South to the urban North, a migration much larger than the "great migration" at the time of World War I. Between 1910 (when the first great migration began) and 1940, approximately 1.5 million blacks moved from the South to the North. In the 1940s alone, 2 million African Americans left the South, and 3 million more moved in the twenty years after that. The migration brought substantial numbers of them closer to the center of the nation's economic, cultural, and institutional life. The number of blacks employed in manufacturing more than doubled during the war. There were major increases in the number of African Americans employed as skilled craftsmen or enrolled in unions. There was a massive movement of African American women out of domestic work and into the factory and the shop. Much of this would have occurred with or without World War II, but the war greatly accelerated the movement by expanding industrial activity and by creating a labor shortage that gave African American men and women an incentive to move into industrial cities.[6]

This second great migration carried the question of race out of the South and into the North, out of the countryside and into the city, out of the field and into the factory. African American men and women encountered prejudice and discrimination in the urban, industrial world much as they had in the agrarian world; but in the city they were far better positioned to organize and protest their condition, as some were beginning to do even before the fighting ended. World War II therefore began the process by which race would increase its claim on American consciousness and, ultimately, transform American liberalism.

Just as the war helped lay the groundwork for challenges to racial orthodoxies, so it contributed to later challenges to gender norms. Three million women entered the paid workforce for the first time during the war, benefiting—like black workers—from the labor shortage military conscription had created. Many women performed jobs long considered the exclusive province of men. Women had been moving into the workforce in growing numbers before the war began, to be sure, and almost certainly they would have continued to do so even had the United States remained at peace. Many of their wartime gains, moreover, proved short lived. Female factory workers in particular were usually dismissed as soon as male workers returned to take their places, even though many wanted to remain in their jobs.

Still, most women who had begun working during the war continued working after 1945 (if not always in the same jobs). And while popular assumptions about women's roles (among both women and men) were slow to change, the economic realities of many women's lives were changing dramatically and permanently—in ways that would eventually help raise powerful challenges to ideas about gender. The war, in short, accelerated a critical long-term shift in the role of women in society that would produce, among other things, the feminist movements of the 1960s and beyond.[7]

Similar, if less dramatic, changes were affecting other American communities during the war. Men and women who had long lived on the margins of American life—because of prejudice or geographical isolation or both—found their lives transformed by the pressures of war. Asian Americans, Latino Americans, Native Americans, and others served in the military, worked in factories, moved into diverse urban neighborhoods, and otherwise encountered the urban-industrial world of the mid-twentieth century. Life was not, perhaps, much better for many such people in their new roles than it had been in traditional ones. For Japanese Americans on the West Coast, who spent much of the war in internment camps, victims of popular and official hysteria, it was considerably worse. But for many such communities the changes helped erode the isolation that had made it difficult to challenge discrimination and demand inclusion.[8]

No one living in the era of multiculturalism will be inclined to argue with the proposition that the changing composition of the American population over the past fifty years—and the changing relations among different groups within the population—is one of the most important events in the nation's recent history. Those changes have reshaped America's economy, its culture, its politics, and its intellectual life. They have forced the nation to confront its increasing diversity in more direct and painful ways than at any time since the Civil War. They have challenged America's conception of itself as a nation and a society. And they have transformed American liberalism. In the 1930s, most liberals considered questions of racial, ethnic, or gender difference of distinctly secondary importance (or in the case of gender, virtually no importance at all). Liberal discourse centered much more on issues of class and the distribution of wealth and economic power. By 1945 that was beginning to change. One sign of that change was the remarkable reception among liberals of Gunnar Myrdal's *An American Dilemma,* published in 1944. Myrdal identified race as the one issue most likely to shape and perplex the American future. The great migration of the 1940s helped ensure that history would vindicate Myrdal's prediction and that American liberals would adjust their outlook and their goals in fundamental ways in the postwar years.[9]

o o o

*P*erhaps the most common and important observation about the domestic impact of World War II is that it ended the Great Depression and launched an era of unprecedented prosperity. Between 1940 and 1945 the United States experienced the greatest expansion of industrial production in its history. After a decade of depression, a decade of growing doubts about capitalism, a decade of high unemployment and underproduction, suddenly, in a single stroke, the American economy restored itself and—equally important—seemed to redeem itself. Gross national product in the war years rose from $91 billion to $166 billion; 15 million new jobs were created, and the most enduring problem of the depression—massive unemployment—came to an end; industrial production doubled; personal incomes rose (depending on location) by as much as 200 percent.[10] The revival of the economy is obviously important in its own right. But it also had implications for the future of American political economy, for how liberals in particular conceived of the role of the state in the postwar United States.

One of the mainstays of economic thought in the late 1930s was the belief that the United States had reached what many called "economic maturity": the belief that the nation was approaching, or perhaps had reached, the end of its capacity to grow, that America must now learn to live within limits.This assumption strengthened the belief among many reformers that in the future it would be necessary to regulate the economy much more closely and carefully for the benefit of society as a whole. America could not rely any more on a constantly expanding pie; it would have to worry about how the existing pie was to be divided.[11]

The wartime economic experience—the booming expansion, the virtual elimination of unemployment, the creation of new industries, new "frontiers"—served as a rebuke to the "mature economy" idea and restored the concept of growth to the center of liberal hopes. The capitalist economy, liberals suddenly discovered, was not irretrievably stagnant. Economic expansion could achieve, in fact had achieved, dimensions beyond the wildest dreams of the 1930s. Social and economic advancement could proceed, therefore, without structural changes in capitalism, without continuing, intrusive state management of the economy. It could proceed by virtue of growth.

Assaults on the concept of economic maturity were emerging as early as 1940 and gathered force throughout the war. Alvin Hansen, one of the most prominent champions in the 1930s of what he called "secular stagnation," repudiated the idea in 1941. "All of us had our sights too low," he admitted. The *New Republic* and the *Nation*, both of which had embraced the idea of economic maturity in 1938 and 1939, openly rejected it in the 1940s—not only rejected it, but celebrated its demise. The country had achieved a "break," exulted the *Nation*, "from the defeatist thinking that held us in economic thraldom through the thirties, when it was assumed that we could not afford full employment or full production in this country."[12]

But along with this celebration of economic growth came a new and urgent fear: that the growth might not continue once the war was over. What if the depression came back? What if there was a return to massive unemployment? What could be done to make sure that economic growth continued? That was the great liberal challenge of the war years—not to restructure the economy, not to control corporate behavior, not to search for new and more efficient forms of management, but to find a way to keep things going as they were.[13]

And in response to that challenge, a growing number of liberal economists and policymakers became interested in a tool that had begun to attract their attention in the 1930s and that seemed to prove itself during the war: government spending. That was clearly how the economy had revived—in response to the massive increase in the federal budget in the war years, from $9 billion in 1939 to $100 billion in 1945. And that was how the revival could be sustained—by pumping more money into the economy in peacetime. What government needed to do, therefore, was to "plan" for postwar full employment.

Those who called themselves "planners" in the 1940s did not talk much anymore, as planners had talked in earlier years, about the need for an efficient, centrally planned economy in which the government would help direct the behavior of private institutions. They talked instead about fiscal planning—about public works projects, about social welfare programs, about the expansion of the Social Security system. The National Resource Planning Board, the central "planning" agency of the New Deal since 1933, issued a report in 1942 called *Security, Work, and Relief Policies.* In the past, the NRPB had been preoccupied largely with older ideas of planning—regional planning, resource management, government supervision of production and investment. Now, in their 1942 report, the members turned their attention to the new kind of planning. The government should create a "shelf" of public works projects, so that after the war—whenever the economy showed signs of stagnating—it could pull projects off the shelf and spend the money on them to stimulate more growth. The government should commit itself to more expansive Social Security measures so that after the war—if the economy should slow down—there would be welfare mechanisms in place that would immediately pick up the slack and start paying out benefits, which would increase purchasing power and stimulate growth.[14]

All of this reflected, among other things, the increasing influence in American liberal circles of Keynesian economics. The most important liberal economist of the war years—Alvin Hansen of Harvard, who contributed to many NRPB reports—was also the leading American exponent of Keynesianism. Keynesianism provided those concerned about the future of the American economy with an escape from their fears of a new, postwar depression. Economic growth, it taught them, did not require constant involvement in the affairs of private institutions—which the 1930s (and the war itself) had shown to be logistically difficult and politically controversial. Growth could be sustained through the *indirect* manipulation of the economy by fiscal and monetary levers.[15]

The wartime faith in economic growth led, in other words, to several developments of great importance to the future of American liberalism. It helped relegitimize capitalism among people who had, in the 1930s, developed serious doubts about its viability. It helped rob the "administrative" reform ideas of the late 1930s—the belief in ever greater regulation of private institutions—of their urgency. It helped elevate Keynesian ideas about indirect management of the economy to the center of reform hopes. And it made the idea of the welfare state—of Social Security and public works and other social welfare efforts—come to seem a part of the larger vision of sustaining economic growth by defining welfare as a way to distribute income and stimulate purchasing power. It helped channel American liberalism into a new, less confrontational direction—a direction that would produce fewer clashes with capitalist institutions; that tried to define the interests of capitalists and the interests of the larger public in identical terms; that emphasized problems of consumption over problems of production; that shaped the liberal agenda for more than a generation and helped shape the next great episode in liberal policy experiments: the Great Society of the 1960s.[16]

○   ○   ○

World War II had other important and more purely ideological effects on American liberalism—some of them in apparent conflict with others, but all of them important in determining the permissible range of liberal aspirations for the postwar era. First, the war created, or at least greatly reinforced, a set of anxieties and fears that would become increasingly central to liberal thought in the late 1940s and 1950s. It inflamed two fears in particular: a fear of the state and a fear of the people. Both were a response, in large part, to the horror with which American liberals (and most other Americans as well) regarded the regimes the United States was fighting in World War II. Both would be sustained and strengthened by the similar horror with which most Americans came to view the regime the nation was beginning to mobilize against in peacetime even before the end of the war: the Soviet Union.

The fear of the state emerged directly out of the way American liberals (and the American people generally) defined the nature of their enemy in World War II. During World War I many Americans had believed the enemy was a race, a people: the Germans, the beastlike "Huns," and their presumably savage culture. In World War II racial stereotypes continued to play an important role in portrayals of the Japanese; but in defining the enemy in Europe—always the principal enemy in the 1940s to most Americans—the government and most of the media relied less on racial or cultural images than on political ones. Wartime propaganda in World War II did not personify the Germans and Italians as evil peoples. It focused instead on the Nazi and fascist states.[17]

The war, in other words, pushed a fear of totalitarianism (and hence a general wariness about excessive state power) to the center of American liberal thought. In particular, it forced a reassessment of the kinds of associational and corporatist arrangements that many had found so attractive in the aftermath of World War I. Those, after all, were the kinds of arrangements Germany and Italy had claimed to be creating. But it also created a less specific fear of state power that made other kinds of direct planning and management of the economy or society seem unappealing as well. "The rise of totalitarianism," Reinhold Niebuhr noted somberly in 1945, "has prompted the democratic world to view all collectivist answers to our social problems with increased apprehension." Virtually all experiments in state supervision of private institutions, he warned, contained "some peril of compounding economic and political power." Hence "a wise community will walk warily and test the effect of each new adventure before further adventures."[18] To others the lesson was even starker. *Any* steps in the direction of state control of economic institutions were (to use the title of Friedrich A. Hayek's celebrated antistatist book of 1944) steps along "the road to serfdom." This fear of the state was one of many things that lent strength to the emerging Keynesian–welfare state liberal vision of political economy, with its much more limited role for government as a manager of economic behavior.[19]

Along with this fear of the state emerged a related fear: a fear of "mass politics" or "mass man"; a fear, in short, of the people. Nazi Germany, fascist Italy, even the Soviet Union, many liberals came to believe, illustrated the dangers inherent in trusting the people to control their political life. The people, the "mass," could too easily be swayed by demagogues and tyrants. They were too susceptible to appeals to their passions, to the dark, intolerant impulses that in a healthy society remained largely repressed and subdued. Fascism and communism were not simply the products of the state or of elite politics, many liberals believed; they were the products of mass movements, of the unleashing of the dangerous and irrational impulses within every individual and every society.

This fear of the mass lay at the heart of much liberal cultural and intellectual criticism in the first fifteen years after World War II. It found expression in the writings of Hannah Arendt, Theodor Adorno, Richard Hofstadter, Lionel Trilling, Daniel Bell, Dwight Macdonald, and many others. Like the fear of the state, with which it was so closely associated, it reinforced a sense of caution and restraint in liberal thinking; a suspicion of ideology, a commitment to pragmatism, a wariness about moving too quickly to encourage or embrace spontaneous popular movements; a conviction that one of the purposes of politics was to defend the state against popular movements and their potentially dangerous effects.[20]

There were, in short, powerful voices within American liberalism during and immediately after World War II arguing that the experience of the war had introduced a dark cloud of doubt and even despair to human society. A world that could produce so terrible a war; a world that could produce Hiroshima, Nagasaki, the Katyn Forest, Auschwitz; a world capable of profound evil and inconceivable destruction: such a world, many American liberals argued, must be forever regarded skeptically and suspiciously. Humankind must move cautiously into its uncertain future, wary of unleashing the dark impulses that had produced such horror.

Some liberal intellectuals went further. Americans, they argued, must resist the temptation to think of themselves, in their hour of triumph, as a chosen people. No people, no nation, could afford to ignore its own capacity for evil. Reinhold Niebuhr spoke for many liberals when he wrote of the dangers of the "deep layer of Messianic consciousness in the mind of America" and warned of liberal culture's "inability to comprehend the depth of evil to which individuals and communities may sink, particularly when they try to play the role of God in history." Americans, he said, would do well to remember that "no nation is sacred and unique. . . . Providence has not set Americans apart from lesser breeds. We too are part of history's seamless web."[21]

But Niebuhr's statements were obviously written to refute a competing assumption. And as it suggests, there was in the 1940s another, very different ideological force at work in America, another form of national self-definition that affected liberal thought and behavior, at home and in the world, at least as much as the somber assessments of Niebuhr and others. Indeed even many liberal intellectuals attracted to Niebuhr's pessimistic ideas about human nature and mass politics were simultaneously drawn to this different and, on the surface at least, contradictory assessment of the nation's potential. For in many ways the most powerful ideological force at work in postwar American liberalism, and in the postwar United States generally, was the view of America as an anointed nation; America as a special moral force in the world; America as a society with a unique mission, born of its righteousness. This is an ideological tradition that is often described as the tradition of American innocence. But innocence is perhaps too gentle a word for what has often been an aggressive and intrusive vision, a vision that rests on the belief that America is somehow insulated from the sins and failures and travails that affect other nations, that America stands somehow outside of history, protected from it by its own strength and virtue.

World War II did not create those beliefs. They are as old as the nation itself.[22] But the American experience in the conflict, and the radically enhanced international stature and responsibility of the United States in the aftermath of the war, strengthened such ideas and gave them a crusading quality that made them as active and powerful as they had been at any moment in the nation's history.

It is not difficult, perhaps, to understand how and why that happened. Fighting a war against Nazi Germany would encourage any nation to think of itself as a moral force in an immoral world, to believe in the righteousness of its cause, to consider itself the champion of freedom and justice in a battle against tyranny and darkness. But it was not just the contrast between America's democratic potential and the autocracies of Germany and Japan that influenced the liberal vision of the postwar world. There was also a strengthened sense that the United States had something worth sharing with *all* nations, that it had a commitment to freedom and justice that could serve as a model for the rest of the world. That was the message of, among others, Henry Luce in a small book he published in 1941, titled *The American Century*. In that book Luce—the crusading founder and publisher of *Time* and *Life* magazines—sketched a picture of the nation's destiny that probably only slightly exaggerated what would, by the late 1940s, be a widely shared and increasingly powerful view.

The American century, Luce said, must be a time when the American people would share with the rest of the world the special virtues of their own society. The "American Century," Luce wrote,

> . . . must be a sharing with all people of our Bill of Rights, our Declaration of Independence, our Constitution, our magnificent industrial products, our technical skills. . . . We have that indefinable, unmistakable sign of leadership: prestige. And unlike the prestige of Rome or Genghis Khan or nineteenth century England, American prestige throughout the world is [based on] faith in the good intentions as well as in the ultimate intelligence and strength of the whole of the American people.

Luce continued with an almost rhapsodic paean to the virtues the United States could share with other peoples:

> Our vision of America as a world power includes a passionate devotion to great American ideals . . . a love of freedom, a feeling for the equality of opportunity, a tradition of self-reliance and independence, and also of cooperation. . . . we are the inheritors of all the great principles of Western civilization—above all Justice, the love of Truth, the ideal of charity. . . . It now becomes our time to be the powerhouse from which the ideals spread throughout the world and do their mysterious work of lifting the life of mankind from the level of the beasts to what the Psalmist called a little lower than the angels.[23]

Luce's vision had obvious implications for America's international role: it must be active and forceful, to ensure that less worthy nations did not shape the future. But it had implications for American domestic life as well. If the American example was to inspire the world, Americans must make sure their own society was worthy of emulation.

Luce was a Republican, an often bitter opponent of Roosevelt and the New Deal, and a man mistrusted and even despised by many liberals, most of whom considered his idea of an American century excessively nationalistic, even imperialistic.[24] Yet even many liberals who disliked Luce and whose visions of the postwar world were strongly anti-imperialist spoke at times in a similar language, imbued with much the same sense of American mission. Vice President Henry A. Wallace, for example, described America's wartime (and by implication postwar) mission to extend democracy, both at home and abroad, in almost floridly idealistic language in a 1942 statement: "No compromise with Satan is possible. . . . The people's revolution is on the march, and the devil and all his angels can not prevail against it. They can not prevail, for on the side of the people [America and its allies] is the Lord."[25] The belief that America had a powerful destiny in the postwar world, that it had special virtues worth sharing with other peoples, that it could (and should) serve as a model to the democratic strivings of all nations—this belief was penetrating deep into American culture and forming the liberal concept of the nation's postwar mission. It helped reconcile liberals (and other Americans) to the active, crusading international role that victory had thrust upon the nation. It enabled liberals (and other Americans) to rationalize the continued development of methods of mass destruction by harnessing that effort to a perceived moral imperative. It made possible widespread public support for the cold war. It helped create considerable support for much of the domestic political repression the cold war later produced and made it difficult for liberals to find an effective position from which to criticize that repression. But by increasing popular sensitivity to America's image in the world (and to the impact of its own social problems on that image), it also created support for some of the ambitious liberal reform efforts of the postwar years.[26] Theodore White, one of the most eloquent and prolific chroniclers of the experiences of the World War II generation, suggested something of the ambiguous impact of this sense of world mission when he wrote very near the end of his life:

> For a proper historian of our times, there was only one overtowering beginning—the Year of Victory, 1945. All things flowed from that victory. . . . The intoxication of [it] . . . lasted for a generation. First, the sense of power which had convinced a peaceful nation that its armed force . . . could and should forever police and reorder the world. Second, the seductive belief that in any contest between good and evil, good always triumphs. We, our soldiers, had proved that Right makes Might. The imperative legacy of Virtue descended from the war.[27]

The war left other ideological legacies for American liberalism as well. In the glow of the nation's victory, in the sense of old orders shattered and a new world being born, came an era of exuberant innovation, an era in which, for a time, nothing seemed more appealing than the new. The allure of the new was visible in the brave new world of architectural modernism, whose controversial legacy is so much a part of the postwar American landscape. It was visible in the explosive growth of the innovative and iconoclastic American art world, which made New York in the 1940s and 1950s something of what Paris had been in the nineteenth century. It was visible in the increased stature and boldness of the American scientific community, and in the almost religious faith in technological progress that came to characterize so much of American life.[28]

Above all, perhaps, it was visible in the way it excited, and then frustrated, a generation of American liberals as they imagined new possibilities for progress and social justice. That is what Archibald MacLeish meant in 1943 when he spoke about the America of the imagination, the society that the war was encouraging Americans to create:

> We have, and we know we have, the abundant means to bring our boldest dreams to pass—to create for ourselves whatever world we have the courage to desire. . . . We have the tools and the skill and the intelligence to take our cities apart and put them together, to lead our roads and rivers where we please to lead them, to build our houses where we want our houses, to brighten the air, to clean the wind, to live as men in this Republic, free men, should be living. We have the power and the courage and the resources of good-will and decency and common understanding . . . to create a nation such as men have never seen. . . . We stand at the moment of the building of great lives, for the war's end and our victory in the war will throw that moment and the means before us.[29]

There was, of course, considerable naïveté, and even arrogance, in such visions. But there was also an appealing sense of hope and commitment—a belief in the possibility of sweeping away old problems and failures, of creating "great lives." Out of such visions came some of the postwar crusades of American liberals—the battle for racial justice, the effort to combat poverty, the expansion of individual rights. And although all of those battles had some ambiguous and even unhappy consequences, they all reflected a confidence in the character and commitment of American society—and the possibility of creating social justice within it—that few people would express so blithely today. Postwar liberalism has suffered many failures and travails in the half century since 1945. But surely its postwar faith in the capacity of America to rebuild—

and perhaps even redeem—itself remains one of its most appealing legacies.

Notes

1. David Kennedy, *Over Here: The First World War in American Society* (New York, 1980), 59–69; George Creel, *How We Advertised America* (New York, 1920).

2. Allan M. Winkler, *The Politics of Propaganda: The Office of War Information, 1942–1945* (New Haven, 1978), 9–42. A recent biography of MacLeish is Scott Donaldson, *Archibald MacLeish: An American Life* (Boston, 1992).

3. Archibald MacLeish, "The Unimagined America," *Atlantic,* June 1943, 59–63.

4. General histories of the American "home front" during World War II include John M. Blum, *V Was for Victory: Politics and American Culture during World War II* (New York, 1976); Richard Polenberg, *War and Society: The United States, 1941–1945* (Philadelphia, 1972); Geoffrey Perrett, *Days of Sadness, Years of Triumph: The American People, 1939–1945* (New York, 1973).

5. For a discussion of changing uses of the word "liberalism," see Ronald D. Rotunda, "The 'Liberal' Label: Roosevelt's Capture of a Symbol," *Public Policy* 17 (1968): 377–408.

6. Arnold R. Hirsch, *Making the Second Ghetto: Race and Housing in Chicago, 1940–1960* (New York, 1983), 1–39; Nicholas Lemann, *The Promised Land: The Great Black Migration and How It Changed America* (New York, 1991), 1–10; Jacqueline Jones, *Labor of Love, Labor of Sorrow: Black Women, Work and the Family, from Slavery to the Present* (New York, 1985), 232–56; Blum, *V Was for Victory,* 182–207; "The Negro's War," *Fortune,* June 1942, 77–80, 157–64.

7. Sherna Berger Gluck, *Rosie the Riveter Revisited: Women, the War, and Social Change* (Boston, 1987), is an important oral history of women war workers. Susan M. Hartman, *The Home Front and Beyond: American Women in the 1940s* (Boston, 1982), is a general history. Alice Kessler-Harris minimizes the impact of the war in moving women into the workplace, although she concedes that the conflict had some important effects on the attitude of many women toward their relation to the economy. *Out to Work: A History of Wage-Earning Women in America* (New York, 1982), 273–99.

8. Ronald Takaki, *A Different Mirror: A History of Multicultural America* (Boston, 1993), 378–401; Ronald Takaki, *Strangers from a Different Shore: A History of Asian Americans* (Boston, 1989), 357–405; Peter Irons, *Justice at War: The Story of the Japanese American Internment Cases* (New York, 1983); Alison R. Bernstein, *American Indians and World War II: Toward a New Era in Indian Affairs* (Norman, Okla., 1991).

9. Gunnar Myrdal, *An American Dilemma: The Negro Problem and Modern Democracy* (New York, 1944). On the making of and responses to Myrdal's book, see Walter A. Jackson, *Gunnar Myrdal and America's Conscience: Social Engineering and Racial Liberalism, 1938–1987* (Chapel Hill, N.C., 1990), esp. chaps. 5–7.

10. Although the bulk of the growth was a result of military production, the consumer economy expanded by 12 percent during the same years. Alan S. Milward, *War, Economy and Society: 1939–1945* (Berkeley, Calif., 1977), 63–65; Blum, *V Was for Victory,* 90–93.

11. Alvin H. Hansen, "Economic Progress and Declining Population Growth," *American Economic Review* 29 (1939): 1–15; Stuart Chase, "Freedom from Want," *Harper's,* October 1942, 468; Theodore Rosenof, *Patterns of Political Economy in America: The Failure to Develop a Democratic Left Synthesis, 1933–1950* (New York, 1983), 39–46.

12. Alvin Hansen, "Planning Full Employment," *Nation,* 21 October 1941, 492; "Is There a New Frontier?" *New Republic,* 27 November 1944, 708–10; "A New Bill of Rights," *Nation,* 20 March 1943, 402; Herbert Stein, *The Fiscal Revolution in America* (Chicago, 1969), 175–77.

13. Lewis Corey, "Problems of the Peace: 3. Boom and Bust?" *Antioch Review* 4 (1944): 449–64; Eliot Janeway, "War Boom or Bust?" *Nation,* 21 October 1939, 432–34; George Soule, "That Post-war Depression," *New Republic,* 20 July 1942, 74–76; Oscar Cox to Harry Hopkins, 10 February 1943, Hopkins MSS 239, Franklin Delano Roosevelt (FDR) Library.

14. Office of Facts and Figures, "War Aims and Postwar Policies," 17 March 1942, Archibald MacLeish MSS 5, Library of Congress; Philip J. Funigiello, *The Challenge to Urban Liberalism: Federal-City Relations during World War II* (Knoxville, Tenn., 1978), 11, 180–85, 197; Otis L. Graham Jr., *Toward a Planned Society: From Roosevelt to Nixon* (New

York, 1976), 52–58; Frederic Delano et al. to FDR, 24 August 1943, Official File 1092, FDR Library; National Resource Planning Board (NRPB), "Post-war Plan and Program," February 1943, Senatorial File 43, Truman Library; NRPB, "National Resources Development Report"; NRPB, *Security, Work, and Relief Policies* (Washington, D.C., 1942); NRPB, "The NRPB in Wartime," *Frontiers of Democracy* 8 (15 February 1942), 143.

15. William O. Douglas to Keynes, 29 July 1937, Douglas MSS 8, Library of Congress; Felix Frankfurter to Alfred Harcourt, 2 February 1939, MacLeish MSS 8; Archibald MacLeish to Keynes, 8 July 1941 and 10 October 1944, both in MacLeish MSS 8, 12; Richard Strout, "Hansen of Harvard," *New Republic,* 29 December 1941, 888–89; Alvin Hansen and Guy Greer, "The Federal Debt and the Future," *Harper's,* April 1942, 500; Alvin Hansen, "Wanted: Ten Million Jobs," *Atlantic* 172 (September 1943), 68–69. See Robert Lekachman, *The Age of Keynes* (New York, 1966), 124–43, for a discussion of the rise of an indigenous American "Keynesian school" of economists after 1937.

16. Further elaboration of some of these ideas is in Alan Brinkley, "The New Deal and the Idea of the State," in *The Rise and Fall of the New Deal Order,* ed. Steve Fraser and Gary Gerstle (Princeton, 1989), 85–101, and Alan Brinkley, *The End of Reform: New Deal Liberalism in Recession and War* (New York, 1995).

17. Winkler, *Politics of Propaganda,* 38–72; Blum, *V Was for Victory,* 45–52.

18. Reinhold Niebuhr, *The Children of Light and the Children of Darkness* (New York, 1945), 117; Rosenof, *Patterns of Political Economy,* 228–32.

19. Friedrich A. Hayek, *The Road to Serfdom* (Chicago, 1944); Theodore Rosenof, "Freedom, Planning, and Totalitarianism: The Reception of F. A. Hayek's *Road to Serfdom,*" *Canadian Review of American Studies* 5 (1974): 149–65.

20. The preoccupation with mass politics, "mass man," and "mass culture" was pervasive in the intellectual life of the 1940s and 1950s, and it remains a pervasive theme in the historical scholarship on that era. See, for example, Christopher Brookeman, *American Culture and Society since the 1930s* (New York, 1984); Richard H. Pells, *The Liberal Mind in a Conservative Age: American Intellectuals in the 1940s and*

1950s (New York, 1985); Stephen J. Whitfield, *The Culture of the Cold War* (Baltimore, 1991); William S. Graebner, *The Age of Doubt: American Thought and Culture in the 1940s* (Boston, 1991).

21. Reinhold Niebuhr, *The Irony of American History* (New York, 1952), 69, 173; Arthur M. Schlesinger Jr., *The Cycles of American History* (Boston, 1987), 19–20.

22. Arthur Schlesinger's 1977 essay "The Theory of America: Experiment or Destiny?" evaluates the tension between the doubting and messianic visions of America. It is reprinted in ibid., 3–22.

23. Henry R. Luce, *The American Century* (New York, 1941), 32–34, 38–39. The essay appeared originally in *Life*, 17 February 1941; it is reprinted in John K. Jessup, *The Ideas of Henry Luce* (New York, 1969), 105–20.

24. See James L. Baughman, *Henry R. Luce and the Rise of the American News Media* (Boston, 1987), esp. chaps. 8–9.

25. Henry A. Wallace, *Democracy Reborn,* ed. Russell Lord (New York, 1944), 195–96; Edward L. Schapsmeier and Frederick H. Schapsmeier, *Prophet in Politics: Henry A. Wallace and the War Years, 1940–1965* (Ames, Iowa, 1970), 32.

26. Alan Brinkley, "Dilemmas of Modern Liberalism," in *Franklin D. Roosevelt and the Future of Liberalism,* ed. John F. Sears (Westport, Conn., 1991), 17–24.

27. Theodore H. White, *America in Search of Itself* (New York, 1982), 3–4.

28. Godfrey Hodgson, *America in Our Time* (Garden City, N.Y., 1976), 6–8.

29. MacLeish, "Unimagined America," 59–63.

CONTRIBUTORS

Alan Brinkley is professor of history at Columbia University. His research focuses on American political history in the twentieth century, and his works include *Voices of Protest: Huey Long, Father Coughlin and the Great Depression* and *The End of Reform: New Deal Liberalism in Recession and War*. He is also the author of a widely used text, *American History: A Survey*.

John W. Dower is professor of history and Henry R. Luce Professor of International Cooperation at the Massachusetts Institute of Technology. His books include *Empire and Aftermath: Yoshida Shigeru and the Japanese Experience, 1878–1954, War without Mercy: Race and Power in the Pacific War*, and *Japan in Peace and War: Selected Essays*. He is currently at work on a broad study of Japanese society and culture in the immediate aftermath of World War II.

Perry R. Duis is associate professor of history at the University of Illinois at Chicago and a specialist in Chicago history and American social history. He is the author of *Chicago: Creating New Traditions, The Saloon: Public Drinking in Chicago and Boston, 1880–1920*, and *We've Got a Job to Do: Chicagoans and World War II*.

Lewis A. Erenberg is professor of history at Loyola University of Chicago. His research brings together popular culture, social history, and gender studies. He is the author of *Steppin' Out: New York Nightlife and the Transformation of American Culture, 1890–1930* and the forthcoming *Swinging the Dream: Big Band Jazz and the Reorientation of American Culture, 1923–1955*.

Edward J. Escobar is associate professor of history and director of the Office of Chicana and Chicano Studies at Arizona State University. His works include "The Dialectics of Repression: The Los Angeles Police Department and the Chicano Movement, 1968–1971" and the forthcoming *Race and Law Enforcement: Relations between Chicanos and the Los Angeles Police Department, 1900–1945*. With James B. Lane he edited *Forging a Community: The Latino Experience in Northwest Indiana, 1919–1975*.

Gary Gerstle is associate professor of history at Catholic University of America and the author of *Working-Class Americanism: The Politics of Labor in a Textile City, 1914–1960*. With Steve Fraser he edited *The Rise and Fall of the New Deal Order, 1930–1980*. He currently is working on a book to be titled "Nationalism and Multiculturalism in the Twentieth-Century United States."

Susan E. Hirsch is associate professor of history at Loyola University of Chicago. She is the author of *Roots of the American Working Class: The Industrialization of Crafts in Newark, 1800–1860* and with Robert Goler of *A City Comes of Age: Chicago in the 1890s*. She is writing a book about the long struggle between Pullman workers and managers to control conditions of labor in the company.

Elaine Tyler May is professor of American studies and history at the University of Minnesota and the 1995–96 president of the American Studies Association. She is the author of *Great Expectations: Marriage and Divorce in Post-Victorian America, Homeward Bound: American Families in the Cold War Era, Pushing the Limits: American Women, 1940–1961*, and *Barren in the Promised Land: Childless Americans and the Pursuit of Happiness*.

Lary May is associate professor of American studies and history at the University of Minnesota. He is the author of *Screening out the Past: The Birth of Mass Culture and the Motion Picture Industry* and the editor of *Recasting America: Culture and Politics in the Age of Cold War*. He is working on a study of the relation between the motion picture industry and modern American nationalism, politics, and private life between 1930 and 1960.

Carol Miller is associate professor in the Program in American Studies and the Department of American Indian Studies at the University of Minnesota. She is the author of numerous articles on American Indian fiction and on multicultural education; she is also a published poet. Currently she is working on a book-length study of collective functionality in contemporary narratives by American Indian women writers.

Shirley Ann Wilson Moore is associate professor of history at California State University, Sacramento, where she teaches African American history and American social history. She is the author of "Getting There, Being There: African-American Migration to Richmond, California, 1910–1945," in *The Great Migration in Historical Perspective,* edited by Joe Trotter, and of the forthcoming *To Place Our Deeds: The Black Community in Richmond, California 1910–1963.*

George H. Roeder Jr. is chair of the Undergraduate Division and professor of liberal arts at the School of the Art Institute of Chicago. He is the author of *The Censored War: American Visual Experience during World War Two* and *Forum of Uncertainty: Confrontations with Modern Painting in Twentieth-Century American Thought.* He is now working on the relationship of the artist and society and the sensory dimensions of history.

Reed Ueda is associate professor of history at Tufts University. He is the author of *Avenues to Adulthood: The Origins of the High School and Social Mobility in an American Suburb* and *Postwar Immigrant America: A Social History.* His current research is on historical turning points in policies on ethnic pluralism.

NAME INDEX

TITLE INDEX

SUBJECT INDEX